NIAAA's Guide to Interscholastic Athletic Administration

National Interscholastic
Athletic Administrators Association

Michael L. Blackburn
Eric Forsyth
John R. Olson
Bruce Whitehead
EDITORS

Human Kinetics

Library of Congress Cataloging-in-Publication Data

NIAAA's guide to interscholastic athletic administration / Michael L. Blackburn, Eric Forsyth, John R. Olson, Bruce Whitehead, editors.
     pages cm
  Includes bibliographical references and index.
  1. National Interscholastic Athletic Administrators Association--Handbooks, manuals, etc. 2. School sports--United States--Management--Handbooks, manuals, etc. 3. Sports administration--United States--Handbooks, manuals, etc. 4. Coaching (Athletics)--United States--Handbooks, manuals, etc. I. Blackburn, Michael L. II. Title: National Interscholastic Association of Athletic Administrators guide to interscholastic athletic administration.
  GV346.N53 2013
  796.043--dc23

                                                2013010169

  ISBN-10: 1-4504-3277-8 (print)
  ISBN-13: 978-1-4504-3277-1 (print)

The web addresses cited in this text were current as of January 18, 2013, unless otherwise noted.

Developmental Editor: Kevin Matz; **Assistant Editor:** Susan Huls; **Copyeditor:** Patricia MacDonald; **Indexer:** Katy Balcer; **Permissions Manager:** Dalene Reeder; **Graphic Designer:** Nancy Rasmus; **Graphic Artist:** Dawn Sills; **Cover Designer:** Keith Blomberg; **Art Manager:** Kelly Hendren; **Associate Art Manager:** Alan L. Wilborn; **Printer:** Edwards Brothers Malloy

Printed in the United States of America   10 9 8 7 6 5 4 3 2

The paper in this book is certified under a sustainable forestry program.

Human Kinetics
Website: www.HumanKinetics.com

United States: Human Kinetics
P.O. Box 5076
Champaign, IL 61825-5076
800-747-4457
e-mail: humank@hkusa.com

Canada: Human Kinetics
475 Devonshire Road Unit 100
Windsor, ON N8Y 2L5
800-465-7301 (in Canada only)
e-mail: info@hkcanada.com

Europe: Human Kinetics
107 Bradford Road
Stanningley
Leeds LS28 6AT, United Kingdom
+44 (0) 113 255 5665
e-mail: hk@hkeurope.com

Australia: Human Kinetics
57A Price Avenue
Lower Mitcham, South Australia 5062
08 8372 0999
e-mail: info@hkaustralia.com

New Zealand: Human Kinetics
P.O. Box 80
Torrens Park, South Australia 5062
0800 222 062
e-mail: info@hknewzealand.com

E5743

Contents

Contributor List   vii

INTRODUCTION   **Challenges in Today's Interscholastic
Sport Administration**   **ix**
Eric Forsyth, John Olson
Initial Field Research of Contemporary
Issues x · Initial Research Findings and
Commentary on Current Issues in High School
Athletics x · Summary xv

PART I   Leadership Orientation

CHAPTER 1   **Professional Foundations**   **3**
Bruce Whitehead, Mike Blackburn
Association With Academic Achievement 4 ·
Contributor to Future Success 5 · Origin
and Framework of Interscholastic Athletics 6 ·
Profile of the Athletic Administrator Position 9 ·
Professional Preparation for the Athletic Administrator
Position 11 · Design of the Athletic
Program 14 · Summary 17

CHAPTER 2   **Guiding Personal Philosophy**   **19**
David Hoch
Benchmarks Beyond Winning 20 · Priorities 23 ·
Decision Making 24 · Change and Flexibility 25 ·
Educating Others 27 · Ethics and Integrity 28 ·
Dependability 29 · Personal Care 30 · Continual
Professional Development 31 · Authority Versus
Power 32 · The Hurdle of Friendship 33 ·
Summary 35

CHAPTER 3   **Communication and Accessibility**   **37**
Warren L. Hagman
Effective Communication 38 · Composure in
Communication 42 · Communications With
Members of the School Community 44 · Perfecting
Communication Skills 52 · Summary 53

CHAPTER 4   Personnel Management   55

David Hoch

Recruiting, Interviewing, and Hiring 56 ·
Mentoring 58 · Evaluating Coaches 60 ·
Terminating Staff 69 · Keeping Records 70 ·
Managing Adjunct Staff 71 · Summary 73

CHAPTER 5   Student-Athlete Development   75

Sheri Stice

Player Management 77 · Building Successful
Programs 93 · Summary 93

CHAPTER 6   Program Management   95

Bill Bowers

Design of the Athletic Program 95 · Goals and
Objectives 99 · Performance Assessments 104 ·
Strategic Plan 109 · Summary 116

PART II   Operational Process

CHAPTER 7   Allied Educational Services   119

Kim Chorosiewski

Allied Services Programs 119 · Student Health
Services 125 · Sports Medicine Program 131 ·
Strength and Conditioning Program 132 · Role of
Nutrition in Student Health 136 · Academic
Support and Precollege Counseling 137 ·
Summary 141

CHAPTER 8   Scheduling Considerations   143

Steve Berseth

Contest and Event Scheduling 144 · Facility
Scheduling 161 · Scheduling Contest
Officials 167 · Commercial Scheduling Programs
and Products 168 · Summary 169

CHAPTER 9   Transportation   171

Tim Graham

Travel Scheduling 171 · Transportation
Options 175 · Safety Regulations and
Recommendations 178 · Budget
Management 184 · Summary 188

CHAPTER 10   Technology   189

Roy Turner

Professional Development 190 · Office
Productivity 193 · Personal Professional
Productivity 195 · Communications 200 ·
Marketing and Promotions 203 ·
Collaboration 210 · Athletic Performance
and Competition 213 · Summary 218

CHAPTER 11   Contest Management   221

Gary Stevens

Contest Staff Management and Duties 222 ·
Game Management 226 · Emergency and
Security Issues 237 · Summary 241

CHAPTER 12   Legal and Safety Concerns   243

Lee Green

Sports Injury Liability 244 · Title IX
Compliance 259 · Constitutional and Civil Rights
of Student-Athletes 262 · Hazing and Bullying
in Athletic Programs 265 · Sexual Harassment
in Athletic Programs 266 · Summary 268

PART III   Financial Matters

CHAPTER 13   Marketing and Fund-Raising   271

Bob Buckanavage

Nontraditional Marketing 271 · Relationship
Marketing 273 · Interscholastic Sport
Marketing Process 274 · Booster Clubs 277 ·
Corporate Sponsorships 280 · Educational
Foundations and Fund-Raising 286 ·
Summary 290

CHAPTER 14   Budgeting and Purchasing   291

John Evers

Budgeting Process 293 · Documentation 305 ·
Summary 315

PART IV   Physical Assets

CHAPTER 15   **Equipment**   319

Joni Pabst

Equipment Management 319 · Rotation
Plans for Uniforms and Consumable Playing
Equipment 324 · Equipment Repair and
Reconditioning 325 · Inventory Control 328 ·
Accountability 329 · Care of Equipment
and Uniforms 335 · Storage 336 ·
Summary 337

CHAPTER 16   **Facilities**   339

Carter Wilson

Physical Plant 339 · Permanent
Equipment 350 · Building Renovation Versus
New Construction 351 · Maintenance 354 ·
Current Athletic Facility Trends 356 · Athletic
Master Plan 357 · Summary 359

CLOSING   **Priority Issues Ahead in
Interscholastic Sports**   361

Eric Forsyth, John Olson

Specialization by Athletes 364 · Budget, Finance,
and Resource Shortfall 365 · Effect of Fees
on Participation Stability 366 · Electronic Social
Networking 367 · Quality of Coaches and
Continuing Education 367 · Summary 368

References   369
Index   381
About the Editors   390

Contributor List

Steve Berseth, MSc, CMAA

Mike Blackburn, PhD, CMAA

Bill Bowers, CMAA

Bob Buckanavage

Kim Chorosiewski, MEd, CSCS, CMAA

John Evers, CMAA

Eric Forsyth, PhD, CAA

Tim Graham, CMAA

Lee Green, JD

Warren L. Hagman, CMAA

David Hoch, PhD, CMAA

John Olson, PhD, CMAA

Joni Pabst, MA, CAA

Gary Stevens, CMAA

Sheri Stice, CMAA

Roy Turner, CMAA

Bruce Whitehead, CMAA

Carter Wilson, CMAA

Challenges in Today's Interscholastic Sport Administration

Eric Forsyth, PhD, CAA

John Olson, PhD, CMAA

Issues in the field of high school athletic administration have been given little attention compared with coverage of the management and administration of Olympic, professional, and collegiate athletics. This is surprising given the impact of interscholastic sports, as reflected in this statement more than a decade ago: "High school sport programs are now the single most significant dimension in the entire sport enterprise" (Robinson et al. 2001).

More than 23,000 high school athletic departments; approximately 300,000 administrators, coaches, and officials (Bureau of Labor Statistics 2009); and more than 7.6 million students participate in interscholastic competitions (NFHS 2011). Surely, any endeavor with that scope of engagement merits interest. When combined with the potential for both positive and negative outcomes in that environment, it rises to the level of demanding close scrutiny.

The National Interscholastic Athletic Administrators Association (NIAAA) appreciates, perhaps more than most, the importance of high school sports in American culture. The NIAAA also recognizes the huge role an athletic administrator can have in enriching that culture and the experiences of participating athletes and coaches. Therefore, we have developed for aspiring and currently employed athletic directors a comprehensive guidebook featuring the very best practices in high school athletic administration.

The chapters that follow present an overview of high school sports operations, written by experienced, successful athletic administrators across the United States. To focus the efforts of the writers, Forsyth first determined several major issues that challenge contemporary high school sport administrators (Forsyth 2007).

After Forsyth's initial research on the major issues in high school sport, a subsequent investigation assessed and ranked the impact of each identified issue (Forsyth 2010). The findings of the second study provided data for the closing section of this book, Priority Issues Ahead in Interscholastic Sports.

Initial Field Research of Contemporary Issues

After interviews with the Minnesota State High School League (MSHSL) executive board, Forsyth (2010) identified 12 categories encompassing 95 contemporary issues as significant problems for U.S. high school interscholastic athletic programs. To gain deeper insight into these contemporary issues, four experienced and well-respected athletic administrators were interviewed:

- Ken Barreras, director of athletics, Albuquerque Public Schools, NM
- Kim Chorosiewski, director of athletics, Fay School in Southborough, MA
- Dave Stead, executive director, MSHSL
- Bruce Whitehead, executive director, NIAAA

Each provided opinions as to what these issues mean for everyday interscholastic athletic administrators at the local, district, state, and national levels. In addition, all were asked to predict the future implications of these contemporary issues. The following interview responses identify the major challenges facing today's interscholastic athletic administrators.

Initial Research Findings and Commentary on Current Issues in High School Athletics

In the following sections, issues are followed by commentary provided during interviews of experienced high school athletic administrators.

Athletic Administrator Training and Preparation for the Complexity of the Task

Current applicants for athletic director positions are lacking in the knowledge and skill proficiencies required for the job. These deficits make it clear that newly hired athletic administrators must have access to state-of-the art knowledge and expertise in order to competently lead contemporary high school athletic programs. Following are the opinions of experienced high school, state association, and national leaders in high school sports on this topic.

Ken Barreras: The ability to recruit and retain competent athletic administrators is becoming increasingly difficult for two reasons. First, the scope of work has increased exponentially, making it necessary for an athletic administrator to be well versed in a variety of areas (e.g., legislative impacts, booster club involvement, budget and finance) beyond the normal, everyday issues of managing people and facilities. Second, the pool of candidates for high school athletic director jobs has become smaller over time, and applicants are less experienced and qualified than in earlier years. To some extent, this phenomenon has evolved because of an increase in the number of nonfaculty coaches who do not have interest in administrative positions. Historically, veteran educators with a great deal of coaching experience moved into administrative positions and used this experience and associated knowledge to administer an athletic program. With fewer coaches remaining in the profession long enough to be considered veterans, the ability to hire experienced and qualified coaches to fill administrator positions has been compromised.

Kim Chorosiewski: As with all roles, a fundamental knowledge base will give an athletic administrator both the competence and confidence to execute the daily duties of the position while being guided by sound principles of education. With experience comes expertise. However, technology and societal demands on sports have undergone massive changes. That being the case, it would be unwise for athletic directors to feel overly confident about the level of expertise they might bring to the contemporary high school athletics setting.

Dave Stead: Given the change in education funding, it's become more frequent that an athletic administrator's responsibilities are combined with student services responsibilities (e.g., assistant principal). Such a combination, regardless of the size of the school, seems to do a disservice to both the administrator and school community. Expertise in the administration of student activities differs widely among educational administrators, and an integral involvement in and working knowledge of athletic and fine arts programs truly is an essential component of a well-constructed school activities position.

Bruce Whitehead: The administration of an interscholastic athletic program today requires a person with broad-based knowledge and training and a passion to serve students and coaches. A school district that employs an athletic administrator lacking these skills creates potential liability exposure. School districts must be committed to providing the best educational opportunities for students by hiring the best-qualified staff in academic subject areas. This same high standard should also apply when seeking an athletic administrator. The NIAAA is the first career, technical, and postsecondary association accredited by the North Central Association Commission on Accreditation and School Improvement. To respond to the needs of employed athletic directors and candidates for administrative vacancies, the NIAAA has developed education and certification programs specific to interscholastic athletic administration. This program provides the knowledge and training athletic administrators need. The enormity of contemporary athletic administration responsibilities has created a mandate for adequate training.

Community-Based Sport Programs Versus School Sport Programs

As more community-based youth sports programs are developed, more student participants are asked to compete for school and nonschool sports teams simultaneously. This arrangement can impose intense demands on students in terms of time and commitment.

Ken Barreras: Athletics and activities, while healthy and recommended for the well-being of the students, have often taken priority over the curricular necessities. As with other health and wellness concepts, participation in extracurricular activities should be limited. It is the responsibility of athletic and school administrators to ensure that the demands imposed on these young people are reasonable.

Kim Chorosiewski: Demand will eventually demonstrate that community and school programs cannot be all things to all people all the time. The economy will force school and community partnerships that will require some political negotiation and grassroots support to sustain educationally sound programs that also meet the needs of all sports users.

Dave Stead: The values gained by students through participation in high school activities are often compromised by coaches whose educational philosophy differs from the foundational beliefs and core values of educational institutions. Care must be taken to support and protect student participants at all levels in order to avoid burnout and overexertion of adolescents whose bodies are still developing.

Bruce Whitehead: Excessive demands on the time and energy of student-athletes both in and out of season are major issues for athletic administrators. Even though student-athletes experience time demands from coaches, many continue to maintain higher grade point averages and have better attendance records, fewer discipline issues, and lower dropout rates than the general student population.

In summary, athletic directors are facing ever-increasing challenges because they are being asked to do more with less. School budget cuts are forcing the elimination of paid positions that support athletic administrators. Budget cuts mean less funding to operate the programs. In addition, the number of responsibilities assigned to contemporary athletic administrators is growing. The position of interscholastic athletic administrator is rapidly becoming a highly challenging job in any school district, requiring the longest workweek and expertise in multiple disciplines.

Parents

Some parents have lost sight, or never knew the purpose, of interscholastic sport programs. The local school athletic program's mission statement should be shared with parents and athletes along with the mission statements of the state association, NFHS, and NIAAA.

Ken Barreras: As with many areas of public education, parental involvement (and lack thereof) and the unreasonable expectations of a small number of parents have created pockets of turmoil in interscholastic athletics. In some cases, a coach's perspective varies greatly from the parents'. Because of emotional responses and challenges by parents, it is my thought that coaches, especially inexperienced coaches, have become hesitant to communicate with parents in any form in order to avoid conflict and dissension. I have witnessed, with increasing frequency, parents intent on extending their decision-making and leadership roles in private-sector community (club) programs to education-based athletic programs. These misunderstandings lead to great confusion and conflict with coaches and athletic administrators.

Kim Chorosiewski: Parents see sports as a social identifier for students while also enabling success as the students proceed through the education cycle. Although there can be a time-demand tipping point in terms of participation in school- and non-school-related sports programs, it is the larger demand on social, physical, and emotional domains that has left player development and growth in question. Some parents are totally entrenched in the culture of immediacy, forgetting all variables that affect sport and education outcomes. Similarly, the line has been blurred by society about the intent of sports and participation at all levels. Educators must never lose sight of the privilege of athletic participation and the organic intent for participating. Athletic administrators must remind parents and coaches that the athletic program should always be compatible with the educational mission of the school, district, state, and NFHS.

Dave Stead: High school activities are not "the other half of education." In fact, high school activities are an integral part of education, and we must continually focus on the educational opportunities provided by state associations and their member high schools. Parents must be taught to focus on the value of participation rather than winning. This commitment must begin with the school board and be fully supported by school administrators in order to support the athletic director in his role within the school community.

Bruce Whitehead: In recent years, dealing with parents has become more time consuming for the athletic administrator and coach. The parental attitude of supporting the school and the coach has completely changed. The adage that "students have changed over the years" is really a myth, but the adage that "parents have changed" is a reality. An increasing number of parents no longer support the school, the team, and the coach. These parents support and encourage only their child at the expense of the team, the coach, and all other participants. They have lost sight of reality with respect to their child and the mission of interscholastic athletic participation. This phenomenon causes the contemporary athletic administrator and coach to devote additional time to educating this growing number of parents.

Sporting Behavior

Considering the worsening spectator conduct and courtesy that coaches, officials, and parents face, there is a clear need to emphasize sporting behavior throughout interscholastic sports. Ongoing proactive educational measures must be a priority for the contemporary administrator. Negative modeling by players, coaches, and spectators at higher levels of competitions creates an image that is emulated in high school sports all too quickly unless consistent preventive measures are taken.

Ken Barreras: Much like educating student-athletes about drug and alcohol use, this is an area that often has a lower priority, with coaches and athletic administrators taking a less active approach. Too often, the teaching and maintenance of sporting behavior are reactive in nature and addressed only after a critical issue.

Kim Chorosiewski: This issue stems from a school and community culture that demands proactive measures in order to protect the sanctity of sport. We are making strides in this area, especially since professional teams are faced with the need to curtail poor fan choices, some of which have resulted in the deaths of spectators.

Dave Stead: Life lessons are learned on the field as well as in the classroom by athletes and fine arts participants. A school board initiative for sporting behavior, supported by parents and community members, is an essential ingredient for a well-rounded school activity program.

Bruce Whitehead: There is no doubt that participation in interscholastic athletics teaches student-athletes character, moral and ethical values, and leadership skills that will serve the students for life. These foundational values may not be taught in private-sector clubs. Of concern to athletic administrators is the growing lack of sporting behavior demonstrated by increasing numbers of students, parents, and other adult spectators at interscholastic sports events. The NIAAA, the NFHS, and most state activity and athletic associations continue to develop advertising campaigns and education programs about the importance of positive behavior. This is yet another issue the athletic administrator of 20 years ago did not need to devote as much time to.

Title IX and Gender Equity

Approximately 4.4 million boys and 3.2 million girls participate in interscholastic sport competitions (NFHS 2011), demonstrating increased opportunities and fairness for both males and females. However, compliance with Title IX appears to have become a double-edged sword. When providing programs for both genders, if there is not enough female interest to warrant adding new competition levels or new sports, this lack of growth can be interpreted as noncompliance unless surveys of student interests can document the reasons for not providing new opportunities.

Ken Barreras: New state legislation in New Mexico has increased awareness of Title IX legislation and gender equity issues in their athletic program. Two positive factors evolved from the increased awareness created by this legislation: (1) better education and instruction about compliance and (2) the sharing of best practices and compliance approaches used by fellow athletic administrators. A negative issue that resulted from publicity associated with the new legislation includes misconceptions and misinterpretations regarding gender equity among parents and coaches.

Kim Chorosiewski: Common sense has distorted the spirit of Title IX in ways that force administrators to support programs that should not exist to satisfy the letter of the law. Revisions should be considered to the Education Amendment Act.

Dave Stead: Schools may be able to turn a perceived negative into a positive by actively reviewing the Title IX three-prong test. By doing so, growth in boys' and girls' athletics may have a positive outcome. The outside-the-box growth of coed teams, collaborative efforts through intramural activities, and other community-generated programs for students who have not yet become connected to standard school offerings may attract an entirely different group of students to athletic involvement at the middle school and high school level.

Bruce Whitehead: For many years, the NIAAA and NFHS have emphasized the importance of Title IX compliance by state activity and athletic associations and schools across the United States. I believe a very high percentage of our schools are in compliance with Title IX because of these education efforts by state and national organizations. However, some needs persist at the interscholastic level.

A school must meet only one of the three Title IX tests, and most athletic administrators work diligently to meet the requirement of accommodating emerging interests. Athletic administrators attempt to offer a sport or new level of competition for both boys and girls when there is demonstrated interest. Factors considered include sufficient ability to field a viable team and adequate numbers to support multiple competitive levels. Athletic administrators who comply with the interest accommodation prong of Title IX usually are found to be in compliance. At the same time, as the director of the NIAAA, I believe we must continue to send the message to our membership that every effort must be made to achieve Title IX compliance by meeting one of the three Title IX tests.

Summary

The contemporary high school athletic administrator faces significant challenges because of increased demands and fewer resources. School budget cuts are forcing the elimination of paid positions that support athletic administrators. Budget reductions also mean less funding to operate the programs. In addition, the number of responsibilities assigned to athletic administrators grows constantly. The position of interscholastic athletic administrator is rapidly becoming one of the most challenging in any school, and the job increasingly demands expertise in multiple disciplines. This book is dedicated to meeting those needs.

PART I

Leadership Orientation

The six chapters included in part I provide an overview of the characteristics of successful leadership. Education-based athletic programs must have student learning, personal growth, and total welfare at their core. The chapters in part I address developing a personal philosophy based on the core principles of education-based athletics and how to manage your program, personnel, and student-athletes in a way that reflects those principles.

CHAPTER 1

Professional Foundations

Bruce Whitehead, CMAA

Mike Blackburn, PhD, CMAA

Hundreds of millions of Americans have participated in organized sports programs, and the educational setting has been the primary source of most experiences. Sports offerings in schools have been a valuable and integral part of education (Stevenson 2007) for well over a century. They served as an agent of change for the nation, contributed to the uniqueness of American competitiveness, have become a cornerstone of schools in the United States, and now entrust each generation with educational traditions. Interscholastic athletic programs have become an essential teacher of fundamental life skills to students.

The significance of interscholastic athletics was evident in the 2010 season when spectator attendance at high school sports events exceeded 510 million people for the top 16 programs participated in by students (Vaccaro 2011). In addition, 2011 marked the 22nd consecutive year for record sport participation in the nation's high school athletic programs, as the total number of participants grew to more than 7.6 million. It has been estimated that 55 percent of students participate in sports programs provided by schools (Koebler 2011). With approximately 23,000 potential athletic departments and 300,000 administrators, coaches, and officials, interscholastic athletics rank as perhaps the United States' most significant contributor to the enterprise of sport (Forsyth 2010). Interscholastic athletic programs have long been considered one of education's best bargains, utilizing only 1 to 3 percent of the total school budget (NFHS 2012).

Education-based athletics are often the fabric that endears a student, a family, and a community to the school. Athletic programs offer equal access to opportunity regardless of race, social class, or culture. As an essential arm of education, athletic programs do not divert attention from student learning but serve as an extension of the classroom. A primary goal of interscholastic programs is to support the academic curriculum and classroom schedule. High school programs must focus on developing the total student from a base of student centeredness while consistently remaining compatible with

> **Education-based athletic programs must have student learning, personal growth, and total welfare at their core. This philosophy drives the programs in all offerings, safety mechanisms, and decisions.**

the academic mission of the school. Education-based athletic programs must have student learning, personal growth, and total welfare at their core. This philosophy drives the programs in all offerings, safety mechanisms, and decisions. An outstanding teaching laboratory exists in sport, and education-based athletics provide the proper atmosphere for student-athletes to become immersed and flourish, committed to cooperative goals larger than themselves as individuals.

School sports are inherently educational (Pedersen et al. 2011), promoting through participation skills that cannot be taught via the formal curriculum. The life lessons taught through education-based athletics cannot be quantified on a written test. A floor burn earned diving for the ball or a blister acquired from an uneven bar routine can be as indicative of future success in adulthood as are standardized test scores. Sport resembles life in a microcosm, and the athletic fields, pools, tracks, courses, and courts of our nation's schools are inspirational classrooms. Sports require working together to overcome difficult individual or group challenges, maintaining perseverance, accepting defeat graciously, learning to sacrifice for others, and cooperatively pursuing victory; these are the life lesson benefits of education-based athletics.

Association With Academic Achievement

High school sports participation is correlated with lower dropout rates, fewer discipline referrals, higher grade point averages, better graduation rates, and improved daily attendance when records of participants are compared with those of nonparticipants. Studies have shown better test scores, lower rates of alcohol and tobacco use, and a positive view of school and the educational process (Roberts 1993).

Longitudinal studies have shown the most beneficial form of involvement for student achievement is interscholastic sports participation, shown to assist in raising students' grades and test scores (Broh 2002). Studies in Colorado (IAHSAA 1992), Indiana (Blackburn 2004), Iowa (Blackburn 2000), Kansas (NFHS 1977), Michigan (NIAAA 1992), Minnesota (Born 2007; NCHSAA 2012), New Mexico (Bukowski 2001), North Carolina (Overton 2003; Whitley 2003), North Dakota (NFHS 1980), Oregon (Mannen 1997) and Texas (California Interscholastic Federation 2009) have all shown significantly better grade point averages, as much as 25 percent higher, among high school student-athletes compared with nonparticipants. Recent studies have further shown that those who participate in multiple sport seasons in high school have higher grade point averages during participation (Sawyer et al., 2012). Trends toward higher grades favored athletes compared with nonathletes among Hispanic, African American, and Caucasian students, both in season and out of season (Jeziorski 1994). Participants were three times more likely to perform in the top quartile of composite math and reading assessments compared with those who did not participate in athletics (National Center for Educational Statistics 1995). Further, sport activities have a great benefit for high-risk youth in reducing problem behaviors (Fredricks 2006).

Factors that contribute to the academic success of multisport student-athletes include better time management by students, academic eligibility requirements for athletics, better school attendance, physical conditioning, sport's positive relationship with brain effectiveness, promotion of academic excellence in athletics, and recognition programs. Regular school attendance required to practice and participate translates to academic performance (Becker 1993). In addition, education-based athletics promote commitment and cooperation, provide many teachable moments that engage learners, foster the development of supportive relationships that serve as a safety net of affiliation, and provide critical-thinking and problem-solving experiences.

Contributor to Future Success

Heath (1992) found that extracurricular participation is a strong predictor of adult success, comparable to academic achievement or standardized test scores. The real measure of success as an adult include positive involvements in and contributions to the community, spiritual organizations, and society, along with a sense of well-being and happiness, achievement in a profession, and providing assistance to other people. High school athletic programs are the ideal classroom for learning real-life skills such as self-worth, confidence, determination, structure, and loyalty.

After graduation, varsity athletes are more likely than nonparticipants to earn a bachelor's degree, be employed full time, have higher levels of income, and participate in physical fitness activities, while being less likely to smoke (NFHS 2006). Participation had a positive affect on future wage earnings later in life (Kosteas 2012). Student-athletes were better prepared for postsecondary education (NASBE 2004), took more rigorous courses, and focused on long-term life accomplishments via short-term goals.

Young women who participated in school-related sports teams were less sexually active and experienced fewer teen pregnancies by 37 percent (OSAA 2012). Female participants also had lower risks of breast cancer, heart disease, and osteoporosis (Indiana Women's History Association 2003).

Other important personal qualities gained through participation in education-based athletics include resiliency, self-motivation, a strong work ethic, self-discipline, and initiative. Participants endeavor to distinguish themselves in citizenship, higher standards of behavior, and respect for self and others. The strengths of determination, dedication, and resourcefulness are prevalent. Additional attributes include integrity, honesty, reliability, and ethical behavior. Athletes in school programs dream big dreams and are goal oriented, thriving on adaptability, positive attitude, self-awareness, and enthusiasm. Leaders promote patience, responsibility, empathy, and compassion. Pride in effort and a willingness to prepare create a foundation on which other areas of success are built (Sheehy 2002). Success is often attributed to perseverance more than talent, and being passionate about athletic programs can promote enthusiasm in later life endeavors.

That is not to say that running, jumping, lifting, catching, kicking, or throwing are more important than academics. Nor is it to suggest that sports participation is more important than family time, spiritual commitment, or assisting those in need within our communities. However, few pursuits have such a high educational payoff as school-based athletics. Ruffin (Michigan High School Athletic Association n.d.) went so far as to say that such activities represent the salvation of schools and perhaps the nation. Education-based athletic programs provide young people a place to belong and be cared for, a place where they can make mistakes and still grow and be accepted.

Origin and Framework of Interscholastic Athletics

High school athletic programs established roots long ago, gaining impetus within the 50 states as well as being influenced by people from across the globe. This unique American experiment of sports infiltrating the educational system evolved over the years and followed quite a nontraditional avenue.

Youth have participated in sporting activities since the earliest settling of the country. Beginning with the Native Americans' form of lacrosse, the settlers' pursuit of recreation was often sport of a subsistence nature including hunting, fishing, and horse racing. Early colonists considered sport idleness when compared with taming the land and personal survival. Although shooting competitions were allowed because of the need for a trained militia, society as well as the church often regarded recreational events as vain. This view of sport as a wasteful pastime existed because gambling often was intricately associated. Among the aristocrats, however, outlets of recreation began to manifest themselves.

As the urbanization of eastern cities continued and as people moved westward and settled in remote geographical areas, each demographic offered unique sporting outgrowths. The competitions in which the inhabitants participated were determined by the natural resources of the land and by the nationalities of the settlers. From rail-splitting contests to cycling, from rodeo events to sandlot baseball, from horseshoe pitching to sailboat racing, and from plowing matches to golf, settlers in each area of the country developed a contest to meet their competitive interests. Eventually, sport gave way to a melting pot of games, rules, and traditions brought by immigrants from around the world, with a strong impact from European countries.

Sport was used as an outreach to curb youth civil disobedience as well as to socialize new citizens and foster patriotism as the country struggled to democratize the influx of immigrants from abroad. Sport flourished in both strong and difficult economic times, displayed by the Work Progress Administration's building thousands of athletic facilities during the Great Depression. New inventions, the advent of electricity, and the manufacturing boom manifested athletic interests. Products and services such as vulcanized rubber, railroad travel, and the telephone related to the athletic interests of both spectator and participant.

Leisure in the Unites States moved from play to recreation, from diversion to a way to incorporate national loyalty, and from sport to a developer of admirable character traits fostered through athletic program participation. Early athletic opportunities in high school communities were often initiated by college students who provided coaching, officiating, and facilities. Colleges also utilized such initiatives for the recruitment of high school athletes to their student-organized college teams (Riess 1995).

World wars prompted education to implement mass activities and become involved in physical training of prospective soldiers. Education gradually adopted sport as an agent to gain control of programs and develop good character traits. High school athletics were both influenced by and bridged the gap in helping the United States address desegregation during the 1950s and 1960s civil rights movement. In 1972, Title IX ensured equal opportunity for participation in educational programs including interscholastic athletics. One result of this act has been the 40-year increase of female participants from 300,000 to more than 3 million at the high school level. Extracurricular activities were accepted in the school as a positive extension of school offerings through a process of conflict and compromise among students, teachers, educational leaders, communities, and politicians. Over the years, the field of high school athletics has served as a positive model for change related to culture, ethnicity, race, religion, and gender.

State governing bodies empowered to oversee the growing high school athletic programs began to form in the early 1900s, and the National Federation of State High School Associations (NFHS) began in 1921 as a rule-writing organization. The developments demonstrated the national scope of high school sports by that time. Just as associations developed competition rules and standards based on foundation beliefs about participation, states began to provide athletic directors with professional growth opportunities to share innovations and ideas. The first such state organization appeared in New Jersey in 1951. In 1977, the National Interscholastic Athletic Administrators Association (NIAAA) was organized for the professional development of athletic administrators.

Professional Foundations

The value of education-based athletic experiences cannot be voiced any more emphatically than when actual program participants tell their stories. Student-athletes possess the perspective and the experiences to best express the benefits of being involved in a school sport learning experience. Each year the NIAAA sponsors the Student Essay/Scholarship Program for all 50 states and the District of Columbia. An important portion of the scholarship application is a written essay titled "How High School Athletics Has Impacted My Life." Listen to the life lessons learned as these students share their heartfelt experiences.

"High school athletics . . . have tested my character, heart, and wisdom through various challenges [and] taught me countless lessons about teamwork, responsibility, dedication, willpower, and leadership. . . . These little miracles happen everywhere in high school athletics. The lessons you learn in athletics can be life changing."

Jace Billingsley, Nevada

"It was through . . . high school sports that I have learned to love being active. It also taught me the importance of eating healthy and taking care of my body in order to perform at my optimum level. . . . The sum of these experiences has led me to choose my future career field."

Michelle Fischer, Iowa

"Most importantly, I acquired an inexorable strength of self-respect. . . . I now understand that success can only be attained if one risks failure. Equipped with this new knowledge and desire to excel, I have since pursued endeavors and leadership positions I would never have imagined in the past."

Stephanie Honig, Maryland

"Through high school sports . . . I have grown to be creative with the choices I have, and I've gained decision-making skills that have enabled me to overcome challenges. . . . My high school sports have immensely helped to express my passion for life. . . . Gaining confidence in my ability to succeed, I am creating new ideas and solutions for my future."

McKenzie Johnson, Idaho

"High school athletics have taken me on a journey the past four years of my life and taught me valuable lessons that no teacher or textbook could have ever touched on. I am truly grateful to have been given the opportunity to grow and develop with such a positive influence."

Erin Kocher, Florida

" I learned from athletics . . . to not give in to temptation. . . . [Athletics] taught me that it is important to stay above peer pressure."

Josepyh Kuiper, Iowa

"To me, sports are . . . mediums for learning lifelong lessons that help build character."

Matthew Letourneau, New York

"An athlete must recognize all of the individual factors in the span of a few seconds. . . . The ability to see problems clearly, deduce the proper solution, and carry out that action . . . [has] particularly helped me in my studies by allowing me to . . . systematically attack problems."

Peter Redgrave, Virginia

Profile of the Athletic Administrator Position

Athletic administration as a profession has undergone significant and continual change over the past three decades. As interscholastic sports has increased participation over the last 40 years (NFHS 2011a), the role of the athletic administrator has evolved into a significant position of professional leadership in secondary schools. This increased participation has resulted in increased sports offerings and more responsibility for the program administrator. Whether one has the title of assistant principal for athletics, athletic administrator, athletic director, athletic coordinator, or athletic liaison, the responsibilities are similar and too numerous to mention in this brief account. The role of the athletic administrator is to provide leadership for the athletic program and to manage its daily operation. Athletic administrators must follow the statement of Warren Bennis (NIAAA 2010, 52): "Managers are people who do things right; leaders are people who do the right thing."

Few could argue the fact that more is expected from today's athletic administrators than ever before. The position of interscholastic athletic administrator is unique and has become one of the most complex positions within the secondary educational setting. It also remains one of the most misunderstood positions. Ever-increasing demands and expectations, new sports additions, the changing parent, fiscal tightening, and managing risk for safety and liability are but a few of the issues that have stretched and challenged today's athletic administrators. Technology continues to alter the profession—both positively and negatively—and in ways that were unimaginable a decade ago. There have been many innovations in the administration of athletic programs; even so, new challenges have increased for which administrators must find solutions. An athletic administrator wears many hats and should possess some degree of expertise in a variety of disciplines. So what is the profile of the position of interscholastic athletic administrator today?

The position requires a person who is a servant leader. As a servant leader, the athletic administrator has a significant impact on the coach and the student-athlete by providing participation opportunities, safety, and leadership. Within this context, this position requires one to be a visionary, a director, a manager, a communicator, and a counselor, while also being knowledgeable in sport law. Athletic administration requires skill in the development, maintenance, and improvement of the total program. The athletic administrator in concert with the coaching staff must be the driving force in establishing the program philosophy and communicating that philosophy to students, coaches, faculty, administration, and the community.

As a director, the athletic administrator oversees and directly addresses all aspects of the program. He must coordinate team rosters and student eligibility as well as the scheduling of contests, officials, transportation, and event personnel. Personal satisfaction of a job well done is derived from directing outstanding events that provide valuable participation opportunities for the students. The administrator is behind the scenes, supporting coaches and athletes and leading others to personal and group successes. It is the attention to detail in the preparation of events that ensures they will be conducted flawlessly. Conducting successful, uneventful activities develops confidence, support, and trust among all members of the school community.

As a manager, the athletic administrator is responsible for facilities, including maintenance, capital improvements, and scheduling. The athletic administrator may supervise the care and safety of numerous venues. Overseeing inspections, scheduling, repairs and updates, preventive maintenance, and major improvements can be quite time consuming. Providing safe facilities for participants and spectators must be the highest priority. In addition, most visitors, whether in or outside the community, will arrive through the gates of the school's athletic facilities. An aesthetic, well-groomed, clean, and safe physical plant provides a lasting impression of the school and of the entire community as well.

The administrator must also manage and oversee the purchase, inventory, and care of such items as uniforms, large equipment, and consumable goods. This is not limited to the equipment used by each sport; it also includes equipment found in the various facilities such as training room equipment and supplies, weight room equipment, seating, lighting, playing surfaces, and concession equipment and supplies.

The athletic administrator must have strengths as a writer and be an articulate communicator. As the athletic disciplinarian, he must assume the development and enforcement of policy, codes of conduct, and handbooks. He should communicate a mission statement, training rules, district policies and department guidelines, objectives, and expectations through publications, preseason parent meetings, awards programs, coaches' workshops, a website, presentations to community groups, and other methods of sharing information. The school's philosophy and governing information must be in harmony with those of the state association and school district.

The athletic administrator is a personnel manager who must constantly strive to recruit, hire, and train coaches and other department staff. All staff must possess educationally sound compatible philosophies, exemplary behavior, and ethical values. While being mindful of equity among staff and in the representation of athletes, the athletic administrator must seek coaches who are good teachers that model these qualities during both practice and competition, in the classroom, and in personal lifestyle. The employment of coaches and related workers, a trend that began in 2008, is expected to increase by 23 percent through 2018, which is higher than the average for all occupations (Bureau of Labor and Statistics 2009).

The administrator's legal responsibilities exceed the scope of previous generations. Today these responsibilities include certification of the athletic administrator, safety issues, ADA guidelines, legal liability, ethical considerations, Title IX, coaches' education, promotion of proper athlete training principles, and sportsmanship.

Finally, as a role model the athletic administrator sets the example for coaches, student-athletes, parents, officials, and spectators. As the administrator works with the media, counsels parents, hosts officials, mentors coaches, and teaches and encourages students, her personal demeanor will set the tone. The interscholastic athletic program is the most visible of all school programs to the public. The athletic administrator must possess strong vision as a positive ambassador and as a beacon in leading the way.

Professional Preparation for the Athletic Administrator Position

No course of study or college degree will adequately prepare an individual to perform the duties of an interscholastic athletic administrator—the position requires a wide variety of skills and a diverse knowledge base in a multitude of subject matters. In fact, very few universities include curriculum leading to a degree related to interscholastic athletic administration. Today's collegiate curriculum is often directed more toward sport management and sport marketing degrees at the collegiate and professional levels. The NIAAA has filled this void and embarked on curriculum development and certifications specific for people desiring to be an interscholastic athletic administrator.

So what does a person do to prepare to be an effective interscholastic athletic administrator? To fully understand the preparation required, one must examine a few characteristics of outstanding athletic administrators. Although having a varied knowledge and background in high school sport is beneficial, the learning curve is less steep for those who have participated, coached, or officiated at the high school level. These areas provide a base understanding of the concept and philosophy of interscholastic athletics; however, this is simply the tip of the iceberg.

A degree in the field of education provides an understanding of the school climate. The athletic administrator must understand how the program fits within the school's total educational offering, and a degree that supplies administrative experiences can be very beneficial. A task-oriented person with a commitment and dedication to the well-rounded education of all student-athletes is much better equipped to be an interscholastic athletic administrator. Much of the job revolves around working with and managing people, and it is incumbent to have some background in related skills.

Perhaps more important than the personal preparation before becoming an athletic administrator is what one does after becoming one. State athletic and activity association mandates and the accompanying work, paired with greater accountability at all levels, point to the fact that continuous professional growth and personal improvement is imperative. How do athletic directors continually improve their ability to cope with or meet the growing list of demands of upper-level administration as well as the needs of student-athletes, coaches, parents, and other community members? The most frequent answer is professional development. Professional development can be defined as the process of learning and remaining current in one's area of expertise while adding to or strengthening the specialized knowledge and skills used in one's profession (NIAAA 2010).

Today's athletic administrators should use multiple options to accomplish professional growth, including university graduate classes, online classes, conference seminars and workshops sponsored by the NIAAA, and state athletic and activity associations. Professional books, journals, and other published materials are made available by and through the NIAAA. Two particular NIAAA-sponsored programs that lend themselves well to professional development for interscholastic athletic administrators are the Leadership Training Institute and the athletic administrator certification program.

The Leadership Training Institute (LTI) is a professional development education program established in 1997 that includes a broad-based curriculum specific to interscholastic athletic administration. Written by athletic administrators and other experts in the field, the LTI curriculum provides the opportunity to become a lifelong learner. The objectives of the LTI are as follows:

- To promote the professional growth and prestige of athletic administrators

- To provide an opportunity for athletic administrators to participate in the nation's largest professional organization, whose activities are directed exclusively to high school and middle school athletic administrators

- To provide education programs as a resource tool for athletic administrators

- To promote quality in all programs conducted at the national, state, and local level (NIAAA 2011a)

The institute continually expands its course offerings and updates existing courses. The program currently consists of 37 courses separated into three categories. Foundation courses (500 level) address the fundamental concepts of overall program philosophy, budgeting, scheduling, legal duties, and organization. Operations courses (600 level) address various management aspects of the program including sports medicine, facilities, scheduling, technology, time management, and event security. Leadership courses (700 level) address strategies and practices involved in personnel and self-management, assessment, communication, leadership, and character development.

A testament to the quality of material for both education and professional growth is the fact that many colleges and universities are currently using LTI curriculum content in either an undergraduate, graduate, or certificate program. Classes are taught face to face in more than 45 states by state athletic administrator associations. In addition, courses available online and via the Internet in a webinar setting give busy athletic administrators the opportunity for professional growth without leaving the home or office.

An important professional recognition program is also provided by the NIAAA for athletic administrators. This program is the multi-level certification program. Tied to the Leadership Training Institute, the certification program offers athletic administrators the opportunity to demonstrate a broad-based knowledge of the duties of athletic administration and to become certified in one of four levels. The objectives of the certification program are as follows:

- To promote professional standards, practices, and ethics
- To encourage self-assessment by offering guidelines for achievement
- To improve performance by encouraging participation in a continuing program of professional growth and development
- To identify levels of educational training essential for effective athletic administration
- To foster professional contributions to the field

- To maximize the benefits received by the school community from the leadership provided by certified athletic administrators (NIAAA 2011a).

To accommodate those currently in athletic administration at the high school or middle school level, and those aspiring to become an interscholastic athletic administrator, the NIAAA offers different certification levels. Registered athletic administrator (RAA) is a certification for those who aspire to become an athletic director or are in the early stages of athletic administration. This certification level gives people the opportunity to demonstrate their professional desire to obtain or grow in a position. RAA requires the completion of two LTI courses. The registered middle school athletic administrator (RMSAA) level of certification is designed for those who are middle school athletic administrators. Many middle school athletic administrators cannot qualify for the certified athletic administrator (CAA) course or do not aspire to become a CAA, making the middle school athletic administrator (MSAA) the credible option for certification. The RMSAA certification requires completing five LTI courses. The CAA certification is designed for high school, and some middle school athletic administrators, and requires successfully completing four LTI classes, attaining a minimum requirement of points on the personal data form, and passing an exam. Athletic administrators who achieve CAA certification demonstrate significant professional knowledge and experiences that set them apart from their peers, serving as a mark of excellence in the profession.

The highest level of certification is the certified master athletic administrator (CMAA). The CMAA designation can be sought only after the athletic administrator has attained the CAA certification. In addition to this prerequisite, the CMAA requires completing an additional six LTI classes beyond the original five courses completed, a minimum requirement of points on a personal data form, and completion of a project that will be, or has been, implemented to benefit an athletic program. About 2 percent of the nation's athletic administrators have demonstrated this level of excellence by attaining the CMAA certification.

Participating in the NIAAA programs of leadership training and certification is the most focused and in-depth interscholastic athletic administration preparation an individual can pursue. Program participants are exposed to the best practices, current law, and most beneficial resources in the profession. They also receive the opportunity to grow by professionally networking with colleagues.

Design of the Athletic Program

Interscholastic athletic programs must continue to be an integral part of the total American educational community. They must be conducted as educationally sound classrooms in which students are taught core values such as personal sacrifice, responsibility, commitment, and cooperation. A quality athletic program is one that provides all students an equal opportunity to experience physical, emotional, and intellectual growth. One goal is for the student-athlete to learn to accept personal responsibility for success and failure, and to recognize the limitations and strengths of both areas.

It is important for everyone related to the program, including students, staff, and parents, to realize that participation in an athletic program is a privilege. The program is for individuals who possess the correct attitude, ability, desire, and competitive spirit. Success defined by wins and losses, while important, do not match the true standards and expectations of quality interscholastic sport. Designed not simply for the elite athlete, education-based athletics support the growth of all participants in overcoming adversity and gaining resourcefulness.

Administrative support is a necessary component when constructing a quality athletic program. Serving as an administrator in the total school setting, the athletic program should complement the classroom curriculum of the school in terms of achievement, success, and standard of excellence. Mentoring of coaches and parents as active participants in encouraging and monitoring the academic progress of the student-athlete is an important role of the athletic administrator.

A proper perspective of winning is an integral component in helping students understand how to accept defeat graciously and lose with character. Winning seems to be of ultimate importance to coaches, athletes, and parents in society today. This perspective bears upon athletic administrators to provide a proper perspective and balance. Competing to the best of one's ability with utmost integrity should be the standard, as compared to a win-at-all-costs philosophy.

Promoting good sportsmanship and citizenship is a lifeblood of every quality program. The lifelong lessons taught via interscholastic athletics will manifest if built upon expectations of proper ethics and conduct. This begins with coaches and the perspective filtered from the athletic administrator. Also, the expectations conveyed to parents and community must include proper actions toward one another, opponents, and contest officials.

Every effort should be made to provide education, resources, and support to the student athlete on the subject of alcohol, drugs, and performance-enhancing substances. Student athletes, first and foremost, need an education and a program that serves as a deterrent for student athletes facing peer pressure, societal mixed messages, and media attention. All should be trained to recognize early warning signs. While a code of conduct, rules, and discipline is punitive, it is an important part of resources for students.

An unacceptable trend that has grown dramatically in recent years is school hazing and bullying. This area requires an extensive education program for all stakeholders since a number of actions that fall under these categories can be accepted in some demographic sectors. No initiation for participation as a "rite of passage" for upperclassmen should be allowed. Violent or nonviolent acts of individuals against other individuals must not be tolerated.

Equal opportunity for potential participants must be a priority. Title IX prohibits discrimination based on gender in educational programs and activities that receive Federal funds. The law directed schools to provide equal opportunities for both male and female students in the school environment. While quality athletic programs should not need a mandate, equal opportunities extend to competitions, scheduling, contests, practice times, access to comparable facilities, comparable coaching equipment, uniforms, transportation, and support services.

Perhaps the single most critical aspect of the athletic administrator's job is doing everything possible to minimize risk for students, coaches, contest officials, and spectators. Risk management involves more than safe facilities and equipment. It requires education of everyone relative to written plans for emergency situations, proper protocol, safety related to practice drills and conditioning methods, teaching of proper skills and techniques, maintenance of facilities, and recognizing dangerous environments.

A quality athletic program works to gain and maintain support of parents and community. Cooperative efforts by everyone will go far to achieve a significant positive impact toward the growth and development of young people. Auxiliary groups, including booster clubs, parent-teacher associations, and civic organizations, can assist in guidance, leadership, and encouragement of students as they mature in their athletic programs.

The athletic administrator is responsible for one of the school's most visible, valuable, and challenging programs. The athletic program, which carries no academic credit, provides numerous opportunities in which the public can see measurable results and monitor accountability through performance. All must ensure that athletic programs not be a diversion, but rather, an extension of educational values.

The board of education or private school governance board is the school or district leadership organization that is responsible for implementing state and federal laws, while also developing directives and policies. The superintendent is responsible for administration of schools according to adopted policies and in accordance with state school code. The official representative of the school is the principal who is directly responsible for the student body and the conduct of the athletic program. In most school environments the principal delegates responsibility for administration of the athletic program to the athletic administrator, who becomes the school representative in matters dealing with the school athletic and activity association and conference, district, or league affiliations. The principal remains responsible for any official school action and for all student activities, and must be in constant communication with the designated district or school athletic program administrator.

As designated by the principal, the athletic administrator has a responsibility for the administration and supervision of the school's interscholastic athletic program. The building athletic administrator is directly responsible to the principal, while the district athletic administrator, in most cases, works closely with the superintendent of schools. The athletic administrator must provide the leadership required for the day-to-day operations of school programs. Head coaches answer to the athletic administrator and act as official representatives of the school as they carry out their interscholastic athletic responsibilities, while assuming responsibility for the operation of their respective sports programs including managing their staff of assistant coaches.

Summary

The phenomenon of school-sponsored sports mirrors distinct political, social, cultural, industrial, and economic eras and draws parallels to the changes experienced as the United States developed as a nation. Throughout U.S. history, such attributes strongly influenced the ideology of sport and the effectiveness with which each sport was introduced and flourished, first independently and then within the public schools of the nation. The experiences of student-athletes today are steeped in years of progress, struggles, and socialization and are all a part of the fabric that makes the United States strong. Sport in schools is a grand hallmark of the United States (University of Maine 2006) and is part of the liberties, education rights, and individual freedoms enjoyed by citizens.

The benefits of student participation in education-based athletic programs are not intended to imply that athletic programs are more important than the traditional setting of the educational classroom. Teaching a student-athlete how to do a forward one-and-a-half somersault pike dive or how to throw a curveball is not more important than the core goal of producing good people and citizens.

The primary purpose of high school sports programs is to provide participation opportunities that contribute to student growth into successful adulthood. Allowing students to be part of programs that enhance maturation is a primary goal. Securing collegiate athletic scholarships is a secondary and remote objective. Athletic scholarships are a byproduct of interscholastic participation. Approximately 126,000 athletic scholarships valued at 2 billion dollars are annually awarded by university programs (NCAA 2012). This represents less than two percent of high school senior athletes who annually participate nationwide. As a further indication of the small number of scholarships awarded to division I, II, and III varsity team rosters for all sports are comprised of only an average of eight percent freshman athletes. The average athletic scholarship amounts to a little over $10,000, compared to the $40,000 annual average cost of a college education in the United States. Thus, the primary purpose of high school education-based athletics is not to create hundreds of collegiate athletes, but rather to enhance the growth of millions of quality American citizens.

Much is expected of contemporary high school athletic administrators. They are asked to be full-time educators and part psychologist, attorney, accountant, and contractor. At the same time, they must possess the wisdom of Solomon, the heart of a tiger, and the compassion of Mother Theresa. Such expectations are, obviously, highly demanding.

Instead of trying to be all things for all people, athletic administrators must focus on what is achievable and what is most important; they need to prepare well, be true to self, grow professionally, and balance time demands with family responsibilities. Through honorable service, athletic administrators realize both the cost and reward of the time they contribute.

One of the profession's greatest joys is the satisfaction gained from striving for personal growth while giving of one's self to the future of young people, our communities, and our nation. Since the efforts of athletic administrators are directed toward students' future success, students' access to athletic participation should not be hindered for the sake of budgets or cutbacks. Only when as many students as possible are involved in as many varied and meaningful participation opportunities as possible will the full potential of schools and students have been tapped (Roberts 1993).

CHAPTER 2

Guiding Personal Philosophy

David Hoch, PhD, CMAA

There should be no doubt that an athletic administrator should embrace and utilize the education-based athletic concept. It is also a certainty that the position entails a multitude of responsibilities and the need to make major decisions in order to lead and manage the department.

To handle all these responsibilities and tasks, the athletic administrator must develop a personal guiding philosophy. This means examining, ranking, and determining how to handle the various elements of the position and how to keep personal values and the philosophy of education-based athletics in harmony.

The number one objective in education-based athletics is the development and growth of student-athletes, not winning. It therefore may be of value to explore what goes into winning on a high school level and what part it actually plays.

Although it is understandable and desirable to want the best coach for all the school's teams, the coach is not the ultimate reason a team wins. The major determinant of winning is the athletic ability of the players on a team. Yes, a good coach will help athletes enhance their ability and reach their potential. But talent is by far the largest component for winning, and this obviously gives larger schools the advantage.

In theory, schools are usually grouped according to size so that larger schools aren't playing smaller schools. However, theory is one thing and practicality is another. In Maryland, for example, there are four classifications according to the size of the school. The enrollments of the smallest school through the absolute largest are put in order—all 280 public schools.

The total number of schools is then divided into four equal classifications—70 schools in each classification. School A could have an enrollment of 1,021 and be in 1-A (the smallest division); the next school, B, with an enrollment of 1,022 would become the first in 2-A and so forth. This means that, other than the 1-A group, the classifications could have an enrollment differential of 800 to 1,000 from the smallest school to the largest in their division.

In Maryland—and the states down through Florida and back to Kentucky—school districts are organized by counties. In Baltimore County, for example, there are 24 high schools, and this means there are three leagues for football. Loch Raven High School is the 4th smallest of the 24. Since one of the schools below them in terms of enrollment did not field a football team, Loch Raven played only two schools smaller than they were.

This also means that five or six schools would have twice the number of students than they did in a sport such as football, this meant a considerable disadvantage for Loch Raven.

Also, some states try to use enrollment to determine their league alignment. However, the largest factor in the formation and maintenance of their leagues is geography—time missed from class, the cost of travel, and so on.

In addition, a reasonable schedule and the lack of injuries to major players have to be included in the formula for winning, and the weather may also play a factor. Having a little luck doesn't hurt either when tallying the number of wins at the end of the season.

The culture, expectations, and values of a community also have a major influence on what sports succeed and which do not attract enough athletes and support. All this highlights the importance of not using wins and championships as the ultimate barometer of success for high school athletics (Hoch 2010).

Nonetheless, coaches and teams should plan, prepare, and strive to win. The individual and group effort—hard work to achieve a desired outcome— is consistent with the underlying philosophy of education-based athletics. It is only when winning becomes the overriding aim, at the expense of other worthy objectives, that priorities need to be realigned. Athletic administrators should remain vigilant to maintain the proper balance and not evaluate their sports programs or the coaches conducting them primarily on the number of wins or championships.

It is important that an athletic administrator help the coaching staff by introducing and consistently reinforcing the basic ingredients of education-based athletics. This includes preparing the teams to win with class and handle the disappointment of a loss with dignity. Both teams—winner and loser—can and should gain from the competition.

Benchmarks Beyond Winning

The most important objective in education-based athletics, as previously mentioned, is the growth and development of the student-athletes. Although there is nothing wrong with preparing for, striving toward, and eventually enjoying a win, other vital achievements measure the success of an athletic program.

The following are a few objectives that should guide an athletic director's efforts to measure success.

Participation Rate

Since winning shouldn't be the barometer for measuring a program's success, it is essential to identify other benchmarks. One indicator of success is the student participation rate. The number of young people involved in a school's teams is a great measuring stick.

An athletic director's goal, therefore, should be to offer as many sports and teams as possible. A greater number of teams will provide more opportunities for young people to experience the educational benefits of athletics. This objective obviously is based on the limitations of the facilities and budget.

Keeping with this approach, no sports should have an elevated or preferential place in the athletic program. The gate revenue produced or the media attention garnered by any team should not influence or alter the athletic department's support for any sports or teams.

The reason all sports are vital is really very simple. Each team is important to the athletes on it, becoming the foundation for their education-based experience. Therefore, no sport is more important than any other, and this has to become part of an athletic administrator's operating philosophy.

Multisport Participation

An athletic administrator should promote broad-based multisport participation. Whether due to the combination of parental pressure and the pursuit of limited athletic scholarships, there is a definite trend away from the two- or three-sport athlete.

Although sport scientists have done a very good job detailing the dangers of specialization, Mom and Dad either don't see this information or choose to ignore it in their pursuit of an athletic scholarship. They increasingly pay for private lessons; trainers for agility, conditioning, and other attributes; sports camps; fees for Amateur Athletic Union (AAU) elite and traveling teams; and so on. Mom and Dad are pouring huge amounts of money into specialization. In Maryland, this is especially prevalent for volleyball, basketball, and lacrosse.

Softball now features specialized pitcher training throughout the winter and has positional camps, clinics, and workouts starting the last week of October, which intrudes not only on winter sports but also on the last few weeks of the fall season.

Although high school coaches *should* know the dangers of specialization and the benefits of multisport participation, there are some who strictly think only in terms of their own sports. The athletic administrator should try to rein in these coaches and keep them in line with the preferred philosophy. This isn't always easy, for two reasons. More coaches than ever before are not teacher-coaches and may actually come from the AAU and community ranks to coach the high school team. Also, it is not uncommon for a person to coach her players in both settings—now that is real specialization!

Coaches cannot or should not be able to dictate to athletes that they can participate only in their sport. Athletes don't belong to any coach or team and need to be free to play more than one sport if desired.

For coaches to understand and follow this principle, the athletic administrator needs to explain it to the staff and intervene if there is ever a problem. The student-athlete and his experience must come first, and sport specialization cannot be allowed to alter this objective.

A few coaches may need guidance with respect to sharing facilities and equipment. The athletic administrator has the responsibility of ensuring that all teams have fair access to the school's facilities. For example, the stadium field does not "belong" to the football team. Although the football team does have to play its games in this venue, other sports such as soccer, field hockey, and lacrosse should also be able to fairly use this space for their contests when there are no scheduling conflicts. And obviously, if there is a track surrounding the stadium field, the track and field team needs to be able to use this facility.

Academic Attainment

The academic attainment of athletes is another measure of success. The school should always honor and promote student-athletes who meet the criteria for academic awards, whether district or state-association standards.

It can be relatively easy to compare the success of athletes against the general student population or other schools in the area. These statistics and rankings are valuable tools to promote the value of a school's athletic programs.

Community Service

Although community service may not be as obvious or as easy to substantiate as participation rate or academic achievement, the extent that student-athletes are involved in these efforts can also be an excellent benchmark. It is essential to encourage coaches to adopt community service projects with their teams.

The most important outcome of community service is the benefits provided to the recipients and the actual experience of the participants. In addition, there can be an ancillary boost in public relations. The athletic director should publish and post photos and articles to highlight the positive contributions of the school's student-athletes (Hoch 2011).

A Disconnect Between Philosophy and Actions

A mission statement from a Midwestern high school includes all the normal elements considered an important basis for education-based athletics. It states that athletics provides educational opportunities for students, and participation will help them grow and develop.

In addition to drafting the school and department mission statements, the athletic administrator created well-written procedures for coaching evaluations, and this document also reflects the education-based philosophy. For example, the evaluation process includes questions to determine if coaches helped student-athletes learn lifelong lessons, promoted sportsmanship, and served as positive role models.

However, the actual coaching evaluation of a relatively new head coach revealed a disconnect from the education-based philosophy and reality. The narrative section of the evaluation started out well enough by mentioning that the coach cared about his athletes, used teachable moments, was encouraging and nurturing, and served as a very good role model.

The tone and message made a sudden turn with the following statement: "But after three years, the honeymoon is over and it is time to start winning more games." Wow! This statement doesn't take into account the many positive contributions the coach made and may not consider the other factors that go into winning beyond the coach's efforts.

In addition, during a recap of the school year, the athletic administrator's first statement, or for that matter the only comment, focused on the championships the school won. Wouldn't it be refreshing if school officials started off with "Our participation rate was the highest in school history this past year." Or "Our teams and coaches participated in more community service projects than in any previous year." Winning championships and team records can be mentioned later, but not as the only accomplishment connected to success.

Unfortunately, what is written in mission statements and other documents is not always truly part of an athletic administrator's personal guiding philosophy. There is in some schools a real disconnect between what is officially stated as the purpose and mission of the athletic program and what is actually done.

Priorities

With an athletic administrator's tasks and responsibilities, there is never enough time to get everything done during the day or week. An administrator can work as hard as possible and possess great organizational skills, but this may not be enough. It is simply next to impossible to accomplish everything.

It is therefore vital to establish a set of priorities in order to complete the most essential items if choices need to be made. Since there will be problems and interruptions daily, what should the athletic director do first, and what can be postponed?

In developing a hierarchy of priorities, consider the following:

1. Anything that concerns the health, safety, and welfare of student-athletes has the highest priority. For example, eligibility reports must be completed at the beginning of a season and filed on time in order for athletes to participate. Some states have a deadline for postseason tournament entry forms, and these need to be filed in a timely manner.

2. All requests or directives for reports, information, or help from a supervisor—whether this person is the principal, superintendent, or someone else—must be seen to. In the corporate world, this would be your boss, and it is always wise to meet his expectations as soon as possible. This person does control your working environment and future.

3. Any requests or arrangements to deal with an emergency that may affect the operation of or ability to host a contest also take priority. This may include helping a coach, and it's wise to clearly explain the importance and value of planning ahead to avoid last-minute items.

In addition to these three priorities, a few others may be critical depending on the setting. The athletic director may want to add these items to the list after conferring with his supervisor and coaching staff.

Even with a system of priorities in place, unexpected problems may necessitate a change in the daily schedule. In the event that the athletic director needs to reorder items on his to-do list, the following question can be helpful: What would happen if I have to postpone this task until tomorrow or later in the week? Usually this question will provide the answer of how to reorder the schedule.

A degree of flexibility in daily and weekly schedules is essential. Unexpected problems must be dealt with as expediently as possible, and these situations may be unpredictable and often occur at the strangest times. Setting priorities and having flexibility may seem to be polar opposites, but they are both necessary to accommodate the time demands of the position.

Decision Making

In addition to determining what needs to be done and in what order, an athletic administrator will have to make important and, in some cases, difficult decisions. The process works best when the decision-maker utilizes a systematic formula in order to develop a solution. Consider the following steps.

1. Define the problem. Although this may seem fairly straightforward, it is important to determine what actually is involved. This initial step includes gathering all the facts, talking to anyone involved, and checking any records from similar problems in the past.

2. Take time to analyze the facts. To gain the necessary background, seek advice from others who may have knowledge of the situation. If there were witnesses, it is always wise to interview them or review their written statements.

3. Refer to district and state-association resources, which include policy manuals, handbooks, and any other pertinent materials. This step ensures that the ultimate decision is in line with established procedures, policies, and regulations.

4. Develop a number of possible responses. Consider as wide a range of alternatives as possible. These solutions can range from "do nothing" up to the other extreme of "eliminate the cause of the problem." Again, input from others often provides additional creative options, a valuable asset in this step of the process.

5. Consider the realistic timeline for implementing each of the possible alternatives. The amount of time required may help determine which solution is selected.

6. Decide which alternative is the best solution. For any critical or major decision, consult first with a supervisor. Without the principal's or superintendent's backing, an athletic director could find himself in a difficult position with some parents, coaches, booster club officers, and community leaders.

7. Communicate the decision to all the individuals involved in or affected by it.

Athletic directors should be prepared and understand that it's impossible to make everyone happy, regardless of their concerted efforts to make an informed decision. All that administrators can do is follow these steps and do the best they can in reaching a decision.

Some difficult decisions may require courage, but athletic administrators should always be guided by doing what will provide the optimal environment for the school's athletes, coaches, and athletic program.

Change and Flexibility

In the demanding world of the high school athletic administrator, new tasks and obligations are constantly being added to the list of responsibilities. In addition, there are always developments with technology, evolutions with equipment, and new regulations that need to be met.

As with other aspects of life, change is inevitable and ongoing. This doesn't mean that change is good or bad, but it does happen—constantly. As an athletic administrator, therefore, it is important to understand that change exists, its role, and how it may affect the position.

Administrators who resist change—whether it is in the form of new regulations or advancements with technology—are likely to face problems. Learning is a lifelong pursuit and not a one-time journey. This means that once an athletic director stops adapting, learning, and moving forward, it is time to leave an athletic administrative position behind.

Throughout their careers, athletic directors will probably encounter a new supervisor—principal or superintendent—at some point. Adjustment to this new person and her particular leadership style is another important element of change.

Principals and superintendents are as varied as any group of people, and this also includes athletic administrators. It is important to understand from a statistical standpoint that for every outstanding one, there is another one at the other end of the spectrum. For every administrator who is easy and enjoyable to work for, there is one who is challenging and difficult.

Some administrators will fall into one of the following categories:

• Micromanager—A person who needs to know what, how, and when employees handle even the smallest task and doesn't grant them any autonomy to do their jobs. Workers must constantly report to this supervisor and provide updates.

• Power monger—Someone who insists on making every decision, regardless of his experience or knowledge, because he is the boss. Seldom will this person ask for advice or input.

• Egomaniac—A person who believes she is the greatest administrator and is not shy about letting you know. This administrator will take credit for every idea, development, innovation, and success within the building regardless of who actually accomplished them.

• Bully—A person who runs the school through intimidation, threats, and vindictive measures. These principals may raise their voices by several octaves and create unrealistic demands in order to get what they want.

Although this is not an all-inclusive list of challenging leadership approaches, it explains several that athletic administrators may need to adjust to. Athletic directors may have a difficult time in their positions if they don't understand and adapt to their supervisors' style, however difficult it may be.

When adjusting to challenging administrators, analyzing the approach they are employing and determining how to negate the impact of this approach is a good first step. For example, with a supervisor who is a micromanager, an athletic director should constantly keep this person informed of any progress toward solving problems and any developments with new initiatives. This can easily be done with e-mail messages or a weekly half-hour meeting.

It may get to the point that athletic directors must politely and professionally remind upper-level administrators to treat them with respect and dignity. Although this may not be an easy discussion to have, it may be needed for an athletic director to continue in the position. This meeting should always be undertaken behind closed doors and, if possible, when there are no pressing problems that could elevate the tension or alter the focus of the conversation.

The people an athletic director works with also do not remain constant. Coaches and staff members will move on to new positions or will retire. Therefore, there is a continual process of adaptation to new personalities. An athletic administrator who can't or doesn't adjust may be asked to leave the position or may choose to move on to another job.

In this environment of change, the ability to be open, receptive, and flexible is important. Responding by resisting change or complaining about it won't help. Successful athletic directors put in the required effort to adjust.

Educating Others

An often neglected or overlooked part of developing a guiding philosophy is the importance of educating members of the school community about the program. It is easy to get bogged down in minutiae and daily responsibilities, but it is essential to explain the critical parts and purpose of the athletic program.

As the leader of the athletic program, the athletic administrator is responsible for communicating the fundamental tenets of education-based athletic philosophy. It would be foolish to assume that athletes, coaches, parents, and other administrators understand what is involved much less embrace this concept.

Every opportunity and all forms of communication should be employed to educate all relevant parties. Preseason meetings with athletes, coaches, and parents are a good start. Websites, handbooks, Facebook, twitter, and blogs can be good communication vehicles. Don't overlook any medium that can be used to communicate with and educate the constituents of the athletic program.

The major topic to be introduced and explained is the concept of education-based athletics. This should include a major dose of fair play and sporting behavior, which means treating everyone involved—athletes, officials, coaches, and fans—with respect. Also, this means playing within the spirit and intent of the rules.

An athletic administrator also needs to provide the rationale for and examples of other outcomes beyond winning that are ultimately more important.

The values of teamwork, perseverance, and leadership are a few examples, but there are also many others. This education process has to be ongoing and not an isolated, one-and-done approach. Every year brings athletes, parents, and coaches who are new to the program, at different times in the athletic season, so the message needs to be repeated often.

The better an athletic administrator does his job of educating everyone connected to the athletic program about education-based athletics, the fewer problems and misunderstandings he should encounter. And this all starts with the understanding that winning is not the ultimate objective of the high school experience.

Ethics and Integrity

Two personal guiding principles that are essential for a leader are ethics and integrity. In the simplest terms, ethics is doing what is right, and this has to be the bedrock for all an athletic director's decisions, actions, and efforts.

An athletic administrator can have enthusiasm, a solid work ethic, charisma, and countless other qualities but isn't worth much without an ethical compass. And ethics tie in with integrity, meaning a person is honest and stands by her word. These two personal aspects are essential in order to be successful in an athletic management career.

All individuals have strengths and weaknesses. There are things everyone can work on and improve, such as organizational skills or communication skills. But without ethics and integrity, it will be difficult to survive and thrive as an athletic administrator. Why?

Ethics and integrity are the foundation for trust and respect. And these two qualities are important components for forming working relationships. Whether the relationship is with staff, supervisors, parents, or any other shareholder in the athletic program, it is vital that these people trust and respect the athletic director.

Doing what is best for the student-athletes, coaches, and program should be an athletic director's guiding maxim. If people know the system is based on sound, honest, and consistent tenets, they will be able to work with the director even if they disagree with a decision. Their respect for the director's philosophical compass will enable this working relationship.

Although an athletic administrator may occasionally have detractors, it is necessary to find the courage to do what is right. It isn't always easy to stand alone, but it may also result in earning trust and respect. An athletic administrator's guiding principles have to include these qualities.

Athletic administrators who are considering or refining their ethical approach will want to refer to the NIAAA Code of Ethics. This document provides the guidelines that all athletic administrators should incorporate into their professional philosophy.

The interscholastic athletic administrator:

1. Develops and maintains a comprehensive athletic program that seeks the highest development of all participants and that respects the individual dignity of every athlete.

2. Considers the well-being of the entire student body as fundamental in all decisions and actions.

3. Supports the principle of due process and protects the civil and human rights of all individuals.

4. Organizes, directs, and promotes an interscholastic athletic program that is an integral part of the total educational program.

5. Cooperates with the staff and school administration in establishing, implementing, and supporting school policies.

6. Acts impartially in the execution of basic policies and in the enforcement of the conference, league, and state high school association rules and regulations.

7. Fulfills professional responsibilities with honesty and integrity.

8. Upholds the honor of the profession in all relations with students, colleagues, coaches, administrators, and the general public.

9. Improves the professional status and effectiveness of the interscholastic athletic administrator through participation in local, state, and national in-service programs.

10. Promotes high standards of ethics, sportsmanship, and personal conduct by encouraging administration, coaches, staff, student-athletes, and community to commit to these high standards.

FIGURE 2.1   NIAAA Code of Ethics.

Copyright ©2005 NIAAA. All Rights Reserved.

Note: The NIAAA Code of Ethics may be updated in 2013. Visit www.niaaa.org.

Dependability

Although ethics and integrity are bedrock qualities for an athletic administrator, dependability is also essential. Meeting the expectations of the position effectively and in a timely fashion is a major requirement. The athletic director's arrangements, efforts, and guidance affect everyone associated with the athletic program.

It is critical, therefore, that when athletic directors say they will do something that they do it. Although this seems like a straightforward and, perhaps, commonsense statement, it is vital for working relationships.

Even after establishing a set of priorities, athletic directors should always consider how much is currently on their plate and be able to accurately predict their commitments weeks or months in advance. It is much better to explain in advance an inability to undertake an additional task or request than to be overcommitted. Not meeting deadlines or expectations greatly affects a person's dependability.

When unable to undertake something, an athletic director should offer an explanation and estimate when it might be possible. "My schedule does not permit me to take on an additional request at this time. However, please stop by in two weeks and I'll be happy to meet with you to discuss your proposal."

Dependability also extends to daily tasks such as answering voice and e-mail messages in a timely manner, even when faced with a deluge of messages. This effort is simply a form of common courtesy. Acknowledging the receipt of a message, even a simple "I got it," is important so as not to leave the person who sent the information or the request hanging.

Personal Care

Considering the time commitment and the ever-expanding responsibilities, an athletic administrator's job can be extremely hectic and demanding, requiring a great deal of effort, energy, and emotion to simply survive every day. It is easy for athletic administrators to overlook their own health, families, and personal well-being because they are so involved with the expectations and responsibilities of their position. In developing a guiding philosophy, an athletic director needs to understand this pitfall and take steps to avoid possible accompanying problems.

As the hours extend each day, it is easy to skip meals and exercise. In an effort to complete every task, it is also common to get less sleep than what is needed. As these three requirements are compromised, health, energy, and outlook can also be negatively affected.

Many athletic directors also have family responsibilities. Trying to find quality family time may be difficult. It is not uncommon for an athletic administrator to become so thoroughly engrossed in his position that his family is neglected.

Trying to create a balance between meeting professional responsibilities, taking care of yourself, and maintaining good family relationships are extremely important. Considering the professional pressure and occasional difficulties that athletic directors may experience, their homes and families can be a protective oasis and sanctuary.

Athletic administrators often encounter people who are challenging, disagreeable, and problematic. On the other hand, they can always count on their families for love and support. Keeping this in mind can carry an athletic administrator through many difficult times and situations.

With so many responsibilities, it can be difficult to develop balance in life. Even with a complicated and demanding schedule, athletic administrators should try to implement some of the following suggestions.

- Arrange for a friend or colleague to cover a few game management responsibilities in order to attend family functions such as children's birthday parties, recitals, and games.
- Use weekends, or at least Sundays if the school has Saturday contests, for family time. This means not taking work home.
- Don't take phone calls or answer professional e-mail over the weekend. Obviously, handle emergency communications, but only in the most extreme situations are calls or e-mails truly urgent. Screening messages can help maintain family time.
- Learn to say "no" in order to avoid taking on any additional or unrealistic requests for help. An appropriate response is "I'd be glad to consider helping when my schedule becomes a little less hectic in a few weeks."

It is also helpful to establish and maintain professional relationships that can provide support, advice, and help when needed. These people can be teachers or department chairs within the school, but often fellow athletic administrators at other schools are the best source of support. Only colleagues totally understand what is involved in the position.

Anyone, however, who will provide an ear for venting or who can offer sound advice can be immeasurably important for surviving the frustrations and pressures of the job. Developing and maintaining a support group is vital.

Continual Professional Development

In the 1980s, Lee Iacocca was the CEO of the Chrysler Corporation and was largely credited with rescuing the company from bankruptcy. A quote often attributed to Iacocca is "You are either moving forward or falling behind, because there is no such thing as remaining stationary."

Although Iacocca was obviously referring to competition in the auto industry, one can easily adopt this philosophy in many other professions including athletic management. With new developments involving technology, regulations, and equipment, along with countless ever-increasing responsibilities, athletic administrators constantly have to update their skills and continue their professional development.

Using websites and social sites such as Facebook, for example, is now a reality for many in the field of athletic management. One cannot exist in the athletic administrator's position without utilizing e-mail, Excel, and PowerPoint computer applications. But these represent just the essential basics.

In only the last year or two, it has become vital for an athletic administrator to be aware of and develop some degree of expertise in the following:

- The research into and efforts made in the care and prevention of concussions
- The application and use of Twitter to communicate with parents and shareholders of the athletic program
- The various programs and initiatives that have been instituted by state athletic associations to enhance sporting behavior
- The development of the NFHS Coaching Education/Certification Program and the implications for the professionalism of a coaching staff

Although these examples are not meant to be an all-inclusive list, they do represent a few from the tip of the iceberg. It is absolutely essential that athletic directors keep pace.

Professional development can and does come in different forms. A degree program in sport management is a possibility, and the National Interscholastic Athletic Administrators Association has a full range of courses and certification program that all high school athletic administrators should complete.

In addition, state athletic director associations and the NIAAA and NFHS host annual conferences. It is important to not only register for the conference but also actually attend the various workshop sessions. These workshops offer practical solutions and ideas for a wide range of common problems athletic administrators face.

There is little doubt that athletic administrators juggle hectic schedules and are overextended for a good part of the school year. Even so, they should still take time during the summer and over breaks to read professional magazines and journals. The content contained in the articles can provide ideas for revising procedures and policies and for implementing new programs and initiatives. The summer can be a great opportunity for visionary thinking and professional development.

Learning isn't a one-time destination, it is a lifelong journey. People who become complacent or believe they have all the answers may fall to the prophecy of Lee Iacocca. Athletic administrators have an obligation to their athletes, coaches, and programs to constantly make efforts to expand their knowledge and background.

Authority Versus Power

Most administrative positions in a school system, and this includes athletic administrators, come with a degree of authority that is defined and delineated in job descriptions, policies, and procedures of the school district. Therefore, authority is neither good nor bad—it is merely a component of the position.

However, how an athletic director views and uses that authority does become a vital issue. An athletic administrator controls and directs the department and program. Any misuse or abuse of the power associated with this position can lead to problems.

Abuse of power may occur when the athletic director uses this authority to advance or protect personal interests and agendas instead of doing what is best for the athletes, coaches, or program. Actions that are self-serving, punitive, or vindictive toward others constitute a misuse of power.

Regardless of the athletic director's leadership style, an excellent leader inspires others to excel. This means helping people attempt to reach their potential and to become the best they can.

Subtly influencing, guiding, and nudging others to learn, improve, and ultimately excel doesn't diminish authority. And rarely does the use of blunt-force power produce positive results. Although an athletic administrator needs to exert control, authority tempered with understanding, consistency, and fairness is the key.

The Hurdle of Friendship

It may seem strange to suggest that friendship could be a problem for an athletic director. Most people in life would prefer dealing with a nice, friendly, positive person.

However, if the athletic director tries to "be a friend," it can actually cause problems. An athletic administrator makes decisions that affect everyone in and associated with the program. These decisions cannot be influenced by or even take the appearance of favoring a group or person, and this is one of the dangers of trying to be a friend.

The issue of being a friend can be especially critical if the director is a former coach who worked with some of the people currently on staff. These former colleagues may not realize that the relationship has changed—and it has. Also, others on the staff may perceive that there is preferential treatment, whether there is or not.

Although most people want to be liked, it is much more important to be trusted and respected as a professional. This may mean outlining and defining new working relationships with coaches who were once colleagues. Being friendly is a good approach, while being a friend may not work.

A friendly approach, which involves being polite, positive, and personable with all members of the school community—athletes, coaches, and parents— also requires being fair and consistent. Athletic administrators must try to be as transparent as possible and communicate effectively with everyone.

Great communication skills may not prevent all problems, but they can go a long way toward eliminating or minimizing many. Athletic directors should let everyone know in a clear, concise, and straightforward manner how they will conduct the business of the department. This can help overcome the possible hurdle of friendship.

Professionally, there is a line that cannot be crossed regarding intimate relationships between teachers and students. This standard also applies to relationships between administrators and coaches and between administrators and student-athletes. As previously mentioned, athletic administrators are in a position of power, and it is inappropriate to engage in a relationship with those working for them or participating in the program.

It is therefore wise to think through potentially dangerous situations ahead of time. When it is necessary to meet with a coach or student-athlete, simple precautions such as keeping the office door open or holding the meeting when an assistant or other school personnel is present can eliminate false, damaging perceptions or accusations.

As mentioned earlier with respect to ethical behavior, doing what is right should always be the athletic director's major goal and guiding principle. By coupling this goal with proactive and preventive measures, an athletic director should be able to maintain a friendly, professional approach without crossing over into inappropriate relationships.

Athletic administrators should consider the following guidelines in their efforts to develop effective working relationships:

- Although you may on occasion need to be firm and in control, temper your approach with courtesy, understanding, and patience.

- Be as consistent as possible. Don't extend preferential treatment to certain coaches or staff members. While you may need to consider extenuating circumstances, standards and expectations should be fair and the same for all.

- Show appreciation. The quick and simple expression of "Great job!" will go a long way toward motivating people to continue to perform at a high level.

- Say please and thank you. It only takes seconds to use these important words, and you are never too busy to incorporate them. These two expressions will reap huge benefits and enhance your working relationships.

- Always give credit to others—assistants, coaches—for their ideas and work. By acknowledging their contributions, you are more likely to get additional help in the future.

- Seek input from your staff and coaches when possible. Providing this opportunity will usually create a feeling of ownership and acceptance on their part.

- Try to handle all interactions with class, with dignity, and in a positive and polite manner. Even in difficult situations, you will be judged on how you react.

Summary

Developing a personal guiding philosophy is a difficult but vital process for any athletic administrator. Athletic administrators can have a great influence on members of the school community, and this impact often can't be immediately measured. It is impossible to survive let alone thrive in this rewarding position without a well-developed guiding philosophy.

To efficiently manage all the job's responsibilities, an athletic director needs to set priorities and make sound, informed decisions. All of this has to be done in an ethical, dependable manner and with the highest degree of integrity while effectively educating and communicating with all members of the school community.

Athletic administrators must also learn how to appropriately use the authority and power associated with this position. They must be polite, professional, and friendly—without falling into the pitfalls of being a friend. It is also important to carve out some recuperative time from hectic schedules to spend with their families.

In spite of the massive demands, guiding an education-based athletic program can be one of the most rewarding and important positions in the realm of secondary education.

CHAPTER 3

Communication and Accessibility

Warren L. Hagman, CMAA

Today's athletic personnel are called on to be first-rate communicators. Athletic personnel include the athletic director, coaches, assistant coaches, secretarial staff, and athletic trainers. This list is not exclusive, as other school personnel from the principal, assistant principals, and deans of students at the school level may be called on to communicate with the athletic community. School personnel at the school district level, including superintendents, assistant superintendents, school board members, and associated support personnel, will also be involved in communicating in the athletic arena from time to time.

People with a direct interest in a school's athletic program include the student-athletes, their parents, the coaching staff, the school faculty, the support staff, sports officials, the school administration, the media, and those in the community itself. They will all be active participants in the communication process, either as receivers of information in a one-way process or receivers and senders in a two-way process.

The bottom line is that the athletic personnel and everyone with a stake in the athletic program will be in communication with each other on a continuing basis. The athletic personnel are on the firing line in today's climate of almost instant communication. Information conveyed through the communication processes must be current and useful to be effective. Conversely, the lack of information—regardless of the communication process—will stifle effective communication between parties. Those looking for information, answers, and agreements have gotten used to instant gratification in a variety of situations. Instant meals, fast food, Internet searches, and instant messaging are a few examples. These people are going to expect the same quick responses from the athletic personnel.

Effective communication helps athletic personnel better understand the parent, student, student-athlete, or community member. It enables them to resolve the conflicts, build trust and respect, and create formative environments where creative ideas and problem solving can occur.

Effective Communication

We hear only half of what is said to us, understand only half of that, believe only half of that, and remember only half of that.—Kathy Walker

Effective communication helps athletic personnel better understand the parent, student, student-athlete, or community member. It enables them to resolve the conflicts, build trust and respect, and create formative environments where creative ideas and problem solving can occur. As simple as communication seems, many athletic directors experience difficulties building successful connections with others when conflict is involved. Much of what one tries to communicate, as seen from the Kathy Walker quote (2002), is only partially heard, understood, and believed. This is a genuine source of conflict and frustration for school personnel, student-athletes, and community members.

Athletic directors send, receive, and process huge numbers of messages every day. To be effective communicators, they must see the process as more than just an exchange of information. Effective communication requires understanding the emotion that is blended into the information. Relationships at home, at work, and in social situations will improve from strengthening connections to others. This will further result in improving decision making, teamwork, caring, and problem solving. Effective communication skills make athletic directors better at communicating negative or difficult messages without creating further conflict or destroying the trust factor. Effective communication requires active listening, nonverbal communication, stress management, and recognizing and understanding your own emotion to create a dynamic and changing set of skills to help you successfully communicate.

Effective communication is a learned skill and not a naturally occurring ability. It should be practiced at every opportunity so that it becomes a habit. It should be experienced as natural to both the speaker and the receiver.

Listening

The number one skill in effective communication is listening. Listening is quite possibly the least considered aspect of communication when one party in the communication process is stressed or agitated. Successful listening is the understanding of the words, the information, and to a greater extent the underlying feeling the speaker has about the information being communicated. If the speaker feels she is being both heard and understood, a stronger connection will be established between the two parties. Successful listening creates positive environments where everyone feels safe to share opinions, ideas, and feelings. The potential outcome may be creative ways to problem-solve the current situation. Successful listening will help clarify information, which will minimize conflicts and misunderstandings. Successful listening will help reduce the negative emotion that comes with conflict. If a parent feels he has truly been heard, he will tend to calm down and is open to better understanding, where problems can begin to be solved.

There are several ways to listen successfully, and these apply to all athletic personnel.

- Fully focus on the speaker, observing body language and other nonverbal cues being given. Avoid at all costs activities such as daydreaming and doodling. You are certain to miss important points. Some speakers are hard to concentrate on. Repeating in your mind what they have said will reinforce their message and keep you focused.

- Avoid interrupting. The parent or student-athlete really wants you to listen. They want to know that you acknowledge their concerns and that you understand them. Be quiet and listen until they are done. When they start to repeat themselves, this is the time to redirect the conversation to your understanding of their concerns. Remember, listening is not the same as waiting for your turn to talk. Take in the information as it is given to you. Avoid forming the ideas of what you want to say when you get your turn. The speaker has the same abilities as you do in knowing that your mind is somewhere else.

- Avoid seeming judgmental. You do not have to like someone, share her opinions, or agree with her ideas and values. You do, however, need to put away for the time being your judgments, blame, and criticism to fully understand the person speaking. You may find that the most difficult communications you have with a person will create the most profound connections over a long span of time.

- Show an interest in what is being said. A positive nod, a smile at the person, and an alert and attentive posture that is open and inviting is necessary. Keep your hands busy with note taking when possible. This demonstrates that you want to take a lasting record of all the facts as they are presented. It is highly suggested that you leave space between facts to provide room to further clarify points. Be sure that what you are writing can be seen. You project the feelings of openness and honesty by doing this.

Nonverbal Communication

Nonverbal communication comes out strongly when we communicate about things for which we care deeply. This wordless communication includes eye contact, facial expressions, posture, body movement and gestures, voice tone, muscle tension, and breathing. It will reflect in the way someone looks, listens, moves, and reacts. This nonverbal communication says more about a person than simple words alone.

The importance of being able to understand and use nonverbal signals cannot be overstated. Using an open body language style—leaving arms uncrossed, maintaining good eye contact, and sitting on the edge of the seat or standing with an open stance—enhances effective nonverbal communication. A person can emphasize or enhance his verbal message with the correct body language. Shaking hands while verbally congratulating a friend on his success will send a positive nonverbal message. A simple pat on the back when something hasn't gone as well as it was expected sends a powerful message of empathy without saying a word.

Even the expert at nonverbal communication can benefit from observing people in public places. Shopping malls, grocery stores, buses, restaurants, and television provide multiple opportunities to observe how others use body language. This teaches people how to better receive and use these nonverbal signals when interacting with others. It is important to notice how people act and react to each other. You can even make a game of it by attempting to guess what they are talking about, what their relationship is, and what feelings are being expressed.

A second exercise is trying to determine what cultural differences exist that you need to be aware of. Among the differences to consider when reading nonverbal signals are age, gender, culture, emotional state, and religion. A typical teenager and a Hispanic businessman will likely differ greatly in their nonverbal signals.

Athletic administrators should work on improving their delivery of nonverbal communication. First, it is important to ensure that the nonverbal signals match and reinforce what the words are saying. Sending a confusing message when the actions and words do not match will paint a picture of dishonesty. A simple example is when a person's words say yes but her body actions say no.

Adjusting nonverbal signals to match the context in which the message is being sent is also important. The tone of a person's voice should be different when addressing a teenager or child than when addressing an adult. This is often referred to as speaking in "your parent voice" versus speaking in "your adult voice." It is critical to take into account the emotional state of the receiver and his cultural differences.

Another way to improve delivery of nonverbal communication is to attempt to use body language to convey positive feelings. This can help turn around a negative situation. An athletic director can use positive nonverbal skills to signal confidence even though she may not be feeling confident (e.g., when speaking to an upset parent or relieving a coach of his coaching duties). Strategies include standing tall, keeping the head up, smiling, maintaining eye contact, and giving a firm handshake. Using these techniques will make the speaker feel more self-confident. It will also put the receiver more at ease.

E-mail, Texting, and Social Media

E-mail, texting, and social media are the predominant communication preferences for technologically connected adults and students. The average person can go months without receiving a written letter in the mail. It is the rare day that news is shared through a written letter, phone call, or visit. E-mail, texting, and social media now fill our lives and shape the way we correspond. Now with a few clicks of the keyboard, we can communicate and share information with everyone in a matter of seconds. Posting updates, photos, and feelings takes only a few moments.

This can be very advantageous to the athletic director, but it can be just as disadvantageous. On the advantageous side, information deemed necessary by the student-athletes, coaches, and administrators is instantaneously available or only moments away. A cancelled game or a team stuck in traffic on the way to an event can be shared quickly and easily through a social media site.

On the disadvantageous side, what was a good idea to share on a social media site a few minutes, hours, or days ago may no longer seem quite as appropriate. Once information is shared with the world, those words are no longer available to be taken back. The analogy to this is "you cannot un-ring the bell."

Technological communication in any of its forms does not provide the nonverbal cues available in one-on-one meetings or even phone calls. Some emotions are possible with technological communication, such as "screaming." Creating the message in all capital letters, underlining critical words, placing them in red font, increasing the font size, and highlighting words all act to "scream" at the intended receiver.

On the whole, however, little emotion can be conveyed through technology. It is easy to read into an e-mail or social media response what you believe the sender meant, but the guarantee of a successful interpretation is limited. An athletic director's response to a parent or student will also lack nonverbal cues and emotion. When confronted with what appears to be a highly charged situation involving a social media contact, consider hosting a one-on-one meeting. This allows the nonverbal skills to come into play along with the emotional assessment skills.

Legal issues and legal answers communicated with e-mails, texts, and social media posts are known as unsettled law. State laws, school district regulations, and school policies leave school personnel subject to being under fire when a court challenge takes place. Keeping laws, regulations, and policies current is nearly impossible with the fast advent of change in communication technology.

The technology of how we communicate is in a state of flux. E-mail has for the most part replaced letter writing. Texting and social media opportunities are on the way to replacing e-mail as a favored communication avenue. What the future holds is uncertain, but it will challenge those responsible for effective communication. Staying current on new technologies will position school personnel to both embrace technology and understand how students will use and abuse it.

Composure in Communication

Keeping your composure in trying situations can be difficult. Your natural impulse is to express your feelings and emotions. This usually happens when you have not considered the consequences of losing your composure. As we look at this issue it will be important to consider why you are losing your composure. Are you reacting rather than responding to emotional triggers?

Communicating During Stressful Situations

Small doses of stress can enhance performance. Effective communication can become hampered, however, when stress is constant and overwhelming. Stress affects a person's capacity to think clearly, to be creative, and to act appropriately. Major stress will lead to misreading other people. It also makes people send confusing and negative nonverbal signals. Because stress is so closely related to time, it can cause people to make knee-jerk decisions or reactions in complicated situations.

In managing stress you need to identify that you are stressed. The stress may be job related, but it will exhibit in your home life in disagreements with your spouse and children. At work it may exhibit in disagreements with your boss, friends, and coworkers. You may even say things you will later regret. It is only when you are calm and relaxed that you will be able to know if a situation requires a response or if the other person's signals indicate no response is necessary.

When a person is faced with stress, it is not always possible to take the time to bring emotions under control before acting. An argument with your boss or spouse is a clear example of this. Learning to reduce stress in the moment through recognition of the feelings and emotions will allow you to behave appropriately. Learning to relax and still be energized will help you safely face the strong emotions you are feeling. When faced with something upsetting, remain emotionally available and engaged.

A number of strategies can help athletic directors deal with stress during communication. The first of these is to recognize you are becoming stressed. Listen to your body communicate with you. Have your muscles or stomach tightened? Have you clenched your hands? Are your nostrils flared? Have you forgotten to breathe? If you answered yes to these and other similar questions, you are probably suffering from stress.

Take a personal moment to calm down. This will give you a chance to decide whether to continue a conversation or postpone it.

Take a few deep breaths, clench and relax your back and shoulder muscles (use a shoulder shrug by shrugging shoulders up and down, forward and backward), and recall a soothing or sensory-rich image. Use the senses of sight, sound, touch, taste, and smell to rapidly and reliably relieve stress. Each person responds differently to sensory input, so in safe environments try one at a time and see what works best for you.

Seek humor in tough situations. Humor is a great stress reliever when used appropriately. When surrounded by people who are under stress, find a way to lighten the mood. Police and medical personnel are adept at using humor in difficult situations. It is important not to make light of the situation because you may appear to the receiver as insensitive.

Look for compromise in the situation. Is there a way to find a common ground that will reduce the stress levels for everyone concerned? If you come to understand that the other person cares more about the situation than you do, it may be easier for you to compromise. Compromise is a good investment in the future of relationships. When compromise is not possible, it is appropriate to agree to disagree. Take stock of time factors that may be in play, and if possible also agree to take a break. Doing so gives each party time to consider possible alternative actions and outcomes for the situation.

Communication and Emotional Awareness

Emotional awareness is a set of tools for understanding both ourselves and others. It creates the real messages being communicated. Emotions play an important role in the way we communicate. How you react to emotionally driven, nonverbal cues affects your understanding of other people and how they come to understand you. Being in touch with your feelings, and understanding how you feel and why you feel that way, will help you more easily communicate your feelings and needs to others. This will result in less frustration, fewer misunderstandings, and less conflict. To understand your feelings, you will need to examine the strong emotions of anger, sadness, and fear. It is also important to understand that your feelings will change from moment to moment.

Having emotional awareness will help an athletic director understand and empathize with what is really troubling others. It will help him understand himself and his own troubles. It will help him stay motivated to understand and empathize even if he does not like the message he is receiving. An athletic director with emotional awareness will be able to clearly and effectively respond even when delivering negative messages.

A positive outcome of emotional awareness is strong in rewarding relationships that will allow the athletic director to think creatively to solve problems and conflicts. When you have developed strong emotional awareness, you will know what you are feeling without having to think about it. It is a practiced skill not unlike any athletic skill. You will understand what someone is really communicating to you, and you will be able to act accordingly.

Communications With Members of the School Community

The school community is an accumulation of stakeholders all of whom have a vested interest in the success of the school and its students. The list of stakeholders is not limited to, but includes the faculty, staff, students, parents, community members, businesses, media, and the school district under which the school functions. Each of these stakeholders and stakeholder groups will have issues and concerns that will need to be addressed primarily through both verbal and written communication.

Communicating With Personnel Within the Athletic Department

An athletic department is a major functioning unit within a comprehensive school. It is staffed by a limited number of personnel in comparison to the academic program. The immediate staff usually consists of an athletic director, coaches, support staff, and athletes. The internal communications between and among these groups will of necessity be greater in number and more ongoing than with other stakeholders and stakeholder groups.

Contact and Relations With Coaches

Communication from the first day of the new school year, typically July 1 to the end of the year on June 30, will be nonstop. The school year should start with a total program meeting of all members of the athletic program. This general meeting is the time and place to provide all the information necessary for successful seasons in each program. New information, changing regulations, and updated procedures are all communicated at this time. As the first seasons begin, a season-specific meeting with the in-season coaches is well advised. The demands on time and the sharing of practice and competition space are arranged. As each season ends and the next season begins, the athletic director will plan and schedule each meeting.

Daily communication with coaches will take a variety of forms. Quick handwritten notes, written memos, phone calls, and one-on-one visits on the fields and courts of play make up the many forms of communication.

One of the strongest and most positive forms of communication is the athletic director's physical presence at practices and events. Too often the only time the athletic director shows up to a practice is when something is wrong. Plan to deliver the good news as well as the bad news in person with the coaching staff of each program. Being on the coach's turf for positive reasons will create an environment of openness and trust. The student-athletes in particular enjoy the recognition received from the athletic director at their practice and play sites.

The early establishment of good communication paths with the coaching staff will make the sending and receiving of good and bad news easier. An athletic director needs to hear both. She also needs to hear it quickly and with as much factual information as possible.

Contact and Relations With Student-Athletes

One of the most frequent communication contacts athletic personnel will have is with the student-athletes. The most familiar situation is between the coach and the athlete, which occurs on a daily basis during the season: multiple times during a practice or event; before practice, during practice, and after practice; during passing time in the hallways of the school; on the bus to an away event; and numerous other times.

A University of Texas study found that people remember 10 percent of what they read, 20 percent of what they hear, 30 percent of what they see, 50 percent of what they see and hear, 70 percent of what they say, and 90 percent of what they do and say (Metcalf 1997). The 90 percent really means people remember 90 percent of what they participate in. For modern coaches, the focus should be on their athletes' "seeing and hearing" and "doing and saying." For modern athletes, the focus should be on participation.

Coaches' communications with their athletes should be high in content and low in quantity. The messages should be short to be the most effective.

Contact and Relations With Staff

It is important to define the term *staff*. Staff are those employees whose tasks include making sure the building, the programs, and the paperwork are in place or running efficiently. The positions may be called something different in every school and school district, but the jobs remain the same overall. The titles of these positions include but are not limited to head secretary, office manager, assistant principal secretary, administrative assistant, athletic secretary, bookkeeper, head custodian, plant foreman, building engineer, assistant custodian, groundskeeper, school resource officer, campus monitor, classroom aide, bus driver, special education aide, and cafeteria manager.

Communications between the athletic secretary and the athletic program coaches is another lifeline in a school. In this age of technology, phone calls are routinely routed to the correct offices by either a live switchboard operator or by a voice choice presented by the phone system. This means athletic questions are going to be routed to the athletic offices. People making those calls expect to be greeted and have their questions answered with few further transfers of their call. This translates into the athletic secretary being the last stop for a phone call. This also means the athletic secretary needs to know virtually everything about a school's athletic programs.

It is important for the athletic director or the person responsible for managing the program on an administrative basis to establish good communication policies to meet the needs of each program.

Communicating With Officials and Officials' Associations

Communication with the sports officials and their associations is usually a routine task. Scheduling events that require a sports official or officials is a straightforward activity. If done in a timely manner, it is just one more job in the busy day. When things go wrong at events, it is usually the aftermath and the multitude of phone calls that come with it that will tax the athletic director. Initiating the first contact with the officials' association after an incident with an official will enhance the proactiveness of the communication from the school.

The relationship established between the school and the officials' associations has long-term implications. The quality and experience of the officiating teams that get assigned to the school, the number of officials who show up ready to work, and the treatment the coaching staff gets in calls are all outcomes of good relationships. It is also important to remember that the coach and school are rarely going to win an argument with the officials' association.

Communicating With School Administration and Faculty

The school administration and school faculty are two groups with whom the sharing of information is extremely important. These two groups are the champions of the sporting programs from within the school organization.

Contact and Relations With School Administration

The administrative team at the school level is made up predominately of the principal, assistant principals, deans of students, and activity and athletic directors. Depending on the size of the school, one person may hold more than one job title and be directly responsible for communicating with a variety of groups other than athletics. At the central office level, personnel staffing can be very simple or highly complex. In small school districts it usually tends toward the fairly simple—a superintendent, secretary, and school board. In this case, the district staff and school boards take a much more in-depth look at the day-to-day offerings and management of the schools. They tend to be extremely responsive to parents and others who approach them with ideas, issues, and concerns. The parents tend to expect to be heard and to receive an almost immediate response. They have firsthand knowledge of the decision-makers in the district.

As the size of the school district increases, the level of autonomy in a school increases, with less direct contact with the upper levels of school district management. This does not stop concerned parents from making direct contact with the superintendent or school board. There are people who want to be heard at the highest levels even though this is rarely where decisions on the operation of a school are made. This disconnect gets mired in the multiple levels of management as the size grows. The parents' frustration increases because they are not able to get the answers they think they deserve. It is not unusual for parents to be referred back to the school level to have their concerns addressed.

Keeping the administrative team updated on all athletic issues is a never-ending job for the active athletic administrator. Simple information such as daily athletic schedules is important for the smooth functioning of the programs. Knowledge of potential problems that may occur during an event is even more critical.

Communication with the administration at rival schools can be an important matter. Information on students who have caused significant problems in the past and who have been denied the right to attend future events is necessary. Communication with rival schools can be as simple as exchanging team rosters for use in publications for the parents and friends of the programs. Most fans find this information highly useful.

Contact and Relations With Faculty

The faculty of a school is the heart line to the success of an athletic program. This is a two-way street that must be carefully preserved. The first direction this street takes is from the athletic department to the faculty. One of the simplest steps on this path is communicating what programs are currently in season, where and when the activities of each program are taking place, and who the responsible parties are to contact for further information. Athletic directors will know they are doing a good job of this when they get no questions about the minor details of the program. Conversely, they will know they are not doing such a great job of sharing information when they are inundated with questions to which the answers seem so obvious.

It is good to remember that the students and student-athletes are with the teaching faculty longer each day than they are with the coaches. A faculty member is often the first person to whom questions get asked. If the faculty member can answer a student's question based on the detailed information that has been provided, the athletic director has saved both himself and his coaching staff time and energy.

Providing faculty with timely information that contains all the facts is essential to good relations. Coaches and the athletic director must also hear from the faculty on several topics. It is suggested that the athletic department personnel meet with the faculty on a regular basis. This should start with the initial meetings at the beginning of the school year and continue throughout the year. It is further suggested that the agenda be short and to the point. The agenda should highlight how to contact the athletic department and the individual coaches of each program when concerns arise.

Communicating With Parents, Booster Clubs, Community Members, and Media

Parents, booster clubs, community members, and the media form the community stakeholder group. The size of a school may have an effect on the involvement in the programs by these stakeholders. Nonetheless, each of these entities care about and have concerns about the athletic program and their cares and concerns will all be positively addressed through good communication.

Contact and Relations With Parents

The contact an athletic director has with students and student-athletes will be very similar to the contacts with parents. Most of this communication will be in regard to their own student-athlete and their child's participation in one or more of the school's sports offerings.

It is unfortunate that the parents will have many of the same feelings as their student-athlete about a coach or program. The parents will have an additional focus on protecting their child. This is a responsibility that is not easily released by the parent and a responsibility that needs to be recognized by the athletic director from the start. Minimizing or trivializing it at the outset of the communication is usually a serious put-off for a parent.

The athletic director needs to have the facts at hand when meeting with a parent. There will be times, however, when this is not possible. The number one example of this is when the parent shows up at the director's office with no forewarning or catches him on the sidelines at a practice or event. The athletic director should determine to what extent he is going to communicate with a parent when he has no facts at hand. Courtesy suggests that he at least listen to the parent if it is at all possible. The athletic director has wide-ranging responsibilities that are usually time sensitive. Suggesting a more appropriate time to meet is a preferred method.

If the athletic director is able to listen to the parent at this time, it is helpful to let the parent know at the outset that the courtesy of listening is being afforded, but the athletic director probably will not be able to provide any guidance or answers until he has had an opportunity to do some fact-checking. Being forthright at the start of the conversation will put some parents off, but the majority will appreciate the honesty. Timely follow-up is the next step. Don't delay!

Developing contingency plans for the parents who will tax an athletic administrator's abilities to maintain a professional demeanor is a good strategy. The plans do not have to be as detailed as the medical emergency plans. They will, however, come in as handy as those medical emergency plans. As time permits, athletic administrators should set aside a few minutes to develop on paper or in their minds the types of quick conversations that will help them deal with difficult situations. It is not easy to think on your

Surprise Visits from Angry Parents

Mr. Edward Smith, father of Billie Smith (athlete), appears in the athletic department's office area bright and early on a Monday morning. The athletic director can hear most of the heated conversation he is having with the secretary, as well as the tone of his voice. The essence of his conversation is, "I demand to see the athletic director right now. I pay his salary through my taxes, and he is going to see me!"

Mr. Jones, the athletic director, steps out of his office and greets Mr. Smith, saying, "Good morning, Mr. Smith. I understand from your conversation with my secretary that you would like to meet with me. I will be happy to do so right after we get our students in class for the morning. My first responsibility is to the students. It should take only 15 or 20 minutes and I will be back in my office. I know you understand the importance of morning supervision duty. My principal expects us to be on duty. Are you able to wait for this brief period of time so I can meet with you?"

Mr. Smith really does not have a choice other than to say, "Yes."

In this brief time, it is prudent that the athletic director quickly gather information from his coaches and advisors so that he will have a clearer understanding of the problem in this initial meeting with the parent. It is also important to acknowledge the parent and to put off the conference for no longer than necessary.

To further emphasize an interest in addressing the issue, the athletic director can instruct the secretary (within earshot of the parent) to clear his calendar for the next hour of other meetings (which may or may not exist). This indicates to the parent that the athletic director is concerned and cares about both the parent and his son or daughter.

To also set the focus of the meeting, the athletic director can ask the secretary to have the student-athlete come to the office. This way he is getting two views of the problem at hand. Often the parent's view is not the same as the student's view.

feet and maintain poise and dignity, especially when emotions are running high. Saying less is saying more in many cases. This is especially true when you say too much and regret it immediately.

Contact and Relations With Booster Clubs

Parental support groups have taken on a variety of names over the years. Popular among the football enthusiasts is the Quarterback Club, the Football Booster Club, and the PTSO of SO High School (Parent Teacher Student

Organization of South Orange High School). Regardless of the name or the sport, these support organizations typically have one or two reasons for their existence. Fund-raising money for the program is typically the first and primary reason for a booster club to exist. The second reason is to bring parents together for a common goal. The term *booster club* is used here for simplicity. Whether the booster club serves a single program within the school or is a master organization for all programs, the club is a function of school philosophy. It does not change any of the needs for communication between the school and the parents who make up the booster club.

The athletic director and the coach are the two primary people who provide the communication link with the booster club. The effective athletic director will establish before the season the protocols for communication, laying out the guidelines for the booster club. This will ensure a united front on the part of the school. It is important to remember that each year a group of parents from the previous year graduated with their student-athletes, and a new group of parents, of the incoming frosh, will be joining the parents who are somewhere in the middle of the process. The athletic director will establish a new relationship and in essence repeats himself on a yearly basis to make sure everyone has the same information and is working toward the same purposes.

It is helpful to develop a list of discussion items with the booster club. Important dos and don'ts should be on the list. The list in reality is a living document that gets added to as rules, regulations, or guidelines change. This list provides the springboard for direct communication with the booster club members by the athletic director.

Contact and Relations With the Public and Community

Communication with the public and community is considered for these purposes large-scale events rather than encounters with individual people. This type of communication is more formalized in its presentation.

Preparing for large audiences takes time and effort. Creating an agenda is a good first step. The ideas of what needs to be included in the presentation can come from the speaker herself, the athletic department as a whole, the outside entities such as parents and general community members, as well as governing bodies.

Parent and athlete nights conducted by the athletic office personnel are a standard contact for most schools. This gives athletic personnel the chance to explain all the paperwork, share rules and regulations, explain medical information and requirements, collect fees and fines, and introduce coaches. This type of event needs a clear agenda so that important items are not missed or forgotten. It is highly suggested that copies of the agenda be provided to each participant. Good communication at these events will alleviate a number of problems after the fact. A sign-in sheet helps document that the parent and athlete were in attendance if it is required by rule or regulation.

Good public speaking skills can enhance a large group presentation. Having a good voice for public speaking is a plus. Learning how to properly use a microphone will provide positive benefits. Placement of the speakers (if they are portable) is very important for quality sound reproduction. If the luxury of a sound mixing board is available, it can also positively assist with the sound reproduction.

PowerPoint presentation tools can be advantageously used for presentations to large audiences. In a small room, the amount of information on each slide can be increased. When a presentation is made in a large facility such as a gymnasium or theater, less information can be contained on each slide and still be read by the audience. The athletic director should not put all the information he wants the audience to see and have in the PowerPoint. Use PowerPoint presentations just to highlight the important facts in the written material being provided.

Contact and Relations With the Media

The modern athletic director has an obligation to maintain good working relationships with both print and television media. Sports news media have taken massive cuts in personnel in recent years. This translates into fewer and fewer people to report on the successes in athletic programs.

The media have been criticized for the lack of coverage for many programs. The smaller programs in particular have been hit hard in not receiving media recognition. The media have also been criticized for enhanced coverage of issues and events that are distasteful and sometimes tragic for a school. With the explosion of reality shows where the public gets to vicariously live out others' misfortunes, it is easy for the media to take the same approach with news reporting. The negative sells ratings and ink.

In a perfect world, the media would report only the positives of a program and its wins, but this is not a perfect world. In a perfect world we would have only winners, but in this world we have both winners and losers.

The athletic director must be a champion of the school's programs. Writing articles for publication and becoming proficient as a writer is necessary in today's media environment. Not everything an athletic administrator submits will get published, but failing to write virtually guarantees that the word will not get out to the public. In addition, an athletic director who takes the time to write is in control of more of what gets published about the school. Small local publications are usually the easiest medium for getting information out to the public. Well-written articles of local interest are quickly edited and included in publications. News is a timed event. The game that happened today is news today and old news tomorrow.

In the technological age we live in, it is easy to spread information. Social media and other upcoming technological advances will challenge current athletic directors to stay on top of their game. What gets posted on school media sites will be a major consideration for the athletic director.

Professionalism will be key because school-based media sites reflect both the school and the school district to the public.

Perfecting Communication Skills

Public speaking is a part of an athletic director's life, and the athletic director should be prepared in advance for public speaking obligations. These obligations include parent night, sports banquets, recognition ceremonies, and pep assemblies as well as off-campus presentations. Community organizations appreciate hearing about school-based programs. The messages sent need to positively promote the school and its programs.

Public presentations need to have adequate public address systems so that even people with hearing deficits can hear and understand what is being said. Microphones are simple by design, yet it is difficult to get speakers to use them correctly. For most systems, the speaker should hold the microphone 3 to 6 inches (8 to 15 cm) from the mouth for good sound reproduction. Having the microphone closer than 3 inches tends to muffle the sound reproduction. Having the microphone farther away than 6 inches will result in only part of the total sound being reproduced. Keep a steady hand on the microphone, and keep it in one place.

Two-way radios, which are the backbone of communication devices for sporting and activity events, are very much like public address systems. The microphones on these radios are usually more sensitive than a public address system. Communications giant Motorola recommends that the microphone be 6 to 12 inches (15 to 30 cm) away from the speaker's mouth. If the microphone is closer than 6 inches, the sound is muffled; if the mouth is right next to the microphone, it becomes totally unintelligible. Two-way radios require some etiquette in their operation. A responsible radio operator will listen before talking into the microphone to make sure he has a clear channel (no one else is using the radio frequency).

Having translators available is necessary for most communications with parents whose native language is not English. In some jurisdictions, it is a requirement to have a translator present. The prudent athletic director will know the local jurisdiction requirements for translators.

The anonymous communications that come to the athletic director, both telephone calls and notes or letters, can be challenging to handle. No athletic director likes to receive a phone call in which the caller will not identify herself. A parent often fears reprisal against a child in the program. So in essence, the athletic director does not know the parent or the athlete. The prudent athletic director can advise the parent at the start of the anonymous call that he may not be able to do anything about the concern without the full cooperation of the caller. It should be a joint decision of the various supervisory levels as to what occurs with the information provided in this anonymous manner.

The same consideration is given to anonymous written communication. The unfortunate part of written communication is the lack of any interaction between the initiating party and the athletic director. The same joint decision making should prevail on how to deal with this type of anonymous communication. Strong, positive messages must be sent to parents and the community at the start of the school year about appropriate procedures for contacting the school and programs with concerns.

Summary

The need to communicate has never been greater than it is today. The timely response to communication requests match this 'greater need'. It is expected that almost instantaneous responses are to be the norm. As an athletic director your communications with the public are expected to be effective. They further expect you to be composed in all your communications. In order to accomplish these serious tasks you will be on a constant mission to perfect your communication skills. Athletic directors should practice using their communication skills at every opportunity. Just like the sports team the coach has out on the playing field, practice makes perfect. Practice, practice, and practice to perfect your communication skills.

CHAPTER 4

Personnel Management

David Hoch, PhD, CMAA

High school athletic administrators tend to receive the most attention when they hire or fire a head coach of a program that has a large following in the community and receives significant media coverage. However, few people outside the athletic department really understand the scope of an athletic administrator's duties. In fact, an athletic administrator serves many roles and performs a wide range of tasks in performing the job.

More specifically, as it relates to working with staff, an athletic administrator must be prepared to do the following:

- Write job descriptions.
- Post vacancies.
- Recruit, interview, and select the best candidate for each position.
- Maintain personnel records and files.
- Mentor or provide in-service professional development activities.
- Communicate new policies and procedures, and reinforce existing guidelines.
- Evaluate staff performance.
- Recommend retention, termination, and compensation.

Although the largest segment of staff members that athletic administrators deal with and lead are the coaches, athletic directors may also supervise several other people. Depending on the size and organizational structure of the district, they may also have an assistant athletic director, an administrative assistant, an athletic trainer, a grounds crew, and a custodial crew under their direction.

In addition, the athletic department probably employs part-time seasonal personnel such as ticket sellers, scoreboard operators, public address announcers, security personnel, and others who are necessary to host events. The athletic director may also have to hire, instruct, and supervise these workers.

Successful coaches enhance the athletes' experience, help young people grow and develop, and teach lifelong lessons.

A good place to start when writing job descriptions is to revise existing ones. If the district doesn't have anything in place, a colleague at another school may be able to provide one for a similar position. After revising any job description, the athletic director must get approval from the principal, superintendent, or board of education as dictated by the organizational structure of the district.

It's often desirable or necessary to initially post all vacancies within the district according to procedural and contractual obligations. When the athletic administrator is ready to extend the reach of the search, posting vacancy notices on district and state-association websites and placing an ad in the local newspaper are standard procedures.

In addition, networking can be an extremely useful technique. Networking? This involves contacting fellow athletic administrators; former coaches; and even former players, parents, and community members. All these people can provide prospects who may not have been readily identified.

Creativity can and does pay off when trying to fill vacancies, particularly those hard-to-fill positions. Local college coaches may be able to suggest one of their former players, a physical education student, or an athlete who has no remaining college eligibility. These young people may be able to fill assistants' positions for a year or two.

Recruiting, Interviewing, and Hiring

In education-based athletics, winning should not be the only or ultimate outcome. Although planning and striving to win should be part of a coach's efforts, winning seasons should not be the barometer of success for the program.

This means that beyond the expected knowledge of the sport, the athletic director should be looking for a coach who is organized, works hard, and can effectively communicate with everyone associated with the athletic program. Successful coaches enhance the athletes' experience, help young people grow and develop, and teach lifelong lessons.

At times, it almost gets to the point in the hiring process that the sport-specific skills and knowledge of the game are a given. For most candidates, the sport-specific aspects of their resumes are usually very apparent, but seeing a connection to helping young people reach their potential and understanding the value of athletics is much more complex to determine.

In the interviewing and hiring process, athletic directors should look for coaches who possess as many of the following traits and approaches as possible.

- Is positive and encouraging with their athletes during the instruction of skills and strategies
- Teaches values, character, and lifelong lessons beyond elements of their specific sport
- Serves as a positive role model for the athletes, fans, student body, and community
- Follows the rules, policies, and procedures of the school, league, and state association and does so with great integrity
- Actively looks for and uses opportunities to enhance teachable moments for their athletes, which may include community service involvement
- Always puts the welfare of student-athletes ahead of winning or their own objectives
- Continually takes courses, reads, and attends conferences to enhance their background and knowledge

These examples are not meant to be all-inclusive, but they do represent a good starting point of what qualities to look for in order to fill coaching vacancies. Take time and determine the traits and qualities that are valued and essential for the school setting. It is important that the questions used in interviews be phrased so that simple, transparent, stock answers are not the result (Hoch 2012).

The following are some suggestions for determining if a candidate is a good fit for the program and for working in an education-based philosophy.

- Always ask the same questions of each candidate. This provides a fair, consistent basis for comparing the answers given by each and allows the responses to be ranked from 1 to 5. After the conclusion of all interviews, totaling the numerical ratings for each candidate will give a ranking of the candidates.

- Don't overlook the simple question "Please tell us a little bit about yourself." This offer is an opportunity for the coach to relax a little, but it can also provide valuable insight into this person.

- Plan and prepare the questions carefully in order to avoid simple, standard answers. For example, almost every candidate would respond that she believes in sporting behavior and that it plays an important role in high school athletics. However, to obtain a better perspective, ask what the coach did to enhance such behavior with her last team.

Once the successful candidate has been chosen, it is important to notify not only the successful person but also all the other candidates. This is a matter of professional courtesy. It may be a little awkward making a phone call to those not selected; a well-crafted letter will also serve the purpose.

Mentoring

In the corporate world, human resource departments are also responsible for helping employees improve their competencies and fit into the operations and culture of the business. Mentoring is helping, guiding, and encouraging a person to grow, develop, and become the best he can be. This effort isn't important just for corporations; it is also critical for an athletic administrator in education-based athletics.

Upon hiring a new coach, the athletic director should schedule a mutually convenient time to cover the basics of the position. This orientation session should cover any and all items this new coach needs in order to get started (Hoch 2012). The athletic director might cover some of the following to ease a coach's transition to a new school:

- The location of where the team's equipment and uniforms are stored and a copy of the current inventory.
- A copy of the upcoming seasonal schedule. Be sure to specifically provide and explain the first legal date for the first practice session and any restrictions or procedures that have to be followed. For example, in football, a player may have to complete a number of practice sessions before he is permitted to put on pads and hit.
- An explanation of how to complete the eligibility form and process.
- The pertinent policies and procedures of the athletic department and school. Especially highlight those the new coach will have to use immediately. If you have a coaches' handbook that includes these documents, provide the new coach with a copy.
- The contact information for the athletic trainer and the department's guidelines for dealing with injuries.

It is fairly common for athletes and parents to want to find out a little bit about the next person who will be guiding their program. You might want to consider scheduling a meeting with both the athletes and parents so they can meet the new coach.

One-on-One Mentoring

Often referred to as the coaches of coaches, athletic administrators are the perfect people to mentor the coaching staff. Since the coaches come in direct daily contact with student-athletes and are responsible for their safety and development, this mentoring role has to be the highest priority for any athletic administrator, in spite of numerous other responsibilities and tasks. The better an athletic director mentors and educates the coaching staff, the fewer problems that should develop.

When a coach stops by with questions or in need of help, it may not always be a convenient time for the athletic director. However, providing feedback and advice as quickly as possible is vital in order to help the coach. An athletic director should either build time into his weekly schedule or postpone items for another day in order to mentor and assist his coaches.

The situations or topics that might be covered in these sessions are almost endless. For many coaches, tops on the list is advice on handling problematic parents or how to handle a discipline issue within the team. But anything that is pressing and causing a coach a problem should be dealt with as soon as possible. Receiving immediate help and support, whenever possible, is critical for the coaching staff.

Buddy System

An established method of mentoring is to pair a new or young coach with an experienced one. When an inexperienced coach has a question or faces a problem, she can seek the answer or advice by going to her mentor.

If this approach is implemented, it may be best to pair a new coach with an experienced person who is not coaching during the season in which he is serving as a mentor. Because of the time demands of teaching, or working, and coaching one's team, a mentor who isn't currently coaching during a season may be more available to help.

There are limitations to this mentoring approach, however. For the buddy system to work, the mentoring coach has to ascribe to the education-based athletic concept and be a positive, helpful example.

If a sound role model is not available for a new coach, the mentoring effort may not produce the desired results. An ineffective mentor may actually inhibit or harm the overall goal of providing a good foundation for inexperienced coaches. Since the athletic administrator is the coach of coaches, the ultimate responsibility falls back on his shoulders.

Ongoing Mentoring: In-Service Education

Part of the human resource function in the corporate world is to provide ongoing instruction and professional development programs in an effort to improve the knowledge and competencies of the employees. And this aspect of personnel management should also be part of every high school athletic program.

This process of continuing education is not intended only for new coaches. All staff members can benefit from the latest information and developments, reminders, and suggestions, all of which will fuel their improvement. With this in mind, an athletic administrator should always look for and embrace opportunities to help the school's coaches.

An e-mail distribution list created for each season can be an excellent method of quickly and effectively providing updated information to the coaches. This arrangement allows the athletic director to send out simple reminders or links to pertinent sites featuring new, practical ideas.

In addition to e-mail attachments and links, the old standby method of photocopying articles and documents in order to share information is always available. Anything that will provide coaches with new techniques, ideas for teachable moments, and help in performing some of their responsibilities will benefit them.

To provide in-service opportunities for the coaches, the athletic director can also schedule specific topical meetings. These sessions can include refreshments and an expert speaker. Typical staff development efforts include the following:

- Tips and guidelines for helping athletes with the college recruiting process
- Cautions and procedures for treating and dealing with concussions
- Ideas and techniques for dealing with challenging parents
- Communication skills for interacting with parents and dealing with the media

Special sessions should cover topics that are relevant to the local community and setting. Anything that will help the coaching staff improve and grow should be seriously considered.

An athletic administrator should also encourage and promote the professional development of her coaching staff. These efforts include more than the traditional sport-specific clinics that focus on teaching skills and strategies.

As the coach of coaches, the athletic director should motivate and guide coaches toward completing NFHS coach education courses that lead to national certification. This certification process is a critical way to demonstrate to the community that the coaches are professionals who embrace the education-based athletic concept.

Some state athletic associations have also developed their own accredited coaching education programs. These programs will also produce the same positive results—a better-prepared coaching staff.

Coaches don't usually consider taking courses unless it's suggested to them, therefore the onus is on the athletic director to get them involved in coaching education. Understandably, more knowledgeable coaches cause fewer problems for an athletic director and provide a better experience for the student-athletes.

Evaluating Coaches

Many school districts have job descriptions for their coaching positions and standard coaching contracts. Although these documents are a good starting point for describing the responsibilities and expectations of the coaching staff, a few additional steps can be taken in order to clarify and strengthen this effort.

Conducting preseason staff meetings for all coaches is vital. In these meetings, an athletic administrator should review important procedures and policies and cover all pertinent responsibilities and expectations that the coaches will be accountable for in their positions. Copies of new material, whether originating from the state athletic association or the school district, should also be distributed at the appropriate point in the meeting.

Although coaches can and should ask questions during these meetings, it is important that the athletic administrator use a detailed agenda and stay on task in order to cover all the necessary items. At the end of the meeting, the agenda should be filed for reference and as a record that everything was covered.

Understandably, job descriptions and standard coaching contracts, which are formal legal documents, normally list the basic expectations and what violations or problems would be cause for termination of a coach's contract. These two documents cannot possibly list every detail of a coach's position.

However, athletic administrators can augment these two important documents, cover loopholes, and emphasize responsibilities that may not have been outlined. One approach is to create a letter of coaching expectations. By using a template for this letter, the athletic director can insert each coach's name and give a copy to every coach. After reading the letter of coaching expectations, the coach signs, dates, and returns the letter.

Contrary to the belief of some, coaching evaluations should not exist solely to provide the basis for termination of a coach. A coaching evaluation should serve as the blueprint for professional growth and improvement. It should also highlight a coach's positive accomplishments.

In concert with the philosophical concept of education-based athletics, coaching evaluations should not be based on wins. This basic tenet was extremely well presented by Robert Gardner and Nina Van Erk in the NFHS Report in the January 2011 issue of *High School Today*:

> While winning as many games as possible is a goal for all high school coaches, the final outcome of a contest—in the long run—is not the all-determining factor for judging success. . . . While some want to measure success by the number of victories or state championships, principals, superintendents and school boards should judge, assess and reward high school coaches based on the successful implementation of the following educational components: citizenship, life skills, healthy lifestyles, learning and sportsmanship. (p. 1)

Considering the ultimate purpose of the evaluation process, it is vital that an athletic administrator take this responsibility seriously and invest a great deal of time in doing it properly. One step that is extremely helpful is to explain the process to the coaching staff. The better an athletic director explains the goal of evaluations and how they will be conducted, the better the coaches will buy into the concept.

The evaluation process can ideally be presented as one of the agenda items in the preseason staff meeting. During this presentation, the athletic director will want to explain the following:

- Coaching evaluations are not based on wins. Detail the outcomes that are valued.
- The main purpose of the evaluation process is to provide a blueprint for improvement for all coaches. Even very good coaches may have something to learn, and they should always work to continually improve.
- The evaluation process should involve a dialogue so the coach is better able to provide the optimal environment for the student-athletes.

It is helpful for the athletic administrator to review a few sample questions from the evaluation form and explain what it takes for a coach to earn the highest rating. This is also the time to point out that merely meeting the normal expectations for the position would earn a rating of satisfactory.

Unfortunately, the concept of accountability is often misunderstood and may be interpreted as being negative. In simple terms, accountability is merely monitoring an employee to ensure she meets the responsibilities of her position. For the benefit of the student-athletes and the athletic program, this should be an obvious objective for everyone involved.

The process of documentation is an integral part of ensuring accountability. Documentation is nothing more than dating and keeping on file items that can be used to substantiate problems, concerns, and accomplishments.

In a high school organizational hierarchy, the athletic administrator is the personnel director for the athletic department and, therefore, is the person to ensure the accountability of the coaching staff. This means a dated copy of the following should be kept in a coach's file:

- Reminders for late submissions of eligibility reports, tournament entries, and all other paperwork associated with the coaching position
- Reports and annotated notes of problems with athletes, officials, or other coaches
- Copies of minutes or scripts from meetings to discuss problems that have arisen with a coach
- A hard copy of any e-mail messages sent to explain a policy or procedure or to remind a coach of a missed deadline or overlooked responsibility
- Agendas for all coaches' meetings; these documents provide a reference of what was covered and the items for which coaches are responsible

Although everyone will occasionally make an honest mistake or forget a task, a number of reminders can illustrate and substantiate an ongoing problem. During the final evaluation at the end of the season, the athletic director should throw away the one or two isolated copies and use only those that represent serious or repeated incidents.

Observe Practice Sessions

In addition to watching games, it is very important to observe practice sessions. This technique is very much like what assistant principals do in classroom observations for teacher evaluations. The athletic director will complete a standard form for recording comments about his observations.

It is not necessary to stay for the full practice session. The athletic director can spend a few minutes watching one team before moving on to another. For example, when the athletic director needs to set up for a game, he can leave for the stadium early and watch another team practice for 10 minutes. During this time, the athletic director should look for the following:

- How are the drills organized? Is the practice space being utilized to the best advantage? Hopefully, all the athletes are active and totally involved rather than waiting for their next turn in a drill. The assistants should also be active and involved in giving instruction during the drills. Is there evidence of a written, well-organized practice plan? Practice sessions should last only two hours because longer sessions result in negative returns. It is extremely important, therefore, that the coach make the best advantage of every minute.

- How do the coaches interact with the athletes? During instruction, a positive, reassuring, and encouraging approach really works best. The old-school approach of getting in an athlete's face and screaming is not effective or acceptable in education-based athletics. Some coaches, parents, and fans may have difficulty understanding this, but there is no place for abusive tactics in a school setting. This should be a basic expectation of all the coaches.

- Are the coaches prepared to handle injuries and emergencies? The medical kits, water, and ice should be at every practice session and within view. If the heat index is high, water breaks should be frequently planned. In sports such as football and boys' lacrosse, practice times should be scheduled to avoid the hottest times of the day; if deemed necessary, specific drills and practice sessions can be altered so the athletes can practice in only shorts and T-shirts.

These three examples are not intended to be an inclusive list, but they give an idea of what to look for. An athletic director doesn't have to be—and most probably isn't—knowledgeable about every skill taught in each sport, but she can learn a great deal by watching or walking by a practice session for a few minutes (Hoch 2012).

An athletic administrator should never leave the office without a notepad and pen. This makes it easy to take notes while circulating through practice sessions. The notes for each coach should be dated and later filed. These notes are extremely useful when creating the narrative section of an evaluation.

While observing practices and games, the athletic administrator should look for the positive things the coaches do, and there should be a lot of them. This is important, since the negatives will always come to light. Whether by a phone call, e-mail message, or face-to-face conversation, parents, athletes, other administrators, teachers, and others will surely let the athletic director know about a problem. Therefore, the athletic director wants to uncover the good things in order to have the proper balance for the final evaluation.

Get Input From Athletes and Parents

Another source of insight into the effectiveness and success of the coaching staff is the athletes and parents. A recent school of thought advocates surveying these members of the school community in order to obtain their perspective of the effectiveness and direction of the program. This usually includes an evaluation of the coach.

On the surface, soliciting viewpoints from athletes and parents sounds like a viable approach, but it should be undertaken with caution. The parents' love of their child often overrides logic and reason, and they may very well have a biased hidden agenda.

An analogy of asking for input from athletes or parents for coaching evaluations can be drawn from student evaluations of college professors. It could be commonly assumed that professors who were thought to be easy graders often received the highest ratings. On the other hand, professors who were demanding and maintained strict grading guidelines may often have received lower ratings.

If there is one other lesson to be learned from the college professor example it is that some universities use student evaluations only as a part of the total evaluation process. This could be how athletes' and parents' opinions are viewed as well. After all, the athletic administrator has professional training, insight, observations, and firsthand information that athletes and parents don't have.

As long as athlete or parent input is considered as only one ingredient in the process, it may be an additional avenue to include. An athletic administrator should know his school and community, and it is up to him to determine whether this is best for a particular setting (Hoch 2012).

Solicit Coach Self-Evaluations

Self-evaluation forms—completed not just by head coaches but by assistants and junior varsity coaches as well—can yield useful information. The athletic director can use the same final evaluation form he fills out for the coaches. For items that apply only to the head coach, the assistant merely records NA, or not applicable.

Completing self-evaluations gives the coaching staff an opportunity to tell the athletic director how they think they performed. This simple step often suggests that the process is a two-way street and that the coaches' opinions also count. It is not surprising, however, that early in the evaluation process there may be a wide gap between a coach's and athletic administrator's viewpoints.

It is also very beneficial to have the head coach evaluate, again using the same form, her assistants and the junior varsity coaches. The success of most programs depends on the working relationship and contributions of the entire staff. It only makes sense to get the head coach's perspective for the final report.

The last step is for the athletic administrator to read through the self-evaluations, read through the evaluations by the head coach, and consult all the notes the director compiled about the coach during the season. With all this information, the athletic director is in the position to produce the final copy, which will be shared with the coach, signed, and ultimately filed.

In the evaluation process, it's necessary to use a standard form for all the coaches. Although it is natural for many athletic directors to want to find the best possible form or to improve the one they use, it is more important to remember the purpose of evaluations. It should be about the process and not about the tool that is used.

When creating an evaluation form or revising an existing one, athletic directors should consider the AAHPERD coaching domains and their benchmarks. These standards clearly define the competencies coaches should have in education-based athletics.

The domains were created in 1995 at a meeting of representatives from more than 100 major national sports organizations. They were revised nine years later in 2006 and provide the basis for coaching education and certification across the United States. For reference, the domains and their benchmarks can be found in *National Standards for Sport Coaches* (NASPE 2006). A scale of numerical answers needs to accompany each coaching evaluation question. The Likert scale, which is based on five responses—usually (1) definite weakness, (2) improvement needed, (3) satisfactory, (4) good, (5) excellent—provides results that can easily be analyzed to find the statistical concept of two standard deviations from the mean, and this makes its use highly desirable. A "not applicable" column may also be good, but this does not become the sixth possibility for statistical purposes.

However, it's important not to get bogged down or obsessed about improving the evaluation form. Although updating the coaching evaluation form is like updating most policies, procedures, and guidelines that athletic directors use, the form is merely the tool. The process—developing a blueprint for the coaches—is the most important thing.

Write an Evaluation Narrative

The narrative part of the evaluation may be the most difficult and time-consuming aspect for many athletic directors. Writing anything can be a daunting task, and having to produce a very good document to support or illustrate the ratings given in an evaluation can be a challenge. The narrative may be, however, the most important aspect of the evaluation process.

If done properly, the narrative section will substantiate and elaborate on the critical numerical ratings found in the evaluation. The narrative should also provide clear, specific recommendations for improvement, and these need to be conveyed in such a manner and tone that the coach understands and is receptive to what is outlined. This is not an easy task, and it takes an athletic administrator considerable time and effort to carefully craft a good narrative.

In public school settings, exemplary coaches can't receive raises because the salary scale is negotiated with the board and predetermined. The athletic director, however, can praise these outstanding people and let them know their efforts on behalf of the student-athletes and program are greatly appreciated.

Words of praise and compliments can be a very powerful motivator, and this extends well beyond the realm of coaching. In many districts, a signed copy of the coaching evaluation also goes to the principal and central office in addition to the coach. Letting these administrators know how much the coach is valued is another important aspect of the evaluation process.

When listing desired improvements in a coaching evaluation, the athletic director wants to be as specific and clear as possible and should include a time frame for the steps to be accomplished. To help the coach and to ensure the improvements are made, there shouldn't be any misunderstanding or ambiguity.

Since the narrative section is so important to the evaluation, the athletic administrator wants to produce the best possible write-up for each coach. They deserve it. As with many tasks, an athletic administrator can improve her narrative-writing skills. The following hints should help.

• Take notes throughout the season, as already recommended, and refer to them during the writing process. Never rely on memory at the end of the season to write a narrative.

• Plan ahead to meet deadlines for submitting or completing the evaluations. Good writing takes time, and with several narratives to complete, it's not a good idea to wait until the evening before they are due.

• Try to consider how the coach will receive any recommended suggestions for improvement or change. The manner and tone in which the information is stated can either aid or hinder the objective. This is another reason for taking time during the writing process so the message is as clear and concise as possible.

- Use the time-honored approach of balancing constructive criticism with areas of praise and recognition of the coach's accomplishments. In this manner, the suggestions may be better received and a little more palatable.

- Always write a draft or two before including the narrative with the rest of the evaluation. As with any good writing, reviewing, revising, and rewriting are essential in order to produce the very best quality. Since this document becomes the blueprint and possible motivational tool for the coach, it needs to be good. Also, the narrative is reflective of an athletic director's professional work. It will usually be read by not only the coach but also the principal and central office staff.

- Have someone else—an assistant principal, department chairperson, or spouse—proof the narratives before including them in the evaluations. This step is important for uncovering any mistakes or typos. In a professional document, it is extremely important for the copy to be as correct as possible.

- Always type the narrative section. Handwriting this vital part of an evaluation is not the proper professional approach. It is difficult to appeal to a coach to improve his professionalism or deficiencies if the document presented to him isn't as professional as possible. Athletic directors who can't type should ask a secretary or spouse for help.

- Make a photocopy of the evaluation before giving it to the coach. If the evaluation is misplaced or perhaps "lost" on purpose by the coach, another copy is available, preventing the need to start over. Unpopular evaluations that detail requests for improvement may be misplaced more frequently than positive and complimentary ones.

Writing a good narrative section can be challenging, but it is an extremely important task that plays a major role in the evaluation process. Very few people in life are overly receptive to recommendations for change and may be in denial or resistant to suggestions. An athletic director's efforts to craft a well-written narrative can make all the difference (Hoch 2005).

Recommend Improvements and Remediation

Although recommendations for improvement and steps for remediation are often found in the narrative section, they are important enough features to warrant a little more detail. As mentioned, very few people like being told that something needs improvement.

Explaining the purpose and process of the evaluation system to the coaches in the preseason meeting is a good start for this step. But it's important to remember that all people are different. Having an understanding of the personalities of and potential reactions from your coaches should also help.

Although it's necessary to be clear about what needs to be improved and how this change can be brought about, the athletic director must be extremely careful how he phrases it. Stating the recommendations in a positive, nonpunitive approach without actually attacking the person is more likely to result in success.

Always try to include remediation that addresses the actual problem instead of recommending vague or general possibilities. For remediation, the stated recommendation could be that the coach complete the NFHS Fundamentals of Coaching course; the athletic director should specifically indicate which section of the course will be of value in order to make the necessary improvements.

In addition, the NFHS has a whole host of courses beyond the fundamentals that would be invaluable for the remediation step. The NFHS offers inexpensive online courses that cover many of the problem areas for high school coaches. For example, the following NFHS courses would be useful in many instances:

- Engaging Effectively With Parents
- Teaching and Modeling Behavior
- Teaching Sports Skills
- Sportsmanship
- Creating a Safe and Respectful Environment

It is important, therefore, to put a great deal of thought into any recommendations for improvement and to provide practical, specific steps to take. When done properly, the end result will be a better coach for your program.

Meet After the Evaluation

Evaluating coaches is a process, and one of the normal concluding steps is to meet with each coach to discuss the evaluation. The athletic administrator should answer any questions a coach might have, but this should also be a time to highlight and clarify the recommendations for improvement for the coach.

As with any meeting, time, effort, and preparation are important considerations. Spending just 30 minutes meeting with each coach will amount to a great deal of time over the course of the year. This means that although athletic administrators should be considerate, they should also be efficient, concise, and extremely clear in order to effectively communicate their recommendations.

In addition to outlining the steps for improvement, it is important to acknowledge positive contributions and accomplishments. Letting coaches know their efforts are appreciated is a very powerful motivator. Considering the desired outcome of the coaching evaluation, being supportive, positive, and encouraging during this meeting is also extremely important.

The post-evaluation meeting has a lot riding on it; it is during this session that the coach receives her blueprint for improvement. If the meeting is successful and the coach is receptive, this is a good first step for the future.

Terminating Staff

Termination should be considered only after an extensive mentoring and professional development program has been implemented. This includes a thorough evaluation process that provides specific, concrete recommendations for improvement over a defined time frame.

The decision to terminate a coach should not be arbitrary or reactionary. As with the mission statement for athletics, all other guiding documents, and the criteria for the hiring of coaches, the basis for termination should be predetermined and part of the school's written policies and procedures.

An athletic administrator can consider the following five areas to determine if there is a basis for termination:

1. Is the health or safety of the student-athletes in jeopardy?
2. Does the coach negatively represent the school in terms of public statements or actions?
3. Does the coach's behavior, attitude, or approach affect the future of the team? A good indicator is when a number of players quit the team and there are fewer candidates trying out in succeeding seasons.
4. Has there been no attempt by the coach to improve on the recommendations listed in the coaching evaluation?
5. Has the coach repeated the same problems, mistakes, or shortcomings after being asked to change or improve?

In addition, since the coaches are not evaluated based on wins, wins should not be the basis for termination.

Clueless About Human Resource Management

Two or three days after the conclusion of the season, a coach was summoned to the athletic administrator's office. The coach was told that a few parents had complained about not winning enough, and she was going to be relieved of her head coaching position.

In her position, the coach always made the development and welfare of her student-athletes her number one priority, used teachable moments, instilled fair play and sporting behavior, and was a great role model. Even though these qualities are deemed essential in education-based athletics, they weren't considered in determining whether to terminate her employment. Only the lack of wins was used to make the decision.

(continued)

(continued)

Four weeks after the coach's dismissal, she received a copy of her coaching evaluation. Since the purpose of a coaching evaluation is to provide a blueprint for improvement and to highlight outstanding aspects, the only reason this exercise was conducted was to meet district requirements. There was no mention of "not winning enough" in the evaluation, and there were plenty of examples of the coach's supporting the education-based philosophy.

Adding to the strange situation was that the athletic administrator was new to the school and had completed only his third month in this position. There was no due process afforded to the coach. There was no effort to provide suggestions for improvement and no opportunity for the coach to make changes.

A week or two after releasing the head coach, the administration asked her for a favor. Would she help out and coach the JV team the next season? In terms of human resource management, the administrators definitely did not take into account the coach's feelings and had no understanding of normal human reactions.

How do you relieve someone of a position she loved and put her heart and soul into? And then ask a favor? When the former head coach said, "No, I'm not interested in the position," both the athletic administrator and principal became irritated.

Resource management of education-based athletics must follow a philosophy in which winning is not the only or ultimate outcome considered for success. Coaching evaluations need to fairly appraise qualities and efforts that are integral to this philosophy and then provide suggestions and time for improvements where necessary.

And finally, good human resource management takes into account the feelings and emotions of the people involved and even the timing and setting of meetings. Since coaches are the most important resource in the athletic program, athletic administrators must become experts in this vital responsibility.

Keeping Records

Although it may not be an exciting task, coaching evaluations and other pertinent documents need to be filed for each coach, and these files have to be maintained. This information may be necessary to confirm or substantiate compliance with district or state standards and regulations. Beyond coaching evaluations, an athletic administrator would normally keep the following items:

- Coaching applications and letters of reference
- Coaching certifications, including the NFHS Level I national certification, completion of concussion training, first aid and CPR training, and other required programs within the district and state
- Coaching contracts with any addendums or specific requirements or expectations that have been added
- Copies of awards and accomplishments the coach has won
- Any other report or document that is relevant to the person's coaching position

A good normal practice is to keep active files—for those currently coaching within the program—labeled in a file cabinet within the athletic administrator's office. In this manner, the files can be quickly and easily accessed when needed and new documents can be added in an efficient manner.

For coaches who have retired or left coaching, their files should be boxed, labeled, and placed in a storage room. These files may not have to be accessed often, but they need to be kept for reference in the event of a problem or in case information needs to be retrieved in the future. How long should these inactive files be kept? For the answer to this question, consult the district's legal department and follow their directives.

Managing Adjunct Staff

Although the largest group of employees an athletic administrator usually deals with is the coaching staff, there may be other employees hired by the district who report to the athletic administrator. These additional personnel could, depending on the structure and size of the setting, include a department secretary, an assistant athletic director, an athletic trainer, custodial staff, and a grounds crew.

With these positions, the athletic director may not actually be involved in the posting of vacancies and the hiring process. They may be covered by district policies, union contracts, and job descriptions. However, regardless of who hired these people, the athletic director will most likely be responsible for supervising and managing them.

As with most working relationships, understanding what these employees do and how much time it takes is important. The athletic director doesn't have to be familiar with every detail or every responsibility, but generally knowing what is involved in terms of effort and pressure is vital.

With this level of understanding, the athletic director should be able to develop a realistic set of expectations for these different positions. Quite often unrealistic expectations create difficult working conditions and relationships. Anything administrators can do to understand their employees' contributions will ultimately help create a better situation for all.

Another key element of developing a good working relationship is to express and show appreciation for what a person does. It is so simple. As with the coaching staff, the athletic director probably doesn't have the latitude to give raises or monetary bonuses, but he can say thank you and show appreciation. If this is done, he will usually get extraordinary efforts in return.

An athletic director can show appreciation by doing a few simple things:

• Give any extra caps, sweatshirts, or other team gear to the secretarial staff, custodians, and grounds crew. These token items will usually be well received and greatly appreciated by these people. They will wear the clothing proudly.

• Provide the best equipment possible for all personnel. Whether it is a new line-painting machine for the grounds crew or a new computer for a secretary, anything to help make their jobs easier will be greatly appreciated. When these people know their efforts are sincerely appreciated, they will often take extra steps to help when there is a problem or emergency.

• Always start by asking, "Would you please . . . ." And definitely always say thank you for a job well done. No matter how busy a person might be, nobody should overlook the importance and power of these two expressions. They are vital for creating and maintaining good working relationships. Never take anyone for granted!

Communication with an athletic trainer is especially critical, should the school be lucky enough to have one. Since an athletic trainer cannot possibly attend all contests, a priority schedule should be developed and periodically updated. When contests are postponed and ultimately rescheduled, it is vital to share this information with the athletic trainer in order to ensure essential game coverage.

When multiple contests are held at the school, all coaches should know which contest the athletic trainer will be attending. In some areas of the country, for example, athletic trainers are required to be present during football games because of the collision contact that is part of the game. It is important, therefore, that all coaches know how and where to contact the athletic trainer if needed.

In addition to full-time employees, it is not unusual for athletic departments to hire people to perform duties at games. This group may include ticket sellers, scoreboard operators, security personnel, and others.

These positions usually don't require contracts, interviews, and formal evaluations. If the person has the ability to perform the task and is dependable, these are usually the only requirements for employment.

Just as with secretaries, custodians, and grounds crews, the athletic director should develop a good working relationship with these seasonal employees. Expressing appreciation is again an important key, and communicating effectively is also vital.

Seasonal employees need to be kept well informed and given as much notice as possible in the event of weather-related postponements, rescheduling, and sudden changes. With schedule changes, there must be some flexibility with regard to an employee's being unable to report for duty because of previous commitments.

Providing complimentary sodas and hot dogs at games is often a nice touch to show appreciation for seasonal employees. Making a brief public address announcement at a game is another simple but valuable technique for acknowledging their contributions.

Even though game workers may be part-time or temporary staff members, keeping some basic records is a good idea. Information to be kept on file includes home addresses, phone numbers, and e-mail addresses as well as an accurate record of payment for fulfilling their game duties. These workers should be paid according to the prescribed payment procedures for the district—whether this involves submitting an accounts payable voucher or paying cash from the gate with a receipt.

Summary

Although an athletic administrator has a wide range of responsibilities and tasks to perform, none may be as essential or important as fulfilling the role of personnel manager. Why? Unlike managing the budget, maintaining facilities and equipment, scheduling, and other responsibilities, this job requirement involves dealing with people. And these people have contact with and great direct impact on the student-athletes.

People are the most important resource of any organization—corporation or school—and the success of a program is largely dependent on them. This makes the athletic administrator's role as a personnel manager one of the most critical and important responsibilities.

CHAPTER 5

Student-Athlete Development

Sheri Stice, CMAA

An outstanding athletic program should teach young student-athletes how to compete, how to win and lose, how to prepare, how to discern strategy, and how to understand the system of values that is inherent in sport. For this to happen, athletes must be presented with multiple opportunities in a safe environment void of denigration and humiliation. Despite criticism directed at competitive sport at all levels, the education potential of positive experiences is powerful.

Several studies (Braddock 1981; Fejgin 1994; Marsh 1993; Melnick, Sabo, and Vanfassen 1977) show the benefits of sport participation and demonstrate that students who participate in sports have better attendance records, lower rates of discipline referrals, and higher academic self-esteem as well as aspirations to enroll in and graduate from college. Additionally, teachable moments in sport and thorough season planning result in life lessons, increased self-esteem, and the ability to build interpersonal relationships, all while building individual leadership skills.

In an ever-changing society, today's athletes' experiences and expectations differ from those of their predecessors of 30, 20, or even 10 years ago. Social issues such as peer pressure, character, accountability, disrespect, and entitlement are among the tough challenges coaches deal with on a daily basis. Teacher-coaches today must have expertise in areas of cognitive, social, and character development to create a successful program. Athletic directors can help prepare their coaches for these challenges by asking them some very important questions:

- Do you know about the cultural and socioeconomic backgrounds of your athletes and the community where they live?
- Do you model respect for those who are different?
- Are you able to recognize and constructively address conflicts that might come up based on race, gender, religion, or socioeconomic status?

A program philosophy is about attitudes, beliefs, and values and defines what is important to the school community; an effective communicator who provides quality growth opportunities merely continues to fertilize and cultivate after the roots have been established.

- How will you motivate athletes to consistently perform to their full potential?
- How will you create a sense of community?
- How will you continue to learn and grow in your field?
- How will you maximize participation numbers?
- How will you set high expectations for classroom performance?
- How will you convince athletes they must always present themselves well?

As coaches take the time to write out the answers to these questions, their own coaching philosophy and objectives for success will evolve or be refined. This philosophy will drive the teacher-coach in all aspects of the development of a successful program. By guiding their coaches, athletic directors play a critical role in the climate of athletic programs. Just as the player–coach relationship is important, so is the relationship between the athletic director and the coaching staff. A program philosophy is about attitudes, beliefs, and values and defines what is important to the school community; an effective communicator who provides quality growth opportunities merely continues to fertilize and cultivate after the roots have been established.

The inability to keep sports in the proper perspective is a failure that leads to conflicting values and is frustrating for everyone. According to Yeager et al. (2001), a number of influences have become problematic in sports today, including pressure to begin competition at too young an age, pressure to specialize too early and focus on one sport, pressure to win at all costs, absence of joy and fun in the endeavor, the presence of sport violence, the presence of negative parental interference, and the presence of too many coaches who are not sensitive to character development in their athletes.

Clearly, these pressures and negative influences result from misconceptions about what is expected and what is important. They not only create unhealthy situations for young athletes but also are confusing.

Empowering athletes to be leaders is critical to the success of athletic programs. Leaders empower others to work hard, and they can be recognized because the players who work with them consistently demonstrate superior performance. Great student leaders encompass confidence, assertiveness, and mutual respect; however they are not necessarily the oldest or most experienced players on the team. Their added strength results in teammates who turn the ordinary into the extraordinary. How do coaches determine "the generals?" Can student-athletes learn to be leaders?

Unfortunately, there is no sure method of identifying great leaders; however, natural leaders walk their talk. Primarily, they are fierce competitors who can balance fun with the will to win. They are self-disciplined, mentally tough, and willing to accept responsibility when things go wrong. This accountability results in a person who is respectful to others, including teammates, officials, and coaches. Lastly, they are unselfish and offer praise to others when it is deserved.

Can leadership be learned? Several resources are available to help coaches develop leadership in their student-athletes as well as provide them with a support network to maintain their skills. These programs address what it means to be a leader; persuasiveness; becoming a good listener; skills in conflict resolution; skills in decision making; and skills in learning to collaborate, compromise, and build consensus. Athletic administrators and coaches desiring to implement this critical piece of successful programming should visit the Janssen Sports Leadership Center at www.janssensports leadership.com.

Player Management

Foremost in the success of any athletic program is the way coaches handle the great deal of power inherent in their position. A coach's actions have an important influence on the self-esteem and self-worth of his athletes; thus, the coach's philosophy affects everything he does, from organizing practices, applying consistent discipline, assigning off-season workouts, and managing and interacting with athletes.

A coach is one of the most important people in an athlete's life (Thompson 2007). *Positive Coaching in a Nutshell* describes the emotional tanks (E-tanks) of athletes and provides a list of ways coaches can fill these E-tanks. The athletic director should make sure all members of the coaching staff are familiar with the following tactics for positive coaching.

- Using names—Every athlete should be greeted and bid farewell by name. Hearing their names spoken in a friendly tone of voice is music to players' ears.
- Smiling—Many coaches regard too much smiling as a negative, but smiling at players is an easy way to let them know you value them.
- Joking—Humor that doesn't make fun of someone causes people to enjoy each other's company, which is important in the often stressful setting of a team.
- Making eye contact—Friendly eye contact communicates caring.
- Appropriate touching—Touching kids needs to be appropriate, but tousling a player's hair, patting players on the shoulder, exchanging high-fives, and so on communicate that the coach likes and values the players.

- Granting influence—Having influence makes kids believe they are important. The coach should ask players advice about what to do in a given situation, which says she cares enough to ask them what they think. Players often want to play a position beyond their ability. Using blowout games to give kids a chance to play their favorite positions lets them know they have influence.

- Listening—There are times when a coach has to make a decision the athlete is not going to like, but it helps to give the athlete a chance to offer an opinion. Listening without interrupting communicates caring and that the player is being taken seriously. Sometimes that is more important than the specific problem a player is upset about in the first place.

- Making apologies—When adults apologize to children for a mistake they make, it sends a powerful message of caring. A coach who finds the humility to apologize to a player is communicating in a direct way that he values the player.

- Forgiving—We forgive because we care about people. Often coaches take it personally when a child misses practice or fails to execute a play. Being able to forgive and move on is an advanced skill for a coach.

- Asking for help—Coaches fill E-tanks by asking players to help. Being asked to help signals to players that they are important members of the team and is a big E-tank filler.

- Showing appreciation and recognition—When someone notices our effort, we want to make more efforts.

- Bragging—Bragging about someone conveys pride in the person. Kids need to be bragged about by important persons in their life. Coaches should try to tell parents something good about their child's play.

- Finding time for individual teaching—All players need individual teaching time. A coach should not spend all her teaching time with the most talented players. Taking time to work with less talented players on an individual basis is a big E-tank filler.

- Gently delivering negative feedback—Athletes often get yelled at when they make a mistake. A gentle word about how they might improve can be the stimulus to improve, whereas yelling mainly allows an undisciplined coach to vent.

- Helping kids see their potential—Most of us will work harder for someone who helps us see our potential.

- Taking photographs—Taking photos is a good way for coaches to connect with their players. The very act of asking them to stand still or pose for a photo sends a message of caring.

Encouragement is the oxygen of the soul. A positive approach to coaching can certainly enhance the atmosphere of the team. Coaches who are having fun and using positive reinforcers, verbally and nonverbally, will certainly experience success.

Successful Coaching

I was relatively new in my role as an athletic administrator when I had a profound realization of the incredible power that coaches possess . . . the good, the bad, and the ugly. Having been a coach for several years, I did not consider myself powerful, only tremendously committed. That commitment was to develop a team with the tools and knowledge I had and to continually try to learn as much as I could to maintain credibility and to have fun. Didn't everyone do this?

As I ventured into the supervisory role, it became evident that coaches who are successful possess attributes that transcend far beyond the most basic. As well, those who struggle continue to miss the mark in getting athletes to move to the next level. Their athletes tend to be perimeter trained, much like circus elephants. Their chains allow them to venture only so far, and once the chains are removed, the level of trust and expertise remains stagnant. This phenomenon is usually rooted in that the coach fails to realize there is life and death in the power of the tongue and they should not be reduced to strategy and technique. Constant and consistent positive affirmation that encourage rather than denigrate yield amazing results. By putting an athlete's needs before their own, coaches can unlock a sense of the human, not just athletic potential of those in their charge.

Successful coaches continue to focus on the basics and stick with them. They capture the hearts of their players by earning their trust and behaving consistently. They are lifelong learners and stay up to date with regard to knowledge of their sports, but they are cognizant that their athletes, *and their parents,* will not care what they know until they know they care. Twenty-first-century athletes are motivated by the relationship between their coach and themselves. They need that connection and guidance, much like that of a shepherd. This style of coaching places great value on the worth of "flock," and it is hard work.

This chapter on student-athlete development is a beginning for coaches to refine their craft. Whether coaches are beginners or experienced, the approach is simple: Focus on the basics and the process; communicate; stay up to date; communicate; failure is part of success; communicate; be direct and honest; communicate; and finally, capture the athletes' hearts and earn the trust of the flock.

Preseason

Although we extol the virtues of high participation numbers, player cuts are a real and unpleasant part of the team selection process. As mentioned previously, the coach's influence on the self-esteem and self-worth of prospective athletes is paramount. Therefore, the selection process should be clear and succinct. As athletic director, instruct the coaches to define expectations, to make clear the skills to be evaluated, to use an evaluation instrument, and to maintain one-on-one communication with the players. The evaluation criteria should reflect the philosophy of the program; therefore, if value is placed on academics and citizenship, the matrix should include these criteria in addition to the obvious skill and athletic rubric. When the team is determined, candidates deserve a one-on-one meeting with the coach. Posting results is ineffective and does not recognize and value the effort made by the athletes.

As with any group or organization, establishing boundaries and creating a set of rules by which the group functions are critical. Giving student-athletes the opportunity to be a part of this process allows them to "own it." Some topics that should be addressed include player language, locker room behavior, behavior at practices and games, behavior with regard to officials, behavior when traveling, attendance and curfews, and dress for practices and games.

Coaches should help team members determine logical consequences that change behaviors. Other team rules may be driven by the philosophy of the athletic administration. Completed in collaboration with the coaching staff, these rules are more serious and must be addressed and communicated to parents and athletes before the season. Such rules cover drugs and alcohol, social media, threats of violence, theft, felony offenses, safety practices, and derogatory comments.

Finally, rules regarding eligibility and lettering criteria must be made clear and concise to athletes and their parents before the season. Nothing can destroy the trust and confidence of a program more quickly than the lack of transparency on the part of the coach or the school; therefore, a preseason meeting with parents and athletes is a necessity. A preseason meeting agenda should include the following:

- An overview of the program
- Introduction of the coaching staff
- The mission and vision of the program
- Eligibility requirements
- Lettering requirements
- Team rules
- Team expectations

- Inherent risks involved in participation
- Practice schedules
- Game schedules
- Nutrition and game-day meals
- Booster club involvement for parents and fund-raising events

Open and clear communication will help eliminate any negativity that may occur because of lack of knowledge, but more important, it sets a standard of expectation and accountability.

Sports hold inherent risks in any environment. A coach's job description should clearly state the criteria and methods by which the community and school system will hold him accountable. This criteria may include documentation of the following:

- A facility inspection checklist (the greater the risk the more regular the inspections)
- Equipment checklist and method of disposal
- Injury report forms and chain of notification
- Medical history and physical exams (frequency)
- Concussion protocol and chain of notification
- Crisis management plans with clearly delineated duties
- Full disclosure of inherent risks for specific sports
- Transportation policy and waivers
- Maintenance of eligibility requirements and academic progress
- Required training in CPR, first aid, and AED

Athletic departments can reduce their risk by ensuring that adequate records are kept, safe transportation is provided, coaches receive proper training, and due process is followed.

Beginning with the end in mind is an important step for any person or team focused on a positive outcome. This concept is expressed all too poignantly in *Alice in Wonderland* as the Cheshire cat exclaimed, "If you don't know where you are going, you will never get there." Although goal setting is a popular topic, few people take the time to write goals down and stick with them. Student-athletes need to understand the process for setting goals because it is a skill they will use for a lifetime. Naturally, student-athletes will ask, why bother with goals? Instruct coaches to take the time to explain how the process will affect success. Goals provide direction, tell you how far you have come, help make the overall vision attainable, clarify everyone's roles, and give people something to strive for.

Team goals cannot be accomplished independently of others; therefore, goal setting is an extremely important process in determining a team's real objectives. It is helpful to have clearly written and visible goals for the group to achieve, and they should be important enough to post throughout the year.

SMART goals is a common acronym used by businesses, but it works equally well with groups attempting to determine outcome-based results.

S = specific
M = measurable
A = attainable
R = relevant
T = time bound

Coaches and athletic administrators want to ensure that the goals they set are related to their roles and that they use their values to guide behaviors. In this case less is more. Choose two or three aspects to focus on and those having the greatest relevance. Naturally the focus should tie most closely to the mission. The following process is a relatively simple one that student-athletes can connect to quickly. It will be up to the coaches and athletic directors to establish a clear vision of how they see athletes working together and then open it up to the team to find out what their expectations are.

1. Why? What makes us a team? What outcomes do we envision? These are known as outcome goals and are basically uncontrollable. Examples might include winning a state championship or going 10-0 in the regular season.

2. What? These are performance goals. They are more within your control and are typically measured against previous performances. Effort and attitude are included here; how athletes respond to situations (e.g., mental toughness) is based on performance, not winning. Additionally, quality preparation plays a critical role in building confidence.

3. How? How will the team practice to get to the Why? These are process goals. Process goals allow you to delineate exactly what you must do each day to reach the outcome you want. Confident athletes provide themselves more confidence building opportunities by focusing on the process more than the outcome.

According to Dale and Robbins (2010), examples of outcome, performance, and process goals might be described as shown in table 5.1.

Athletic directors and coaches cannot assume that once the process of goal setting is complete, it is final. Goals need to be revisited constantly, and they should be written down and viewed daily. That which is valued is measured, and what gets measured gets done. *We are what we repeatedly do* is an adage that speaks loudly to the effects of goal setting.

TABLE 5.1 Outcome, Performance, and Process Goals

Outcome	Performance	Process
Make the all-state team as a wide receiver in football.	Catch every ball that is thrown my way during each game.	Run 10 extra passing routes after each practice.
Win a championship in golf.	Improve the number of fairways hit from 12 to 15.	Follow my preshot routine for every shot during the round.
Be an all-conference point guard in basketball.	Improve assist-to-turnover ratio from 3 to 1 to 5 to 1.	Practice dribbling drills for 20 minutes, 3 days a week, after practice.
Start every game in volleyball.	Increase my serving percentage by 20%.	Work on tossing the ball to the same height at least 30 times before and after practice.

In Season

Several physiological principles must be followed if athletes are going to progress and avoid injury. Inherent in these principles is the notion that all athletes must be treated individually, resulting in a huge responsibility for coaches. The maturation process of adolescents is evidenced in Tanner's five stages of development, as shown in table 5.2, which is uniformly accepted to describe the onset and progression of pubertal changes.

Boys accelerate more slowly but continue to grow for about six years after the first visible signs of pubertal changes, while girls complete the puberty process between the ages of 15 and 17. Variations in height and weight, muscle mass, cardiovascular endurance, skeletal and connective tissue maturity, and endocrine activity are apparent within any adolescent population and across grade levels. The demands of growth require considerable energy and rest.

The athletic director must ensure his coaches understand the maturation process and the principles of training. Those who do not may harm athletes rather than help them. Before puberty, athletes simply are not physiologically ready to respond fully to training. Thus, coaches need to be particularly mindful of the training methods for young athletes. Their neuromuscular skill is a function of practice, not age or maturation; therefore, the focus should be on skill development and fun, while the more serious training should wait for physiological capacity to increase.

The value of training depends on the readiness of athletes, and this readiness comes with maturation. Using the information in Tanner's chart for

TABLE 5.2 Tanner Maturation Stages

Tanner maturation stage	Physiological description	Related development of other systems	Implication for parents, athletes, and athletic supervisors
1	Pre-pubescence Age 10 and younger	The skeleton, cardiovascular system, lungs, and muscle tissue are immature.	Consider individualized activities aimed at building endurance, large muscle group strength, and overall coordination (e.g., swimming, gymnastics, low-organized soccer).
2	Early pubescence Age 12-13	Skeletal growth rate exceeds increase in muscle mass and strength. Skeletal growth rate for girls may exceed rate for boys. Epiphyses not ossified. Cardiovascular growth is gradual but responds well to gradual conditioning.	Use caution with high-impact sports. Play controlled-contact football, with a rigorous and controlled sequence to teach safe blocking and tackling. Emphasize aerobic-based training for all sports.
3	Pubescence Age 13-14	Male skeletal growth accelerates. Endocrine maturation may produce other body changes. Menarche commences (if it has not already done so).	Skeletal growth exceeds muscular growth and thus may create awkwardness and inability to perform explosive actions with efficiency. Encourage conditioning of both the cardio-respiratory and skeletal systems. Menarche may be delayed with intense activity for extended time.
4	Late pubescence Age 15-16	Muscle mass in boys begins to develop. Better coordination is apparent. Females extremely conscious of body composition and appearance.	Effect of practice begins to surface. Excellent time to promote off-season conditioning and proper nutrition. Supervised powerlifting can begin.
5	Young adult	Signals maturation of all systems.	Quickness, strength, endurance, and coordination approach maximal levels with conditioning.

stage 2, training for early pubescent athletes should emphasize stretching and avoid activities that stress the epiphyses. As the chart indicates, the epiphyses have not ossified; therefore, deep knee bends, curveball pitching, and repetitive stops and starts may be harmful. As the athletes mature, more resistive strength regimens and the use of a high number of repetitions rather than powerlifting should be incorporated.

Without question, training improvements are most dramatic when the initial fitness level is low. As fitness improves, it takes extended periods of time and effort to achieve even the smallest changes. Unfit athletes fatigue easily and are more prone to injury; therefore, a major responsibility of the coach is to develop programs that help athletes achieve the levels of fitness demanded by sport. Athletes must be fit to optimize performance and to avoid injury.

According to Sharkey (1986), fitness is described in two ways: energy fitness and muscular fitness. Energy fitness involves storing and using fuels to power muscle contractions. It also involves the development of important supply and support systems, including the respiratory, cardiovascular, and endocrine systems. While others speak of aerobic or cardiorespiratory training, Dr. Sharkey uses the term *energy fitness* to describe the training of specific aerobic and anaerobic energy systems and to focus on how such training enhances the muscles' ability to use the body's available energy.

Muscular fitness encompasses flexibility, strength, muscle endurance, power, and speed. It also involves the nervous system, which controls muscle contractions, and therefore training for muscular fitness cannot be separated from neuromuscular training. Properly designed training programs follow the principle of specificity: Energy and muscular fitness activities should support the skills involved in the sport.

Each training session should begin with a warm-up designed specifically for the sport of choice. An adequate warm-up is an essential part of injury prevention because it decreases the incidences of strains and sprains. Before competition, the warm-up is a good time for athletes to review and practice the psychological skills of imagery, relaxation, and concentration and to review their strategy for the event. The stretching part of a warm-up reduces soreness and the risk of injury and increases the range of motion around joints. Beginning on a comfortable surface, slowly stretch the lower back, hamstrings, and other muscles to prevent soreness or injury.

Coaches should practice being lifelong learners, especially with regard to keeping up with advanced training principles. For instance, ballistic, or bobbing and bouncing movements, to increase flexibility have been proven to cause a reflex muscle contraction that makes stretching difficult and risky. After exercise, athletes should be encouraged to cool down and hold a stretch until they feel a slight pull in the muscle but no pain. As they hold the stretch the muscle will relax. Recent research indicates that warming up by itself has no effect on range of motion, but when the warm up is followed by stretching there is an increase in range of motion. If injury prevention is the primary objective, the evidence suggests that athletes should limit the stretching before exercise and increase warm up time. Studies also support that range of motion can be increased by a single 15 to 30 second stretch for each muscle group each day. Naturally, some athletes will require longer duration and more repetitions.

Well-informed coaches know the major energy sources and pathways used in their sports and how to help athletes achieve the energy fitness they need in order to compete successfully. They understand how muscles use the energy available to them and how inefficient energy use hastens fatigue. By matching training regimens to the energy demands of a sport, coaches can help athletes meet these differing demands more effectively. Using Dr. Sharkey's analysis of energy training, establishing an aerobic foundation, and developing an anaerobic threshold can be studied in more detail in *Successful Coaching, Fourth Edition*, by Rainer Martens.

Dealing with the stress of competition, training, and the perception of others is reality for athletes. In recognition of this, coaches should include opportunities for athletes to process ways to identify the triggers that cause the stress. Symptoms of stress are manifested in many different ways. Physical manifestations include frequent stomach aches, trouble sleeping, injuries, backaches, constipation, headaches, and exhaustion. Trouble concentrating, difficulty making decisions, forgetfulness, and making mistakes are all mental manifestations of stress. There are also emotional manifestations: feeling grumpy, tense, impatient, hopeless, hostile, easily upset, lonely, or depressed.

Athletes should be able to recognize the choices they have when situations are not working for them. Providing a list of their alternatives for relieving stress gives them the freedom to make choices that will improve their performance or reignite their passion for the game.

More critically, stress can influence an athlete's confidence level. The most powerful tool for building confidence is for an athlete to be successful; unfortunately, the player must perform on his own to accomplish this. Coaches can help players experience success by doing the following:

- Being a good coach who constantly looks for ways to help the athlete get better
- Defining success in terms of things the athlete has control over, such as effort, and rewarding the athlete accordingly
- Simplifying practice drills as much as necessary to let a struggling player experience at least some success
- Setting up the game schedule to give the team a good chance of being successful early in the season

Rarely does an athlete have everything going just right. Players often make the mistake of simply letting their performances or how they happen to feel that day dictate their confidence level. Although past performance is certainly a very powerful determiner of a player's confidence level, there are several methods of increasing confidence—it does not have to be left to chance. One of the most powerful ways is simple positive reinforcement. Also, coaches who model confident behavior tend to have confident athletes. Finally, helping athletes meet challenging goals that they set for themselves can certainly elevate their confidence level.

Preparing athletes for competition is what coaches do. Without question, mistakes will be made. Janssen and Dale (2001) offer 12 tips that will help coaches preserve an athlete's confidence when they need to give feedback after mistakes. The athletic director should discuss these tips with his coaches to ensure they are prepared to give appropriate and effective feedback to student-athletes.

1. Be understanding. The vast majority of mistakes that athletes make are not intentional. Athletes want to play well for themselves, and they want to please their coaches and teammates. They usually make mistakes because they have not sufficiently mastered the skill, do not understand the strategy, or are overwhelmed by pressure.

2. Allow athletes to play through mistakes whenever possible. One of the best things a coach can do to demonstrate confidence is allowing the athlete to play through her mistake. Give her the chance to correct herself within the game rather than pulling her out or offering immediate feedback. Athletes who are pulled or chastised every time they make a mistake may begin to play tentatively.

3. Avoid making it personal. Criticize the behavior, not the person.

4. Limit the use of profanity. There are many ways to get a point across without swearing. Cursing at athletes does little for a coach's credibility, and athletes will not respect coaches who curse at them personally.

5. Never embarrass an athlete in public. Praise in public, criticize in private.

6. Avoid using sarcasm to embarrass athletes into performing better. Making unnecessary comments undermines the coach's credibility. Coaches who do this give the impression they do not know how to handle their frustrations with an athlete.

7. Use the "sandwich approach" when providing feedback. In this approach, the coach begins an interaction with something positive, then instructs the athlete on what needs to be corrected or changed, and then ends with another positive statement.

8. "I know you are better than that." This is one of the best things coaches can say to athletes when they are making mistakes and not performing well.

This simple phrase tells them they are capable of performing much better than what they are currently showing.

9. Focus on the solution. When athletes are struggling, coaches need to help them focus on the physical and mental adjustments they need to make in order to be successful.

10. Make it a "we" project. This shows athletes that their coach is willing to partner with them to help them improve.

11. Remind them of their strengths, past successes, and preparation. One of the best things a coach can do is remind athletes what they already have going for them. Coaches should refocus athletes on their strengths, remind them of past games or practices where they were successful, remind them of all the work they have put in, and assure them they deserve to be successful because they have paid the price.

12. Don't give up. Don't ever give up! Coaches must adopt this mind-set when it comes to their athletes. If an athlete senses a coach has given up on him, he will give up on himself or lose all respect for the coach and give up on the coach as well.

One of the most significantly difficult tasks of a coach is the ability to influence an athlete's eating habits. Short of a sterile environment wherein athletes are all living together, eating together, practicing together, and competing together, coaches will need to depend on many others who are responsible for selecting and preparing food. As well, a seemingly constant influx of nutrition studies makes it hard to be accurately informed. There are some very basic rules of good nutrition for athletes that athletic directors should share with the athletes, their parents, the coaches, and the school cafeteria.

When an athlete's diet fails to meet energy needs, the body will burn its own protein or muscle tissue for energy. It is critical that athletes understand the importance of eating enough calories—failure to do so simply wipes out any training they are doing. The average female needs 2,000 to 2,400 calories of energy daily, the average male 2,500 to 3,000. These values can fluctuate depending on age and body size.

Normally, people eat more protein and fat than they need. A high-performance diet for athletes should include more carbohydrate and less fat according to sport scientists. Table 5.3 compares the typical teenage diet with a high-performance diet (Eisenman, Johnson, and Benson 1990).

TABLE 5.3   Components of Teenage Diets

Component	Typical teenage diet (% of total calories)	High-performance diet (% of total calories)
Fat	40	20
Protein	15	15
Carbohydrate	45	65

Fat does little good for athletic performance; however, some fat is essential in a healthy diet. An athlete's fat intake should stay at the recommended level of 20 percent of daily calories.

As indicated in table 5.3, the protein level in high-performance diets is 15 percent. Athletes need this amount for the development of muscle tissue in strength training, for the stimulation of aerobic enzymes during endurance training, and for tissue repair. Young athletes in particular need extra protein to provide for normal growth and development. Athletes should be encouraged to eat a variety of foods to meet protein and other nutrient needs; however, they should select foods from low-fat sources (e.g., soft versus hard cheese, skim milk versus whole).

Carbohydrates are a leading source of energy in high-performance diets. It is a common myth today that all carbohydrates are fattening. Carbohydrate foods such as potatoes; corn; beans; rice; and whole-grain cereals, breads, and pasta are nutritious and healthy. Complex carbohydrate foods such as corn and beans contain protein, vitamins, minerals, and fiber, thereby providing a more balanced nutrition along with energy.

Regardless of age, the best diets for athletes are low in fat and high in carbohydrate. Intense energy expenditure during practice and competition draws energy from the carbohydrates that are stored in muscle. The high-carbohydrate diet refills the muscles so they are ready to work again the next day. A low-carbohydrate diet will result in an athlete who "runs out of gas" during practice or competition.

If an athlete is practicing good nutrition, the pregame meal should not really be an issue. This meal should be easily digested and out of the stomach before the competition starts; therefore, eating approximately three hours before a contest is sufficient. Athletes should eat enough to feel satisfied but not overly full.

The critical attributes of player readiness, physical fitness, and nutrition are central to in-season team development. One final objective to address in order to meet the ultimate goal of success is clarity of focus. Individual growth involves training minds to focus and concentrate. This focus helps with patience, control, and the development of a mental calmness. Learning how to focus can cultivate positive emotions and states of mind in young athletes.

What should be the object of an athlete's focus? Unfortunately, this focus is sometimes directed toward unproductive things such as negative thoughts (e.g., "I'm not ready" or "There is no way we can win"), irrelevant information (the score, trash talk, verbal abuse), or energy-sapping emotions (e.g., fear, anxiety, or worry). Naturally, focusing on these areas can cause a decline in performance. A competitive event has a timeline of its own, and the key is to stay focused only on the things that contribute to success in the moment. An important feature of mental training is simplification of the thought process. For many situations, there is usually a routine that leads to or unlocks improved behaviors or correct performance.

How is focus achieved? One way to quickly recover focus is to develop performance routines that identify key elements such as symbols, focal points, and cue words that lead to achieving greater awareness.

Symbols are tangible items in the environment that redirect attention to the present moment. Coaches and athletes can use symbols in their sport to increase performance focus. For instance, the pitching rubber on the mound, the free-throw line, the strings on a tennis racket, or even a sign from the coach can serve as a signal for the athlete to think in the present moment and in a positive direction.

Focal points can be visible targets that are important for the implementation of certain behaviors. Pitchers may target the catcher's glove; basketball players may locate the center of the rim. However, looking at the target may not be beneficial if done for long periods because it may give away an action. Athletes need to be careful not to inhibit flow or follow-through of the movement. Learning to identify a focal point and develop imagery skills to maintain focus in the absence of a target will help eliminate distractions.

Cue words represent the way athletes would like to be seen or how they would like to feel while performing and can be used to initiate or trigger the correct movement responses. Adversely, negative thoughts may trigger a negative response as well.

Symbols, targets, and cue words can remind athletes of the things they need to focus on in the immediate moment as well as remind them that they have done the things necessary to get ready to perform successfully. In sports, key elements must be identified and practiced before competition, and this can easily be accomplished with the assistance of the coach. Focusing is a skill, and like any skill, it can be improved with practice. Developing and practicing routines while being positive and staying in the moment can help provide clarity of focus for performance success.

Postseason

The season may be over, but much of the work of a coach has yet to begin. Aside from the managerial aspects of the job (e.g., checking in equipment, planning for a banquet, ordering awards, conducting inventory), an important step for future success lies in evaluations.

Athletes and parents who are given the opportunity to evaluate a program after the season play an important role in the future success of the program and the success of the coach. Athletic administrators should encourage and expect an evaluative instrument that addresses the critical attributes of programming and student-athlete interaction. The information that is gleaned from these evaluations will pave the way for the next season. They will also assist in the development of the off-season program and assist in pinpointing areas of concern.

Evaluations can be simple or complex. The more simple instruments allow the participants to express their thoughts in simple sentences; the more complex instruments pinpoint specific criteria requesting Yes or No answers, or they use Likert scales. Likert scales are frequency scales using fixed-choice responses designed to measure attitudes or opinions. The simple instrument shown in figure 5.1 is an example that requires athletes to be specific about their experience.

Why are evaluations necessary? Athletic administrators may face some resistance from their staffs; however, their leadership in making coaches understand the need for evaluation is vital. The results of evaluations will give the school or system the ability to collect data over a period of time, focus on student-athlete experiences, determine strengths and weaknesses, and determine where improvements are needed or where accolades should be shared. Evaluations should be systematic and controlled, with the ultimate purpose of putting a program in a position to be enjoyable and successful.

Name_____ Position_____

Desired Change_____

Personal

1. What is one thing you like best about the program?
2. What is one thing you liked least about the program?
3. How can we improve team chemistry? Did you feel a part of the team?
4. What is one relationship you are having a tough time with?

Sport Related

1. Provide two of your strongest points.
2. Provide two areas where you need to improve.
3. What role do you see yourself playing on this team next year?

Staff Feedback (completed by coach)

1. This is your best attribute as a team member.
2. This is an area I think you need improvement in as a team member.
3. Here is what you need to do to fulfill your role.
4. How I see you right now as a player and why.

Rank yourself in each of the following three areas:

1. Academics
2. Physical habits and conditioning
3. Team member

FIGURE 5.1   Program evaluation questionnaire.

An ongoing responsibility for coaches lies in the talented athletes who are recruited or choose to participate in athletics at the college level. NCAA eligibility requirements and college scholarship protocols are succinct and must be followed accurately. In most cases, the guidance counselor has the necessary knowledge to assist student-athletes in this endeavor; however, the coach needs to be cognizant of the rules as well in order to guide athletes and their parents down this straight path.

It is not uncommon for incoming freshmen to have a dream of eventually securing an athletic scholarship. Coaches should take advantage of this teachable moment with their teams and share some scholarship facts.

- Only 3 percent of high school students receive a scholarship.
- Less than 1 percent receive a four-year Division I scholarship.
- 26 percent of students who enter college on a scholarship are no longer on scholarship entering their sophomore year.
- 80 percent of scholarships are not on a Division I level.

These facts are not intended to diminish students' aspirations or goals but to present the reality of scholarships. Athletic scholarships are admirable, but they are a by-product of interscholastic participation available to a few through the gift of talent and hard work. Approximately 126,000 athletic scholarships amounting to $2 billion are awarded annually in NCAA Division I and II university programs (NCAA 2012); however, this still means that less than 2 percent of high school senior athletes receive such an award. An average of 8 percent of Division I, II, and III team rosters for all sports are made up of first-year athletes.

Basically, there are four sports that provide full athletic scholarships; these are men's and women's basketball, football, and women's volleyball. The average athletic scholarship amounts to a little over $10,000, and when excluding football and men's basketball, the normal athletic scholarship decreases by another $1,700 on the average. Compare this with the average annual cost of a college education in the United States ($40,000 annually). The true and primary purpose of education-based athletics in high schools is not to create hundreds of collegiate All-Americans in their respective sports but rather to raise millions of stellar American citizens.

The NCAA Eligibility Center is the gateway to collegiate athletics. Its job is to ensure athletes are prepared for the rigors they will face in college. The goal of the athlete is to become a qualifier—a prospect who has satisfied the specific academic requirements that allow him to practice, compete, and receive athletic aid during his first year. The certification process occurs in two parts: academics and status as an amateur.

During the academic phase, assessments are done by reviewing transcripts and college entrance exams. Early registration will prevent problems later, and an official sealed transcript from all high schools attended is required. In reviewing transcripts, the Eligibility Center will look at grades or credits in 16 core courses. They will calculate the best product of SAT or ACT scores in relation to the core course GPA to identify the qualifying status. This works as a floating scale—the higher your test score, the lower your required core course GPA and vice versa.

The second part of the process is certifying the athlete's status as an amateur. This is determined by completing a survey that assesses whether athletes have professionalized themselves. To stay informed with updated policies and procedures, candidates, coaches, and athletic directors should visit http://web1.ncaa.org/ECWR2/NCAA_EMS/NCAA.jsp on a yearly basis.

It is unfortunate that many talented athletes loose the opportunity to meet the qualifying criteria for college eligibility because of their lack of knowledge about the rules. Simple steps, when taken early, can prevent the pitfalls of disqualification.

Building Successful Programs

A description of a successful program or person might include the word *motivated*. Whether a coach is instructing a team of student-athletes or a team of coaches, motivation is important for the team's atmosphere and success. Thompson's *Positive Coaching in a Nutshell* and Janssen and Dale's *The Seven Secrets of Successful Coaches* are excellent sources for coaches and athletic directors to use in pinpointing the criteria necessary for effective motivation. Four criteria that should never be overlooked include (1) having fun, (2) encouraging input, (3) gaining respect, and (4) setting goals.

Great organizations thrive on momentum. Although difficult to see in the beginning, small successes begin to pick up speed over time, much like falling dominoes. Just as this linked sequence of events is small in the beginning, the chain reaction grows exponentially at a swift pace. As the momentum builds, the impact widens and the support continues. Teams develop in much the same way. Athletic departments and coaches need to build momentum, maintain momentum, and never stop moving forward.

Summary

Coaching young athletes is an honorable and rewarding profession but contains elements of difficulty. Coaches often enter this field not realizing the scope of influence they will have on the athletes they serve, nor do they all understand the reason they become coaches. They should remember that they are character educators and through action or omission have an effect, be it positive or negative, on the athletes and programs they serve. Good coaches aspire to reinforce and teach good character, are consistent in their own actions, live in the skin of their athletes, and are self-disciplined, patient, and persevering. Coaches that make a difference are individuals who guide with principles that not only make better athletes but help athletes form a sense of who they are and what is important in life.

CHAPTER 6

Program Management

Bill Bowers, CMAA

Challenges exist to keep education-based athletic programs, as we know them now, alive and well. Generally, extracurricular programs—which include athletics—are one of the first items to be considered for budgetary reductions in a school district.

The importance of a comprehensive education-based athletic program can be seen in how the athletic program helps define the identity of a school and, often, an entire community. The athletic program can be a rallying point that simply does not exist in any other academic arena. Accomplishments on the athletic field, gym, or court are indeed academic achievements, based on fundamentally sound teaching techniques executed by the athletes, where four walls and a door do not define the classroom. Positive values learned from participation in athletics encompass an entire school and community.

Design of the Athletic Program

Interscholastic athletic programs of the 21st century must be an integral part of the total education community, with the purpose of providing educational experiences not otherwise provided in the academic classroom. They are classrooms in themselves, where students are taught basic core values such as responsibility, commitment, and cooperation. A high-quality athletic program provides all student-athletes an equal opportunity to experience personal growth and development, both physically and mentally, while managing and minimizing their risks. The student-athletes learn to accept personal responsibility for success and failure and to recognize the limitations and strengths of both. Interscholastic athletic programs are not solely for elite athletes but are intended to provide equal participation opportunities for all students in the school setting.

Contributors to this chapter include: Margaret Sturza, CAA; Michael Maghan, CMAA; Scott Garvis, CMAA; James Perkins, CAA; Ron Simmons; Roy Turner, CMAA; Dale Bachman; Rod Molek.

■

A high-quality athletic program provides all student-athletes an equal opportunity to experience personal growth and development, both physically and mentally, while managing and minimizing their risks.

It is important for everyone related to the program, including students, staff, and parents, to realize that participation in an athletic program is a privilege and not a right. The program is for those people who, regardless of their physical abilities, possess the attitude, desire, and competitive spirit to participate. Success defined by wins and losses, while important, does not match the true design standards and expectations of first-rate interscholastic sport, which promotes an attitude of eagerness and confidence to face and overcome adversity.

There are many other necessary components of a high-quality athletic program:

- Administrative support. The administrator of the athletic program is also an administrator in the total school setting. The athletic program should complement the curriculum of the school in achieving academic success and must demand the same standard of excellence of athletes in the classroom as it does on the fields of competition. Coaches and parents must be mentored regarding how to be active participants in encouraging and monitoring the academic progress of the student-athletes.

- Proper perspective on winning. An integral part of this component is learning how to accept defeat graciously and with character, since any athletic competition results in a winner and a loser. In society today, winning seems to be of ultimate importance to coaches, athletes, and parents; so it must be the role of the administration to place winning in the proper perspective. The win-at-all-costs mentality must not be a part of the program, as the goal should be to compete to the best of one's ability with utmost integrity and exemplary sporting behavior.

- Fair play and citizenship. Promoting good sporting behavior and citizenship must be a part of every program. The lifelong lessons of interscholastic athletics will be lost if we do not insist on a display of proper conduct at all times. This starts with coaches and the mentoring they receive from the athletic administrator in order to help them understand and teach the same to their student-athletes. The expectations must also be conveyed to the parents and community, with an understanding that those who support the athletic program will always act in the proper manner toward one another, opponents, and contest officials. Athletic personnel must abide by the rules at all times, whether affiliated with a team, in the classroom, or in their personal lives. Those who are part of a high-quality program understand the meaning of the adage "Thoughts become words, words become actions, actions become habits, habits become character, and character becomes destiny."

- Chemical-free environment. Every effort should be made to provide education, resources, and support to student-athletes on the subject of alcohol, drugs, and performance-enhancing substances. A discipline code is not enough to deter student-athletes in the face of today's peer pressure, societal mixed messages, and media attention. A comprehensive education program that demonstrates to student-athletes and parents the dangers of use and abuse of these substances is imperative. Parents can be a great ally in deterring their child-athlete and supporting a program that has student interest first in mind. The availability of assistance programs for those who need help is another aspect of a complete drug and alcohol education program. Coaches must be trained to recognize early warning signs of drug and alcohol use. A discipline code that is only punitive in nature and does not address rehabilitation of the athlete is unacceptable. Student-athletes in the program are people first and need to be treated as such.

- Zero tolerance for hazing and bullying. A trend that has grown dramatically in our society in recent years is hazing and bullying. This subject requires an extensive education program for all, as it is an accepted norm in many sectors. Coaches must be educated that what once may have been considered a rite of passage or an initiation is no longer acceptable. Violent or nonviolent acts of people against other people must not be tolerated. Students and parents must also receive education that confirms there is no place in the athletic program for acts of intimidation toward students. Such demeaning and degrading acts must be brought to the attention of the school administration.

- Equal opportunity. Title IX prohibits discrimination based on gender in education programs and activities that receive federal funds. The law directs schools to provide equal opportunities for both male and female students in the school environment. However, top-quality athletic programs should not need a Title IX mandate. Equal opportunities extend well beyond competition to include scheduling contests, practice times, access to comparable facilities, comparable coaching, equipment, uniforms, transportation, and support services including weight and training facilities.

- A safe environment. Perhaps the most critical aspect of the athletic administrator's job is doing everything possible to minimize risk for student-athletes, coaches, contest officials, and spectators. Risk management involves more than safe facilities and equipment. It requires educating everyone about written plans for emergency situations, outlining proper protocol, using proper practice drills and conditioning methods, teaching proper skills and techniques, properly maintaining facilities, and generally recognizing dangerous environments.

- Parental and community involvement. A top-quality athletic program must enjoy the support of parents and the community. The development of well-rounded student-athletes requires a combined effort by school personnel, parents, and members of the school community. Working together can result in a significant positive impact on the growth and development of young people. Auxiliary groups including booster clubs, parent–teacher associations, and civic organizations can assist in guidance, leadership, and encouragement of student-athletes as they support athletic programs in various ways.

The athletic administrator is responsible for one of the school's most visible, valuable, and challenging programs. The athletic program, which carries no academic credit, provides numerous opportunities for the public to see measurable results and monitor accountability through performance. The athletic director must ensure that athletic programs are not a diversion but rather an extension of educational values. The positive value of high school athletics and its impact on the lives of young students are immeasurable.

At the top of the school district chain of command is the board of education. The board is the governing body for the school district and is responsible for setting policies that follow state and federal laws as well as those of the department of education. The board also provides the vehicle by which policies are administered by staff. It has the ultimate responsibility of evaluating the athletic program, its value to the community, and how it fits into the mission of the school district.

The superintendent of schools answers to the board of education. The superintendent is responsible for the administration of schools according to adopted policies and in accordance with state school code. As the school district's chief executive officer, she is responsible for enforcement of policy. The superintendent is the school district representative in relationships with other school systems, social institutions, and community businesses. The superintendent is ultimately responsible for all phases of the public school program and will delegate authority for the administration of the interscholastic athletic program, through the high school principal to the athletic administrator.

The principal is responsible to the superintendent of schools. The principal is the official representative of the school and is directly responsible for the student body and the conduct of the athletic program. In most school environments today, the principal delegates responsibility for administration of the athletic program to the athletic director. By delegation and by established precedent, the athletic director becomes the school representative in matters dealing with school athletic and activity associations and conference, district, or league affiliations. The principal remains responsible for any official school action and for all student activities. The principal must be in constant communication with the designated administrator of the athletic program.

As designated by the principal, the athletic director's primary responsibility is the administration and supervision of the school's interscholastic athletic program. The athletic administrator is directly responsible to the principal, and his duties are those listed in the job description as well as others assigned by the principal. The athletic administrator must provide the leadership required for day-to-day operations as well as mentor the coaches of school programs.

Head coaches answer to the athletic administrator and act as official representatives of the school as they carry out their interscholastic athletic responsibilities. Head coaches shall be responsible for the total operation of their respective sports programs, including managing their staff of assistant coaches. Head coaches will perform those duties outlined in their job descriptions and other duties as delegated by the athletic administrator. Assistant coaches are responsible to the head coach of the sport they are coaching and assist that head coach in all duties required to coordinate the respective sports teams.

Goals and Objectives

Successful athletic programs are based on a foundation of goals and objectives. These become the road map by which a high school athletic department will operate and function. In establishing goals and objectives for a school's athletic department, the director must determine how they relate to an established mission statement. Before any discussion of goals and objectives, we must first define the two terms. *Webster's* defines a goal as "the terminal point of a race." It defines an objective as "something toward which effort is directed: an aim or end of action." These two terms have relevance in athletics. Athletic programs are about the race, how to run it, and how to finish strong. How each program "runs" the race and how it "finishes" will largely be influenced by its goals and objectives.

Each school's athletic department should base its goals and objectives on a mission statement. The school's mission statement should follow directly from the school district's mission statement. When beginning to develop the athletic department's mission statement, the athletic director should take care to include all shareholders: administration, coaches, student-athletes, and parents. This mission statement will give direction and purpose to the athletic program. It needs to be viewed as an ongoing document that has checks and balances to ensure each aspect of the statement is addressed. The entire athletic department must work to implement it throughout all the individual programs. The mission statement, goals, and objectives should be reviewed at least every five years and revised when needed.

A school's mission statement will describe the who, what, and why of the athletic program. The document helps define expectations for all involved. Typically the mission statement articulates what the school wants to accomplish or achieve and adheres to the philosophy of the school board and community. There needs to be integration between the vision and goals of the school district and those of the high school, the athletic department, and ultimately the individual sports teams. The mission statement should focus on those aspects that are important to all parties.

The athletic administrator is the leader of the department and charged with overseeing the operation of all programs. The ultimate goal of a leader should be to get all people to work together toward a common goal. To accomplish this, the personnel must trust the leader. To earn trust the leader must be honest, be "in the trenches" with them, admit mistakes, be very organized, and work alongside them on tasks. Leadership strengths must be modeled. It is not a case of having a written statement independent of the day-to-day routines and the commitment to achieve the goals established for everyone in the department. Effective leaders must use a variety of styles and methods to lead because they are working with a variety of personalities. A strong leader must exhibit confidence, flexibility, patience, honesty, and a vision for the future.

Each sport should set goals before the season based on the mission statement and the athletic program's goals and objectives. The head coach in each sport should meet with her staff to discuss how the program goals tie into the school's and district's goals and objectives. Goals should be set for each level in the program as well as the program in general. The goals should all be measurable and include action steps. The head coach should confer with the athletic administrator concerning these goals and objectives to ensure continuity exists throughout the department.

The goals of the individual sports programs should be based on instruction: What do you want your student-athletes to know and do by the end of the season? Once these goals and objectives are in place, they should be shared with the parents and student-athletes at the preseason meeting. Student-athletes in each program may also be asked to write their personal goals based on those of the program and individual sport.

Goals are effective only if they are measurable. How do you know if a goal has been met? By writing an action plan for each goal. Each goal may have one person or more assigned to it. Timelines for each goal and its evaluation should be set to provide evidence of accomplishment.

An example of an athletic program goal might be as follows:

Goal: All coaches will be trained in the area of basic first aid.

Assigned to: The athletic director.

Resources: Local Red Cross first aid classes and NFHS First Aid for Coaches.

Timelines: Before the start of each season.

Evaluation: Each coach will present a current first aid card to the athletic director. A copy will be kept on file by the school. Coaches may not have contact with student-athletes unless this certification is current.

A sport-specific goal might be written in the following manner:

Sport: Volleyball.

Goal: All players will know how to serve using proper technique.

Assigned to: All coaches in the program.

Resources: USVBA clinic, NFHS volleyball instructional videos, coaches.

Timelines: Varsity players are proficient by the first game, JV players by midseason, and frosh players by season's end.

Evaluation: Varsity players will serve with 95 percent accuracy each game. JV players will serve with 80 percent accuracy each game. Frosh players will serve all serves overhead with 65 percent accuracy by season's end. Statistics will be kept on each player so the goals can be assessed at season's end.

One of the most important elements of goal setting is review and assessment: What are our goals (where are we going), and how are we meeting them (are we getting there)? Review and assessment should be performed throughout the season. At the end of each season, the coaches and players must evaluate and assess their goals to determine the overall success of the program. Perhaps not all goals will have been met, but there should be evidence of movement toward meeting these goals. The athletic administrator may also use this process when evaluating the coaches and the overall program. Some goals may be carried over to the next season.

Although school athletic programs offer many benefits, ultimately they all need to reflect strong, positive, educationally sound values. Examples of values that can be found in successful programs include dedication, commitment, responsibility, cooperation, trust, integrity, discipline, sporting behavior, loyalty, respect, and accountability. When developing a mission statement, the athletic director should focus on what can be done to define these positive values and communicate them to all members of the school community, even those who do not participate in the athletic program but are still directly affected, either as a student or community member. The athletic department's road map should not be strictly limited to athletes and coaches in the program. The following two mission statements serve as examples (figures 6.1 and 6.2).

Loveland High School, Ohio

The Loveland City School District athletic program will provide a wide variety of athletic opportunities that will aid in the overall development of our students. Participation in athletics will provide students with a significant opportunity to become involved with other students and their coaches in an educational experience that takes place outside of the classroom.

Athletic department philosophy: The Loveland City School District believes that a dynamic program of student activities is significant to the educational development of the student. The Loveland City School

(continued)

(continued)

District athletic program provides a variety of experiences to aid in the development of favorable habits and attitudes in students that prepare them for adult life in a democratic society. Athletics play an important part in the life of the Loveland City School District student-athletes. Young people learn a great deal from their participation in interscholastic athletics. Lessons in sportsmanship, teamwork, competition, and how to win and lose gracefully are integral parts of team goals in our athletic department.

Athletics also play an important part in helping the individual student develop a healthy self-concept as well as a healthy body. Athletic competition adds to school spirit and helps students, spectators, and participants develop pride in their school.

The Loveland Board of Education further encourages the development and promotion of sportsmanship, ethics, and integrity in all phases of the educational process in all segments of the community, including administrators, participants, adult supervisors, parents, fans, spirit groups, and support/booster groups.

Athletic department goals:

- Promote the development of favorable habits and positive attitudes in students that will prepare them for adult life.
- Promote academic excellence in the classroom.
- Recognize and promote the lessons learned regarding good sportsmanship, ethics, teamwork, and the value of competing—win or lose.
- Ensure a safe and secure environment for practice and competitions.
- Recognize and promote the accomplishments of athletic teams and individuals.
- Encourage coaches to be leaders, role models, and people of character.
- Emphasize and encourage positive lifestyles that will assist in striving to be the best.
- Promote cooperation throughout the athletic department, while supporting all athletic and extracurricular programs.
- Ensure that everyone involved with the athletic department adheres to the rules and policies of the Loveland City Schools, the Ohio High School Athletic Association, the Fort Ancient Valley Conference, and the Loveland Athletic Department.

FIGURE 6.1 Mission Statement of Loveland High School, Loveland, Ohio.

Reprinted, by permission, from Loveland High School, Loveland, OH. Available: www.loveland.k12.oh.us/lhs/athletics/pages/Mission_Statement.pdf

Eugene Ashley High School, Wilmington, North Carolina

Mission statement: Consistent with North Hanover County Schools (NHCS) and Ashley's mission and values, the athletic department provides student-athletes with opportunities for success in education-based athletics while supporting their personal growth as students, citizens, and leaders. In drafting a new mission statement for the athletic department, the committee reviewed mission-appropriate documents from a number of sources and developed the following mission statement for Ashley Athletics:

Athletics' mission statement: The mission of Ashley Athletics is to guide our student-athletes to become better people both on and off the court and to enhance their critical-thinking skills.

Beliefs: We believe that high-level competitiveness is a by-product of strong leadership, focused discipline, and a commitment to pursue excellence.

Vision statement: Using similar methodology, including efforts to align, control, and motivate all stakeholders of the athletic department, we developed the following vision statement for Ashley Athletics:

Athletics' vision statement: Ashley Athletics will be recognized as a model program and as a source of campus and community pride and respect by inspiring every athlete to pursue excellence.

To achieve this vision we are committed to building traditions and our reputation through the creation of an environment and culture characterized by:

- Student first, athlete second
- Culture of excellence, integrity, and character
- Eagle pride and respect
- Nationally certified coaches and staff
- Quality facilities and equipment

Statement of core values: Using similar methodology we developed the following statement of core values for Ashley Athletics that we will never compromise:

Core values of athletics:

- Excellence: pursuit of excellence and inspiring others
- Achievement: using educational athletics as an extension of the classroom and creating educational partnerships
- Honor: always showing Eagle pride and respect for opponents, officials, teammates, coaching staff, fans, and themselves
- Success: players accepting responsibility for outcomes and looking to themselves first when improvement is needed

FIGURE 6.2   Mission Statement of Eugene Ashley High School, Wilmington, North Carolina

Reprinted, by permission, from Eugene Ashley High School, Wilmington, NC. Available: www.ashleyathletics.org.

Action Plans in Action

An interest survey of students determined there was sufficient interest to add boys' and girls' lacrosse teams to the athletic program. But this was only the first step. Before the school began to buy equipment, hire coaches, and schedule games and officials, a few other important groups needed to come on board.

The school board, superintendent, community leaders, and school administration needed to see the overall benefits of adding these sport offerings. Many factors had to be discussed, including where and how to acquire financial funding as well as how to schedule practices and games in already overused facilities.

The athletic administrator had to develop a blueprint showing he could ensure equitable access for both the existing programs and the new lacrosse program. Success hinged on establishing program goals that fit the school district's mission and philosophy statements, developing a five-year strategic plan, and working with community members who had previously operated a club-level recreational lacrosse program.

The school held community-wide meetings where all potentially interested people had the opportunity to offer suggestions and critique proposals. All these considerations led to the successful implementation of both a boys' and girls' varsity lacrosse team for the next school year.

Performance Assessments

As discussed with goals and objectives, performance measures should also be related to the mission statement. Performance measures should quantitatively reflect the goals and objectives of the program and be used as a tool to improve the program. Typically, performance measures will indicate how well the program is doing, if it is meeting the defined goals, where improvement is warranted, and if the involved parties are satisfied with the program. This improvement can come about only after observation, evaluation, and correction of the desired performance.

An old adage states, "You can't manage what you don't measure." This axiom has many undocumented sources, one of which traces back to Galileo, who was quoted as saying, "Count what is countable. Measure what is measurable. What is not measurable, make measurable." The verb *measure* means to ascertain the measurement. Collecting data and assessing the findings is a form of measurement. This raises a question of why a school and athletic department would want to gather data.

Some desired outcomes associated with gathering assessment data are identifying the needs of the program and the involved personnel. This can be accomplished by setting realistic goals for those being assessed within the scope of what they can control. Assessment goals, like building or district goals, should be used to improve performance levels for coaches and athletic department personnel; to improve operational aspects of the program; and ultimately to improve satisfaction among players, parents, and athletic department personnel (e.g., coaches).

The sequence involves developing a plan to assess the mission statement, implementing a plan of action to look at the goals and objectives, and assessing or measuring the effectiveness of how all these meet primary established criteria.

Athletic directors should observe performance over time and not rush to a conclusion. Basing an evaluation on a one-time occurrence may give incorrect feedback. Constant monitoring of a program is needed for accurate measurement. Feedback is also needed while monitoring, whether it is feedback to student-athletes or coaches. When observing a program, the administrator should give frequent feedback about his observations, thus allowing for correction of errors or reinforcement of positive behavior. This feedback must be specific. Telling someone the program has terrible communications is not effective. Telling someone the program needs to improve communication with parents and student-athletes through the use of a parent and player expectation guide and preseason meeting is specific and allows for positive improvement. The collection of data during the observation is essential to the evaluation process. Upon seeing an issue, the athletic director should give clear expectations so positive change can occur.

During the evaluation phase, all parties must look at the goals and objectives established at the beginning of the season to determine if they were attained or if there was at least some movement toward their attainment. Measurements can be obtained through statistics, player and parent surveys, coaches' comments, and perceived attitudes from all relevant parties within the program. Emphasis should be focused on factors over which a coach has control. These factors include, but are not limited to, communications, coaching strategies and methods, efficient use of time, effective use of resources, and relationships with players and parents. Although the win–loss record may be a factor, it should not be the most important criterion used to evaluate the effectiveness of a program. Overemphasizing the win–loss component often diminishes the purpose for having the program and the true value of developing an athlete's skill and the educational aspect the program provides.

The final step of performance measurement is to determine if the program is moving forward in the desired direction and to correct any undesired performance. The correction process may include setting new goals for the next season or requiring that coaches attend clinics or seminars related to their sport program or enroll in one of the sport-specific classes of the NFHS Coach Education/Certification Program. In extreme cases, a change of personnel may be warranted. The process must correlate to the educational compatibility of the program and how it transcends to those participating in the program.

Quantitative Analysis

Factors to be considered when assessing a program include coaching strategies, efficient use of time and available resources, sound education-based methods of instruction, and effective open communication among all involved parties in the program. Other factors to be considered are student behavior agreements, regular eligibility checks throughout the season to ensure academic accountability, completion of an annual sport-specific rules quiz, preseason parent meeting, preseason player–coach meeting, and regularly scheduled coaches meetings.

Since athletic programs have a much higher visibility in the community than a math class or foreign language class, it is important when assessing the overall program to ensure coaches are acting professionally and maintaining a caring atmosphere for those involved. Evaluation should focus on the goals and objectives set forth at the end of the previous season or the beginning of the current season. In this process, coaches and administrators can develop strategies to work on areas needing improvement, while not neglecting those necessary to provide competitive balance.

A program's effectiveness can be determined using quantitative evidence. Parents, coaches, community members, and athletes can fill out satisfaction surveys that include questions developed to get a true overview of the program. The type of questions asked can validate observations and provide strong evidence for an administrator assessing the program's effectiveness. Ultimately these surveys may become part of the coaches' evaluations in terms of continued employment. Just as important, the surveys can expose areas that need improvement. The job for the athletic administrator is to assess the findings based not only on input from those taking the survey but more important from the personal observations and evaluations the athletic director has made throughout the season. This emphasizes the need and importance of making numerous observations and providing feedback on a continual basis during the season.

Designing a survey can be both time consuming and laborious. Commercial surveys are available from numerous sources. Finding samples used by other athletic administrators who are willing to share is another means of developing a survey that meets specific objectives. The National Interscholastic Athletic Administrators Association Leadership Training Institute program includes the LTC 707 class, Assessment of Interscholastic Athletic Programs and Personnel (NIAAA 2008), which has forms available that athletic administrators can use to gather data on programs and coaches.

From the LTC 707 presentation we learn the following: "That which is measured can be changed and improved" (NIAAA 2008). The key when developing an assessment tool, or using one already in place, is making sure the tool will assess how effectively the program is meeting those educational standards outlined in the goals and objectives of the school district's mission statement. Additionally the tool must assess students' growth as well as how effective coaches are in their leadership position as it relates to their job assignment requirements. Coaches tend to gather and use statistical data in a variety of ways as they assess the athletic ability of their players in the program. Coaches should assess player development regularly to evaluate the players' speed, agility, sport-specific skill level, and knowledge of the sport. These data are used to place players at the appropriate level, determine the amount of playing time, diagnose knowledge of the sport and skill, and structure practices and skill-building activities. The objective is to sort through and evaluate the data to assess the program's effectiveness in meeting educationally established standards.

When using an assessment tool to solicit information from community members, parents, and players, coaches ideally should be involved with the athletic director in developing the criteria. Emphasis should be on how frequently the assessment tool is being used, who is involved in the process, and what specifically is being assessed. The tool should focus on how the assessment can provide data to support continual improvement in the program. This process reflects a contemporary and best-practice approach to evaluating the program from the educational viewpoint.

Program Evaluation

James L. Kestner discusses six steps for an effective program evaluation. He breaks these six into two groups, those dealing with the planning stages and those dealing with the review and revision of the plan (Kestner 1996). Each of the six stages relates back to the basic plan that is crafted from the school district's mission statement, goals, and objectives. This process identifies the district's philosophy and the coaches' personal philosophies as well as formulates how the personal and district philosophies align to fit the mission statement. The key, as mentioned previously, is for the athletic director to ensure there are no philosophical conflicts between the district and individual coaches, players, parents, or administrators.

Evidence for Growth and Development of the Program

Many factors enter into the assessment of a school's athletic program. Finding areas that need attention and developing a procedure to gather information to assess growth can be accomplished through many avenues. For example, surveys can illustrate trends within the athletic department. The specific type of survey used can vary from a participation survey to a satisfaction survey. Choices include those that indicate and assess a growth or decline in the number of participants and teams over a five-year period. Many factors can lead to change from one year to the next. Five years gives a better picture of any increase or decrease in participation numbers. These data can be used to help determine the optimal number for player-to-coach ratios. Sports with high risk factors such as football, soccer, lacrosse, gymnastics, swimming, and wrestling must have a lower ratio than other sports such as basketball, volleyball, or cross country.

With an ever-increasing number of coaches who are not certified teachers, it is important for districts to have specific policies to ensure that the hiring process for classroom teaching positions includes the opportunity to interview potential coaching candidates. Every school district should have a goal of hiring on-staff coaches whenever possible.

Once coaches are hired, keeping them abreast of district and school policies can be challenging. Regularly scheduled coaches meetings should be planned throughout the school year, with the school athletic director presiding. At the beginning of each sport season, a preseason meeting allows coaches, players, and parents to review policies related to the schools' goals and objectives.

Personnel are generally evaluated using objective- or performance-related instruments that compare performance to various standards or criteria assessing the level of achievement, productivity, or progress accomplished during the evaluation period (NIAAA 2008). The evaluation program must focus on gathering information to improve the quality of the program. Individual personnel should be assessed based on the expectations and performance benchmarks outlined in the original job description. The evaluative instrument must measure their effectiveness and level of performance against educationally sound instruction techniques.

Typically, school districts use summative evaluations as a form of personnel assessment. Many districts have begun using self-assessments or formative evaluations filled out by the coaches and in some cases the players. This form of assessment requires that the coach be dedicated to improvement through performance throughout the course of the season. Regardless of the assessment form, the athletic administrator should conduct a formal evaluation with each head coach after the season has concluded. Before this meeting, the athletic director may utilize information gathered from players or parents through surveys.

The desired outcome of surveys should be an indication of how effectively the coach is meeting the pedagogical best practices for their sports. Ascertaining the relationships between the coach, players, and parents is important to determine how effective communication is among all involved. Collecting information from surveys or personal interviews allows the athletic director an opportunity to glean a perspective about the growth of the program, the effectiveness of the techniques used by the coaches, and how informative and communicative the coaches are with everyone involved in the program.

Districts and schools must continue to find funds for coaches to attend clinics and seminars in their sports to ensure proper teaching fundamentals are being taught. Decreasing professional development opportunities prevents coaches from learning current coaching trends and techniques. The NFHS Coach Education/Certification Program has developed a list of sport-specific courses that can be accessed through their website (http:// nfhslearn.com). These online courses offer coaches the opportunity to enroll without leaving their home or office.

Strategic Plan

A school's athletic department rarely has a strategic plan uniquely designed for the department. Most school districts will have a district strategic plan as well as one designed for the high school in general. To emphasize the importance of an education-based athletic program, the athletic department needs to develop its own strategic plan that provides a road map showing relevance and continuity for all programs offered. It is important to clearly define the goals and objectives the department wishes to accomplish in a three- to five-year cycle. This long-range plan can directly guide the athletic department in day-to-day planning. The short-term decisions will have relevance because they will be measured and evaluated against the overall school and district strategic plans.

To begin the process, it is important to consider who will develop the strategic plan for the athletic department. A planning committee divided into subgroups of possibly three or four different focus areas should include members from the school's community, which may include parents of students as well as key people from the community who have a vested interest in and knowledge about the school.

The staff members who represent the academic department staff and the athletic department programs at the high school and feeder program (middle and junior high school) levels should be included. Students should also be on the planning committee, including those involved in a school activity or athletic program as well as students who are not. These groups need to ensure equal gender representation. The leadership of the planning committee must be made up of administrators from the athletic department as well as others on the administrative team.

Before a planning committee meets, a generalized blueprint is developed from questionnaires soliciting information about how the athletic department functions. The results will give a clear picture to guide the planning committee. Ultimately, the strategic plan must be developed with the school's mission statement clearly in mind. The goals and objectives listed within the mission statement will be the foundation of the plan. Clearly, the strategic plan does not focus solely on athletic programs and athletes. Consideration needs to be given to students who are involved in club activities and other nonathletic groups. The strategic plan needs to be comprehensive to encourage a robust schoolwide activity program.

It is important to involve members of the community in the planning process. These groups must be in agreement and support the philosophy of the school's and district's mission statements and their goals and objectives. In today's economic climate, businesses want to know what benefit they can expect for their involvement. The businesses need to see a return for their investment. It is important in that regard to research a school's needs to determine what product lines, goods, and services offered by the local businesses that school programs can utilize or consume. Many business owners may be alumni, parents of current or former students, board members, or active members of the chamber of commerce who share a vested interest. In putting together a strategic plan, focus on providing a vision and clearly defining what is needed from the business community. This process will enable the athletic administrator to find businesses that can align themselves with the school programs to benefit both.

According to Scott Garvis, CMAA, athletic director at Eastside Catholic High School in Sammamish, Washington, "Today's more savvy businesses are focused on cultivating loyalty to their products, which is a huge buying factor among families and teens." Garvis points out that a study conducted by Turnkey Intelligence shows "over 89 percent of surveyed youths are likely to switch from one brand to another if the second brand is associated with a good cause, such as a high school." With that in mind, it is imperative that the school's strategic plan focuses on ways to attain buy-in from alumni, parents, and students. The vision and strategic plan of the school must be written to attract and solicit the community's support. Examples include developing sponsorship programs that promote a business by distributing fliers for special discounts or events, displaying advertising at school events and in game programs, holding special drawings for products, or sponsoring a ticket back for an event.

The athletic department's steering committee charged with developing a strategic plan will determine the priorities that must be in place. The direction the department takes should encompass the best interests of all students in the school, not just those involved in the athletic department programs. The following are 12 common priorities presented by James Perkins Jr., CAA, director of wellness, fitness, and sport at Metropolitan School District of Pike Township in greater Indianapolis, Indiana, outlining critical areas that need to be addressed in developing an athletic department strategic plan.

1. Organization: This includes the structural organization of the athletic program that provides progressive flow from the elementary and grassroots athlete to the well-trained interscholastic athlete. Specific areas of responsibility must be identified within the structure. These will be designed to fit the school's and district's mission statements and the goals and objectives of the high school and athletic department.

2. Staffing: Staff assignments and the number of available staff, both paid and volunteer, need to be outlined along with the specific duties and responsibilities of each position. Attention needs to be given to ensure that coaching and support staff receive proper training in all aspects of their

assigned duties. This is not limited simply to sport-specific technical training; it should also include those skills necessary to develop character as well as skills necessary for each sport program. These coaching methods must reflect best practices as defined by the NFHS through the NFHS Fundamentals of Coaching course. Always maintain a ratio of coaches to athletes that will ensure a safe environment.

3. Participants: Care should be taken to nurture participation throughout a student's educational experience. This should start at the elementary level or, in the event an athletic program does not exist at that level, at the first opportunity an athletic program is offered by the school district. Identify and encourage participation in athletic programs throughout the K through 12 school years while attempting to keep students involved as long as possible. Statistics show there is a point when students' interests and attention may turn away from competing in athletic programs; the focus needs to be on providing an active plan and opportunities to retain those participants who do wish to stay involved and to hopefully convince those who are thinking of turning away to reconsider.

4. Skill and fitness development: The school district must develop organized and systematic methods for training fitness, developing sport-specific skills, and providing high-quality instruction that reflects best practices for each sport program. Although it is increasingly difficult to find highly qualified coaches, the responsibility of the school district and the athletic department staff is to ensure that all coaches are provided with sufficient training to effectively instruct and lead all skill levels, from the beginner through the highly advanced athlete.

5. Plan for competition: The school district and athletic department must encourage districtwide discussions and collaboration among coaches, administrators, parents, community youth sport providers, and others who may become associated with the sport programs to maintain continuity through all levels. There is a need to develop a district-inclusive plan for teaching sport philosophy as it relates to the goals and objectives used in competition strategies. These plans should reflect the mission statement and athletic department goals.

6. Academics: Athletic programs based on best practices will show a strong emphasis on maintaining high academic standards throughout all levels. It is important to develop a philosophical, practical, and collaborative approach to these academic standards. The foundation years in early elementary and middle school set the tone for promoting and emphasizing the importance of academic achievement for all participants in the school's athletic program. Attention should be placed on working with not only the students but the parents as well, even when the students are participating in a youth league or club program.

7. Character development: Beginning with the earliest level of participation, it is important to focus attention on, encourage, promote, and

model good character traits by all participants at every opportunity. Strong character development at every level is key to making everyone—coaches, players, parents, and spectators—recognize the importance and need for high moral values, strong civic standards, and exemplary behavior traits beginning at the lowest level of participation and continuing throughout the high school experience.

8. Parental involvement: Typically in youth programs, parents and guardians are relied on to be coaches, team representatives, program directors, fund-raisers, and car-pool drivers. Although it is important to encourage this volunteer participation at the youth sport or community program level, it is equally important to elicit support when students enter school-sponsored programs, where the parental involvement focuses on other areas often not associated with coaching or running the program.

9. Facility and equipment planning: Youth sport providers, community-sponsored programs, and school athletic programs often share school facilities. It is important to develop an efficient and equitable usage plan that addresses the needs of all groups. Outlining a priority level when more than one group wishes to use a facility will reduce frustration and disagreement. Collaborative methods need to be in place for the maintenance and care of school athletic facilities. The plan should include facility and equipment improvement along with replacement and purchase of materials needed to effectively maintain and operate the facility. Although certain equipment will become obsolete and nonusable over time, a plan must be in place to replace and update the equipment and facility to ensure they meet the standards of comparable programs in the area and state. This plan is integral to the success of the overall program.

10. Community involvement: Participants need to look beyond their own sport-specific teams or programs. Encouraging and promoting participation in community service projects, either during the season or outside the season, can accomplish this. Seek out opportunities for players, coaches, parents, and other interested parties to partner with community programs to lend support, provide leadership skills, and mentor younger age groups or to lend a hand in other community service projects that exist outside their own sport involvement.

11. Public relations: School districts and programs must find ways to market and promote positive images of themselves throughout the local community. This may mean finding ways to work collaboratively and constructively with organizations and agencies that might be in competition for athletes at lower levels or even club programs at the high school level. Social networks such as Twitter and Facebook can be used to connect with the community.

12. Administration: The first key to success is to gain support from board of education members; school district leaders, including the superintendent

and his staff; and building-level administrators in order to maintain and strengthen relationships. The benefit to all participants is reliance on open communication that allows everyone input (including members of the community and school sport programs) in the decision-making process.

The next step for the steering committee is to implement the plan. The committee must identify and secure any resources necessary through school or community funding. This might involve use of in-kind services, private and public funds, donations, fund-raisers, or procuring support to put a bond levy before the community. This plan must take place within a reasonable time schedule, not to exceed two years, that will ensure the plan can succeed.

The National Interscholastic Athletic Administrators Association (NIAAA) through the Leadership Training Institute (LTI) has developed a course titled LTC 799, Standards of Excellence in Interscholastic Athletic Administration. The course teaches best practices in the administration of high school sport programs for superintendents, principals, athletic directors, and board of education leaders (Olson, J. and Blackburn 2010). According to Dr. Mike Blackburn, CMAA, Associate Executive Director of the NIAAA, "these 'Standards of Excellence' were intended as a guide for long-range planning, program improvement, and professional growth for coaches and athletic administrators." School teams can use these 10 standards as a measuring stick to help formulate a strategic plan.

Ten Standards of Excellence

1. Athletic philosophy
2. Educational implications
3. Mentoring
4. Risk management
5. Program access and equity
6. Budget and fund-raising
7. Program assessment
8. Technology
9. Sports medicine
10. Innovation

LTC 799 is a survey course that covers more than 11 different LTC courses. It is not intended to cover any of these standards in great depth but rather uses the information from each to show evidence that an individual school's or school district's programs operate on sound education-based values. The course takes participants along a pathway to ascertain the degree of proficiency an individual school or district program has attained based on these 10 standards of excellence. Figure 6.3 serves as a paradigm.

Athletic Department: Strategic Plan

Mission: We are an athletic community dedicated to providing a competitive athletic environment that empowers and inspires student-athletes.

Vision: The Glenbard Township High School athletic department is committed to developing student-athletes that are:

- Dedicated learners
- Unselfish teammates
- Multisport athletes
- Role models for a healthy lifestyle
- Role models for sportsmanship
- Leaders who develop pride in their school
- Committed to excellence

Core Values

Academic success: Athletes should be held to high standards in both athletics and academics. We believe student-athletes need to develop time management skills to balance success in both areas.

Teamwork: All student-athletes can be positive contributors to the team. Each teammate can be responsible, accountable, and dependable.

Multisport athletes: Student-athletes should strive to be well-rounded athletes who are committed to development in various sports, especially at lower levels, in order to reach their maximum potential.

Healthy lifestyle: Athletics fosters a healthy lifestyle year round, encouraging students to make good choices. Student-athletes should maintain a chemically free lifestyle in order to achieve optimal performance.

Sportsmanship: All student-athletes demonstrate sportsmanship by respecting teammates, opponents, officials, and the game.

Leaders who develop pride in their school: We believe student-athletes should demonstrate pride, respect, and commitment to their teams, schools, and community through quality play and a positive attitude.

Commitment: Every student-athlete should demonstrate the commitment and work ethic necessary to be successful. Every student should have the opportunity to participate in the athletic program.

Priorities

Create systems for regular communication and collaboration to discuss student achievement:

FIGURE 6.3 Strategic plan for Glenbard Township High School, Glen Ellyn, Illinois.

- Develop specific, measurable, aligned objectives and realistic goals.
- Develop an instrument to review athlete, parent, and community levels of satisfaction.
- Identify key data sources to guide improvement efforts.
- Develop a systematic evaluation program that is aligned with staff development opportunities.
- Use stakeholder input to develop three- to five-year plans.

Develop a culture that values extracurricular participation and student success:

- Create an environment that values sportsmanship and commitment.
- Engage as many students as possible in extracurricular opportunities.
- Promote a competitive environment that teaches team success and personal growth.
- Recruit and retain quality in-house staff.
- Set clear expectations for coaches, parents, and students.
- Foster opportunities for minority and at-risk students in extracurricular activities.
- Promote a nurturing environment that allows athletes to take risks and to learn from their mistakes.

Foster an environment that makes efficient, effective, and equitable use of the building resources:

- Devise a long-term facility plan to address the indoor and outdoor athletic needs.
- Provide a three- to five-year financial commitment to address athletic department physical and programming needs.
- Utilize facilities for maximum efficiency.
- Create outstanding feeder programs.
- Develop flexible off-season training programs.
- Continue to monitor male and female participation and Title IX expectations.
- Encourage multisport athletes.

Summary

Developing an education-based athletic program requires the design to include administrative support, a consensus perspective on the importance of winning, strong citizenship principles, a chemical-free program, zero tolerance for bullying and hazing, equal opportunities for both genders, a safe environment for participant and spectators, and involvement from both community and parents.

In forming the goals and objectives for the athletic program, involving multiple groups in the school community is highly encouraged. Athletic department philosophy and mission statements must align with those of the school district. Develop department goals, staff assignments, vision statements, action plans, performance objectives, and evaluation tools to follow the philosophy and mission statements.

Multiple sources exist to assist in setting up quantitative evaluation models to evaluate the program, provide evidence of growth, and develop a multiple year strategic plan. Twelve critical areas need to be addressed in developing an athletic department strategic plan. These include organization, staffing, participants, skill development, competition, academics, character development, parental involvement, facility and equipment planning, community involvement, public relations, and school district administration.

PART II

Operational Process

The six chapters in part II address the day-to-day duties of the athletic administrator. Chapter 7 covers allied educational services. Chapter 8 covers event scheduling. How to arrange transportation while keeping in mind budget and the safety of students is discussed in chapter 9. Chapter 10 provides an extensive look at the various technologies available to athletic administrators to help make their job performance and programs more efficient. Contest management and legal and safety concerns are covered in chapters 11 and 12.

CHAPTER 7

Allied Educational Services

Kim Chorosiewski, MEd, CSCS, CMAA

In recent years, public and private school educators have agreed that middle and secondary school students need support services that are not provided by the instructional program. In previous years, nonacademic school services were often considered auxiliary services, which suggested these support systems were ancillary to state-mandated instructional programs. Education and medical professionals now refer to nonacademic services that support the health and well-being of students and student-athletes as allied services.

By definition, allied services are support functions that augment the efforts of faculty and administrators to achieve the mission of schools and the educational goals of interscholastic athletic programs (*Merriam-Webster* 2012).

Allied Services Programs

A comprehensive program of school and school district allied services addresses a range of topics of concern to students and student-athletes. These include student health; sports medicine; strength and conditioning; nutrition; academic support; and counseling for college-bound athletes.

Because allied services providers have direct affiliation with schools and students, these professionals must take guidance from and operate in compliance with legislative mandates, local school board policies, legal standards, and professional best practices. Although professional standards and guidelines are published by each allied service governing body, there can be no departure from accepted legal standards and local education policies.

Although all enrolled students may benefit from one or more allied services, the injuries, illnesses, and stressors associated with athletics may necessitate greater access to these support resources than many realize. Thus, students who choose to participate in athletics may increase their exposure to physical demands and injury and thus require one or more allied services to prevent loss of school time.

A comprehensive program of school and school district allied services addresses a range of topics of concern to students and student-athletes. These include student health; sports medicine; strength and conditioning; nutrition; academic support; and counseling for college-bound athletes. Allied services are implemented by trained professionals who are state mandated or certified within their field or practice.

In many cases, the delivery of allied support services may require cooperative interdependence, and integrated services from multiple agencies. In addition, these cooperative efforts require coordinated policies and procedures along with cooperative chains of command and decision-making practices. As an example of cooperative interdependence, a school health nurse (health department) may administer various medications to an injured athlete as prescribed by the team or family physician. In a cooperative effort, a certified athletic trainer (sports medicine department) may administer a program of postinjury rehabilitative exercises prescribed by the same physician.

All allied support activities must align with the educational mission of the school, the school district, and the state athletic and activity associations. This alignment is essential so that allied services policies and practices are consistent with the mission of the school and various governing bodies.

Allied services are implemented by trained professionals who are state licensed or certified within their field or practice. Licensure and certification of these professionals provide assurances that the delivery of care and services will meet or exceed nationally recognized standards and practices.

Professional growth associations (e.g., National Interscholastic Athletic Administrators Association, National Athletic Trainers Association) and nationally accredited training institutions provide guidelines and training that are often referred to as standards of professional practice. These standards ensure that practitioners fully implement the guiding principles of a professional organization, training institution, or certifying agency. The standards also provide a professional assessment framework for judging minimum levels of professional competence, performance, and effectiveness.

Standards of professional practice may also help members of the public and various professional communities by providing information regarding the specific services provided. Standards of professional practice may be better understood by researching one of more of the following:

- Knowledge and experience of the practitioners
- Minimum degree requirements needed to achieve certification
- Certification requirements
- Code of ethics of the organization
- Accepted definition of the allied service

- Definition and scope of practice of the allied service
- Affiliated practices and professionals
- Continuing education requirements for allied service providers
- Professional responsibility and competencies of service providers
- Statutory requirements for certification and recertification

Professional standards of care may also give direction to athletic directors regarding risk management procedures, employment guidelines, and supervision practices. In addition, these standards give direction to emergency planning and service delivery methods. Such standards assure consumers of quality while providing assessment standards that athletic directors can use to monitor, manage, and evaluate the practices of allied service providers.

It is also imperative to understand that attorneys who represent injured athletes often research the professional standards of care and best practices published by a professional organization. In this way, lawyers attempt to determine whether an allied service professional has been negligent or partially negligent in the delivery of services.

As contributing professionals in the chain of allied educational services, athletic directors must implement professional standards to ensure appropriate certification or licensure. The professional standards and expectations associated with each service role might include the following:

- Prerequisites for employment (transcript, proof of current certifications, letters of recommendation)
- Minimum education requirements (undergraduate, graduate from accredited institutions or programs)
- Proof of successful completion of a certification exam or similar competency assessment
- Acknowledgment of, and agreement to, scope of practice (and limitations)
- Agreement with a professional code of ethics (see figure 7.1 for an example)
- Continuing education requirements to maintain licensure or certification credential(s)
- Continued commitment to professional standards of practice

Allied services professionals who are employed by universities, hospitals, and clinics often have obligations to serve the public by providing support and free educational services. These obligations may consist of public presentations that address drugs, eating disorders, steroids, and sports medicine services.

The role of volunteers in both public and independent schools has become more important as budget pressures have increased. Historically, volunteers

---

NIAAA Code of Ethics

The interscholastic athletic administrator:

1. Develops and maintains a comprehensive athletic program that seeks the highest development of all participants and that respects the individual dignity of every athlete.
2. Considers the well-being of the entire student body as fundamental in all decisions and actions.
3. Supports the principle of due process and protects the civil and human rights of all individuals.
4. Organizes, directs, and promotes an interscholastic athletic program that is an integral part of the total educational program.
5. Cooperates with the staff and school administration in establishing, implementing, and supporting school policies.
6. Acts impartially in the execution of basic policies and in the enforcement of the conference, league, and state high school association rules and regulations.
7. Fulfills professional responsibilities with honesty and integrity.
8. Upholds the honor of the profession in all relations with students, colleagues, coaches, administrators, and the general public.
9. Improves the professional status and effectiveness of the interscholastic athletic administrator through participation in local, state, and national in-service programs.
10. Promotes high standards of ethics, sportsmanship, and personal conduct by encouraging administration, coaches, staff, student-athletes, and the community to commit to these high standards.

FIGURE 7.1 National Interscholastic Athletic Administrators Association (NIAAA) ethical standards.

Reprinted from NIAAA. Available: www.niaaa.org/Certification/caa_ethics.asp

Note: The NIAAA Code of Ethics may be updated in 2013. Visit www.niaaa.org.

have assisted in classrooms, in lunchrooms, with student activities, and as helpers for special events. Athletic directors who use volunteers within the educational allied services realm must first thoroughly examine school needs, policy constraints, and liability issues.

Volunteers should be able to perform specific job requirements before a contract or letter of agreement is issued (see figure 7.2 for a sample volunteer agreement). The role of a volunteer should be clearly defined in a contract that meets state and local regulations, including appropriate background and reference checks. Also, the conduct expectations for volunteers should be clearly communicated through an employee handbook or other formal means.

Volunteer Guidelines

All volunteers will be expected to observe the following regulations and standards that the _____ School District has established in order to protect our students and to ensure a successful contribution by the families and community members to our students' achievement.

Standards and Expectations

1. For security purposes, upon every arrival at a school site, volunteers must check in with the front office to sign in and present a district-issued ID badge. The ID badge shall be worn at all times while on campus. Remember to sign out after every visit.

2. Volunteers will treat students, staff, and the general public with respect and consistently be models of decorum and courtesy. Volunteers should not promote commercial products, religious beliefs, political parties, or candidates while on campus.

3. All information, including but not limited to student grades and academic progress, to which the volunteer has access to in the school is confidential.

4. Being under the influence of or having possession of illegal substances, alcohol, or firearms is grounds for immediate dismissal, and notification to _____ Police Department will be issued.

5. Volunteers must seek the aid of a school administrator in case of student discipline problems. Volunteers are encouraged to model positive behavior to students, but the role of enforcing disciplinary action belongs solely to school administrators.

6. Volunteers may not administer medication or give medical treatment to students. In case of medical emergency, the volunteer is to notify school personnel immediately.

7. Volunteers are expected to contact the parent coordinator and teacher if unable to follow through with their volunteer schedule or they wish to discontinue their volunteer service.

8. Volunteers are expected to clean up after themselves while helping at school sites.

Regulations and Procedures

1. Volunteers must submit the required documents to the school site and undergo the required background checks according to the category of or tier of volunteer service.

(continued)

(continued)

2. Volunteers are required to complete required training sessions and are expected to attend all general volunteer meetings.

3. Volunteers shall work only under the direction and supervision of a teacher or other certificated staff member of the school. The relationship between staff and volunteer is one of mutual respect and trust. Volunteers shall initially take matters of concern to the school administrator.

4. Volunteers are expected to clean up after themselves while working in classrooms, offices, or school grounds.

5. Volunteers are responsible for the safety of their own personal property. We recommend that all valuables be left at home. Cell phones are to be turned off and not in use while on school grounds except in nonstudent areas.

6. Approved volunteers are not guaranteed automatic participation in school field trips. Participation will be at the discretion of site administrators and teachers.

I understand that any violation of these volunteer guidelines/standards/regulations will initiate immediate revocation of my volunteer rights.

_____   _____
Signature of volunteer   Date signed

FIGURE 7.2   Sample volunteer agreement.

Reprinted, by permission, from San Jacinto Unified School District, San Jacinto, CA. Available: www.sanjacinto.k12.ca.us/documents/studentsupport/volunteer_contract.pdf

Although volunteers do not receive payment for services, they must abide by legal requirements and school district policies. All details of the arrangement should be clearly defined and mutually understood before a memorandum of agreement is completed. Athletic administrators should determine what state requirements exist with regard to volunteers, tax implications, background checks, and other matters of employment law and student care.

When choosing allied services volunteers, athletic directors should take the following into consideration: personnel restrictions and limitations, parents as volunteers, role delineation, personnel policies (hiring, dismissal, deportment, and so on), and background and related training and professional affiliations.

Student Health Services

Contemporary medical research indicates that health-related factors can greatly influence student performance. According to a report issued by the U.S. Centers for Disease Control and Prevention (CDC), student health in some school communities is a paramount concern because of its relationship to academic achievement. In this report (CDC 2012), the agency further suggests that school health services are important because they contribute to the physical, mental, and social well-being of children and youth; help children and youth fully participate in school through prevention, health promotion, early identification, and intervention of disease; and contribute to healthier students who are more likely to succeed in school and to make healthy lifestyle decisions.

A network of allied health services providers may include school nurses, health aides, consulting physicians (pediatricians, specialists), community or public health providers, or any public health service available to the school.

Student Health

Student health refers to the physical, mental, emotional, or intellectual health of students. These health factors may individually or collectively affect students' overall well-being.

In some schools, the physical health of students is initially managed through annual collection of information on their current health status (e.g., physical exams, inoculations, medications, and prescriptions). In addition, school personnel have responsibility to observe, inspect, and control the school environment to prevent injury or the spread of disease. School health personnel also have responsibility to alert community health officials to potential contagious disease outbreaks. Finally, school health providers may help prepare an emergency response plan for crises involving individual or multiple injuries. These plans must be developed and exercised to address the health and welfare of one or more injured students along with the overall safety of the student body.

Physical Health of Athletes

Managing the physical health of the student-athlete may be shared with the school health office, which may collaborate with the athletic department's sports medicine staff. To integrate these services, student information may be shared by these two departments. This level of cooperation ensures that preexisting conditions, injuries, illnesses, and other health concerns are evaluated in a comprehensive manner. This cooperation enhances the care and prevention of additional injuries whether through athletics or routine school activities. Sharing of information may require written parental permission.

Mental and Emotional Health Services

In some cases, a student's physical health or athletic injuries can negatively affect the mental, emotional, and intellectual components of her overall health profile. As an example, a student-athlete who experiences a season-ending knee injury might demonstrate emotional effects that are disruptive in other areas of school and personal life. Referral to a school counselor, school psychologist, or joint referral to a school resource person and the family's choice for mental health assessment and response could be considered.

Coordination and Interdependence

Key professionals in a coordinated response may include the athletic director, coach, parents, student's family physician or medical specialist, school nurse, school athletic trainer, and school counselor or administrators. This potential group of support personnel must engage in coordinated discussions and make timely decisions to ensure a continuum of care for the athlete while preventing loss of school time.

The student with the season-ending knee injury may be riding an emotional roller coaster as she begins to adjust to various limitations imposed by the injury and a medical management protocol. Medically appropriate rehabilitation responses are well defined for the physical injury. However, it may not be clear that mental health services are also needed. As another example, a student-athlete with diabetes might require a least-restrictive 504 accommodation plan (Section 504 of the Rehabilitation Act of 1973) to ensure proper physical functioning in both the classroom and in athletics. Contributors to this student's accommodation plan may include the family physician, school nurse, coaching staff, athletic director, certified athletic trainer, parents, and teachers.

School Counselors as Mental Health Advocates

School counselors are occasionally considered nonessential service providers until there is a school or community crisis or a student with mental health issues requires assistance. As with other allied services, the policies and procedures related to the school counseling service must be consistent with school district and other allied services policies.

The pressure of competition in a highly visible public arena may precipitate athlete behavior against opponents or among team members that warrants an examination of the stressors the athletes face. In that role, school counselors can be extremely important.

The ability of adults and student peers to recognize changes in an athlete's emotional state is important when coordinating school or district health practices. In that regard, an important role for professional counselors is to conduct an orientation to make employees and community members aware of the symptoms of potentially harmful or dangerous changes in student behavior.

Concussion Management and Student Safety

A student came to school late on Monday. The soccer coach saw him in the hallway and asked whether a head trauma suffered at the previous weekend's competition was the cause for his late arrival. The student acknowledged that he had been to the doctor that morning, and he said he was "fine." The coach mentioned the conversation to the athletic director in passing while talking about upcoming games on the schedule.

Because of a recent medical emphasis on concussion management, the athletic director contacted the athlete's parents to obtain more specific information. The conversation revealed that the student was being "checked out" for a possible concussion. In accordance with school policy, the athletic director informed the parents that the physician's diagnosis or a clearance to practice and play would be required. On receipt of the physician's diagnosis, the school would initiate its concussion management guidelines. These medical guidelines were implemented to ensure the athlete's safe return to classroom and sport activities. In addition, the school nurse, certified athletic trainer, and soccer coach were informed.

In this case, the student began experiencing some latent effects of the concussion. The initial concussion management post-test demonstrated information-processing deficits, and the student was disqualified from play. In addition, the student's academic schedule was modified until his assessment responses returned to normal. The school nurse took responsibility for notifying staff about the need for schedule modifications.

This incident had potential to endanger the student. Communication among allied health service providers and the athletic staff served to intervene in a situation that, in the past, could have gone unnoticed or jeopardized the athlete's health.

Administration of Student Health Services

A strong justification for allied services programs is documentation that multiple providers regularly cooperate to enhance the care and well-being of student-athletes.

The legal term *in loco parentis* refers to the responsibility of school personnel to serve as a surrogate parent when applicable. This includes various aspects of health that relate to the physical, mental, and emotional well-being of student-athletes.

All support services and policies must comply with the confidentiality mandates of the Family Educational Rights and Privacy Act (FERPA) and the Health Insurance Portability and Accountability Act (HIPAA). Religious concerns might also have an impact on policy development and enforcement in secular schools or among populations that resist medical care on the basis of religious beliefs.

In managing the overall care and well-being of students, administrators within a school or district must consider and address several issues. These include program management, personnel management, communications and chain of command, accountability, program assessment and evaluation, legal considerations, and policies and procedures.

Policies are a link between the athletic department and members of the school community. Policies help define the goals, objectives, and practices of the sport programs while providing guidance for program operation. Policies that support student health may be critical in protecting athletes from abusive and inappropriate practices. As such, these policies must reflect federal and state legal mandates as well as state association and league directives.

The following components must be built into allied services policies:

- Planned evaluations and assessments of allied services based on user feedback, site visits, and observations
- Defined mechanisms for changes in policy
- Defined procedures for communicating policy changes to ensure they are implemented

Procedures are an outgrowth of policies that determine how daily operations are conducted within an agency. The functions and operational procedures delineated by organizational policies might include information sources, record-keeping requirements (including data management), resource management, system protocols, daily operational methods, decision-making functions, and conflict resolution functions.

Policies provide a description of operating procedures and identify those employees responsible for implementation. School and program leaders must make certain that procedures ensure fair and equitable access to services by constituents. Thus, changes to policies should also be addressed as priority items during routine staff meetings. In addition, orientation programs for new employees must include a review of an updated department policy manual.

Policy Sources

Policies and procedures can be found in multiple locations including policies and procedures manuals, employee handbooks, emergency or crisis plans, and parent and student handbooks. Providing multiple media formats for these documents ensures portability in compliance with access to regulations and best practices.

Policy Components

Policy expectations define the operation of a program while enhancing the supervisory functions for department managers and executives. This measure begins by identifying a chain of command that addresses policy and procedure. Listing a hierarchy of executive authority and the duties of each leadership level provides clarity and transparency with regard to the support functions of each work group or department. Program management and leadership authorities define how departments work internally and in coordination with other departments. Another important orientation component is defining how communication occurs within and outside the school organization. Defining the relationships and interdependence of various allied services further enhances the supportive functions within a school while creating an environment of accountability and sustainability in support of student-athletes.

Functional Leadership Chain of Command

1. Roles and responsibilities defined by policies
2. Decision-making authority
3. Formal and informal organizational communications related to decisions, policy development, and resource allocations
4. Performance objectives assigned to various levels
5. Assessment of the degree to which objectives are achieved

Sample Chain of Command for School or District Athletic Allied Services

1. Governance board
2. Superintendent or school executive
3. Supervisors (principals, assistant principals, deans, athletic director, department chairpersons)
4. Staff (team physician, certified athletic trainer, school nurse, rehabilitation specialists, coaches)

Emergency Planning

School responsibility for health, safety, and well-being extends to all areas of a school and to all employees and students. Proper planning for emergencies is at the forefront of crisis management along with facility and classroom management. School staff and administrators are charged with making sure emergency plans and protocols are defined and practiced to ensure readiness when required. These plans should address emergency situations that may arise from unpredictable events including injury, illness, death, building intruders, evacuation, and major student disruptions.

Planning should ideally involve all staff members. Staff and students must be involved in rehearsal and execution of preparedness drills to ensure efficiency and familiarity with emergency procedures. This type of preparation also extends beyond the classroom and includes all campus and off-campus athletic venues. The athletic director must formulate site-specific plans for each facility, whether contests are played at the home school or other public venues (NIAAA 2010).

Staff Readiness

For emergencies, staff readiness requires appropriate training and certification in first aid, CPR, and AED usage. Numerous states mandate that coaches maintain their certification in order to be eligible to work with students. This should be a mandatory policy for coaches who work in off-campus and isolated situations.

Staff readiness may include areas such as the following (NIAAA 2009, 2010):

- Event security
- Event staff and officials
- Public address announcements
- Coaching certifications (see NFHS, *Fundamentals of Coaching*, www.nfhslearn.com/coreCourseDetail.aspx?courseID=1000)
- Certified athletic trainer and emergency service provider coordination
- Facility and equipment safety inspections and maintenance

Informed Consent and Sport-Specific Warnings

It is a responsibility of the athletic director to ensure that parents and students are made aware of potential dangers associated with sports participation. This information should include a general statement or warning indicating that competitive athletics can be a cause of serious, catastrophic, or even fatal accidents. Warnings should also include sport-specific hazards and cautionary guidance to students and parents.

After the orientation to sport hazards (general and sport specific), parents and students should be required to sign an informed consent document indicating they have been warned about and are aware of the sports injury risks associated with participation. All school districts should seek legal advice regarding appropriate language and terms that should be included in such a document (NIAAA 2007).

The awareness or comprehension agreement should do the following:

- Generally indicate dangers and injuries that can be associated with sports
- Acknowledge the risk of serious or catastrophic injury or death
- Indicate the need for participants to follow instructions of coaches, officials, and other school personnel

- Indicate the need to use equipment as intended by the manufacturer and under appropriate supervision
- Require athletes to report injuries to coaches or a certified athletic trainer
- Include a dated signature line for the athlete(s) and parent(s) or guardian(s)

Signatures of participants and parents or guardians should indicate their comprehension of the warnings. The document should be dated and retained by the school. Informed consent documents will be of primary interest in the event a serious injury or death that results in litigation.

Sports Medicine Program

The sports medicine program is an allied service with several roles: preventing injuries, providing immediate care for injuries, implementing postinjury rehabilitative procedures, and preventing reinjury to the degree possible. Although increasing numbers of schools are fortunate to have a licensed or certified athletic trainer on staff, many schools do not. This does not reduce a school's responsibility to have a sports medicine service plan in place to manage the following:

- Medical clearance of athletes before participation
- Care and prevention of athletic injuries
- Emergency care plan for athletic events and specific facilities
- Decisions about the student return-to-competition policy after injury, illness, or suspension
- Concussion management protocol and policy
- Education concerning related medical and health issues such as hydration, illegal substances, or performance-enhancing drugs

Sports Medicine Department Hierarchy

The supervisor of the sports medicine program may be the athletic director or an administrator assigned overall supervision of extracurricular programs. Often the designated sports medicine program manager is a certified athletic trainer (ATC). As with other allied services, appropriate policies and procedures are necessary.

Sports Medicine–Related Tasks

Initial screening of student-athletes may be assigned to a certified athletic trainer. This process begins by determining that a medical exam has been completed as required by the state association. The process may continue with completion of a health information questionnaire. This information-gathering procedure helps determine physical and medical eligibility for sports participation. Additional preparticipation requirements may include drug-screening programs, basic fitness assessments, and initial baseline testing as a foundation for a concussion management program such as ImPACT.

Team Physicians

One or more physicians from a local clinic may volunteer to support student-athletes within an allied services model. These physicians may coordinate efforts with the school's health office. Team doctors may also serve as a point of contact for response to an initial injury and follow-up care. They may also provide consultation for postinjury rehabilitation and participation.

Community Clinics

As part of a prearranged agreement for service, community clinics may provide free or low-cost medical and dental exams and aftercare for families affected by poverty.

Strength and Conditioning Program

A strength and conditioning program is an allied service that provides specialized conditioning support for the athletic department. Conditioning programs can improve the performance of athletes and decrease the likelihood of injury. The program can also develop, teach, and monitor safe methods and techniques. Appropriate training allows athletes to achieve better overall fitness levels that may lead to advanced strength and conditioning programs. Educational values may include warnings about the use of performance-enhancing drugs.

The strength and conditioning program also supports the goals and objectives of a sports medicine program by enhancing the general health and well-being of student-athletes. The athletic director approves policies and procedures regarding practices, facilities, and staff. Further, all conditioning activities should comport with legal mandates regarding gender equity, the Americans with Disabilities Act, and affirmative employment practices.

Certified Athletic Trainers (ATCs) and Certified Strength and Conditioning Specialists (CSCSs)

ATCs and CSCSs have completed professional training and certifications that qualify them to provide research-based nutrition information to student-athletes in support of their health and performance.

Many schools acquire certified athletic trainer services on a contractual basis. See figure 7.3 for recommended guidelines governing this practice. As with all hiring efforts, the athletic director should follow policies and

Components of an Allied Services Site Agreement

- Date of agreement
- Types of Service and Schedule
  - Specified activity or activities
  - Specified location or locations
  - Purpose: educational or other
  - Service providers and service recipient(s)
  - Inclusive dates of services
- Authorizing agencies and personnel
  - Scheduling confirmation
  - Permit requirement
  - Lease or Rental Payment requirement or
  - facilities exchange agreement
  - Agency requirements re: legal and mission
  - Criteria for agreement (fair and equitable). Examples: instructional, educational, organized, adult-led, managed and organized, scheduled and supervised, athletic, social, community-related, etc.
  - Stipends for Service Providers and Payment Schedule
  - Cite Relevant Agency and Site Policies and Directives
- Types of Service and Schedule
  - Specified activity or activities
  - Specified location or locations
  - Purpose: educational or other
  - Service providers
  - Inclusive dates of services
- Specific site requested/needed (inclusions and time/date exclusions)
- Any specified or required language relative to union agreements, staffing and funding
  - Coordination, permitting, record-keeping and chain-of-command for mediation/problem resolution
- Change in facility request or facility availability
  - Policy
  - Timing
  - Decision-making

(continued)

(continued)

- Chain-of-command
- Fiscal responsibility
- Rescheduling
- Facilities Access, Maintenance and Repair
  - Responsibilities, costs—janitorial, damage, physical plant set-up, electrical, water, etc. Preparation before and after an event.
- Security Provisions
- Requests for services outside of initial agreement and fees for additional special services
- Liability Responsibilities and Coverage(s) (generic statement)
- Public Information and Notification
- Required signatures (Service Provider and Services User) and Date of Agreement

FIGURE 7.3 Recommended components of an allied health services site agreement.

procedures to ensure the contractual employee meets all the requirements of the vacant position. This includes scope and limitations of practice, affiliations, chain of command (authority), and on-site requirements.

These arrangements can be beneficial for all parties. The athletic director should check with legal counsel before drafting an affiliated site agreement (figure 7.3) or similar for-hire agreement on behalf of the school. Often hospital or clinic providers of athletic training services will issue a contract, which should be carefully evaluated by the school, district legal counsel, or business manager.

Strength and Conditioning Department Hierarchy

The supervisor of the strength and conditioning program may be the athletic director or an administrator assigned overall supervision of extracurricular programs. In most cases the sports medicine program manager (certified athletic trainer or certified strength and conditioning specialist) is assigned to oversee the program. As with other allied services, appropriate policies and procedures are necessary.

Strength and Conditioning Organizational Chart: Chain of Command and Supervision

1. Athletic director
2. Athletic trainer (certified athletic trainer, ATC)

3. Head strength and conditioning coach (National Strength and Conditioning Association–certified strength and conditioning specialist, CSCS)

4. Assistant strength and conditioning coach

5. Facility supervisor

(from 2011, NIAAA LTC 627, and NSCA)

Strength and Conditioning Program–Related Tasks

Initial screening of student-athletes may be shared by a certified athletic trainer and the strength and conditioning program director. Additional assessments are performed by the strength and conditioning coaches as part of normal protocol before physical activity.

Developers of strength and conditioning programs must take into account ethical considerations (NSCA code of ethics and principles, NSCA 2008), educational requirements and expectations, and research-based program design that is developmentally and biologically appropriate (Tanner's stages, Child Growth Foundation 2012).

Athletic directors must ensure that the strength and conditioning coaches working with the school's student-athletes understand the following:

- Key terms associated with strength and conditioning and general methods used to improve performance such as proper exercise prescription, periodization, plyometrics, speed, agility, strength, and power
- The guiding principles for strength and conditioning programs (NSCA code of ethics and principles)
- The role and methodology of testing, screening, and goal setting within strength and conditioning programs
- Nutrition
- The dangers associated with performance-enhancing drugs (PEDs)
- The proper technique for resistance training exercises
- Appropriate assessment and evaluation of programs, personnel, and student-athletes

Other duties of head strength and conditioning coaches specified by the National Strength and Conditioning Association (2012) may include the following:

- Directing all facets of staff, program, and facility operations
- Designing (or having final review of) all training programs
- Overseeing the athletic performance improvement operation to ensure compliance with institutional and conference rules and regulations

- Developing and submitting the annual budget and ensuring budgetary compliance through efficient financial management
- Generating income
- Budgeting funds for maintenance and improvement of the facility
- Overseeing the selection, installation, and maintenance of performance equipment including inspection, cleaning, and repair
- Conducting orientation meetings for student-athletes on such issues as facility rules, the value of proper training and nutrition, and the dangers of banned substances
- Developing staff work and supervision schedules, assigning duties, and evaluating performance
- Coordinating time schedules for use of the facility by each sports team and individual athletes
- Assisting with on-campus recruiting activities for prospective student-athletes
- Serving on various departmental, institutional, conference, governing body, and professional committees and task forces
- Working and communicating with coaches in the athletic department
- Traveling with sports teams (if applicable) and providing remote-site training programs, including the pregame warm-up
- Maintaining a performance training library for professional development
- Achieving and maintaining professional certifications through continuing education
- Abiding by a code of ethics
- Performing other duties and special projects as requested by the athletic director

Role of Nutrition in Student Health

Nutrition professionals within and outside of the school network are fully capable of providing instruction and direction to student-athletes to help ensure that nutrition needs are met and performance considerations have been addressed.

Dietitians and nutritionists operate within specific roles and areas as defined by the Bureau of Labor Statistics (BLS) (2012). These professionals plan food and nutrition programs, supervise meal preparation, and oversee the serving of meals.

School dietitians can provide guidance to parents and coaches while providing scientific direction to the school or district food services department. Special programs can further inform students, parents, and coaches on food choice, nutrition needs, caloric intake, energy expenditure, and appropriate diets for demanding aerobic and anaerobic activity.

Dietitians and nutritionists from medical clinics, universities, and food-marketing agencies can also be called on to help educate students, parents, coaches, and the entire school community at little to no cost to the school. Many food-marketing agencies such as the National Dairy Council, the American Beef Producers Association, and the American Beverage Association employ nutritionists who make public presentations and offer printed materials and other resources. The U.S. Government also offers nutrition information and guidelines (see www.nutrition.gov) for food intake, exercise expenditure, and other important areas affecting health and nutrition as well as resources and handouts for use.

Within the chain of allied services professionals, it is important to note that *coaches must not give nutrition advice unless it is scientifically documented.* Athletic administrators should make their coaches aware of this directive.

Academic Support and Precollege Counseling

Many student-athletes have learning differences. If not addressed, these deficits can have an effect on class performance, high school athletic eligibility, and post–high school success. The obligation to recognize and manage learning differences and educational functioning issues is mandated by the Individuals with Disabilities Education Act (IDEA). Administrators are required to implement individualized education programs (IEPs) for qualifying students. Early implementation is important in order to establish an education plan that can enable the student-athlete to succeed in high school academics, participate in sports, and prepare for college academics and athletics.

In cases where eligibility is denied because of age or the number of semesters of enrollment, the student and his parents or guardians may appeal to the state association. Appeal petitions have been granted under the auspices of the Americans with Disabilities Act of 1990. When special-needs students have exceeded the age of 19 or have been enrolled for eight previous semesters, eligibility requests have been granted if certain criteria have been satisfied. These include school documentation that the child has had limited previous competition, that the school will not gain a competitive advantage, and that other athletes will not be at risk because of physical mismatches.

Precollege Counseling and Planning

Understanding the changing landscape of intercollegiate sports is a valuable tool for college counselors. High school counselors may offer precollege counseling and planning to students who are considering participating in intercollegiate athletics. The counselor can help the student-athlete and her family by establishing timelines and by managing and monitoring achievement of academic prerequisites for intercollegiate athletics eligibility.

The ever-changing landscape of collegiate sports and the emergence of new sports demand that allied services professionals stay informed. In addition, they must communicate these changes to ensure the needs and interests of student-athletes are met.

Student-athletes who are interested in competing in intercollegiate athletics must achieve qualifying standards to be eligible to compete and receive financial aid. Each collegiate association publishes these core requirements. Also, the NFHS and NIAAA have combined to offer *A Guide for College-Bound Student-Athletes and Their Parents* (2011). The NCAA also publishes *Guide for the College-Bound Student-Athlete* (2012) and mandates that student-athletes wishing to compete at the NCAA level register with the NCAA Eligibility Center online to ensure that course work has been validated, grade point test scores have been recorded, and minimum NCAA academic standards have been met.

It is imperative that college counselors frequently check for changes in eligibility standards and requirements. College coaches now recruit and sign some high school prospects as early as the sophomore year. Informing students of appropriate resources and guidance can prevent possible issues with eligibility, financial aid, athletic grants-in-aid, and academic accommodations. Past litigation against the NCAA has caused the association to create a sliding-scale index that is used to determine initial eligibility standards (Bakker 2005). These changes help balance school curriculum options, learning differences, and other factors to ensure that qualifying student-athletes are treated equitably throughout the recruiting process and beyond.

College counselors and informed coaches can provide guidance to student-athletes soon after their high school careers begin. In fact, the NCAA considers ninth-grade student-athletes as official prospects. For that reason it is imperative that the college recruiting process begin with an orientation to the NCAA's strict guidelines and rules. Student-athletes who are successful early in their high school sports careers or in club sport competition may decide that playing intercollegiate sports is an important goal in their long-range plans. It is thus important that counselors research and make available important information regarding academics and athletic recruiting.

When a student-athlete expresses an interest in intercollegiate sports, counselors should develop an academic and athletic plan to address the following requirements and considerations:

Academics

- Core course selection (annually)
- Advanced placement course selection and completion
- PSAT and PLAN (ACT) prep and testing

- SAT, SAT IIs, and ACT prep and testing
- Advanced placement courses and precollege exam schedule
- Extracurricular activities (other than sports)
- Sports participation
- Leadership experiences
- Special skills, experiences, opportunities
- Consideration of a post–high school educational experience before college
- College selection process
- College application process
- College visits to campus(es) of interest
- Learning support services (centralized, decentralized, formalized)
- Federal student aid (FAFSA)
- Other financial aid
- Committing to a school

Athletics

- Contacting coaches
- Letter to coaches
- Online questionnaire
- Reasonable expectations as a collegiate athlete
- Collecting videotapes (school AV department, for-hire service)
- Distributing game tapes (online web page, DVD, direct access)
- Recording and registering times (for rowing, track, and so on)
- Coach evaluation opportunities (high school games, club games, camps, showcase events)
- Junior prospect visit days and clinics (on college campus)
- NCAA eligibility certification registration
- Visiting coaches and schools
  - Unofficial visits
  - Official visits
- College coaches visiting schools
- Scholarship versus nonscholarship
  - Academic and athletic commitment to school or university
  - Invitations to try out as a walk-on
- National letter of intent
- Athletic grants-in-aid

Role of Coaches and Athletic Administrator

The degree to which high school coaches and the athletic administrator are involved with student-athlete recruitment varies. It is essential, however, that the athletic administrator and coaches fully support the academic mission of the school and maintain highest expectations for students who might be recruited.

Visiting the College, Coach, and Team

College coaches and potential college teammates work diligently on image enhancement when a prospective student-athlete comes to campus for a visit or overnight stay. This is a great opportunity for the student-athlete to get a good feel for the atmosphere of the school, the team, and the competitive culture. Similarly, campus visits allow college coaches and team members to develop a relationship with the prospect.

College Sports Environment

When contemplating intercollegiate sports participation, it is imperative that students carefully consider the time commitment required during and after a season. College coaches may require year-round training, conditioning, and skill development. In addition, film study, sports medicine treatments, travel to and from practice and game venues, study hall, meal check-ins, and academic advising meetings can be additional time demands.

Academic Support

High school counselors, coaches, parents, and athletes should ask about the academic support provided by a college athletic department that supplements the traditional student support services provided by colleges and universities. Athletic department support services might include tutoring as well as additional advising to ensure that student-athletes understand school and eligibility requirements, specific course requirements, and graduation requirements. These services help guide student-athletes toward successful degree completion while balancing the rigors of intercollegiate athletics.

Injury or Illness

The college-bound athlete and her parents should ask probing questions about the health care provided before and after an injury. In addition, they should ask about the support provided in the event an injury prevents the student-athlete from participating for the remainder of her collegiate career.

Summary

Students and families face many challenges throughout the high school years and beyond. Allied services professionals can enhance the educational growth and athletic experiences of high school students by supporting the comprehensive educational mission of schools and interscholastic athletics. Athletic support activities that may be helpful include:

- Athletic training services for injury prevention, response, and rehabilitation
- Sports medicine referrals for medical interventions that are beyond the services of the athletic trainer
- Strength and conditioning specialists
- Mental health professionals, including counselors and school psychologists that can address various stressors in the lives of athletes
- Sports administrators for eligibility questions in cases of divorce, college eligibility determinations, state association regulations, and school athletic code interpretations for parents and athletes
- Dietitians that can recommend dietary considerations and plan pregame meals for athletes

CHAPTER 8

Scheduling Considerations

Steve Berseth, MSc, CMAA

The administration of interscholastic athletics is a complex task that requires multiple types of scheduling as a primary and continual responsibility. Whether scheduling duties are assigned to an athletic director, an activities director, or a department secretary, this responsibility usually includes contests, events, and practices; athletic facilities; contest officials; team transportation; and contest personnel (NIAAA 2010a).

The last two items—scheduling transportation and scheduling contest personnel—are addressed in chapters 9 and 11, respectively. This chapter focuses on the first three topics in the list.

Scheduling responsibilities are interrelated and should be integrated and coordinated for the benefit of the instructional and extracurricular programs, student participants, and other members of the school community. Typically, athletic schedules have implications for the scheduling of other school and community events. For that reason, it may be advisable to communicate with nonschool groups to ensure that significant school and community events do not conflict. Proactive planning is an absolute requirement to prevent unexpected schedule conflicts and negative consequences.

Scheduling events and access to facilities is a leadership responsibility that necessitates collaboration, compromise, and communication with athletic personnel from other schools; local school staff; affiliate organizations; and community groups. These individuals and groups tend to share a common characteristic. Many have a passion for a specific activity and may have a personal agenda that the athletic director must address.

Although league schedules largely dictate the annual contest dates and opponents, coaches will occasionally pressure for certain nonconference games and tournaments depending on the make-up of a squad in a particular year. Independent schools may have the luxury of scheduling opponents that fit their open schedule dates and may try to schedule advantageously in early games to help younger teams develop.

■ **Proactive planning is an absolute requirement to prevent unexpected schedule conflicts and negative consequences.**

By comparison, implementing well-defined protocols for scheduling event personnel and transportation is a management task that may be delegated to an appropriately trained administrative assistant or department secretary. In this case, the athletic director must provide adequate supervision of these important responsibilities to prevent undesirable outcomes. It is important for athletic personnel to be aware that educational sports and activities provide a window to the school district for many citizens and members of the school community.

Contest and Event Scheduling

Prioritizing school events and schedules can be a challenge for athletic and activity administrators. Conference and state-association schedules for specific sports and assignments for contest officials must often be contracted long before the calendar for an upcoming school year is approved. State high school association tournaments, fine arts events, and academic contests are also scheduled independently of local school calendars.

The athletic director is generally responsible for scheduling athletic contests at all levels of high school competition (varsity, junior varsity, sophomore, and freshman). In some school districts, the athletic director may also schedule contests for the middle school or multiple high schools. Organizational structures differ from school to school, and scheduling duties for subvarsity sports are sometimes delegated to other athletic department personnel. Regardless of the division of duties, the athletic administrator is ultimately responsible for the contractual details of all athletic competitions (Giebel 2003).

Eight-team conferences enjoy the benefits of exemplary single and double round-robin sports schedules and tournament seeding. Conference membership can also result in enhanced schedules for individual sports teams that don't compete within a conference schedule. Conference schedules that feature 7 football games and 14 basketball games also afford an opportunity to schedule contests with nonconference opponents.

Developing athletic schedules is not a unilateral exercise. Athletic directors quickly learn that they will need occasional scheduling accommodations. When a school has a genuine scheduling need, conference membership can be beneficial with regard to adjustments by other schools. Although an even number of teams facilitates round-robin schedules and tournament brackets, a conference with an uneven number of schools can create workable schedules and conduct sports tournaments by utilizing techniques such as byes, seeding criteria, and tie-breaking formulas.

With experience, school administrators will anticipate potential conflicts and avoid incompatible events and dates when developing local schedules.

School Calendar

Whenever possible, athletic contests should be scheduled so student-athletes and teacher-coaches are able to attend important school events. The school calendar should also be developed so students and faculty can participate in significant school functions. School officials must be aware of events on the state-association calendar and plan so that local and state schedules are compatible and students and families aren't forced to resolve event conflicts.

Increasingly, administrators who provide leadership to high school athletic programs are assigned titles such as director of student activities or cocurricular activities director in recognition of additional duties. When the job description includes supervision of other extracurricular activities such as fine arts programs and student organizations or facility management, an administrator may be assigned the responsibility of coordinating or actually developing the annual school calendar.

Once the school calendar is published, inaccurate information is difficult to correct or adjust, even with a multimedia approach. It is also challenging to make late changes to event dates or times without causing schedule conflicts. The calendar coordinator or committee will often place events on a comprehensive school-year calendar by employing the following or a similar calendar development progression:

1. State-association and substate events
2. Athletic conference competitions
3. Varsity nonconference athletic contests
4. Major events that are scheduled annually on corresponding dates (speech tournaments, music festivals, academic competitions)
5. School district calendar dates approved by the local governance board (first day, last day, vacation dates, teacher in-services, graduation)
6. Academic events (registration, back-to-school event, parent–teacher conferences, semester exams, standardized testing schedules)
7. Other school events (homecoming, concerts, theater productions, awards ceremonies, formal dances, subvarsity athletic contests, PTA meetings)
8. Large events that are hosted on a rotating schedule (area music concerts, conference athletic tournaments, qualifying tournaments)
9. Events of affiliate organizations that are appropriate for inclusion (booster club meetings, youth sports activities, city recreation programs)

Once the school calendar has been finalized, adding contests or performances often requires the approval of school administrators. Consideration of additional events may focus on potential conflicts with previously scheduled events and the availability of facilities and transportation.

State-Association Calendar

Generally, all accredited schools are eligible to become members of the state high school association. The board of education often approves local school membership in the high school association on an annual basis. When a school elects to be a member, it agrees to abide by the rules and regulations of the state association. In most states, schools may compete only with other schools that are members of a high school athletic association during the in-season period.

Local scheduling and calendar development must consider events and dates that are set for member schools by the standardized calendar of the state association. Scheduling considerations include the following:

- Dates of the first allowable practice and contest for each sport
- In-season contest limitations
- Out-of-season regulations
- Prohibited days and dates (e.g., Sunday, religious observations, specific holidays)
- Enrollment classification
- Travel restrictions
- Potential dates for hosting state tournament qualification contests
- State events sponsored by the state association
- Regular-season schedules in specific sports that some state associations develop

Conference Schedule

Although the administration of educational sports has evolved in many respects, some practices have not changed over time. Most coaches and administrators still agree that affiliation with a sports conference (sometimes called a league) offers multiple benefits. The alternative to conference membership is scheduling and competing as an independent, which is usually a challenging and ongoing process. The majority of schools are satisfied conference members or are seeking membership in a conference that will fulfill the needs of their teams and communities. There is little indication that school preference for conference affiliation will change in the future.

In addition to having a set schedule for many sports, a common advantage of conference membership is reductions in transportation costs and lost classroom time. An eight-member athletic conference of similarly sized schools with geographic proximity is often considered to be an ideal affiliation for interscholastic sports teams. Conversely, many conferences have operated for years with fewer or greater than eight schools or issues such as significant travel. Regardless of the number of member schools, a sports conference composed of peer institutions with similar enrollments, interests, and core values should be well positioned to enjoy numerous benefits and stability.

A conference's constitution might specify how sports schedules are to be developed within a league. In addition, bylaws may define scheduling procedures in specific conference sports. The constitution may also facilitate scheduling by defining the conditions of league membership. The bylaws commonly state that member schools must participate in each sport that competes within a round-robin schedule. The implication is that current and prospective members must sponsor each conference sport and all additional sports that are adopted in the future. Such bylaws are intended to provide full schedules for team sports. They also become the basic criteria for adding new members and force current members to exit if they eliminate a conference sport.

Some conferences develop schedules only for varsity teams, but many also schedule subvarsity contests as part of the same session. Other conferences schedule contests between subvarsity teams during the week their varsity teams compete. To facilitate football scheduling, conferences may specify that JV teams play on Monday or Tuesday and frosh teams play on Thursday.

Although schools usually delegate scheduling duties to the athletic director, the task of drafting schedules may be assigned to a conference executive secretary or other official. Conference bylaws may provide a framework for scheduling contests by stipulating a

- multiyear schedule (i.e., specific number of years or ad infinitum),
- formula for rotating opponents and hosting during specific weeks,
- policy for rescheduling contests if the outcome affects the championship,
- start time for varsity contests (unless opponents agree to a different time),
- procedure for conducting tournaments (e.g., hosting rotations, format, seeding criteria, tie-breaking protocols),
- protocol for determining championships,
- scheduling meeting,
- timeline for signing annual master contracts, and
- review of schedules and confirmation of tournament arrangements during regular meetings.

Despite changes to educational sports, some of the constitutional bylaws of athletic conferences may still reflect the value system of the original members. It is normal that values endure while issues evolve, but the implication is that change to conference operating procedures is often difficult and slow. Constitutional amendments may not be easy to enact because approval commonly requires a two-thirds (67 percent) vote of current members. It can be challenging for a conference to obtain the necessary votes for significant change such as adding member schools, adjusting sports schedules, or revising procedures for determining championships.

Divisional Schedules

Athletic conferences of 10 or more schools frequently separate into two equally sized divisions based on a combination of factors such as geography, rivalries, and competitive balance. Some aspects of divisional play may be controversial. Potential sources of conflict arise when division members do not participate in an equivalent number of contests with all conference opponents. In addition, other sources of conflict are related to loss of traditional rivals, relative strength of divisions, and the implications for determining the conference champion.

Football teams (and sports that play a similar number of contests) frequently compete in a single round-robin schedule within each division. Divisional play is often supplemented with rivalry contests so that schools in different divisions can continue to play traditional opponents. Member schools determine the number of rivalry contests and specific opponents. The schedule may include a placement round that features a matchup of the top-ranked team from each division to decide the conference champion. When the placement round also matches other schools according to divisional rank, each team is provided with a competitive contest before the state playoffs.

There are concerns with a placement week in football. The placement round alters the balance of home and away games because both the opponent and site are to be determined. It is also possible that teams will be opponents for a rivalry game and play again in the placement round. These issues are inherent to the use of a placement round, but some concerns may be addressed by establishing procedures. Tie-breaking rules for matching teams and a rotation or competitive criteria for determining host schools can be approved for placement games.

The following provides a sample schedule for a 10-team athletic conference that employs two five-school divisions and a placement round:

- Each team plays four contests within its division.
- Each team plays two rivalry contests with schools in the other division.
- The placement round adds one contest for a total of seven conference contests.
- If the state association allows a nine-contest regular season, each school is able to schedule two nonconference contests.

For basketball, volleyball, and other sports that play a greater number of competitions, approval of a double round-robin schedule depends on several factors. Considerations include the number of conference schools, the contest limitations of the state association, and the number of nonconference contests preferred by member schools. A double round-robin schedule in a 10-team conference provides each school with 18 contests.

When conference members decide not to play a double round-robin schedule, play within two divisions is often adopted. The following is a sample 10-team basketball or volleyball schedule with a placement round:

- Each team plays two contests with each division opponent (8 contests).
- Each team plays one contest with each team in the other division (5 contests).
- The placement round adds one contest (total of 14 conference contests).

Member schools may prefer to determine the conference champion with a tournament. In that case, conference contests may be used to seed teams within the tournament bracket. The number of additional competitions depends on the format of the tournament.

An alternative is to declare the champion of each division as cochampions. A second option is to adopt a plan for determining the conference champion (e.g., establishing a hierarchy or combination of criteria such as head-to-head competition between division champions, winning percentage against all conference opponents, or strength of divisions). Both options may be controversial and a source of strained relations within the conference.

Nonconference Schedules

The great majority of high schools are affiliated with a conference. Hence, the schedules for most athletic programs will consist primarily of contests between league members. Teams in every conference also need to supplement their schedules with contests against teams outside the league.

In most cases, nonconference athletic contests are scheduled after conference schedules have been developed. When scheduling nonconference competitions, the following factors and contractual terms may be considered:

- Balance of home and away contests—short term and season—for team sports
- The importance of hosting competitions and invitational meets to develop a local fan base for individual sports
- Classification, student enrollment, and competiveness of potential opponents
- Importance of a matchup for seeding or team preparations for substate play
- Fair play, crowd conduct, or safety issues related to specific opponents

- Frequency of contests and time for team preparations between contests
- Recovery and warm-up time between multiple contests (e.g., double duals and tournaments) in the same sport
- Time to clear the facility, clean up, set up the competition area for the next event, and sell tickets when multiple events are scheduled on the same date
- Length of travel and avoidance of back-to-back lengthy trips
- Coach's scheduling preferences at various times of the season

In addition to conference schedules, schools may also have nonconference scheduling obligations to provide contests for specific schools or conferences. Many athletic directors and coaches prefer set schedules. Independent schools have fewer scheduling constraints due to lack of affiliation, and coaches may be asked to collaborate with the athletic director in order to fill schedules with appropriate opponents. Athletic schedules of independent schools often aren't characterized by the scheduling factors identified.

Assisting Schools in Remote Locations With Contest Scheduling

The process for contest scheduling varies depending on factors such as school location and distance between schools within a region or state. Because many athletic conferences or classifications in the Northern Plains and Southwestern states are characterized by sparse populations or remote communities, travel time and costs can be significant. Despite these concerns, every school wants appropriate sports schedules, which may require assistance from distant schools.

As an example, a Northern Plains conference modified its scheduling procedures to help the state association provide nonconference competition to schools that are widely separated. To accommodate the competition needs of remotely located schools, members of a large school league chose travel partners from within their conference and scheduled nonconference contests in boys' and girls' basketball and volleyball with schools on the opposite side of the state.

Conference partners travel across the state for Friday nonconference contests and then switch opponents for Saturday afternoon contests. The early start for the second competition on Saturday afternoon facilitates earlier return travel. A multiyear home-and-home schedule is developed to equalize the travel costs.

This is a challenging travel itinerary, but it limits lodging to one night while helping remote schools that are unable to schedule competition in their sports classification because of their locations.

Football Scheduling

Football is immensely popular among male athletes as evidenced by annual sports participation data published by the National Federation of State High School Associations. The NFHS High School Athletics Participation Survey demonstrates that almost twice as many boys participate in football in comparison to the interscholastic sport that is second with respect to participation (Fellmeth 2010).

Relative to other sports, football appears to be a salient factor in determining whether a school joins or remains a member of an athletic conference. Some schools seem to regularly explore membership in new conferences in a search for football compatibility. Similarly, many high school associations routinely investigate potential changes to football classifications. Study and decision making by state associations usually focus on school enrollment disparities. With respect to football compatibility, there are two main concerns—competitiveness and risk minimization—for school officials.

Football enjoys widespread spectator interest in the United States. The significance of football is illustrated by its traditional connection to homecoming. In addition, Friday night football games are frequently the main attraction of a community gathering and often includes tailgating, booster club activities, band shows, and student dances. An inspection of the athletic hall of fame in many high schools also reinforces the notion that football is a major influence on sports heritage (Purdy 1973).

Unfortunately, lack of football competitiveness sometimes results in negative perceptions by alumni and other members of the school community that may place external pressures on local school officials. In many communities, considerable effort is required of school administrators to maintain an appropriate educational sports perspective.

The primary football concern must be risk minimization. The specific issue is the legal duty, emanating from court rulings, to properly match and equate athletes and teams. This issue may arise when games are scheduled between teams with significant enrollment differences. Because football is a collision sport, participants and their parents need to be warned of the inherent risk of participation and a higher incidence of serious injury (NIAAA 2010b, NIAAA 2007).

Football has been referred to as a "numbers sport" because high levels of player participation are desirable. Eleven players participate at all times, but coaches of schools with large enrollments try to gain greater advantage by preparing additional players so they are able to platoon on offense and defense, substitute freely, and insert extra players on special teams. Larger squads enhance depth by position, which often results in improvement of specialized skills, reduction of player fatigue, and fewer injuries, with a resultant increase in team success.

(continued)

(continued)

Schools with larger enrollments are often able to field teams of greater maturity, skill, size, and speed in comparison to smaller schools. These traits create a cumulative physical advantage that may exacerbate the inherent risk of football injury. Such personnel differences must be considered in conjunction with enrollment disparities when scheduling football games.

The duty to match and equate is also a priority when conducting scrimmages involving subvarsity teams of players at various stages in the development of football skills and techniques. Although the difference in chronological age between most frosh and JV players is only 12 to 18 months, the physiological differences may be significant and result in assertions of negligence in the event of injury to less mature and less skilled players during football scrimmages and contact drills.

The duty of athletic directors to consider risk minimization when scheduling football games cannot be overemphasized. Matching teams with large enrollment disparities may lead to allegations that inappropriate pairing was the primary cause of a player injury, and that such an injury was also foreseeable. Contemporary standards—related to prudent professionalism and reasonable care—must play a prominent role in decisions about membership in an athletic conference and about scheduling nonconference football games with schools of significantly greater enrollment.

Some veteran or highly successful coaches lobby for specific nonconference opponents or select tournaments. They may even request a schedule that varies from year to year based on the competitive needs of the current team. In some situations, the athletic director may be in agreement and able to accommodate a coach. The athletic administrator needs to consider the equitable treatment of all programs within the athletic department during the scheduling process. Budgetary limitations are also a factor in decision making for many schools.

In some cases, a nonconference athletic contract will not provide a home contest for both teams. This is also the case for invitational tournaments. Depending on the considerations, a financial guarantee by the host school may be necessary to persuade the visitors to agree to the competition. Visiting team negotiations may include inducements from the home team such as a cash guarantee, meals, or lodging reimbursements that offset travel expenses and loss of gate and concessions revenue by the visiting team. All financial terms should be documented on the contract before it is signed by school officials from the visiting school.

Budgetary pressures have limited long-distance, non-conference games and tournaments. Out-of-state tournament play may be possible for schools and cities that border adjacent states.

Competition Contracts

Written contracts document the terms of athletic contests. Athletic contracts can also be used to confirm contest information before the publication of sports schedules and the school calendar. The practice of exchanging athletic contracts, signed by authorized officials from participating schools, minimizes scheduling errors.

When a conference secretary coordinates the development of sports schedules, the resultant league schedule can be utilized as a master contract between member schools. In that case, athletic directors need only issue contracts for nonconference and subvarsity contests.

Dual competitions typically involve a two-year contract (home and home) to guarantee that each school has the opportunity to host a contest. Dual competitions are often contracted for corresponding dates in both years if the necessary facilities and dates are available. Multiyear contracts are frequently utilized to confirm the dates and terms of double dual (three teams competing in dual competitions) or quadrangular contests as well as jamborees and invitational competitions.

Most athletic administrators utilize electronic contracts that are easily modified for specific competitions. State athletic associations often provide contest contracts to member schools. Rather than mailing hard copies of athletic contracts, school personnel commonly forward electronic documents as attachments to e-mail messages. Participating schools have the option of signing and returning contracts electronically or printing the contract and mailing a signed copy. Whether paper or electronic contracts are preferred, copies may be organized by sport and kept in three-ring binders or filed.

Many athletic directors renew expired contracts by sports season on a weekly basis or at the end of the season. Scheduling contests a minimum of one year in advance ensures that future schedules for each squad in every sports program are confirmed. Athletic personnel who delay scheduling until the end of the school year risk not filling all sports schedules and a poor relationship with other schools. Incomplete schedules are a disservice to coaches and student-athletes and may constitute a gender equity issue.

Some athletic conferences employ a multiyear scheduling formula that periodically rotates schools and opponents in a specified manner. Sports schedules still require annual revision because of conflicts with special events, homecoming adjustments, and facility issues. An appendix to the conference constitution may include the scheduling formula, future schedules, and a hosting rotation for tournaments.

Conference athletic schedules may be used to create an annual master contract. Once member schools have agreed to the dates and times for all contests, the executive secretary prints master schedules for distribution. The agenda for a subsequent conference meeting includes a master contract signing ceremony (Eastern South Dakota Athletic Conference 2009).

The master contract may be used by a supervisor of officials for assigning contest officials to conference competitions. It can also be used by coaches for conference-regulated scouting. Once the master contract has been signed, changes usually require the host school to inform the executive secretary and supervisor of officials of the details of any rescheduled contests. When arrangements have been confirmed, contest officials and athletic administrators of member schools are notified of the change.

During conference meetings, athletic directors regularly discuss the format and details for tournaments and dual contests in the single and double round-robin schedules. Varsity schedules are routinely reviewed to ensure that all schools are in agreement. Discussions may involve the number of squads or contests per session, opportunities for nonconference scheduling, travel partners for overnight trips involving multiple contests, time schedules for early return from overnight trips (e.g., getaway contests on the second day of competition), scheduling basketball games by gender at opposite locations or mixed doubleheaders at a common site, facility use (gymnasiums, fields, locker rooms, support areas) for special events, and arrangements for championship tournaments.

Additional Competition Scheduling Considerations

The athletic administrator also has additional things to keep in mind when scheduling events. Budget, gender equity, the need for rescheduling an event, and a number of other issues are all important considerations. They are discussed here.

Release of Varsity Schedules

After school calendars are finalized for the subsequent year, opponents may still request rescheduling of athletic contests that conflict with school events. Athletic directors can usually identify an alternative date that is acceptable to both schools. On occasion, schools can't agree on a new date for a contest. When rescheduling isn't viable, the host school may have a local option. If the conflict is facility related, moving the contest to a different facility may be a solution.

Another option may be to switch sites if the visiting team can host the contest on the original date. A conflict-free date, availability of facilities, and acceptable balance of home and away contests often enables schools to switch the location of a contest. Switching the site for one contest also requires an acceptable date for the opponent to host the second competition. Switching sites is rarely an option when opponents play only one contest during the season unless it balances the schedules of both teams in future years.

Many athletic directors delay the release of varsity schedules until the schedules of all opponents have been confirmed. Once the school year has concluded, it is usually safe to release athletic schedules for the following year to the media and to post them on school websites. By mid-June, varsity schedules can be sent to the printing company for development of sports posters. Athletic department personnel should carefully proof commercial schedules before they are printed. Errors may be minimized if electronic schedules are forwarded to the printer. The emphasis should be on accuracy because sports schedules often don't need to be distributed in the community until late July.

When the school calendar isn't published until August, unexpected contest changes may be compatible with the all-school calendar print schedule. When circumstances result in late changes to athletic schedules, print dates may not permit revisions to fall sports schedules or the school calendar. If poster schedules are printed for each sports season, corrected athletic schedules can be published for winter and spring posters.

Many state athletic associations set deadlines for member schools to submit varsity sports schedules and team information. Schools are usually required to enter and submit the required information online and update it as changes occur during the season. State associations typically post varsity schedules on their websites by sport, gender, and school classification for easy access.

Maintaining a link on the state-association website for athletic schedules is a convenience for member schools and the public. Host schools can quickly find the information required for printing team rosters and contest programs. Coaches can check the schedules of opponents and develop a scouting schedule. Media, families, and fans also have easy access to schedules for all schools. The result is fewer inquiries and disruptions to athletic department operations.

Rescheduling

The cancellation and postponement of athletic contests and extracurricular activities can be a challenging and time-consuming task for the athletic director. In some areas, events are frequently jeopardized by inclement weather and poor travel conditions. Hazardous playing fields may also be a concern for outdoor sports. In northern states, outdoor athletic seasons are typically short, and teams often adapt to difficult weather conditions rather than routinely canceling contests.

Technology such as fax machines, cellular telephones, e-mail messaging, websites, and other electronic devices has enhanced access to information and communication for school officials. These technological innovations have reduced some of the challenges of decision making and rescheduling.

Invitational tournaments are difficult to postpone because the schedules of most teams won't allow their participation on alternate dates. If several schools need a competition and agree to a new date, the event may be rescheduled. Other schools can easily be invited to join the contest with a mass e-mail communication.

Extended weather forecasts have become quite accurate, which facilitates decisions about competition and travel. When the administration of a conference tournament is in doubt, the constitutional bylaws may define a makeup date and abbreviated format. When the weather forecast is unfavorable and bylaws don't provide direction, athletic directors may decide to reschedule the event in advance if there is a date that enables all member schools to participate with minimal conflict for student-athletes and schools.

In some states, lengthy travel is necessary to compete with schools of similar size. In remote areas, weather conditions such as snow, ice, fog, and wind may also cause poor visibility and treacherous roads. These conditions occasionally force the cancellation or postponement of contests because of safety concerns. When possible, cancellation of varsity competitions should be avoided if the outcome of the contest has a bearing on conference championships or seeding for state-qualifying tournaments. If a competition can't be conducted, the bylaws may clarify the expectations for rescheduling conference athletic contests.

There are often general procedures for postponing competitions in areas where rescheduling is common. When weather predictions are worrisome, athletic directors typically communicate to discuss weather and road information as well as bus departure schedules and then agree on a timeline for decision making. After telephone conversations, the host and visiting schools follow different protocols.

The host school needs to determine alternative dates when the competition area will be available. Preferably, the contest won't need to be rescheduled to the date of another school event. Multiple events may be possible but can cause undesirable consequences such as conflicts for student participants, overcrowded parking lots, and ticket sales for multiple events. Another concern is increased hallway traffic that may disrupt a fine arts performance because of excessive noise. Such consequences may lead to the perception that athletic programs are conducted without consideration for other school activities.

The primary communication for the visiting school should be with the transportation department or the dispatcher of a commercial carrier. The transportation director often consults multiple sources of current and forecasted weather conditions during the trip as well as road reports along the route. For risk management and liability reasons, school district officials may expect the athletic administrator to defer to transportation department personnel if they believe travel isn't advised. If travel begins, the bus driver may be responsible for determining whether conditions warrant returning home, stopping along the route, or continuing to the destination.

Both athletic directors should also consult with their head coaches to determine dates that are compatible with existing team schedules. Coaches usually prefer not to play too many games or travel too often within a short period. Rescheduling early in the season generally offers several options. Despite coach preferences, athletic directors are occasionally forced to postpone contests and reschedule for dates that are less than ideal for teams.

Late in the season, schools may decide to play when the weather forecast isn't favorable if conditions enable safe travel to the site of the contest. An earlier departure is often indicated, and subvarsity games may be cancelled in such cases. In these situations, athletic personnel may need to prepare for team lodging because conditions may not permit return travel.

School district policy may prohibit practices and school events if there is an early dismissal or cancellation of school because of inclement weather. Strict policy eliminates administrative decision making and minimizes risk, but it occasionally results in unnecessary postponements. In rural areas, school cancellation is usually determined by early-morning weather and country-road conditions that may cause school bus routes to be hazardous for students. There may be little relationship between a sound decision in the morning and weather and road conditions in the afternoon. If conditions improve and travel would have involved a short varsity trip on an interstate highway, a rigid policy may seem to be a poor substitute for prudent decision making, based on current conditions.

If school is not in session when athletic contests are cancelled or postponed, the athletic director may be required to work alone in the office. In this case, alerting numerous people and media outlets can be challenging. The immediate task is to communicate about events that will not occur as scheduled. School officials must decide which events to cancel and reschedule so that media outlets can be notified. The task is more difficult when key school personnel are not available for discussions.

Many people and groups are involved in the administration of educational sports. Once competitions have been cancelled or postponed, athletic personnel must promptly notify all relevant parties. The athletic director's first telephone call should be to the supervisor of officials so that contest officials can be contacted before they begin risky travel. The next call should be to cancel same-day transportation. If a department secretary is available, simultaneous calls can be made to officials and transportation agents. Although athletic directors from participating schools are usually involved in decision making, a follow-up e-mail message should be sent so they have the opportunity to confirm a postponement and the specifics of rescheduling before it is distributed to the media and general public.

As soon as the details of rescheduling have been verified by opponents, the athletic director should send out a media release by e-mail message so that radio stations and newspapers can quickly and accurately communicate the cancellation or postponement of school events. Prompt notification helps keep the telephone lines open for athletic department use by reducing weather-related calls. Relevant parties should know to listen to specific radio stations for event announcements.

The athletic director's next contacts should be with coaches, event managers, law enforcement personnel, and support personnel such as the athletic trainer, equipment manager, sideline cheer coach, and concessionaire. If there are special events scheduled in conjunction with a sports contest, personnel such as the pep band director, student council advisor, monogram club officers, booster club officials, or sponsor of half-time entertainment may also need to be advised.

Immediate notification is facilitated by the involvement of several people. An administrative assistant or athletic department secretary may be assigned to contact bench officials, contest support personnel, and event staff such as ticket sellers and takers and faculty supervisors. A secretary in the principal's office can alert school administrators, faculty, and other school offices to indicate that students and teachers need not be released as scheduled and that substitute teachers can be cancelled.

Phone calls should be followed by e-mail messages that can be forwarded to other interested parties. Rescheduling checklists are recommended so that all interested parties will be quickly notified of pertinent information by specific athletic personnel.

Subvarsity and Middle School Schedules

Conference schedules may involve more than varsity contests. Schools often use multiple gymnasiums and manage contests for junior varsity, sophomore, and ninth-grade squads when hosting basketball and volleyball competitions. Smaller schools may schedule high school and middle school teams during the same competitive session.

Many athletic personnel consider the purpose of all subvarsity teams to be developmental and establish goals and procedures that differ both philosophically and in applied practice from varsity teams. Learned competitiveness is an important goal, but team success is secondary; the primary focus of subvarsity squads should be the development of sport-specific skills and knowledge by individual players. Although significant player development occurs during well-planned practices, competition schedules that are commensurate with skill and maturity are necessary to optimize personal and team growth.

Middle school competitive experiences should emphasize the growth of student-athletes rather than winning or losing contests. Coaches should motivate athletes to develop their sports skills by stressing the relationship between good practice habits and improved play and progressing from one squad to another. Ideally, a fulfilling sports experience will result in perseverance that enhances the development of skill and knowledge until they are matched by the physical growth of the student-athlete.

Middle school athletes will demonstrate improvement by competing in one or two contests per week, and teams will progress with a total schedule that is approximately two-thirds those of varsity squads. School sponsorship of multiple teams at the middle school levels has the potential to increase the success, enjoyment, and confidence of student-athletes by providing developmentally appropriate competition. The terms of athletic contracts should include contests for all squads (Bates 2003).

Most state high school associations have in-season regulations that prohibit dual participation by student-athletes on a school-sponsored team and a non-school-sponsored team in the same sport. Such rules are even more logical for middle school participants because young athletes rarely benefit from conflicting schedules, multiple coaches, or an excessive number of competitions during any period. When middle school sports aren't regulated by the state association, the athletic department should consider implementing similar rules for middle school participants.

When possible, middle school practices and contests should be scheduled in middle school facilities to enhance access by student-athletes, develop student body interest, and facilitate supervision by school administrators. Middle school tournaments may need to be scheduled at a high school or community facility to accommodate a larger number of participants or teams and provide concessions and other support facilities.

Gender Equity

The legal framework that defines gender equity for educational sports is Title IX of the Education Amendments to the Civil Rights Act. Compliance with Title IX requires gender equivalency with regard to various types of scheduling and related issues. Equity considerations include scheduling of athletic contests, participation in sports tournaments, scheduling of team practices, travel and mode of transportation, lodging and per diem meal allowances, access to practice and competition facilities, and support programs.

As a specific reference to scheduling, the law mandates equity with respect to prime dates and start times for games and practices as well as the quality of facilities in which games and practices are conducted. If homecoming is traditionally associated with a home football game, the athletic director should also strive to schedule a home match for the volleyball team so a high-profile girls' sport is similarly recognized and associated with homecoming festivities (NIAAA 2010c).

Conference membership can facilitate the development of equivalent schedules in sports that are sponsored for both genders. For example, a double round-robin basketball schedule that assigns girls' and boys' teams to play the same opponent—but at opposite locations—affords both teams a full schedule for all squads and balance between home and away contests. Scheduling in opposition also provides girls' teams with prime-time scheduling with respect to both day and time.

Budget Concerns

Insufficient funding has frequently been a problem for public schools in the United States, but it has reached critical proportions in many states because of contemporary economic pressures. When funding is inadequate to support curricular programs and school operations, educational sports and activities appear to some school stakeholders—including decision-makers—as luxuries that schools can't afford. Severe financial constraints usually require athletic directors to implement budget-reduction strategies that include scheduling.

Transportation expenses can be decreased by reducing mileage and driver hours if area teams are scheduled for nonconference athletic contests rather than distant schools. Travel costs may also be decreased by reducing or eliminating meals and lodging. It is common for schools to curtail athletic schedules for subvarsity and middle school teams as a budget-reduction measure. Schedule reductions also result in lower costs for officials' fees and contest personnel stipends (NIAAA 2009b).

Several state high school associations have reduced travel expenses by decreasing the number of allowable athletic contests. School personnel may discover, however, that lost gate receipts and concessions revenue negate the reduced personnel and transportation expenses. Other state athletic associations have restricted travel by permitting higher-seeded teams to host substate contests rather than conducting central-site tournaments. Some state associations have also enabled teams to stay closer to home during the regular season by minimizing the seeding factor for "strength of schedule."

Transportation sharing is another expense-reduction strategy. If baseball and softball teams have matching schedules, they may be able to share a bus. Urban schools have scheduled transportation so their golf, tennis, or gymnastics teams can travel together to competitions. When multiple contests are scheduled at the same site, all high school basketball and volleyball squads often share transportation. Smaller schools could schedule in a similar manner, with joint transportation for high school and middle school teams. On other occasions, boys' and girls' varsity basketball teams might be scheduled for a doubleheader with the same opponent in order to share transportation (Dyer 2009; Lamb 2011).

A number of school districts have adopted a four-day school schedule as a budget-reduction measure. A four-day week has several implications for scheduling student activities. A large majority of school events are scheduled for Thursday, Friday, and Saturday when school isn't in session on Fridays. Practices and events on school nights may also be expected to conclude by 8:00 p.m. A benefit of the four-day school week is a reduction in lost school time due to participation in educational sports and activities. A potential disadvantage is that longer school days often require a later start for subvarsity contests, which may affect outdoor sports because of daylight limitations (Vachlon 2009).

Difficult decisions may be necessary in response to a budgetary crisis. School officials need to be aware, however, that if they decrease opportunities or benefits for student-athletes or athletic programs, reductions must be implemented without discriminating on the basis of gender (Pennepacker 2010).

Facility Scheduling

Coordinating the use of school facilities is an important and challenging task that is complicated by issues such as inclusion, control, safety, and security. Facility scheduling focuses on the prioritized integration of school-sponsored programs and community users within school facilities. Access to indoor athletic facilities is appreciated by many citizens and an expectation of some user groups, especially during the winter months.

Because athletic contests often make up major portions of school calendars during the winter sports season, there is increased demand for facility use. This factor creates a higher demand for access than available space permits during many weeks. When a group thinks it has reserved a school facility and arrives to find others using it, frustration and resentment are frequent outcomes. Appropriate policies and procedures are necessary to coordinate schedules and communicate with relevant parties so that access to facilities is provided with minimal conflicts (Olson 1997).

The athletic director is often responsible for providing access to athletic facilities such as gymnasiums, playing fields, pools, and weight rooms. Scheduling other school facilities is a logical task because in addition to administering sports programs, the athletic director may have related responsibilities and supervisory or liaison duties for other groups that are frequent users of school facilities:

- Fine arts programs
- Leadership organizations
- Student academic and interest clubs
- Arena management
- School liaison to community recreation or a local college athletic department
- Chairperson of the physical education department
- Intramural sports director
- Monogram club advisor
- Liaison to school affiliates or the area convention and visitors bureau

It is essential that school personnel and community organizations with a joint-use relationship receive the facility schedule on a regular and timely basis. Because the facility schedule may change frequently as a result of multiple user demands, distributing a weekly facility schedule is required.

Toward the end of each week, it is advisable to send an e-mail message with a preliminary facility schedule to all user groups so the events of the following week can be reviewed. Users should be instructed to report additions or changes to the schedule to avoid facility conflicts. The facility schedule can easily be corrected or updated and redistributed by e-mail.

Scheduling events in facilities that are most appropriate for an activity can enhance the performance for both student participants and the audience. If a school does not possess facilities such as an auditorium, studio theatre, or commons, school performances and community events are often scheduled in a gymnasium. Some gymnasiums include a stage on one end so that chairs on the court and sideline bleachers can be positioned to accommodate an audience for graduation ceremonies, music concerts, and theater productions.

Transition times for takedown and setup of equipment between activities are essential considerations when scheduling facility use. A checklist that indicates a timeline and specific tasks for the physical education staff, event manager, custodians, equipment manager, athletic trainer, and activity supervisors is recommended.

Athletic Practices

When schools possess dedicated practice facilities for most indoor sports, equitable schedules of boys' and girls' practices may be readily integrated with physical education classes, intramural sports, open gym sessions, youth sports, and community recreation programs. Few public schools are capable of providing sufficiently dedicated facilities to enable all varsity and subvarsity basketball or hockey squads for both genders to practice in the same facility at the same time, every day. A similar limitation may involve the use of outdoor fields by football and soccer squads.

Consequently, a practice schedule that involves facility sharing is commonly needed. In many schools, scheduling sports practices for multiple programs is a collaborative effort of the athletic director and head coaches during specific sports seasons. In other school districts, a committee of administrators, physical education teachers, and coaches may be assigned the responsibility of developing practice schedules that are fair for all sports.

In schools with limited athletic facilities, teams may be forced to regularly practice in different locations and at different times of the day. This challenge may require scheduling practices before school or in the evenings as well as immediately after school. Scheduling athletic facilities is particularly challenging during seasons that include practices and competitions for several sports. A protocol is necessary to equitably provide access for multiple user groups (Hoch 2002).

The initial task of facility scheduling is establishing priorities. Sports facilities are generally scheduled for use outside of the school day according to a progression that is similar to the following:

1. In-season athletic programs before out-of-season sports
2. Varsity sports contests before subvarsity contests
3. Athletic practices, with priority for varsity squads
4. Fine arts performances and school events
5. Intramural sports
6. Fulfillment of formal joint-use agreements
7. In accordance with memorandums of understanding
8. Out-of-season athletic programs (use may be regulated by the state association)
9. Occasional use by student clubs and organizations
10. School-affiliated organizations (e.g., PTA, booster clubs, Boys & Girls Clubs)
11. Community use of facilities (e.g., rental agreements)

A quick review of the school calendar reveals that most school events are scheduled in athletic facilities. Once conflicting events have been identified, coaches will be aware of the facility implications for scheduling practices. Many coaches prefer to develop practice schedules by focusing on a weekly calendar of athletic contests and practices. There are multiple factors to consider when creating a practice schedule:

- The schedule for hosting athletic contests and school events in athletic facilities will affect practice schedules.
- Equitable use of the competition and auxiliary gymnasiums by both genders is a must.
- Teams or squads that are scheduled to compete—either at home or away—don't need a practice facility on contest days.
- When both boys' and girls' teams are scheduled to play—either as a doubleheader or one gender at home and the other on the road—neither team needs to practice.
- Teams that compete one day—especially when they travel—usually prefer not to practice the next morning.
- Practices the day before a contest may be shorter.
- Preference may be given to teams that are preparing for an upcoming contest.
- Practice times for middle school or ninth-grade teams should consider that participants may depend on transportation from others.

School Programs, Student Organizations, and Affiliates

The principal's office typically maintains the schedule of school facilities usage during the academic day. Physical education classes, wellness activities, and open recreation during noon-hour are generally conducted in athletic and physical education facilities. When the principal's office schedules facility use during the school day, the athletic director will be responsible only for scheduling facilities before and after the curricular day and on weekends. In most cases, school-sponsored programs will have priority for use of school facilities.

The principal will also conduct numerous public events each year such as registration, back-to-school events, community meetings, parent–teacher conferences, student body dances, and graduation ceremonies. In addition to actual use, each of these events will require time for preparation and maintenance of specific facilities. Some major events may require special consideration when creating the school calendar. Other important school events can be coordinated with the schedule of educational athletics and activities.

Nonathletic programs generally meet and practice in facilities such as auditoriums, theaters, cafeterias, and large classrooms. Many practices or rehearsals for fine arts activities and student organizations occur outside of the school day.

On occasion, school groups need to perform or host events in athletic facilities. Athletic practices may need to be scheduled in alternate facilities or at different times to accommodate the setup and hosting of these special events. Music teachers or drama directors may also need to schedule a class period in a gymnasium for rehearsal when a performance is scheduled for the facility.

Preferential use of facilities may also be extended to affiliates of the school district. For example, the community recreation department may provide the school district with a list of preferred youth sport and cultural groups under its auspices. The parent–teacher organization, booster clubs, and other organizations that support the mission and goals of the school district or educational sports are also candidates for school-affiliated status. School affiliates often avoid rental fees when using school facilities, but reimbursement of personnel expenses may be required.

Intramural Sports

In some schools, student participation in intramural sports is an important extension of physical education instruction. The intramural sports program commonly includes a round-robin schedule for several team sports. Tournaments for team and individual sports and special events are often components of the intramural program.

Intramural sports are frequently scheduled several times per week in the late afternoon, evenings, or before school, depending on the availability of facilities. Elementary and middle school intramurals are usually conducted immediately after school to avoid transportation issues. Where middle school interscholastic sports have a "no cut" policy, there may be minimal student interest in intramural sports. When the middle school class schedule includes two lunch periods, students may also have the opportunity to enroll in a specific sport or recreational activity during the period opposite their lunch period.

In some high schools, intramural sports are scheduled immediately after school. In that case, providing prime time for intramural play causes a delay in the start of practices for some interscholastic sports. Such a schedule also has implications for scheduling subvarsity practices and athletic contests.

In many schools, intramural sports are conducted either on weekends or after the conclusion of sports practices when there are no athletic contests. Some schools also schedule open gym, which offers a variety of recreational activities available to all students on weekends or free school nights (Krotee 2007).

Joint Use

A shortage of practice and competition courts and fields provides justification for the construction or renovation of sports facilities. When a referendum election is required to construct sports facilities, the potential of increased public access to school gymnasiums, fields, and pools may encourage taxpayers to vote for approval. Generally, joint-use agreements afford evening and weekend use for community recreation when school events aren't scheduled.

In some instances, school district and municipal officials develop a formal joint-use relationship. When a joint-use document is adopted by both government agencies, the details of facility availability and community use are specifically defined. Joint-use agreements are often characterized by an exchange of services rather than an exchange of funds. For example, the city may agree to develop parks and maintain athletic fields at school sites in exchange for free use of school gymnasiums and pools for youth and adult recreation programs. In some cases, the community recreation department also agrees to sponsor open gyms, intramural sports, and sports camps for the school district. The joint-use relationship may also include community cultural programs.

Memorandums of understanding (MOUs) may be employed in instances where one entity wishes to use athletic facilities that are owned by another entity. For example, some schools sign an MOU that grants use of a National Guard Armory. Conversely, a Boys & Girls Club may wish to use school athletic facilities. Cities, school districts, and local colleges may also share athletic facilities. Typically, the owner of the facility creates an MOU that defines conditions and responsibilities—periods of access, supervision, cleaning, and damages—of both organizations. Rental fees are often waived, but an MOU may include reimbursement for custodians, facility supervisors, and field preparations. Certificates of liability insurance are typically exchanged between parties to a joint-use agreement or memorandum of understanding.

Community Use

The promotion of construction projects for increasing community access to athletic and performing facilities may explain occasional misunderstandings about the conditions for use of school facilities. Some people assume that community use of school facilities is free of charge because taxpayer revenues funded the construction. Community members frequently don't understand that public access to school facilities results in increased operating expenses for the school district. Many business managers periodically determine custodial, utility, and support staff costs so that the school district will be reimbursed for the expenses related to community use of specific facilities (Floyd 2011).

Use of school facilities is often governed by a board of education policy that includes a schedule of rental rates. The policy may refer to equal access and risk minimization considerations. Groups are generally required to sign a facility agreement, provide a certificate of insurance, and submit payment of the rental fee before use. Local groups may be permitted to pay personnel expenses after the event. In most cases, rental agreements aren't issued to user groups until the calendar of school events has been confirmed.

School district policies should clearly define the terms of use and be consistently administered for all user groups. Facility agreements typically include the following:

- User group
- Name of contact person or event manager
- Name (and type) of event
- Facilities needed
- Date and time
- Equipment and services provided by the school
- Conditions of use
- Rental fee
- Reimbursement of personnel expenses
- Certificate of liability insurance
- Assumption of user responsibility and liability
- Hold harmless statement
- Signature of authorized school and user representatives

The requirements of rental fee, reimbursement of personnel expense, and certificate of insurability are often obstacles to school use by people or organizations. A joint-use agreement with the local recreation department may allow community users to schedule court time in school facilities at an affordable rate if the municipality agrees to provide supervision and liability insurance. Such arrangements may be compatible with the philosophy and purposes of community recreation departments.

Scheduling Contest Officials

The scheduling and contracting of contest officials is a primary responsibility and time-consuming task for many athletic administrators. Contest officials—who are registered or certified to referee, umpire, or judge contests in specific sports by the state association—are typically required for all levels of high school competition. Contest officials should be contracted as soon as athletic schedules are confirmed because officials are often much in demand. Lay officials are frequently assigned for middle school competitions (NIAAA 2009a).

There are several considerations when selecting officials appropriate for specific levels of athletic competition:

- State-association licensing and other qualifications. Open-book exams and clinic participation are often required to become a registered official and be assigned to regular-season contests. Sports officials may need to pass a supervised closed-book exam to be certified for state-qualifying tournaments.

- The residence of an official. It isn't appropriate to assign local officials for varsity contests in some rural areas. Because impartiality is a must, officials shouldn't be assigned to a contest if they have a relationship with either school.

- Because mileage is reimbursed, contracting area officials reduces expenses.

- Scheduling the same official or crew for numerous contests during a season isn't recommended because of the perception of excessive familiarity.

- Officials should be well versed on the rules, interpretations, and points of emphasis; work hard; and be properly positioned as per the size of the crew.

- It is appropriate to hire a crew of officials rather than individuals. Officiating crews are accustomed to specific assignments and to working together.

- Officials should be in proper uniforms, be well groomed, and arrive on time.

- When assigning new officials, athletic directors should ensure that the skill and experience of sports officials and players are comparable. For subvarsity contests, it is advisable to pair new officials with veteran officials to facilitate their development.

- Efforts should be made to assign officials who enjoy administering the competition and the interactions with players and coaches.

- Arrogant or confrontational people should be avoided. Crude language is unacceptable for a participant in educational sports.

In the past, athletic directors were responsible for assigning contest officials who were mutually agreeable to the participating schools. Varsity and even subvarsity officials are increasingly scheduled by a conference supervisor of officials or assigner from an area officials association.

Contest official assigners may also be responsible for observing referees. Assigner evaluations and coach rankings may be combined to make recommendations about retention and future officiating assignments. When a coach consistently ranks an official poorly or their interactions are difficult, it is advisable to keep them apart for a period.

Officials are commonly assigned from a conference-approved roster. New officials are typically added to the pool as a result of recommendations from coaches, athletic directors, and assigners. The supply of contest officials is inadequate to meet the needs of schools in many states. Athletic directors in college towns should actively recruit and schedule young officials who may continue to officiate once they graduate and join the work force.

Whether implemented under the auspices of an athletic conference or an officials' association, assigners usually conduct initial and replacement scheduling more efficiently and economically than the athletic director because of access to the entire schedule of each official in the pool. Contracts for athletic contests may be issued to individual officials or indicate "John Doe and Partner" or "John Doe and Crew." Conferences commonly determine the crew size and rate of pay for specific sports. Officials typically meet and travel to the competition together, and the driver commonly receives mileage at the state rate for reimbursement.

Athletic directors who independently contract sports officials are often challenged by a small pool of officials. The situation may be exacerbated when competing with larger schools for capable officials. In remote areas, schools sometimes deal with shortages by contracting contest officials early, paying higher fees and mileage, and providing lodging on occasion.

Commercial Scheduling Programs and Products

Electronic products are available that can coordinate multiple scheduling tasks for the athletic department. The operations of these programs have become increasingly friendly to users. Commercial scheduling programs typically offer time and cost efficiencies for athletic personnel through a combination of minimal data entry and the capability of automatic integration of many administrative tasks in real time. Operations such as contracting athletic contests and sports officials, creating athletic schedules and school calendars, and scheduling facilities, event personnel, and transportation are attractive features of commercial programs.

Commercial programs can also be utilized for tasks related to student-athlete eligibility, team rosters, department websites, and state association functions. In some cases, athletic conferences and all member schools use the same program to enhance operations. Special features of these programs include paperless contracts, multiple views of facility schedules, batch e-mail messaging, and automatic notices and routing. Most commercial programs are 100 percent web based and Macintosh and Windows compatible. Automated notification of schedule conflicts as well as game alerts and e-mail reminders to participating schools, sports officials, contest workers, and media outlets have made these products appealing to athletic department personnel.

Summary

The contemporary athletic director has numerous and diverse responsibilities, including several important scheduling tasks. The scheduling of sports competitions, school facilities, contest officials, event workers, and transportation occupies a significant amount of time for most athletic administrators. The topics discussed in this chapter illustrate the connection between different scheduling elements and emphasize the need for their integration.

The leadership and management duties of the athletic director may be the most varied and challenging of all school administrators. Athletic directors endure frequent interruptions and consistently devote 60 to 70 hours per week in service to participants in educational sports and activities. Because every event represents a deadline, stress is inherent to the position even when other pressures aren't evident. Many athletic administrators would benefit from professional development opportunities as well as organizational techniques that improve efficiency (see chapter 10).

Exemplary athletic directors often function as athletic facilitators who strive to provide necessary resources for athletic programs while efficiently managing athletic department operations. This combination of administrative tasks enables coaches to focus on developing student-athletes and preparing athletic teams for high levels of achievement. Focused attention to scheduling considerations by the athletic director also has the potential to significantly enhance other school operations.

CHAPTER 9

Transportation

Tim Graham, CMAA

The task of scheduling and coordinating sports transportation is an ongoing and important responsibility for interscholastic athletic directors. High school athletic directors typically schedule bus, van, or automobile transportation for at least half of all annual contests as well as some team practices that are conducted on off-campus sites. The result is that millions of high school athletes are safely, efficiently, and effectively transported to a variety of events and locations throughout the United States each school year.

Most observers would be surprised by the detailed procedures and requirements involved in scheduling athletic contests and transportation. Those protocols and guidelines have been developed to ensure proper and safe transport of young athletes.

The task of transporting athletes involves numerous individuals in an elaborate process that requires significant cooperation from all involved. The many aspects of transportation the athletic director must consider include local school and athletic department travel budgets; district, state, and federal school bus laws. Those guidelines that govern safe transportation of student-athletes to an event; district and athletic department limitations on travel distance and loss of school time; equity factors under constitutional and federal laws; and communication with interested parties are additional factors.

Travel Scheduling

Communication is the most important procedure when scheduling buses and vans. In many school districts, up to 50 percent of high school sports coaches are not employed at the schools where they coach. Thus, written communications by way of a faculty mailbox is not possible, and electronic communications become imperative in these cases. Getting the athletic transportation schedule to all relevant parties—the district transportation director or dispatcher, all in-season sports coaches, the athletic secretary, and all parents of traveling athletes—serves multiple purposes.

Generally, the task of scheduling sports team transportation is assigned to the athletic director. This assignment is made because of the director's comprehensive knowledge of the department's operational requirements and his awareness of the importance of communications about transportation with coaches, other faculty, parents, and athletes on a regular basis.

Indirectly, these multiple communications create a system of checks and balances: If one of the informed parties notices an inaccurate date or time or a date conflict, she can easily inform the athletic director; the problem can be quickly cross-checked and referenced for accuracy and changes made if needed. Other benefits include an accurate, concise listing of upcoming events for coaches, parents, the school or district website manager, and school and community media representatives. The information is also a planning tool for interested school parties such as spirit squads, pep bands, and cheer squads.

Athletic department personnel often send transportation documents by sport or activity only to those coaches or supervisors involved. Schedules should also be sent to the program heads (e.g., directors, department chairs) and a designated school administrator. Many athletic departments circulate or post travel information on a website or media site or initiate a phone-tree message system with a weekly plan that details all travel events. A review of upcoming travel dates allows all interested parties to confirm or modify transportation arrangements. Coaches should advise players of travel schedules in a timely manner to enhance squad communication and to ensure parents or guardians are notified as well.

Generally, the task of scheduling sports team transportation is assigned to the athletic director. This assignment is made because of the director's comprehensive knowledge of the department's operational requirements and his awareness of the importance of communications about transportation with coaches, other faculty, parents, and athletes. In some large school districts and athletic departments, one or more of the following may be assigned transportation scheduling responsibilities:

- A high school athletic secretary
- A high school assistant principal
- A high school extracurricular director
- A district travel coordinator
- A district business administrator

On any school day and some weekends, the athletic department transportation coordinator makes use of a variety of skills, methods, and procedures to transport numerous teams to various locations in a timely, organized, and safe manner. Whether the transportation assignment is performed in a public or private school setting, the scheduling agent must always consider the most practical, safest, and least expensive way to transport athletes.

Regardless of the type of transportation, athletic department personnel generally initiate a transportation request that includes pertinent information related to travel. An electronic scheduling program can greatly improve efficiency, reduce overall costs, and increase customer satisfaction. Numerous scheduling software programs are available. Choices can be narrowed through Internet research or by seeking opinions from other athletic directors. Sources of information and recommendations include the district transportation office, the state athletic director association, a professional growth organization (e.g., NIAAA), and the state interscholastic athletic association. Each may have suggestions based on usage, successes or issues, and personal experiences.

The type of scheduling program chosen must fit specific program needs. The athletic director should seek out a program that conveniently allows him to schedule a variety of events quickly and easily. These programs should integrate data such as the following:

- Travel dates
- Departure and return times in a readable format
- Number of athletes and adults who will travel to the event
- Team destination, which may require a map or GPS equipment
- Name of coach or supervisor, including a cell phone contact number
- Team dismissal time along with the roster of those traveling
- Group or sport category
- Whether the bus can be released upon delivery of a team to the competition site or whether a time charge will be required for holding the bus at the site
- Meal plan, if necessary
- Amount and type of equipment to be transported
- Safety concerns such as the need for undercarriage transport of equipment
- Special needs (wheelchairs, large equipment items)

When private-sector transportation providers are used, the transportation coordinator must find out from the bus company whether charges encompass departure and return times of the bus to and from the company headquarters or whether charges begin when the driver leaves and returns to the school property.

When calculating school departure and site arrival times, the athletic director must build in the time required for a squad to dress and properly warm up. It is also important to check with the host school to see what the earliest access times will be for usage of locker rooms and other parts of the opponent's facility.

An often-forgotten item when scheduling athletic transportation is the equipment that must be carried to a competition site. Sports equipment can range from football equipment bags to track items such as throwing implements, poles, and crossbars. It is important to inventory and account for all equipment that will be needed for the specific travel event and choose an appropriate carrier that can accommodate specific needs.

With regard to equipment volume, undercarriage space can be important. Undercarriage storage permits a team to transport all required bulky equipment to an event site without infringement on the seating compartment, aisle space, emergency exits, or number of available seats. If compartment or seating space is limited, a coach or driver should supervise the loading of all equipment and supplies so that safety and efficiency requirements are met. Some special considerations include separate transportation (vans where the seats have been removed, station wagons, or box vans) for javelins, pole-vault poles, cheer boxes, bats, hockey sticks, and other large equipment that will not fit into the undercarriage of a bus. Safety is a paramount consideration because many sports equipment items can become a missile or a barrier to rapid escape in the event of a highway collision or other emergency situation. If more space is needed, a cargo box van or similar vehicle could be used and an assistant coach assigned, trained, licensed, and insured to drive.

Some buses are designed for transporting large squads while also carrying large volumes of bulk equipment (e.g., football, track, and other teams that have extensive gear issues). Squad size and equipment volume are important considerations when scheduling transportation because larger buses may not be available during intense scheduling or rescheduling periods. Most scheduling programs have the capability to set a "trigger point" bus number and warning statement when a bus's equipment limit is approached or exceeded.

A frequently overlooked time frame for transportation schedulers is weekends and holidays. These are when most school offices are closed and athletic directors, secretaries, supervisors, and dispatchers are not available or are difficult to reach. A brief e-mail on the morning of competition or the day before holidays and in-service dates can be used to confirm weekend transportation schedules and times. This procedure can help prevent upset parents, athletes, and coaches.

Other important information that should be included in the e-mail communication is a listing of cell phone contacts for the transportation coordinator and the athletic director. This information should be made available to all coaches, drivers, and administrators in the event a bus does not arrive at school for pickup or return as scheduled.

Canceling or changing a previously scheduled transportation date must be carefully handled so that mistakes and other miscommunications do not occur (e.g., teams double-schedule the same bus, two buses arrive for the same team or contest, no bus arrives for a rescheduled date). A defined process for rescheduling transportation is a critical prerequisite to success and is one of many items to discuss at seasonal coaches' meetings. This process should also be part of the school coaches' handbook and discussed during orientation programs for new coaches. Procedures must be consistent with those of the school's transportation department and dispatcher so that changes are mistake free.

Transportation Options

In an era of pressured budgets, it is important to consider transportation costs and scheduling efficiencies. Doubling up on buses by several sport teams, use of vans, personal automobiles, and parent transportation are options that have developed out of financial necessity. Strategies are discussed in the following sections.

Bus Travel

The physical maturity of athletes as well as the size and number of seats required to accommodate a team comfortably are significant considerations when scheduling an athletic trip. A bus designed for elementary children may not be adequate for a varsity squad and could make a long trip uncomfortable and potentially unsafe. These decisions must be made on an individual team basis.

Because of bus and seating capacity variances, the bus selection process can be enhanced by visiting the district or private-sector bus facility to conduct size assessments of the bus compartment and seating capacity. Records of the satisfaction levels of various squad coaches should be maintained for quick reference when selecting buses of various capacities. A football team may not be transported comfortably or safely in certain carriers, whereas a cross-country team may be comfortable in a smaller carrier or may travel in a larger bus with multiple teams as a cost-saving measure.

The athletic director should check with the district transportation coordinator to determine whether seating size standards have been identified and coded in state law or transportation policies. If so, the appropriate code or size specification should be entered into the scheduling program database so the athletes are able to ride, study, and relax comfortably and safely. These considerations are particularly important for extended bus travel.

As the athletic director schedules contests and monitors travel, she must pay attention to the limitations of the transportation department when sports events are postponed or rescheduled. When events must be rescheduled as a result of inclement weather, the availability of buses and drivers may not be sufficient to support all travel needs for a particular date or dates. This can be especially problematic if the director is located in a multiple high school district and must compete with other directors for limited transportation assets.

If using an electronic scheduling program, the athletic director should enter a trigger number into the software database to identify the maximum number of carriers and drivers available on a specific date. These limitations become particularly important when a district-level scheduling agent is not directly associated with the school athletic department.

Passenger Vans

Besides being more economical, 10-passenger vans and SUVs are a practical and convenient alternative to full-size bus transportation, especially when transporting teams that are smaller in number.

School districts may purchase new or used federally approved vehicles for athletic uses. If owned by a school district, these vans are maintained by district maintenance personnel and scheduled for use through the district transportation coordinator. When initiating a rental contract, the athletic director should check with the district insurance carrier or risk manager about the need for additional rental-company insurance coverage for the driver and all passengers.

Charter Coach Service

For traveling an excessively long distance, a charter coach service may be not only more economical but also more comfortable than a regular school bus. Charter coaches often have amenities such as a lavatory and video monitors throughout the seating area. These additional amenities can save time by eliminating typical bathroom stops usually associated with long bus trips. The coach may also use this opportunity to show training or highlight videos for the upcoming competition or simply choose an appropriate movie to occupy the time.

These conveniences are appealing, but there are potential problems. Although charter coaches are among the safest vehicles on the road today and rarely are involved in highway accidents, when those accidents occur, they often involve significant injury and loss.

Before engaging in a lengthy, complicated contract negotiation with private-sector carriers, the athletic director and transportation coordinator should check with the local drivers to determine whether it is legal to use a charter service. Local union contract language may prohibit the use of charters except in specific situations. Checking to be sure private-sector rentals are approved by the local transportation department, American Bus Association, or United Motorcoach Association is an important starting point.

Creating a locally approved charter service list, as well as the steps needed to secure their services, allows for quick reference. This type of district-required paperwork can be completed in advance, along with emergency contact phone numbers, in case buses do not arrive when scheduled.

If private-sector coach rental is approved, the athletic director should read and discuss details of the specific trip with local legal counsel, the business administrator, and transportation coordinator. The following are among the important considerations:

- The cost of fuel and any meal and lodging costs for a driver that may be incurred on the trip
- Stipend for the driver or drivers
- The length of time any driver can be at the wheel before a defined rest period is required

Creative contest scheduling may save money and enhance comfort and overall satisfaction when arranging trips through a charter service.

Shuttle Buses

Another cost-saving measure is to schedule buses in a shuttle system. This method works well for both weekday and weekend events that are scheduled in relative proximity to the traveling school. Shuttle scheduling refers to making coordinated use of a regularly scheduled city, private-sector, or school bus route and drivers to provide dual service for athletic events. In this system, drivers and vehicles are used for both regular school or city routes and coordinated for dual use by school teams by the athletic director or scheduling agent.

There are two variations for this strategy. First, the athletic director and transportation director can stagger schedules so the same driver who provides service for a regular city or school route picks up and delivers a team to a competition site before the driver's regular city or school assignment. That same driver and bus complete their regular school or city route and then return to pick up the school team when an event is completed.

In the second shuttle method, the driver delivers a school team to a competition site, performs any contracted service other than a city or school route, and then returns to pick up the team when competition is finished. This method is most advantageous for sports teams that participate in weekend tournaments or events that are lengthy such as swimming, volleyball, and wrestling. In all cases, cost savings are realized because the driver and bus are used for regular services, and the school or district avoids paying for an idle bus and driver during the competition.

Cost savings may also be realized by avoiding holidays, weekends, and other off-duty driver hours. During these periods, driver contracts may require hourly compensation 1.5 or 2 times greater than regular pay. Not planning ahead or using a system that leads to scheduling buses in an emergency mode at a time when regular drivers are given overtime assignments will exhaust the transportation budget before the regular season ends. Coordinated schedule planning can help athletic directors operate effectively within a limited transportation budget.

Safety Regulations and Recommendations

Compliance with federal, state, and local laws, regulations, and district guidelines is imperative. Future changes to these legal directives will require ongoing research and communications. A valid source for this information is the district transportation director or other designee. These administrators are briefed annually about current laws and regulations that must be implemented before and during the transport of students. Other regulatory sources include the National Transportation Safety Board (www.ntsb.gov) and the National Safety Council (www.nsc.org). Their websites provide federal regulations and links to other useful sites.

An emergency contact card with the names, titles, and cell phone numbers of pertinent contacts such as the athletic director or secretary, transportation director, and superintendent (or designee) is extremely helpful to coaches throughout the season (see figure 9.1). This document can be especially important on nonschool days and during emergency situations (e.g., bus accident, stalled bus, or late return) when contact information must be immediately available. Coaches should keep this contact card with them at all times (e.g., in the first aid kit). The front of the card should contain transportation communications information, while the back could contain a list of emergency procedures that will quickly assist the coach in a time of crisis.

Once a squad is seated on the carrier, many states require a safety statement to be read or a simulated procedure to be conducted before departure. Coaches can assist by reading a safety script while making sure all athletes are paying attention as directions are given. This will help expedite the process, allowing the driver time to go through her mandatory readiness checklist.

Following is an example of a scripted statement that may be read before departure:

> May I have your attention please. For your personal safety, state regulations require me to ensure that all bus riders are aware of the emergency exits available on this bus. In the unlikely event that we have to evacuate the bus, you should be prepared to evacuate as quickly and safely as possible. Do not attempt to bring any items with you. Passengers should evacuate using the front entrance door whenever possible. [Point out its location.] In the event that this is not possible, you should use the emergency door located in the rear or side of the bus. If we need to use all exits,

the passengers in the first eight rows will exit out the front door, and the remaining rows will exit out the rear or side door. Please look around you to see where the exits are located.

Other state laws mandate that the script reader explain how to use the service door release, the emergency escape windows, and the roof hatches. In a manner similar to airline travel, it is important to ensure the passengers sitting at the exit rows are capable of opening the hatches or kicking out the windows. It may also be mandated to explain that the roof hatches are equipped with an emergency alarm and should be opened only in case of an emergency requiring evacuation.

Emergency Phone Numbers

Card Front

Name, Athletic Director:

Office Phone Cell Phone:

Name, Athletic Assistant:

Office Phone Cell Phone:

Name, Director of District Programs:

Office Phone Cell Phone:

Name, Transportation Director:

Office Phone Cell Phone:

Card Back

Emergency Procedures

- Have training kit checked regularly
- Have emergency clearance forms in training kit
- Require a doctor's note to return to play
- Keep your 1st Aid/CPR card current

In Case of Injury

1. Stabilize student from further injury and call 911 if needed
2. Call parents as soon as possible
3. If ambulance is called, have someone meet them
4. Send an adult with the student if transported
5. If ambulance/hospital required, call building administrator
6. Fill out accident report within 24 hours

FIGURE 9.1   An emergency contact card, front and back.

If the bus is equipped with seat belts, it may also be necessary to explain that in the event a seat belt will not unlatch, there is a seat belt cutter located on the bus (identify the location). Mandated announcements often include references to state transportation and personal safety laws requiring that the bus aisle and exits remain free of obstructions such as coolers, band instruments, book bags, or other items at all times. These items must be stored within the baggage compartments or secured within the seats and must not block any passenger exits.

The athletic director should review safety scripts and other emergency procedures, including any checklists required by the director's specific high school or middle school athletic department. Athletic administrators should establish and document clear expectations and operating procedures that are consistent with district procedures. It may be important to include these expectations in the school or district athletic code or handbook for parents and athletes. To ensure a comprehensive document, these policies should be developed cooperatively by the athletic director, the district transportation director, a panel of experienced coaches, and, when applicable, a private-sector transportation manager.

Under state law, athletes must remain seated while the bus is in motion. It has been scientifically demonstrated that passengers who are standing are not afforded the benefit of the engineered safety structure of the vehicle (National Transportation Safety Board 2009). More important, failure to enforce seating requirements could be a source of negligence litigation in the event an athlete is injured while standing at the time of a traffic accident. This no-standing policy must be enforced by coaches. It may be helpful to place a sign or placard on the bus in full view of all athletes and coaches.

Excessive noise should be curtailed during travel so that directions can be heard by all passengers when needed. Unnecessary and excessive noise is also a distraction to the driver and could pose a safety risk. In addition, as a public relations procedure, the supervisor or coaches should announce that all trash and personal items must be cleared from the bus as the team exits on return to the school.

Coaches or supervisors should have a personal checklist of items to be completed—such as reviewing emergency procedures, ensuring equipment is properly stowed, and checking cleanliness of the bus before and after travel—as well as directions to the event site and the number of athletes and coaches traveling. Distributing the coaching staff throughout the bus will help prevent horseplay, hazing, and other unacceptable behaviors. Doing this can also provide time for players and coaches to interact about contest strategy and tactics.

An accurate, organized travel checklist will save time and ensure that rider attention is directed to important safety regulations. It should be mandatory for coaches traveling without assistants or a certified athletic trainer to carry a fully stocked first aid kit. For travel to a remote site, a portable AED is

Planning for Potential Transportation Emergencies

Transportation is one of the more overlooked responsibilities of a high school athletic director. Yet, considering the small amount of time it takes to properly address transportation when compared to the risk management issues that could potentially arise, transportation emergencies should be carefully assessed and appropriate training implemented.

One of my first fall out-of-town football games as a new athletic director was in a nearby town less than 30 minutes away. The trip to the game was uneventful. The ride back was much different. On our way out of town after a hard-fought game, we proceeded under a roadway bridge, an underpass. At that point, debris was hurled at our school buses. Rocks and large chunks of wood smashed into the windshield and top of the buses.

The professionally trained drivers got all the buses safely to the side of the road. At that point, we implemented our well-rehearsed emergency procedures. To provide contacts for parents and media representatives, we notified school administrative personnel while the injuries were being assessed.

One of our drivers received cuts when the glass windshield shattered on her face and into her arms. The coaching staff began performing first aid techniques as previously trained. In the final analysis, a potentially critical incident was defused because of the emphasis placed on making sure we had covered all aspects of transportation safety, including unforeseen emergencies.

highly desirable but requires *current* certification of user competence. In the event advanced emergency care is needed, at least one coach should carry a cell phone with a fully charged battery.

A checkout and accountability system should be in place for school equipment items that could place a financial burden on an athlete or family if lost or stolen during out-of-town competition. Items such as contest jerseys and warm-up gear must be the responsibility of the individual player. This accountability information should be part of the preseason orientation and should be published in the school athletic code. Comprehension of the code should be acknowledged in writing by the athlete and parent or guardian. Along with equipment accountability, these procedures and guidelines should address travel behavior and dress expectations, emergency procedures, and contingency plans in the event of an accident or delayed return for any reason.

Local, State, and Federal Guidelines

Athletic directors and coaches are assigned a large number of responsibilities in their respective positions including arranging transportation of athletes and other activity participants to events and activities. Thus, for either district-owned buses and vans or private-sector carriers, critical considerations include the following:

- The statutory mandate for professionally trained drivers and maintenance staff
- The need for professionally maintained vehicles that meet state motor carrier standards
- Compliance with state standards for vehicles and driver capabilities

Due in large part to strict state and federal guidelines, school buses are held to the highest-level safety standards by state motor vehicle standards and legislative mandates. These standards and laws have made school bus travel one of the safest forms of transportation. Although school bus transportation has been shown to be safer than most vehicle travel, local school transportation departments and private-sector carriers must remain vigilant and committed to enhancing school bus safety. This can be accomplished through ongoing research of best practices, thorough driver training, and proper equipment maintenance.

State-Specific Examples of Safety Requirements

Certification of bus drivers is commonly regulated by state agencies charged with implementing state and federal transportation laws. For example, certifications such as a class C commercial driver's license (CDL) may be mandated by law in order to operate a school bus or a 15-passenger van. Because of risk management concerns, it is increasingly rare for coaches to operate buses unless they are certified as bus or van drivers by local and state licensing departments.

Examples of various state-specific driver safety standards include but are not limited to the following:

- Ongoing driver training related to the safest methods of transporting athletes is a necessity.
- School district drivers must pass both federal and state driving tests. In some areas this is an annual requirement.
- Drivers must pass a yearly medical exam (e.g., Michigan) before getting behind the wheel of a bus.
- Many school districts require a valid first aid and CPR certification.
- A current chauffeur driver's license (CDL), background checks, state patrol fingerprinting, and other mandated certifications are required.

- In Rhode Island, bus drivers must take at least 10 hours of annual training.
- West Virginia school bus drivers are required to successfully complete a 30-hour bus operator program.

This is a quick overview and sampling of current requirements for various states. Athletic directors and transportation directors should check with the state transportation department for specific driver certification and equipment requirements in their area. It is extremely important to strictly adhere to any local, state, or federal standards and guidelines in place for student transportation.

If a school or school district solicits competitive bids for private-sector transportation rates, proof of meeting driver's licensing and equipment standards must be stipulated as a prerequisite for bidding. Current proof of compliance with state standards should be required as part of the vendor's bid documentation. Your school district will have Request for Proposal forms for requesting transportation bids available for use upon request.

If coaches are authorized to drive sports teams as a cost-saving measure, they may also be required to have appropriate state licensure or type II certification, meet all physical exam and emergency care requirements, undergo regular in-service training related to student supervision and highway safety, and hold a valid first aid CPR certification.

District-owned buses must also be kept in excellent mechanical condition and may be subject to frequent unannounced inspections by the state patrol's or motor vehicle department's mechanical inspection personnel. In addition, all school-owned equipment must pass rigorous federal inspections and checklists. Thirty-five National Highway Traffic Safety Administration standards directly apply to the structural and mechanical safety of a school bus. A quick review of these standards through their website, www.nhtsa. gov, is strongly encouraged for all transportation coordinators.

Federal Regulations on Van Usage

In 2002, the National Highway Traffic Safety Administration outlawed the sale of 15-passenger vans to schools. These vehicles had been traditionally used for transporting smaller groups of students for school-related travel. Federal regulations do not categorically prohibit the use of vans to transport students and athletes. However, these legal mandates require any van of a capacity greater than 10 to meet safety standards applicable to those of a school bus. This mandate also pertains to driver training and general safety. Although most vans and SUVs are allowed for the transportation of athletes, these additional federal safety legislations and recommendations are the result of numerous rollovers in 15-passenger vans and the potential for catastrophic injury.

The National Association of State Directors of Pupil Transportation has indicated that the safety standards of a 15-passenger van are not in line with those of student-related activity travel (NASDPTS 2011). Although vans with a seating capacity of 10 or fewer do meet federal safety standards, a recent survey determined safety inconsistencies among state regulations on the use of 12- to 15-passenger vans. Twenty-nine states have passed laws or regulations that prohibit the use of these vans for transporting students to and from school-related activities. These states are Alabama, California, Delaware, Florida, Iowa, Kansas, Kentucky, Louisiana, Maine, Maryland, Michigan, Minnesota, Missouri, Montana, New Hampshire, New Jersey, New Mexico, New York, Ohio, Oklahoma, Oregon, Pennsylvania, Rhode Island, South Carolina, South Dakota, Utah, Virginia, Washington, and Wyoming.

This same report identified 21 states that do allow the use of 12- to 15-passenger vans for school activities: Alaska, Arizona, Arkansas, Colorado, Connecticut, Georgia, Hawaii, Idaho, Illinois, Indiana, Massachusetts, Mississippi, Nebraska, Nevada, North Carolina, North Dakota, Tennessee, Texas, Vermont, West Virginia, and Wisconsin.

This survey of authorized van use further amplifies the original findings of the NHTSA of 2002 (NASDPTS 2011). Although there are restrictions and recommendations for discontinuing the use of 15-passenger vans, the option of using vans that carry 10 or fewer remains a viable cost-saving choice. These regulations are federally mandated and therefore need to be adhered to only by public entities that accept and use federal funding in their school district budgets. It is imperative to check with the district transportation supervisor for adherence to this law.

Budget Management

As will be seen in chapter 14, an athletic administrator must consider budget ramifications when scheduling transportation. The overall athletic budget will obviously need to include transportation but cannot consume the entire pool of funds earmarked for athletics. As the cost of transporting athletes continues to increase, it is important to be creative.

Prudent budget management is expected of athletic administrators, even when scheduling travel to correspond with league schedules set three or four years in advance of the game dates. This expectation includes some form of controlling recurrent transportation costs and perhaps could include finding alternative funding. Sound financial management of the transportation budget during stable and challenging economic periods enhances public confidence along with that of the senior administrators and the school board directors.

Not every school district situation is similar, but commonalities exist that should be examined and implemented when prudently managing an athletic transportation budget. Leagues and conferences should include idea-sharing opportunities on their meeting agendas at least twice a year.

A growing and popular choice for funding athletic departments is the "pay to play" model. This model can be formulated to have a specific role that may include funding the transportation of athletes. This strategy along with fund-raising is increasingly used to balance transportation budgets. Athletic directors should exercise caution when implementing this model. In some cases, events are canceled and not rescheduled. In this case, patrons may ask that contributions be refunded. Conversely, contributors may also indicate a desire to contribute their unused funds to the entire athletic transportation budget for transporting athletes instead of a specific sport fund.

Transportation costs are typically one of the largest athletic budget categories, usually second only to salaries and benefits. Because there are some discretionary cost-reduction measures that may be instituted with transportation budgets, the following sections discuss some practical cost-saving measures currently in use throughout the United States.

Pairing Teams

A common technique used to create savings is to place two or more teams together on the same bus when traveling to the same contest site or to locations that are in reasonable proximity. This method can be implemented and enhanced through analysis, creative scheduling at the league or conference level, specific vehicle selection, and making sure the paired teams will be in the same area on a specific date and time. These arrangements must be discussed with the involved coaching staffs and the bus driver so all understand the intent and level of cooperation needed to efficiently coordinate efforts. It is important to plan and publish paired-team transportation schedules well in advance because squad numbers can be used to determine a compatible match. In addition, pairing opposite-gender teams may require dedication of various bus seating sections to a particular team, with coaches distributed accordingly and expectations stated.

Delivery or Drop Only

As a more austere measure, athletic directors have been forced to adopt a system wherein sports teams are picked up at school and delivered to the competition site by a school or contracted carrier. Upon delivery, the bus and driver are released from further responsibilities. In this system, parents or other adults are responsible for meeting and returning athletes to the home school after a contest.

If this method is selected, care must be taken to ensure safety and security of the athletes. To begin, the athletic director should consult with the school or district legal counsel and risk management team or insurance carrier to determine the risk exposure of the school or district when implementing this model. In addition, an attorney must develop a document used for preseason orientation meetings and in handbooks for coaches, parents, and athletes to clearly explain the responsibilities of all involved. Along with other contents of the school athletic code, the entire "delivery or drop only" process should be acknowledged in writing by a parent or legal guardian and kept on file in the athletic office.

Risk management efforts must be followed by extensive publicity through school and public media outlets. Preseason team and parent orientation meetings present another opportunity to ensure all parties understand the requirements. In this model, school personnel, parents, and athletes must make cooperative efforts to monitor the security of athletes after competition. After an event, one or more members of the coaching staff must remain at the competition site to ensure no athlete is left without a confirmed, safe ride.

Student Self-Transport

The least desirable and most drastic measure is to have athletes transport themselves to off-campus events. This measure should be clearly defined in terms of approved destinations. In most cases, out-of-town driving is prohibited, while in-town transportation may be authorized. In addition, there may be need to curtail student drivers from transporting other students to a competition or practice site.

In any case, the entire concept of student transportation requires extensive discussion with legal counsel, insurance carriers, parents, senior administration, and the governance board before implementation. Existing models include the following:

- Defining a suggested mileage radius within which athletes are allowed to transport themselves
- Completely prohibiting student driving as a school transportation policy
- Prohibiting student drivers from transporting other athletes
- Allowing convoys of coaches and parents to drive to and from various sites but requiring vehicle maintenance certifications and minimum insurance levels

In all cases, the athletic director must provide clear driving directions to the opponent's facility, the required time of arrival, any special or required group travel, and parking directions. In addition, school personnel should conduct pretrip research to ascertain the potential for imminent hazardous weather conditions or highway detours so that prudent decisions can be made and accurate directions given.

Reduced Rental Agreements

Another potential cost-saving choice is to create a business contract with a national or regional rental company for rentals throughout a school year.

For these contracts, a negotiated rate, unlimited mileage, vehicle usage limitations, and the overall process should be agreed on. This type of contract can be very effective if gasoline prices fluctuate significantly, although the rental company may include an escalator clause to account for changes in fuel price. This may be the most cost-efficient method in the sense that the rental company has responsibility for vehicle maintenance and compliance with federal and state safety regulations. Coaches who transport athletes in rental vehicles may be required to acquire certain licensure.

The school or district may be required to submit a driving abstract that clears district personnel to drive vans for athlete transportation. As a related matter, some states require a type II bus driver certification, which allows a designated school official to transport athletes in a vehicle that has a capacity of more than 10 persons but fewer than 16. Athletic personnel should make regular use of school and rental agency forms and agreements that document dates, purpose of vehicle use, usage times, mileage, number of passengers in the vehicle, destination, rental cost of the vehicle, and the number of gallons of gasoline used. The athletic director or transportation coordinator must ensure that specific state laws and guidelines are implemented in addition to all existing federal mandates when renting or using vehicles other than regulated buses.

Comprehension and Acknowledgment

A written comprehension and acknowledgment statement should be retained at the school or district that specifies parent or guardian understanding and approval for an athlete to transport other students or be transported in a student-driven private vehicle. This statement and comprehension acknowledgment may be especially important when a student driver or passenger has not achieved the state-defined age of majority. For efficiency and convenience, permission to transport and permission to be transported may be published on a single school form but should be reviewed and approved by the school or district risk management team and school district attorney.

Many states have enacted graduated licensing laws that prohibit newly licensed drivers from transporting any persons other than immediate family for a period of six months after state issuance of the initial (probationary) license. This law would supersede any district agreement. Guidelines for students or parents transporting athletes should be published in the all-school handbook, the handbook or code for parents and athletes, and the coaches' manual and should be an orientation topic to be reviewed at the beginning of any extracurricular season.

Ongoing Assessment

Documentation and data collection can be used from previous transportation budgets to create the next year's schedule. With previous knowledge and experience, an athletic director can be better prepared to face obstacles during the upcoming sports year. New and veteran athletic administrators must dedicate time to review and evaluate current policies and practices related to the transporting of athletes to school district–approved events.

Constantly seek innovative ideas and best practices to enhance safe student-athlete travel. Institute a process for assessing, monitoring, and adjusting the transportation program to minimize risk to athletes and coaches. Count on the fact that change is inevitable, and continuously research the most efficient and effective practices in the area of transportation.

Summary

Documented vehicle and driver safety, transportation bid solicitation methods, cost containment, resource management, efficiency in the selection of transportation options, gender equity in the selection of transportation methods, behavior of athletes during transportation, and accounting for the welfare of athletes following return from competition at opponent sites are important topics for athletic administrators. Following the guidelines presented in this chapter will help ensure that your athletes are safely, efficiently, and effectively transported to their events each school year.

CHAPTER 10

Technology

Roy Turner, CMAA

With the number of tasks athletic administrators face on a day-to-day basis, it is imperative that they utilize today's technology to its fullest extent. Huge amounts of information move through e-mail and digital communications each day. User-friendly software, applications, and other recent innovations in technology have potential to make the task of athletic administration more effective and efficient than ever.

Access to technology has changed significantly in the past few years. E-mail, the Internet, tablets, and smartphones are standard tools of the trade. Technology touches every facet of our lives, and professional administrators must continue to learn and adapt to it.

Still, some athletic administrators have been slow to embrace change. That's unfortunate because today's technology can make a person a better teacher, student, coach, athlete, spouse, parent, manager, or leader. What is first needed is a willingness to explore the available software, hardware, and applications and learn how to use them.

When technology is correctly applied, it provides a competitive edge and improves efficiency. Athletic directors must take advantage of and embrace the technology available or lose opportunities to communicate with administrators, coaches, athletes, faculty, parents, media, opponents, and others.

But technology itself is neutral. It's a tool, neither good nor evil. The payoff comes only to administrators and coaches who take advantage of it. The use of technology in athletic administration, and education-based athletics in general, can be of great assistance to those who grasp and maximize its potential.

This chapter is intended to help readers do exactly that. It highlights seven areas of significance to athletic administrators and details the technological tools that can be of benefit in each.

> Athletic directors must take advantage of and embrace the technology available or lose opportunities to communicate with administrators, coaches, athletes, faculty, parents, media, opponents, and others.

Professional Development

The educational value of any new technology hinges on the ability of teachers to use it effectively to engage students. Putting technology in the hands of administrators and coaches to promote lifelong, authentic, collaborative learning should be our objective. According to John Maxwell, "If you can help them to become lifelong learners, you will have given them an incredible gift" (Maxwell 1995, 136).

There is no doubt that technology has dramatically expanded access to learning opportunities. The Internet has all but eliminated the barriers to active learning and personal growth (time, distance, cost, equipment, and so on).

Faculty members and instructors should learn how to use technology without completely relying on it. Instead they should be able to identify and recognize the strengths and deficits of technologies and select the most appropriate delivery mechanism for their lessons (O'Quinn and Corry 2002).

Online Instruction

The ever-increasing diversity of the nation's student population, the advancement of educational technology, and competition in the workplace have combined to increase the popularity of online instruction.

According to *USA Today*, more students are turning to online classes in order to balance work, internships, and a personal life. For many people, online learning is associated with working adults or students with disabilities. But with internships, part-time jobs, and other commitments, a growing number of traditional students are choosing to take online courses in addition to courses in the traditional classroom setting (DeMaria 2012).

Nearly 12 million postsecondary students in the United States take some or all of their classes online right now. But this number will skyrocket to more than 22 million in the next five years, according to data released recently by the research firm Ambient Insight.

According to Ambient Insight's chief research officer, Sam S. Adkins, already some 1.25 million students in higher education programs take all their classes online, while another 10.65 million take some of their classes online. The two groups are still outnumbered by students who take all their courses in physical classrooms, which Ambient Insight estimated at 15.14 million as of 2009 (Nagel 2009).

Learning Technology for Athletic Administrators and Coaches

Athletic directors often need to renew administrative licenses with relevant course work from colleges, universities, or professional growth organizations (e.g., NIAAA). Similarly, coaches need to engage in ongoing training in areas such as risk management, injury prevention, conditioning, nutrition, tactics, and strategies specific to a sport. The following innovations allow personal home study through a variety of electronic media.

E-learning (electronic-based learning) allows people to learn anywhere, anytime, with a properly configured computer. E-learning can be CD-ROM based, network based, intranet based, or Internet based and can include text, video, audio, animation, and virtual environments. It can be a very rich learning experience that can even surpass the level of training received in a crowded classroom. It's self-paced, hands-on learning.

Blackboard is a web-based course management system that allows students and faculty to participate in classes delivered online or to use online materials and activities to complement face-to-face teaching. It can include course materials, discussion boards, online quizzes, exams, a grade center, and more. The instructor can provide links to groups, discussion boards, chat rooms, virtual classrooms, and other tools (e.g., blogs, wikis). Students are also able to e-mail instructors and classmates from within the course.

Increasingly popular and easily accessible, blogs are personal websites for sharing ideas and information online, packed with features that are as easy to use as e-mail. Examples include WordPress and Tumblr, which are both free software programs.

Wiki is a database of pages that visitors can edit live. Additional features include calendar sharing, live AV (audio-video) conferencing, RSS feeds, and more. RSS (rich site summary) is a format for delivering regularly changing web content that users subscribe to.

Web-conferencing programs such as Centra enable a group of people to interact with one another in a virtual online meeting environment. Centra can be accessed "live" anytime from anywhere attendees have access to a computer and an Internet connection. All meetings using Centra are automatically recorded, so those unable to make the live meeting are able to play back the meeting from an archive at a later time.

Taking and sharing notes has never been easier. Evernote provides digital note-taking software in both a free and premium version. A teacher or student can easily capture, save, and share notes (written and audio) and sync them across multiple devices.

Tools are also available to make presentations easy to create and share. Slideshare is a free application that allows users to upload presentations, documents, and videos; share privately or publicly; and receive feedback. SharePoint is Microsoft Office software that allows users to easily communicate and collaborate with colleagues and groups. Both are web based and accessible from anywhere. These innovations have potential use during coaches meetings and strategy sessions.

Technology tools available to support and enhance professional development are available across multiple platforms (e.g., Apple, Microsoft, Mac, PC, Android).

Technology Tools for the Classroom

These tools can be used with teams and coaching staffs when presenting scouting reports, new strategies, and techniques.

Interactive whiteboards are used in many schools as replacements for traditional whiteboards or flip charts. They provide ways to show students anything that can be presented on a computer's desktop (educational software, websites, and others). In addition, interactive whiteboards allow teachers and coaches to record their instruction and post the material for review by students at a later time. This can be a very effective instructional strategy for students and players who benefit from repetition, for students who need to see the material presented again, for students who are absent from school, for struggling learners, and for review for examinations.

PowerPoint presentations using TurningPoint and Poll Everywhere become powerful data collection and assessment tools that collect real-time audience responses and dramatically improve productivity and results for businesses or educational organizations. Coaches can insert diagrams, stream videos, and refer to archived material (e.g., old scouting reports) through the hyperlink device provided within the PowerPoint program.

Quality assurance is an obligation of all educators but especially athletic directors, who have accountability to senior administrators, governance boards, and the public. This is especially important when using technology innovations for instruction. Ensuring the quality of online instruction, the qualification of instructors, and the method of delivery should be the first considerations. Those who teach online courses should understand their roles and be able to adjust to the ever-changing world of technology and differentiated instruction. It is also imperative that instructors master the design and delivery methods for teaching online courses. Finally, sponsoring organizations and school administrators should focus on recruiting and retaining the most qualified and motivated instructors for their online courses. If instruction is to be moved forward, it is crucial for educators to engage in ongoing research and to implement innovative technologies.

Office Productivity

Years ago, routine interruptions in the office meant an unexpected phone call or visitor, and the U.S. or school mail was delivered once daily. Conversely, today's office workers are continually barraged with e-mail, instant messages, texts, drop-by traffic, blog updates, news feeds, tweets, websites with enticing links, and calendar reminders—and the phone still rings, people still drop by, and paper mail is still delivered. In response to these challenges, technology applications provide for expedited, multi-media communications for individuals and groups. Today's technology provides the ability to research thousands of topics using the Internet, access to live streaming video demonstrations, budget development templates, and a convenient means of filing historical information. One of the greatest benefits of technology is the capability to pull compact yet detailed information efficiently and in a timely manner.

The following are useful technology applications to improve office productivity.

Online file sharing: Online file sharing ("cloud storage") allows online storage of everything from documents to photos to videos. It is especially useful as a secure source when working out contracts or agreements with third parties. Access is provided to multiple people and companies without compromising local internal IT (information technology) security. Dropbox is the most popular cloud service, but other alternatives include Amazon, Google Drive, and iCloud. Using "the cloud" means that a coach or athletic director can have access to free storage, numerous personal-use services, and file sharing 24 hours, 7 days a week. Dropbox, an online storage site, provides two gigabytes (500 MP3 songs, 175 pictures) of free storage and allows users to synchronize all their devices simultaneously whenever a file is uploaded or downloaded. Amazon provides five gigabytes of free storage. Google allows users to create forms, presentations, slide shows, surveys, spreadsheets, documents, calendars, and e-mail, all for free.

Electronic faxing: The once-ubiquitous fax machine is taking up less and less desk space in fewer and fewer offices. But faxing itself, the actual sending of documents back and forth, is still alive and remains a crucial tool for many programs. The Internet fax replaces reams of paper with PDF (portable document format) files. Machines are replaced with websites that allow users to send, store, and receive faxes from anywhere.

Business card scanners: Athletic directors and coaches are visited by numerous sales personnel, equipment reconditioners, transportation agents, and other entrepreneurs. Each usually carries a business card for future reference. A business card reader allows quick storage of these cards, uses portable tablet technology, and eliminates manual entry. There are several on the market, such as Business Card Reader (iTunes).

Document scanners: With the aid of digital scanners, athletic directors and coaches can easily manage receipts, business cards, and any other documents or scraps of paper they need to digitize. Numerous models and capabilities are available from any of several office supply outlets.

Technology Innovations Save Time and Money

Technology innovations have proven effective in saving time and money for ongoing tasks such as conference meetings, orientation and instruction of coaches, online instruction for professional growth, and graduate degree programs. The NIAAA has utilized TelSpan (www. TelSpan.com) for ad hoc meetings of its executive board as a major cost-saving initiative. The NIAAA executive board consists of representatives from eight geographic regions of the United States, and so travel for traditional meetings at the NIAAA home office in Indianapolis would be costly. Another commonly used tool is GoToMeeting (www. GoToMeeting.com).

The NIAAA has also used TelSpan to provide interactive streaming video instruction for its Leadership Training Program. During any instructional session, students from Maine to Hawaii may be involved. Some adjustments in the start times must be made to accommodate time zone differences, but the cost savings are immense. School districts in Wisconsin and Colorado have also used Skype to conduct personnel interviews at significant savings in time and travel funds.

The National Federation of State High School Associations (NFHS) makes its Coaching Principles program available in an online format, allowing people seeking NFHS coaching certification to access the curriculum from home (www.NFHS.org).

Ohio University at Athens makes use of Blackboard (www.Black board.com) for interactive instruction as part of its sport administration master's degree program, including streaming video and text readings. The university doesn't use live interaction at this time.

A number of school districts across the United States utilize various cell phone applications to warn of hazardous weather conditions. This technology can be an especially important risk management tool for coaches who work in off-campus or remote sites, where timely warnings may not otherwise be possible. Following are some of the web addresses where these phone applications can be researched:

www.weather.com/services/mobilesplash.html
www.emergencymgmt.com
www.weather.gov

Printers: Standard printer or multifunction printer? Multifunction printers often include a document scanner that can also work as a stand-alone copier. These specialty printers aren't much larger than regular office printers, but they're more versatile, especially when one needs to keep a copy of a letter, a bill, or any other important document. Inkjet or laser? Lasers are usually associated with office environments, where they produce sharp, smudge-free printouts quickly, quietly, and economically, but they can be just as useful at home or in a home office. In addition, color laser printers are now very affordable, and multifunction laser printers are also available.

Personal Professional Productivity

In this contemporary era, people work all day in front of computers. Because of the expanded capabilities of computer technology, it's easy to be distracted by items from the web or e-mail or social media—at the expense of work quality or project deadlines. In today's workplace it's absolutely fundamental to differentiate oneself not only with knowledge but also with an ability to manage time and make deadlines.

The development and availability of technology can use up time (e.g., junk e-mail, tweets, Facebook). But there are many simple and easy ways to implement techniques for improving efficiency at work. These skills will help athletic directors identify and focus on the most relevant tasks.

Prioritize Tasks

Athletic directors have many important tasks to accomplish that require organization and priority setting. The first thing these administrators should do each day is organize their list of pending tasks by priority (e.g., 1, 2, 3 or high, medium, low) and then select those that will be morning tasks and those that will fill the afternoon. As soon as a task is completed, they should mark it as accomplished. Each day, the daily "to-get-done" list must be reorganized and prioritized. Mind-mapping software can help athletic directors set priorities. (For more information, see NIAAA professional development course LTC 608, Management Strategies and Organization Techniques).

Wunderlist is one of several free task-reminder tools that can help athletic directors organize tasks and get a better view of what and how things need to be done. This application is free for all platforms and allows for collaboration and detailed task management. Another is Remember the Milk, a feature-packed app that allows the coach or athletic director to take a personal to-do list anywhere; never forget the milk (or anything else) again.

One of the simplest mind-mapping tools is MindMeister. Once logged into the service, the user can create a fully functional mind map using little more than the directional arrows and the "insert" key to add new nodes to the mind map. Additional customizations such as font size and node colors are available beyond the basics.

XMind is another free application. The interface is simple and intuitive to use. An athletic director can quickly move through an entire mind map with only a handful of keystrokes or jump over to the outline view for even quicker navigation. In addition to a basic mind map, one can also create fishbone, organizational, tree, and logic charts. Charts can be exported as HTML (hypertext markup language), images, or text. XMind provides a free account that allows users to share charts online or embed them into blogs and websites.

Athletic directors and coaches are encouraged to use digital time and task management techniques and software to automate as much as possible.

Manage the Inbox

For all electronic communications, administrators should manage the inbox in a way that expedites finding needed information. One method is to organize the inbox through folders (Outlook Folders) or labels (Gmail Labels).

If the message has a related task, add it to the to-do list or flag it (Outlook). If it is a meeting, mark it on the calendar; if it's a reference, print it. If it's something that isn't immediately required, archive it.

Google Calendar is a simple but effective calendar app with multiple features to help people remember important dates, create schedules, and synchronize entries across multiple devices. The coach or athletic director can set reminder tasks for future events and due dates (e.g., seasonal reports, monthly payroll, state-association eligibility) while also focusing on current priorities.

Athletic administrators should set a particular time each day to review and answer the large volume of e-mail they receive, and they should stick to that schedule as regularly as possible. Time management experts recommend establishing four separate time blocks each day to check e-mails and answering immediately only those that are urgent. All others should be filtered by one's daily task filter.

To help manage their e-mail, athletic directors can create rules. A rule is an action that a web browser performs automatically on incoming or outgoing messages, based on conditions the user specifies. Users can create a rule from a template, from a message, or using one's own conditions.

Sample rule conditions and actions can be found at the Rules Wizard: http://office.microsoft.com/en-us/outlook-help/create-a-rule-HP005242897.aspx. (For more information, see NIAAA course LTC 613, Advanced Computer Application Skills, "Outlook.")

Don't Multitask

Multitasking is the process of working on several tasks simultaneously, switching back and forth as time allows or as pressure demands. Efficiency experts suggest that multitasking is *not* a good idea. If one constantly switches tasks, a huge percentage of available time can be lost getting into the mind-set to solve each task. Some tasks require in-depth thoughts, while others require dialogue with coworkers. Jumping from task to task raises the risk of not finishing any. Limit the multitasking habit because it will end up jeopardizing productivity. Give each task undivided attention and do it once.

Use Office Applications

Microsoft Office (Word, PowerPoint, Excel, Outlook, Publisher, Access, and OneNote) offers essential tools that athletic directors can use to increase personal productivity. The athletic director can choose from thousands of templates, forms, applications, cards, spreadsheets, animations, and backgrounds.

The most common word processor on the market is Microsoft Word. Because it is so common, the .doc format has become the standard for text documents. Word files can also be the starting point for other files, such as PDF and HTML. (For more information, see NIAAA course LTC 612, Basic Computer Application, "Word.")

Athletic directors can use PowerPoint when visual information might be helpful, such as in preseason meetings with coaches or parents. PowerPoint is presentation software that is typically used to display slides during face-to-face meetings and presentations. It is also used on the web and with distance education technologies. Slides used in a live presentation may be given to others for later review. This often occurs by sending the PowerPoint presentation as an e-mail attachment or by posting the presentation on the web and providing a link to the presentation.

PowerPoint presentations can be integrated with live audio or video broadcasts or conferences. Slides are synchronized with the instructor's overall presentation. This can occur easily with many web and electronic communication devices. The sessions can also be integrated with prerecorded audio presentations that are viewed in an anytime, anywhere manner from the web. These presentations could also be e-mailed to students as a very large attachment. PowerPoint presentations might be used as a stand-alone lesson without audio. (For more information, see NIAAA course LTC 612, Basic Computer Application, "PowerPoint," and course LTC 614, Enhancing Public Presentations.)

Microsoft Excel is a commercial spreadsheet application written and distributed for Microsoft Windows and Mac OS. It features calculations, graphing tools, pivot tables, and a macro programming language called Visual Basic for Applications. Excel has the basic features of all spreadsheets, using a grid of cells arranged in numbered rows and letter-named columns to organize data manipulations such as arithmetic operations. It has a battery of supplied functions to respond to statistical, engineering, and financial needs. In addition, it can display data as line graphs, histograms, and charts as well as a very limited three-dimensional graphical display. Using pivot tables, the program allows sectioning of data to view their dependencies on various factors from different perspectives. Excel allows the user to search, sort, and filter information to run reports. Filtering in Excel provides the user a quick and easy way to find and work with data in a range of cells on a spreadsheet. Budget development and budget management are primary uses for EXCEL. However a number of data storage and reference items can be incorporated, such as equipment purchase dates and current inventories (For more information, see NIAAA course LTC 612, Basic Computer Application, "Excel").

Outlook is Microsoft Office's personal information management software. Microsoft Outlook allows searches in folders and manages the POP, IMAP, Hotmail, Exchange servers, and MSM. It also integrates e-mail which is a primary tool for most athletic directors. Built-in calendars, reminder notes, and reminder alarm tones are also features that can enhance the efficiency of busy athletic directors. The program is useful for storing data in different files. (For more information, see NIAAA course LTC 613, Advanced Computer Applications, "Outlook.")

The user-friendly Publisher program lets athletic directors create newsletters, brochures, fliers, banners, and so on. Templates provided within the program allow users to customize everything from content to color layout. This program is perfect for creating a weekly newsletter or a monthly calendar for a school program.

Student Information Management System (SIMS) (e.g., Powerschool) is a stand-alone system that athletic administrators can use to keep track of student data and to ensure student information is not entered more than once. All staff members will need training in order to use the software. Numerous reports can be run in this program including master eligibility, physical exam dates, attendance reports, grade point averages, and scholar athletes. Student data can be exported into a CSV (comma-separated values) file to be uploaded into scheduling software and AlertNow.

School administrators are increasingly under pressure to enhance school safety and security, increase parental involvement, improve student achievement, and build community engagement. AlertNow is an industry-leading rapid notification service designed specifically for the K-12 community. This tool can be used to send out messages to a large number of people quickly and effectively. AlertNow, a service of Blackboard Connect, is implemented in thousands of schools throughout all 50 states to provide a cost-effective, reliable, and user-friendly communication solution to educators.

With AlertNow, educational administrators and leaders can send out voice calls, e-mail messages, or SMS messages to students, parents, and staff. Establishing a reliable channel for communicating helps schools and districts share information effectively and efficiently. In time-sensitive situations, parents and guardians can receive information and details directly from the school. Although useful in emergency situations, AlertNow is also beneficial for sending out routine school messages, such as attendance reports, low lunch balance alerts, and event and meeting reminders.

Take Advantage of Time-Saving Software

Athletic administrators can use scheduling software (e.g., Schedule Star, rSchoolToday, LeagueMinder, SchoolsRus, DigitalTown, 8to18) to assist with game and event management, transportation, officials, game workers, and postgame and media reports. Most of these provide multiple calendar views (by day, week, month, season), are web based, and notify members of the school community when schedules are modified. The key to efficient scheduling is to enter the information once and be able to use it anywhere it is needed.

For an annual fee, the athletic management program Schedule Star puts all the information in one place. The Schedule Star Corporation provides websites and technical support.

The software company rSchoolToday makes web portal programs and activity and facility scheduling programs for K12 schools and colleges. The web-based activity scheduler automates all scheduling and administrative functions while also providing a very powerful web calendar for the whole school or district. It also shares schedules intelligently across the entire conference or league.

LeagueMinder simplifies the job of an athletic director and saves both time and money. Virtually every administrative and communication-based task is easier and more efficient with this user-friendly system designed to decrease one's workload.

SchoolsRus is a web development company. *Web development* is a broad term for the work involved in developing a website for the Internet (World Wide Web) or an intranet. This can include web design, web content development, client liaison, client-side and server-side scripting, web server and network security configuration, and e-commerce development. Computer websites are no longer simply tools for work or commerce but are used most for communication.

DigitalTown, a marketing and website development company, combines the high school name with the school mascot to capture the high school spirit in every local community. DigitalTown has purchased more than 27,000 high school domain names, of which 25,000 are in .com format and 2,000 in .net format, and now represents more than 99 percent of the high schools in the United States.

Stay Connected

Mobile telephones permit sports administrators to operate in the field on various outdoor projects or at league meetings while remaining immediately accessible by the department secretary or school administration.

Smartphones (e.g., the iPhone) are built on a mobile operating system platform, with more advanced computing ability and connectivity than feature phones. Today's models also function as portable media players, low-end compact cameras, digital cameras, pocket video cameras, and global positioning system (GPS) navigation units. Modern smartphones typically include high-resolution touch screens, a web browser that can access and properly display standard web pages rather than just mobile-optimized sites, and high-speed data access via Wi-Fi and mobile broadband.

All mobile telephones require installation of an operating system (OS) within the phone to enhance communications, functionality, and accessibility. The most common mobile operating systems used by modern smartphones include Apple's iOS, Google's Android, Microsoft's Windows Phone, Nokia's Symbian, Research In Motion's (RIM's) BlackBerry OS, and embedded Linux distributions such as Maemo and MeeGo. Such operating systems can be installed on many different phone models, and typically each device can receive multiple OS software updates over its lifetime.

Communications

"When we change the way we communicate, we change the culture." The truth to this axiom can be discerned from an overview of communications through the ages:

1. Drum signals
2. Smoke signals
3. Pony express and stagecoach
4. Electric telegraph
5. Telephones and short-wave radios
6. Television and satellite communications
7. Computers, personal communication devices, and specialized applications
8. Electronic textbooks, instruction, coaching, scouting, and data analysis
9. Facebook, Twitter, text messages

In the 21st century, communication comes in many forms. These include face-to-face interactions, a letter sent by mail, a handwritten note, a quick e-mail, a phone call, a text message, and a message sent through social media (Twitter) or a social network (Facebook). Although some administrators may be wary of utilizing these options, if social media and network sites are used in an appropriate, professional manner, they can provide information and data about local school sports programs that the public greatly appreciates.

Other methods for connecting to constituents and improving internal communications include cell phones, Internet access, e-mail, business applications, and social networking.

Text Messaging

Text messaging allows athletic directors to send a text communication from a mobile telephone. Cell phones are equipped with a keyboard to facilitate text messaging.

Athletic directors should think before they text, however. Questions to ask include "Should I e-mail this information instead?" "Would it be better if we spoke about this topic over the phone?" "Would a face-to-face conversation be more appropriate?" The last thing an administrator should do is waste time sending a text that no one will understand. The information to be communicated must be simple enough for a text message. Following are some best texting practices:

- Keep excessive shorthand for personal text messages only. Text shorthand is a completely different language that not everyone knows how to speak. If a word is shortened, make sure the recipient will know exactly what is meant. As a rule of thumb, if in doubt, spell it out.

- Keep text messages concise. No one wants to read a four-page text. If the message does not fit into one page (about 140 characters), either call or send an e-mail.

- Send texts at appropriate times. Keep business-related text messages close to working hours.

- Check for spelling and grammatical errors. Text messaging is a more casual mode of communication; however, do not embarrass yourself, the athletic program, or your principal by being too casual. Make sure to proofread the text before sending it.

Social Media

Social media includes web-based and mobile technology used to turn communication into interactive dialogue. Andreas Kaplan and Michael Haenlein define social media as "a group of Internet-based applications that build on an ideological and technological foundation that allows the creation and generation of user generated content. Enabled by ubiquitously accessible and scalable communication techniques, social media has substantially changed the way organizations, communities, and individuals communicate" (Power 2010).

Twitter is a communications technology that permits access to activities as they occur; thus a game result or a record-breaking effort could be immediately communicated to a large constituency. Twitter and Facebook are also viable and manageable social media conduits for sharing information and for promoting various athletic teams within the school.

Positive Impact of Social Media

One of the most powerful advantages of utilizing services such as Twitter and Facebook is that both provide *instant* access to content. An audience is no longer limited to sitting in front of a computer monitor and searching the web for data or updates about its sports teams. With social media, event outcomes, a change in dates, or an interesting update about a team, athlete, or contest can be conveyed to a large audience within moments.

High School Today reports, "Your school or team can disseminate a message with very limited resources. Without additional funding or personnel, information can be provided as often as a sender chooses. The school is in control of the message and no longer is at the mercy of the media in getting vital information to stakeholders" (Frombach 2010).

"Twitter may continue to rise or it may go away, but its characteristics—real-time conversation, instant links, and groups of followers—will affect the communications platforms that come after. There's a lesson in that for all of us in the media, for we must adapt to new technology, and not simply by putting the same old wine in new bottles. We need to adapt by creating our content in a way that is organic to those new mediums" (Stengel 2009).

Potential Negative Impact of Social Media and Internet Usage

A study by the University of Maryland suggests that social media services may be addictive and that using social media services may lead to feelings of depression and isolation by many students and working professionals (Ottalini 2010). Excess use of social media has also been proven to erode the time required to accomplish detailed tasks that require precision in development, reporting, and publication. Facebook is now the primary social medium for communication by college students in the United States. Facebook permits individuals or groups to place biographical information on the website and communicate with other members who have also placed their personal and background information on the site.

What to Communicate

Although there are several directions to take when using Twitter or Facebook, it is important to make the appropriateness of the material the highest priority. The following are examples of timely information that athletic administrators and coaches can share. These examples illustrate how such messages can keep members of the school community informed.

- Provide game, practice, and departure or return time reminders.
- Inform about cancellations, postponements, time changes, rescheduled events, and so on.
- Provide score updates—especially popular on Friday nights when community members or those living out of town want current information about their team.
- Share news feeds from local papers. It is possible to create direct links with newspapers when they cover or feature the school's teams.

- Convey honors and awards earned by student-athletes or teams. Local media often miss such notices or don't have enough room to print them.
- Any other relevant information an audience would like to see.

Cautions When Using Digital Technology

Be aware that all communications content must be timely. Because media clientele have become accustomed to receiving current data (often within the hour), the information disseminated must be fresh and new. If there is a delay in providing the latest data, viewership may drop off.

Keep messages short, basic, and to the point. These measures will minimize editorializing and will reduce the effort necessary to maintain outgoing messages.

Another issue of which coaches and athletic directors must be cognizant of is the perception some community members may have about Twitter and Facebook. What some people have read about social network mishaps or misuses may cause concern or hesitancy to join in. These concerns obligate athletic personnel to use appropriate information at all times and to assure all parties that the content will always be suitable for all viewers. The rule of thumb should be "Is a posting that is placed on Twitter or Facebook something all constituents would be comfortable reading about on the front page of tomorrow's newspaper?" (Frombach 2010).

Learning how to communicate with coaches, student-athletes, and parents in the 21st century is one way to keep all members of the school community in the loop. We live in an instant communication age, and the ability to positively communicate electronically has made the job of an athletic administrator easier. At the same time, the speed, the amount of information, and the lack of human interaction have created additional problems. Face-to-face communication is often the best format when dealing with emotional issues. We have two ears and one mouth. We should listen twice as much as we speak. Listen so people will speak, and speak so people will listen. That is true communication, and social and digital media might change our culture.

Marketing and Promotions

The high school athletic program is an integral part of a local community. The marketing and promotional roles of the athletic director or coach are to help keep the community informed about, involved in, and invested in the success of the program.

Most athletic directors and coaches accepted the job because they love sports, they enjoy working with athletes, and they want to give something back to the local school and community. Occasionally, the position requires dealing with unrealistic parents, handling personnel issues, resolving schedule conflicts, making the most of shrinking budgets, and promoting the value of athletic programs.

As a result of budget cuts, tax cuts, inflation, and competition for the entertainment dollar, schools and school districts have found it necessary to increase revenue streams to maintain programs. The current economy has necessitated supplemental fund-raising at all levels of interscholastic athletics. Marketing an athletic program is more important now than ever. Once a rarity, marketing an athletic program to a local community is now a necessity.

There are two goals for successful athletic marketing:

1. Develop personal relationships with community members.
2. Create enthusiasm for programs that enhances gate receipts and booster club activities.

Because of the World Wide Web and digital and social media, today's event and program marketing has shifted to interactive online software and user-generated reviews. Websites that once saw their traffic dominated by search queries are seeing an increase in traffic from social media and link sharing. Three elements may change the way sport administrators market and promote athletic programs and student-athletes: (1) social networks, (2) live searching, and (3) link sharing.

The Internet has brought about a cultural shift in marketing. Internet marketing (websites, newsletters, texting, digital signage, and social media) is an effective and inexpensive way to reach a large group of people. Creating and sharing videos through media such as iMovie, Photo Story 3, Animoto, YouTube, and Vimeo is an effective strategy that can create an emotional awareness for an event or a season.

Mobile phone marketing is a relatively new medium that connects people through texting, social media, and advertising. Visual networks such as Pinterest, Google+, Quara, Instagram, SlideShare, and Flickr are emerging applications that combine digital video and pictures with social networking. Marketing companies (e.g., DigitalTown, Foxwood Sports, Home Team Marketing) have emerged as vendors that provide integrated marketing, promotions, and branding potential. Return on investment (ROI) is based on branding the value of a program, customer service and satisfaction, and relationships (focused on customer needs).

A coach or administrator need not be a technology or Internet expert, but it is essential to be alert to emerging trends and what is happening in the IT world. It is not necessary to implement or embrace every new technology or fad as it is developed. However, one must not be resistant or reluctant to embrace change in the case of new technology that can rapidly change an athletic program.

Website (Building the Brand)

Web addresses are effective because they are short, memorable, and directly tied to the brand (e.g., school identity). The athletic administrator should keep the athletic department web address short, purchase the .net and .org versions, and research search engine optimization to help drive traffic to the school sports department site.

The web address or URL (uniform resource locator) is essentially a name to identify an address on the Internet. The first step is to find a domain registrar (e.g., GoDaddy.com, Register.com, Maddogdomains.com) where one buys and registers a school URL.

Begin with the department goals in mind. Will there be an adequate number of advertisers? Will products sell through site-based e-commerce (spirit wear, season tickets, banquet tickets, ticket packages, tournament tickets, and so on) on the department site? What type of content will be posted, and how will this information be formatted?

Great content, however, drives the message forward, engages site visitors, and creates a conversation between the coaches and athletic directors and a world of current and potential supporters or sports enthusiasts. Great content will help communicate passion and core values with excellence. Assess the type of content interested members of the school community want to see (e.g., current schedules, directions to contests, scores, upcoming events, forms, NCAA information). Content for digital media may consist of videos, blog posts, links to newspaper articles, images and photos, surveys, polls, instant and text messages, and Twitter and Facebook updates. It is important to create, manage, monitor, and constantly evaluate the relevance of all content.

The best customer service is derived from providing what the customer wants, not what the site owner wants the customer to have. Show the site visitors how important they are, and how significant it is that they be a part of the local program.

Search engine optimization is the process of improving the visibility of a website or a web page in various search engines (e.g., Yahoo!, Google) or search results. In general, the earlier (or higher ranked on the search results page) and more frequently a site appears in the search results list, the more visitors it will receive from the search engine's users. To increase the number of visits, it is important to understand that search engines thrive on content. If high-quality, relevant content is posted regularly and is easy to access on the department site, then the World Wide Web will route more traffic to a school site through search results. Search engines index web pages by keywords, so make sure the site content contains all the important, specific words and phrases for which interested persons would search.

E-Mail Marketing

E-mail marketing is the most cost-effective advertising available today. It provides immediate access to the athletic department's entire database of supporters, and it is incredibly targeted and easy to customize. Team and family e-mail addresses are typically sought at the beginning of each sport season to facilitate notifications about changes in schedules, contest locations, cancellations, or other important information. Administrators should never assume someone wants to receive an e-mail, however. Always provide an "opt out" provision, meaning the customer can actively refuse the communication in the future.

With e-mail, the sender has an opportunity to send a message straight to someone's inbox. That means e-mail marketing should communicate the whole athletic department brand (vision, mission, and core values) and the department's passion.

Social Media and Marketing

Social media services capture the art of sharing stories and ideas through interactive communities such as Twitter, Facebook, and YouTube. Social media come in a variety of platforms, but in its purest sense, using social media is simply entering into an active conversation. News spreads infinitely faster and farther than ever before.

Key advantages of social media include the following:

- Allow direct communication and conversation
- Distribute relevant content and information
- Provide a service to interested community residents
- Encourage engagement and sharing (personal and digital word of mouth)

The true value of social media is about how followers share school information with their networks and friends. The question is not *whether* athletic directors and coaches should embrace social media; the question should be *how well* athletic personnel will embrace social media. Social media have changed the culture by altering the way contemporary society communicates.

Facebook has quickly risen to the top of all social media. No other social site has the credibility, market share, recognition, or sheer "cool factor" that Facebook has.

As an administrator or coach, it is important to understand that the recommendations people get through Facebook carry more weight than anything, because they come from supporters and members of the community. Personal recommendations always carry more weight, and Facebook is all about personal recommendations.

Facebook gives an athletic director two options for creating a page:

1. Create a personal page, which is designed for discussing one's personal life and connecting with friends and family.
2. Create a fan page, which is ideal for athletic programs and schools.

Athletic directors can use fan pages to inject the school brand and program into the social conversation and to promote student-athletes. Users simply need to click the Like button on the department page, and from then on, they'll see any updates or comments that are made on that page. Just as important, all their friends will see that they've "liked" the department page, which will carry the fan page into other social networks. It also gives members of the school community an opportunity to defend the athletic program in public on behalf of the school.

Generating Social Media Traffic

Pinterest is a content-sharing service that allows members to "pin" images, videos, and other objects such as events, interests, hobbies, and more to a virtual pinboard. Pinterest does not use written context to drive traffic; it uses images and video to engage the user. Pinterest allows its users to share "pins" on social media sites and to interact in a global community bulletin board.

Google+ is a social network that focuses on sharing and collaborating within subsets of groups called circles. Circles are simply small groups of people who can share information, such as friends, family, paraprofessionals, colleagues, and staff.

Using Video for Social Media Marketing

Athletic directors have several choices if they want to create movies for marketing purposes. iMovie imports video and digital images from digital video cameras, video discs, jump drives, and hard drives. Users can edit video and pictures; use video enhancement tools; and insert transitions, titles, and music. (For more information, see NIAAA course LTC 614, Enhancing Public Presentations.)

Another video program is Photo Story 3, a Microsoft product that allows users to create a visual story with digital photos and movie files that are enhanced through various visual effects. The software allows for the addition of narration, transitions, enhancements, and titles. Users can either import music or create their own music soundtrack. (For more information, see NIAAA course LTC 614, Enhancing Public Presentations.)

The free application Animoto allows users to input images and video clips to create a 60-second video. The software allows the user to input text, music, transitions, and effects, and the video can be uploaded directly to YouTube. (For more information, see NIAAA course LTC 614, Enhancing Public Presentations.)

Three Ways an Athletic Director Can Enhance Marketing in 15 Minutes a Day

Build a relationship and promote brand (local school athletic programs) equity with parents and other community residents through an athletic department website. On a monthly basis, write a 300-word blog or newsletter highlighting athletes or teams or discussing current issues. Starting this dialogue with parents is a key first step toward developing a long-term relationship between them, their extended family, their friends, and a local program. Build equity with other entertainment attractions through a proactive approach to fortify the reputation of the school and athletic program.

Develop a Facebook fan page. Most students and many parents are on Facebook, so it is an ideal way to reach them. Keep them involved on an ongoing basis by posting accomplishments, news, scores, trivia, and more right to their news feeds. This creates an ongoing informal connection with the local community, and anyone who visits will feel the enthusiasm. Don't forget to respond to "likes" and other comments.

Use Twitter for quick promotion. Twitter is the social network for quick updates and connections. Many parents use Twitter to connect with their virtual friends. Parents, students, and community residents want to be excited about the program, but they need information and details.

Social media and mobile technologies have improved collaboration and engagement in the personal lives of contemporary society. So, too, does social media have the potential to create new platforms of communication and engage community constituents within a local high school athletic program.

YouTube (www.youtube.com) is a video-sharing website owned by Google that allows users to upload, view, and share videos. YouTube displays a wide variety of user-generated video content, including how to develop and use videos, movie clips, TV clips, music videos, and short personal videos. Only registered users may upload videos to the site.

Another website that allows users to upload, share, and view videos is Vimeo (www.vimeo.com). Vimeo was the first website to support high-definition video sharing, and numerous musicians have made use of this feature.

Print Media

Two of the simplest templates for newsletters are Microsoft Word and Publisher. Administrators and coaches can use one of these programs or create their own templates using school colors and a logo. Creating a newsletter allows an athletic director to engage and inform members of the school community with timely and interesting content. (For more information, see NIAAA course LTC 612, Basic Computer Application.)

Digital Signage

Digital signage is a form of electronic display that shows digital programming, menus, information, schedules, upcoming events, videos, and slide shows. Digital signs in the form of LED (light-emitting diode) televisions, plasma displays, and message and video boards can be found in stadiums, gymnasiums, offices, and cafeterias. Numerous companies are taking advantage of the benefits offered by LED advertisement billboards, which have had a major impact on the advertising industry. LED billboards have proven to be among the most effective ways to attract the interest of spectators and have the potential to enhance local school athletic department revenues.

Most digital displays are controlled by personal computers or servers by way of proprietary software programs with monthly usage fees. The reduction in cost of digital flat-panel HD (high definition) televisions has made this an affordable alternative or supplement to stadium video or message boards. Athletic directors can engage the community and energize a program with digital signage. By including local business advertising in the digital signage program, the director may also develop a potential revenue stream.

Marketing Services

Foxwood Sports provides a marketing solution designed exclusively for high school athletic programs. This company works with athletic directors to reach merchants, raise funds, and enhance business relationships. By organizing and unifying the various marketing opportunities associated with the athletic program and by offering merchants one point of contact to promote their business, Foxwood offers an efficient way to increase a school's return on investment (ROI).

Home Team Marketing (HTM) is a network of thousands of high schools across the country united together under one platform. HTM provides clients with integrated marketing campaigns that occur at high school athletic events, customized to the school's program and community needs.

As stated before, an athletic director need not be a technology or Internet expert. Nevertheless, it is imperative that administrators keep a close eye on emerging trends. When it comes to using technology in the future, athletic personnel will all fall into one of these classifications:

1. Those who made it happen.
2. Those who let it happen.
3. Those who don't know what happened.

Prudent athletic directors will take advantage of the software and applications available in the profession by learning how to use them, embracing them, and working hard to promote their athletic programs and the value of educational athletics with this technology.

Collaboration

Administrators and coaching staff must work interdependently, sharing knowledge and experience to build consensus as opposed to working independently. To run an effective athletic department, the team must set common goals, and everyone must be mutually accountable. Through such collaboration, all team members can share their strengths and talents. The effectiveness of a collaborative effort is driven by four factors: (1) cost, (2) communication, (3) convenience, and (4) content management.

Staff members can use online collaboration tools (any technology that facilitates linking two or more people to work together for a common goal can be considered a collaborative tool), such as Google Docs, Wiki pages, blogs, and Twitter, to exchange ideas, distribute information, control and share workflow, and communicate. Technological tools for groups of people to work together include social networking, instant and text messaging, and web sharing as well as audio and video conferencing. The most common form of online collaboration is web conferencing using tools such as Cisco WebEx Meetings, GoToMeeting, Microsoft Live Meeting, Skype (LiveMinutes), and Microsoft SharePoint. Following is a list of useful technology resources.

3D Sports (www.3dsportstech.com)

8to18 Media, (www.8to18.com/dashboard/land)

AlertNow (www.alertnow.com)

Amazon CloudFront (aws.amazon.com/cloudfront)

Animoto (http://animoto.com)

Apex Sports Software (www.apexfootball.com)

Athleon (www.athleon.com)

AthleteMonitoring (www.fitstatsweb.com)

Athletic Trainer System (www.athletictrainersystem.com)

Cardiac Science (www.cardiacscience.com)

Cisco WebEx Meetings (www.webex.com)

Cloudon (http://site.cloudon.com)

Coachboard (www.coachboard.com)

CoachSmart (www.vanderbilthealth.com/orthopaedics/38467)

Coach's Eye (www.coachseye.com)

Colorado Time Systems (CTS) (http://coloradotimesystems.com)

Cramer Sports Injuries 3D (www.cramersportsmed.com/products/educational-products/sports-injury-3d%E2%84%A2-software)

Digital Scout (www.digitalscout.com)

DigitalTown (www.digitaltown.com)

DirectAthletics (www.directathletics.com)

Dropbox (www.dropbox.com)

Evernote (http://evernote.com)

Facebook (facebook.com)

FinishLynx (http://finishlynx.com)

FirstDown Playbook (http://itunes.apple.com/us/app/firstdownplay-book/id481108289?mt=8)

Foxwood Sports (www.foxwoodsports.com)

FreeConference (www.freeconference.com)

GameChanger (www.gamechanger.io)

Garmin GPS watches (https://buy.garmin.com/shop/shop.do?pID=11039&ra=true)

Gmail Labels (http://support.google.com/mail/bin/answer.py?hl=en&answer=118708)

Google+ (https://plus.google.com)

Google Calendar (http://support.google.com/calendar)

Google Cloud Storage (www.google.com/enterprise/cloud/storage)

GoToMeeting (www.gotomeeting.com/fec)

HeartStart (www.heartstarthome.com/content/heartstart_featured.asp)

Home Team Marketing (HTM) (www.hometeammarketing.com)

Hudl (www.hudl.com)

iMovie (www.apple.com/imovie)

ImPACT (www.impacttest.com)

imPACT Concussion Awareness Tool (imCAT) (http://impacttest.com/imcat)

Intellicast HD (http://itunes.apple.com/us/app/intellicast-hd/id408451987?mt=8)

LeagueMinder (http://digitalsports.com/leagueminder-your-complete-athletic-management-solution)

LiveMinutes (http://liveminutes.com)

MaxPreps (www.maxpreps.com/national/national.htm)

Meet Manager (www.hy-tekltd.com)

Microsoft Live Meeting (www.livemeetingplace.com)

Midland (www.midlandradio.com)

MindMeister (www.mindmeister.com)

NOAA (www.nws.noaa.gov/nwr)

Outlook Folders, (http://office.microsoft.com/en-us/outlook-help/mailbox-management-3-file-your-stuff-in-folders-RZ102685240.aspx?CTT=1)

Photo Story 3 (www.microsoft.com/download/en/details.aspx?id=11132)

Pinterest (www.pinterest.com)

Poll Everywhere (www.polleverywhere.com)

Powerschool (www.pearsonschoolsystems.com/products/powerschool)

Remember the Milk (www.rememberthemilk.com)

rSchoolToday (www.rschooltoday.com)

Rules Wizard (http://office.microsoft.com/en-us/outlook-help/create-a-rule-HP005242897.aspx)

Schedule Star (www.schedulestar.com)

SchoolsRus (www.schoolsrus.co.za)

SharePoint (http://sharepoint.microsoft.com)

Skype (www.skype.com)

SkyScan (http://skyscanusa.com)

Slideshare (www.slideshare.net)

Sports Film Exchange (www.sportsfilmexchange.com)

StrikeAlert (www.strikealert.com)

SurveyMonkey (www.surveymonkey.com)

Tumblr (www.tumblr.com)

TurningPoint (www.turningtechnologies.com)

TweetDeck (www.tweetdeck.com)

Twitter (https://twitter.com)

Vimeo (http://vimeo.com)

WordPress (http://wordpress.org/download)

XMind (www.xmind.net)

XOS Digital (www.xosdigital.com)

YouTube (www.youtube.com)

Zoll AED Plus (www.zoll.com/medical-products)

Google Apps offers simple, powerful communication and collaboration tools for most applications, all hosted by Google to streamline setup, minimize maintenance, and reduce IT costs. Google Drive is securely powered by the web, giving an athletic director the flexibility to be productive from an office desk, on the road, at home, and on a mobile phone.

Cisco WebEx Meetings allows constituents to meet wherever and whenever it is convenient. Meetings can be recorded and replayed and can be shared with colleagues to ensure no one misses a meeting. Similarly, the program GoToMeeting allows directors and coaches to enjoy the freedom of online meetings with web conferencing that allows users to present, collaborate, and integrate ideas right from a PC or Macintosh computer. Athletic personnel can hold as many meetings each month as needed for one monthly fee. Microsoft Live Meeting is another easy-to-use and reliable web-conferencing solution that lets users connect up to 1,250 attendees with just an Internet connection and web browser.

Athletic directors who make frequent long-distance phone calls will benefit from Skype, a free web-chat software that can be downloaded to a computer. As long as the user has a webcam and a microphone, Skype makes it simple to share text, voice, and video with colleagues in any location. Skype can be used to conduct live candidate interviews at immense cost savings in travel and accommodations for job applicants.

LiveMinutes is a real-time collaboration tool that gives professionals the audio conferencing capabilities of Skype while providing interface technology to share and collaborate on documents and presentations. The maximum collaboration capacity is around 20 participants, with whom a presenter can share documents, PDFs, or earlier presentations while streaming a live video. LiveMinutes is a free program.

To use FreeConference (www.freeconference.com), the user enters a personal name and e-mail address and is instantly provided with a dial-in number and access code for immediate phone conferencing. The teleconferencing line is available 24/7, and there is no need to schedule or make reservations. Each conference call account accommodates 96 callers for an unlimited number of free six-hour conference calls. Administrators can also record and share the call with colleagues who were unable to attend.

Athletic Performance and Competition

Technology has brought about a significant change in the world of sports. Originally, the use of technology in sports faced resistance because it was widely believed it would slow down or take away from sports competition. Instant replay capability and analysis of officiating calls have shown this assumption to be incorrect. Technology, when applied correctly, can help coaches and athletes improve performance.

Visual Learners

Today's athletes and coaches are visual learners, many of whom have been trained and educated via innovative technology. If coaches do not embrace emerging technology, they risk not only giving a competitive edge to opponents but also possibly inhibiting the development of their own players and their teams' performance. Today's coaching must be rooted in cutting-edge technology, best practices, and proven fundamentals.

Video Analysis

Technology has allowed coaches to improve players' tactical and technical knowledge along with analyzing their performance. Programs such as Coach's Eye, Apex, XOS Digital, and Athleon assist the coach and athletic director by recording performance for review and analysis.

Coach's Eye permits convenient, user-friendly review and analysis of individual frames within a contest video. Video is imported directly into the software, allowing for slow-motion, frame-by-frame, or fast-forward analysis using the flywheel within the program. Coach's Eye also has a built-in telestrator and allows for audio comments to create a video for feedback.

APEX Sports Software offers football video-editing software that can be used at all competitive levels. It is one of the premier video editors for scouting and for developing highlight films, specific football reports (offense, defense, kicking), and video cutups. Apex's patented voice-recognition software allows users to quickly add voice-over to video while breaking down game film.

XOS Digital is a leading provider of content management solutions and digital media services for collegiate and professional sports organizations. XOS Thunder provides high-definition video at a decreased file size, which decreases time spent capturing, editing, and distributing practice and game footage used by the coaching staff. The system allows coaches to enter data and share reports with video on a shared network. Reports are customizable with playlists, graphics, play drawing, video skills, and cross-tabs to related information (e.g., team defense cross-tabbed to an individual player's defensive techniques).

Finally, Athleon enhances athlete learning through visualization and interactive technology to improve game-day performance. The Athleon Playbook feature is perfect for today's players, many of whom have been raised and educated via innovative technology. The software is simple to use and very effective for showing the progression of a play along with real movement and timing for better visualization and learning.

Game-Film Exchange

Coaches are now able to exchange game film online (e.g., Hudl, Sports Film Exchange) rather than meeting and sharing analog or digital video face to face. Password-protected software allows coaches to view game and practice video on a secure site. Coaches can cut, edit, and convert the video format to reduce storage requirements.

Hudl makes videos, play diagrams, and coaching presentations securely available to an entire team or coaching staff over the Internet. Sports Film Exchange allows users to easily upload and share games from any computer that has broadband Internet access. Using Sports Film Exchange, coaches are able to share game film without having to copy games to VHS tapes or DVDs and send them through the mail.

Proprietary Training Equipment

The next generation of training equipment will use proprietary technology to train coaches; instruct and condition players; and measure explosive power, dynamic stability, sustainability, endurance, speed, and quickness. Because of today's visual learners, and the need for immediate feedback, video feedback is essential for accelerating the process of learning sport skills, optimizing practice, and enhancing the athletes' training progress. Most of the software and applications have been designed by administrators or coaches with extensive experience in the profession. Athletic directors should consider proprietary training technology for their coaches.

Coachboard is designed to be used on an interactive whiteboard; however, all applications and software can run on a laptop or desktop computer. The following tools are available on Coachboard:

- Play design
- Scouting reports
- Depth charts
- Team and individual statistics
- Scouting scheduling

3D Sports has added 3D PlayBook to its line of sports software products. 3D PlayBook is a powerful and affordable tool for competitive programs at all levels. A coach simply draws plays in the system or imports drawings from other popular drawing systems, and with the click of a mouse, the coach and players can see the play run in 3D animation.

GPS watches (e.g., the Garmin Forerunner) provide a one-piece training assistant that provides athletes with precise information on speed, distance, pace, location, and route sharing. Most watches provide training software that allows users to download workout data for a detailed analysis.

Data and Event Entry Software

Software is available to help athletic directors track data and manage athletic events. Meet Manager for swimming and track offers an easy-to-use display, editing features such as drag and drop for entries and relays, scrolling browsers with in-cell editing, hundreds of reports with extensive export and customization options, extensive online help, the ability to import meet entries electronically from other products as well as the web, and much more.

In collaboration with Hy-Tek, DirectAthletics offers a web-based meet entry system that simplifies the meet entry and declaration process for swimming and track. The software sends instant e-mail entry confirmation receipts to coaches and allows real-time monitoring of the entry process. Meet results are available during and after the meet for rapid distribution.

Event Timing Systems

Colorado Time Systems (CTS) provides precise timing, scoring, and display systems for aquatics. Throughout the years, CTS has maintained a steadfast commitment to provide cutting-edge scoring and display products for all venues. Similarly, FinishLynx provides a sophisticated laser timing system that can be used for any photo-finish activity.

Statistical and Game Updates

GameChanger is a free mobile software app that enables baseball and softball coaches to keep stats, provide live streaming video plays, and share game summaries from a mobile device. GameChanger integrates with MaxPreps, Twitter, and Facebook to quickly distribute postgame reports. MaxPreps is a professional-grade communications tool designed to help athletic directors promote their teams. This free, user-friendly service levels the playing field by allowing every team in the nation to share schedules, results, rosters, and detailed player statistics.

Digital Scout was created by coaches for coaches. This app and program allow users to collect sports statistics, track performances, and analyze opponents and tendencies at any time during or after the game. The statistics-tracking programs are fully customizable and offer more than 30 in-depth player and team reports.

Athletic Training and Sports Medicine

The athletic training room is a place for planned, orderly assessment; treatment of athletic injuries; and rehabilitation. Having immediate access to proper equipment could be the difference between rapid recovery, extensive rehabilitation, or even death. This section describes a few of the technological tools that athletic directors may wish to invest in for their trainers. (For more information, see NIAAA course LTC 617, Administration of Interscholastic Sports Medicine Programs.)

Automated external defibrillators (AEDs) are electronic devices that deliver an electric shock to a victim of sudden cardiac arrest. Ventricular fibrillation may be restored to normal rhythm up to 60 percent of the time if treated promptly with an AED, a procedure called defibrillation. Models include Zoll AED Plus, HeartStart, and Cardiac Science.

A lightning detector is a device that detects lightning strikes in a concentric radius of up to 20 miles (30 km) from a competition or practice site. There are three primary types of detectors: (1) ground-based systems using multiple antennas, (2) mobile systems using a direction and a sense antenna in the same location (often aboard an aircraft), and (3) space-based systems.

Ground-based and mobile detectors (e.g., SkyScan, Strike Alert, CoachSmart) calculate the direction and severity of lightning and its distance from the current location. Ground-based systems use triangulation from multiple locations to determine distance, while mobile systems estimate distance using signal frequency and attenuation. Space-based lightning detectors on artificial satellites can locate range, bearing, and intensities by direct observation.

Hand-held lightning detection devices can be purchased economically and are useful for cross country, golf, track and field, and all other outdoor contests.

Injury-tracking software programs such as Cramer Sports Injuries 3D, SportsWare 2011, the Athletic Trainer System, and AthleteMonitoring can be useful for coaches and trainers. Information they should track includes the following:

- Individual athlete injuries
- Types of injuries
- Treatments and medications
- Insurance
- Referral and doctor recommendations
- Surgery
- Equipment sign-out
- Physical, history, weight, inventory
- Equipment issued
- Concussion response and management
- Databases and related reports

Software is also available for evaluating concussions. ImPACT is a 20-minute test that has become a standard tool in the comprehensive clinical management of concussions for athletes of all ages. The test battery consists of a near infinite number of alternative forms by randomly varying the stimulus array for each administration. This feature was built into the program to minimize the practice effects that have limited the usefulness of more traditional neurocognitive tests.

The ImPACT Concussion Awareness Tool (ImCAT) was developed to educate athletes, parents, and coaches about concussions and their typical signs and symptoms. This free, easy-to-use application contains educational material on the prevention of concussions and mild traumatic brain injuries. It includes a brief quiz to teach athletes, parents, and others involved in sports about concussions and to correct some of the misconceptions about this type of injury.

Emergency Alert Systems

The Emergency Alert System (EAS) is a nationwide warning system in the United States that was initiated on January 1, 1997. The EAS alerts the public of local weather emergencies such as tornadoes and flash floods. Athletic administrators and coaches can also sign up for local severe weather e-mails and texts through local media outlets.

A weather radio service (e.g., Midland, NOAA) is a broadcast service that airs weather reports. When the radio is on and tuned to the weather band, it airs both normal and emergency weather information. If the radio is off or tuned to another band, it automatically turns on or goes to the weather band for emergency weather information.

Intellicast HD is an app that allows a coach or director to pick a location and view current weather information, extended forecasts, hour-by-hour forecasts, local radar loops, storm trackers, and weather alerts. The app will provide temperature, precipitation, UV Index, and wind speed graphs.

Exit Interviews and Satisfaction Surveys

Help is also available in the event that an athletic director needs to terminate the employment of someone on staff. SurveyMonkey provides free online questionnaire and survey software, enabling users to create their own web surveys, create useful reports, and run data analyses.

Survey software can also be used to assess employee, parent, and student satisfaction with various aspects of a high school athletics program (See NIAAA course LTC 707, Assessment of Athletics Personnel and Programs). By using advancements in technology, coaches and administrators can improve personal performance and efficiency in daily operations and management.

Summary

Athletic directors must constantly look for ways to refresh or update existing technology to help them efficiently complete the multiple responsibilities inherent in the job, including communicating with members of the school community. This research may range from learning about new school or district technology requirements to incorporating new software or applications. In all cases, the goal should be to find out how technological tools can enhance efficiency by setting SMART (specific, measurable, attainable, realistic, and timely) goals to get more done each day. Keep exposing yourself to new ideas, new thoughts, new applications, and new technology.

Marketers promote product innovations that can transform professional lives, improve productivity, create more personal time, and enhance quality of life. New technologies are a powerful way for athletic directors to take their programs to the next level, from good to great. The director's willingness to embrace technology may be one of the biggest challenges of a profes-sional commitment. With more than 500,000 applications that improve the function of the iPhone and iPad and new versions of computer programs, continuing research of new hardware, applications, and product upgrades is a mandate for the contemporary athletic director.

CHAPTER 11

Contest Management

Gary Stevens, CMAA

For individuals who aspire to a career in athletic administration, the ability to plan and coordinate the details related to athletic contest management is essential. Often, the quality of the sport experience for both participants and spectators is a direct result of an athletic administrator's management of a variety of factors.

Contrary to the advice given in a best-selling book, athletic directors must "sweat the small stuff." An athletic administrator's skills, philosophy, and values are never more visible than when he manages a home athletic contest. Spectators entering a gymnasium, stadium, or other athletic facility for the first time develop immediate impressions about a school and its athletic program based on their perceptions of how well an event is organized and managed.

Versatility and organizational skills are required when managing home contests. Today's high school athletic director must be a "jack of all trades." In effect, high school athletic directors simultaneously hold a series of temporary or part-time jobs. While hosting a school athletic event, the athletic administrator plays the roles of event coordinator, box office manager, master of ceremonies, and spectator supervisor.

In this latter responsibility, the athletic director must always maintain poise and self-control in the event that spectators demonstrate unsporting, disruptive, or dangerous behaviors. Spectator management can be particularly challenging because many contests attract large groups of people and are scheduled during the evening, when the athletic director has already completed a 10-hour workday. Frequently, athletic administrators are required to make judgments while managing difficult personalities or disruptive situations when their energy level is lowest.

To ensure safe and orderly management of a sports event, many athletic administrators develop venue- and sport-specific checklists. These lists cover many components, such as personnel assignments and locations, equipment needs, and procedures for supervision and for intervention in the case of unacceptable behaviors.

While hosting a school athletic event, the athletic administrator simultaneously plays the roles of event coordinator, box office manager, master of ceremonies, and spectator supervisor.

Evers (2012) observed that frequent turnover among high school administrators and contest supervisors requires athletic administrators to develop clear and concise plans for conducting events. He also noted that "written plans for hosting athletic contests ensure more consistency and higher quality supervision and management" (p. 14). To achieve those goals, Evers developed a handbook for conducting home athletic contests and placed it on a compact disc for distribution to event personnel. The event management handbook includes a departmental philosophy related to holding school athletic events, checklists identifying necessary activities before the contest, a list of game-day management strategies, and postevent evaluative procedures.

Contest Staff Management and Duties

Although the task of school administration can be a lonely job, the athletic director does not work in isolation on game day. Whether it is a contest attended by only a few dozen parents or a highly anticipated rivalry game that draws hundreds of spectators, hosting an athletic contest requires the assistance of a number of personnel in various support roles. Well in advance of the day of an event, athletic administrators must do the following:

- Identify the number of staff required to assist in managing the contest.
- Develop and communicate job descriptions for each person involved in the effort.
- Select and train people and substitutes who are willing and able to accomplish the assigned tasks.
- Provide contest supervisors with the necessary equipment, materials, and support needed to successfully perform their assignments.

At times, event workers may be assigned to supervise or monitor contest sites in relatively isolated locations. In cases such as these, the workers may experience a variety of pressures, including interactions with members of the public that can range from subtle to intense. Cumulatively, these incidents have the potential to affect the performance of contest workers. Therefore, throughout the course of an event, the athletic administrator should routinely check in with the people working in these remote areas to identify and resolve problems they may be facing. The morale of these workers may be a critical factor in their ability to effectively perform their jobs. Ultimately, their experience may also affect their interest in filling these positions in the future.

As previously suggested, the number of workers required to staff a particular contest will vary depending on a number of factors, including the importance of the game, the projected attendance, and the history between the participating schools. Following is a basic list of personnel assignments for use as a starting point when building a contest supervision staff:

- Ticket sellers and ticket takers
- Security or law enforcement personnel
- Game management positions (certified contest officials, timers, scorers, statisticians, shot clock and possession arrow personnel, stadium sideline workers)
- Certified athletic trainer services
- Emergency management services
- Public address announcer
- Host and visitor administrators (depending on the nature of the contest)
- Spectator supervisors

Each position requires a different type and degree of training and supervision, but all are integral to the success of the event. For a number of these positions, the athletic administrator is required to secure personnel with appropriate licensing or credentials to perform their assigned duties. For example, the state high school athletic and activity associations and local school district typically require the employment of state association–certified people to officiate state-sanctioned contests. Similarly, personnel who respond to contestant injuries may need to be certified athletic trainers. In either case, liability issues may develop for both the school system and an individual athletic administrator, particularly in cases where students are severely injured, when noncertified personnel are assigned to work.

Ticket Office

Ticket sellers, ticket takers, and gate supervisors must have two major personality attributes: (1) a disposition conducive to positive public relations and (2) unquestionable integrity. For most people attending an athletic contest, the people selling and taking tickets are their initial points of contact with the host school and therefore are important school representatives who can shape initial public impressions. Having a warm, engaging personality is an asset for any ticket seller, particularly when confronted by patrons who may complain about admission prices. A common approach and an effective strategy is to instruct personnel at ticket sale locations and entry gates to adopt a "Walmart greeter" approach by welcoming each spectator who attends an athletic event (Stevens 2011).

Ticket sales personnel are also in a position of trust because they handle and exchange potentially large sums of money during transactions with spectators entering the athletic complex. Ticket number and revenue calculation mistakes will occasionally occur, particularly when large crowds attend. Nevertheless, ticket sellers must take pride in and have a strong commitment to efficiency and accuracy, enabling them to process many monetary transactions in a short time.

The number of ticket sellers and gate personnel required will vary depending on the anticipated size of the audience. Athletic directors who host large events, such as football or basketball games; major tournaments; or rivalry games should consider utilizing multiple ticket sellers to reduce lines and to move spectators quickly and efficiently. In some cases, it is advantageous to establish express lines to service patrons who hold complimentary passes and season tickets or who have exact change for the number of tickets they require. In addition to adequately staffing the box office operation, athletic administrators should ensure that working conditions are appropriate and that ticket personnel have adequate materials to support their work. Ticket takers should be located in secure, well-lit areas and must have access to communication devices, such as radios or cell phones, so they can contact the athletic director or event security when necessary.

Ticket prices for adults, students, and senior citizens should be prominently displayed at all major entrance points and outside each ticket booth. To assist gate personnel with admitting nonpaying customers, copies of all complimentary passes being honored (such as faculty or staff cards, coaches' passes, and state association identification cards) should be posted at all entry gates and adjacent to each ticket window. Each ticket seller should be stocked with an ample supply of numbered tickets and start-up cash, including extra money in smaller denominations such as one- and five-dollar bills. Starting and ending numbers for all ticket rolls should be recorded on a standardized report form. It may also be helpful to have other supplies on hand, such as change aprons, writing utensils, pads of paper, and calculators, to assist ticket sellers in performing their work.

Athletic directors utilize a variety of sales and marketing strategies to facilitate ticket sales. Some schools sell season ticket packages that offer access to games at a reduced rate. This form of sales approach can be a positive public relations strategy and may contribute to increased attendance. Similarly, many athletic administrators conduct advanced sales for rivalry or championship events to reduce lines and to provide needed start-up cash. Using colored rolls of numbered tickets helps improve accounting efficiency and provides game management with an ongoing tally of attendance. In the event a school facility has a specific spectator capacity set by the local fire marshal or the original design architects, this information will be vital for making any decisions to limit attendance. The athletic director may also wish to communicate this information through media releases to participating communities in the week leading up to the competition.

Ticket takers and other gate personnel should arrive at the game site at least 45 minutes before the start of the event to receive materials and final instructions for the contest. The athletic administrator should monitor sales personnel to assess the need for additional workers or express lines, check on ticket and money supplies, collect large sums of money and large-denomination currency for safekeeping, and remind ticket personnel of the time the box office will close.

When ticket sales are concluded, the athletic administrator should collect all cash boxes, unsold tickets, and materials and place them in secure storage. The director must also follow all school, district, or state accounting procedures to ensure that gate proceeds are deposited and accounted for in a timely manner.

Security

When an athletic director prepares the annual budget for conducting home athletic events, a funding item of major importance is the need for security services. Although some governance board members or the public may see game-day security as a luxury, it is an investment that can pay huge dividends for an athletic administrator, particularly when a crowd is large or attracts unruly spectators. As always, the athletic director and other administrators in attendance are accountable for health, safety, and good order during an athletic event. Contracting law enforcement personnel and assigning them to strategic locations can prove to be an important preventive strategy. Their visibility enhances orderliness, and their involvement can be critical in the event it becomes necessary to remove a spectator.

Of major importance is defining the law enforcement authority and jurisdiction for police working at the contest venue. Local municipal police officers are usually appropriate for contests played in a city high school facility. However, if competition is conducted in a county facility or a state university venue, law enforcement personnel employed by these agencies may be required. Also important is whether contracted security personnel have law enforcement authority for arrest and citation issuance.

Whether utilizing the school's student resource officer, members of the local police or county sheriff's department, or a private security agency, the athletic administrator should meet with a designated security or law enforcement representative before the season to outline duties for all pregame, contest, and postgame activities. These responsibilities must be communicated in writing and reviewed with each member of the security detail employed for each contest. Among the security duties that may be assigned are the following:

- Managing vehicular traffic flow before and after the contest
- Directing drivers to available parking places
- Pointing out spectator access points to the athletic complex

- Assisting elderly or disabled patrons
- Intervening when spectators engage in inappropriate or unsafe conduct
- Patrolling assigned locations within the venue (i.e., walking patrols)
- Communicating with police assigned at the contest site or when support is required from local patrols
- Performing general spectator supervision responsibilities
- Assisting in the removal of or issuing citations to disorderly spectators
- Being visible in areas where there are cash transactions, such as the ticket booths and the concession stand
- Accompanying the athletic administrator when transporting money to the school safe or to a bank's night deposit box

Game Management

Athletic directors are also responsible for securing additional workers to assume various management, operational, and support roles during a contest. The number and type of management and support personnel vary by sport but may include any or all of the following:

- Clock and scoreboard operator
- Official scorers and statisticians
- Game officials and referees (shot clock and possession arrow in some states)
- Music coordinator
- Ball retrievers (field hockey, soccer, lacrosse)
- Football sideline personnel (line-to-gain crew and down-box operator)
- Track and field officials (starter, electronic and manual timers, clerk of course, relay exchange judges, finish judges, field event judges)

These workers ensure that a contest is conducted according to the specific rules prescribed for the particular sport. Because the performance of these people contributes to the perceptions of the public and other participating schools, athletic administrators must ensure that these important contest workers and officials are appropriately trained and qualified for the duties they must perform. In most cases, state or conference rules require that these workers be adults.

An approved officials' governing board recognized by the state athletic association is responsible for certifying officials in most sports. Certification by a board or state association signifies that the contest officials have successfully participated in the training and assessment program required by the state or national certification organization. Equally as important, certification of officials helps protect schools in the event negligence is asserted after a student injury.

To promote a sense of impartiality and provide more equitable opportunities for officials, many high school athletic conferences negotiate with representatives of each officials' board to designate a person to serve as the assignor for each sport. Athletic administrators should work closely with each sport assignor to ensure that all schedules are accurate and include the correct date, time, and venue. In addition, any contest date changes, postponements, and cancellations must be reported to the assignor along with the assigned game officials to ensure game coverage.

Sports Medicine and Allied Services

An essential support position for contemporary high school athletic programs is the certified athletic trainer (ATC). Although many state athletic associations require coaches to have training in CPR, AED, and sports first aid in order to be certified, those credentials demonstrate a rudimentary knowledge of the sports medicine field. Certified athletic trainers are graduates of intensive university programs that combine classroom experiences, school-based internships, and rigorous testing. Furthermore, ATCs are licensed specialists with expertise in injury and reinjury prevention and maintenance, sport nutrition, and rehabilitation. Once considered a luxury found only in schools with large athletic programs and significant financial support, athletic trainers are now considered an integral asset for all high school athletic programs. They are also important professionals required for comprehensive contest management.

Given the speed and intensity of their athletic practices and contests, today's high school student-athletes are susceptible not only to a wider range of injuries than ever before but also to severe or chronic conditions that may threaten to impair other life activities. In particular, certified athletic trainers can play an integral role in assessing and responding to potentially severe injuries such as concussions. Their specialized training enhances their ability to make critical decisions concerning an athlete's readiness for return to play. In addition, from both a child advocacy and risk management point of view, the protection afforded by employment of a certified trainer for games and practices has become an indispensable part of high school athletic operations.

Public Address Announcements and Music

Historically, the responsibilities of the public address announcer at high school athletic events were limited to reading the starting lineups, identifying substitutes, and describing plays during a contest. More recent and challenging trends in spectator management have mandated careful recruitment and quality training for the public address announcer. To address those needs, the Leadership Training Institute of the National Interscholastic Athletic Administrators Association has published a course of study (LTC 623) that focuses exclusively on the role of the public address announcer in the larger context of contest management responsibilities.

The Voice Above the Crowd is a guidebook that describes important components of the craft of game announcing. In this manual, author Brad Rumble asserts that high school announcers differ greatly from their counterparts at collegiate and professional events in a number of ways (Rumble 2003, 39):

• The major function of the public address announcer at high school events is to inform, not entertain. Introductions of players and coaches and game play-by-play announcements should be made with the same voice and inflection for both the home and visiting squads.

• Neutrality is key. Announcers who celebrate scoring plays for the home team while understating the efforts of opponents may create a hostile environment that is not in the true spirit of interscholastic athletics.

• Announcers should maintain a strong degree of authority and credibility with all participants and spectators. These attributes can become particularly important in the event of an emergency. When it becomes necessary to make an announcement related to a safety concern or to evacuate a facility, the "voice above the crowd" can be critical, maintaining order while providing spectators with safety instructions and information about routes of egress.

In addition to selecting and training the high school game announcers, athletic administrators have a number of related responsibilities in this area of contest management. Many athletic directors provide carefully worded scripts for pregame and contest announcements and provide their announcers with a binder containing scripts for various scenarios. These scripts establish guidelines for announcements that set a positive educational tone for competition (e.g., pregame statements about sporting behavior, introduction of starting lineups, announcement of scoring players) and set performance expectations. Other standardized announcements are provided for the closing minutes of competition and the period immediately after a contest. These include reminders for spectators to remain off the playing surface, warnings about the dangers inherent in climbing goalposts or hanging from basket rims, and instructions for accessing major exit points. In addition, the athletic administrator should provide the public address announcer with prepared statements outlining procedures in the event that it becomes necessary to evacuate the gymnasium or stadium.

Similarly, the athletic administrator should work closely with the game-day music coordinator to monitor and approve all music to be played over the public address system during pregame warm-ups and at halftime. Lyrics that contain profanity or innuendos have no place in a high school athletic event. For that reason, the athletic director must screen all material being considered for the playlist. To address this concern, many high school athletic directors have adopted the approach utilized in many college arenas: limiting pregame and contest music to instrumental selections.

In addition, the athletic administrator should work closely with the music coordinator to ensure that the music being selected for timeouts and other intervals during the game is appropriate. For example, when ice hockey players are sent to the penalty box, music selections that use words such as *bad* or *crime* would be in poor taste, as would be the themes to popular television programs such as *Dragnet* or *Cops*. Although some high school programs utilize themed music during the introduction of player at-bats during baseball and softball games (similar to professional baseball games), such an approach may create a perception of an unfriendly or inhospitable environment for visiting players and spectators and is discouraged.

Preevent and Game-Day Communication

An athletic administrator must demonstrate leadership and attention to detail by effectively communicating with head coaches, game officials, and other support personnel to create a sense of order and purpose. Similarly, using a variety of media to promote and communicate relevant details related to the scheduling, postponement, and rescheduling of athletic contests is an essential component of an athletic administrator's public relations efforts.

The communication process begins from the moment the event is scheduled. One of the fundamental components of proper contest management is ensuring that all parties involved in the contest have a common understanding of all details pertaining to that event. Among the people or groups with whom the athletic director should communicate are participants and parents, the general public, game officials, and support personnel.

An athletic administrator should communicate directly with her colleagues to confirm the essential details about the event, including the date, time, specific game venue, and bus parking details. Once confirmed, that same information should be communicated to members of the print and electronic media and should also be available through a number of formats, such as the school website and on pocket schedules and calendars.

Many athletic administrators utilize scheduling software, such as League-Minder or Schedule Star, to cross-reference schedules with other members of their conference and to provide the public with a master schedule of all athletic events. Others post directions to specific campus and off-campus game venues along with driving directions to other schools with whom they compete during each athletic season.

The athletic director should provide the maintenance and custodial staffs with a complete schedule of all home contests. In addition, the host school should ensure that locker room facilities designated for both the participating schools and the game officials are clean, secure, and stocked with supplies.

If possible, the guest locker room should be equipped with a whiteboard and markers to facilitate the communication and teaching needs of visiting coaches.

Courtesy is another hallmark of successful athletic administrators. An athletic director or his designee should greet each team involved in a contest being hosted once they arrive at the game venue. The director should introduce himself to the head coach of each participating school and communicate the following information:

- Location of the team locker room facilities
- Details related to securing that facility during the contest
- Location of the team bench
- Name of the athletic trainer and her location during the contest
- Availability of other game services (e.g., warm-up balls, water, and cups)
- Special activities, such as senior recognition events, homecoming extended halftime, or halftime youth exhibition games

Pregame protocols, such as the amount of warm-up time and the process for introducing the lineups or playing the national anthem should also be reviewed at this time.

A similar process should occur when game officials arrive at the venue. The athletic director should welcome each official shortly after entry and accompany them to the dressing room area, which should be kept secure at all times. Athletic administrators or their appointed game managers may need to gather contest officials before a game to review the following details:

- Information required for the payment voucher (e.g., address, social security number, round-trip mileage)
- Approximate date on which they can expect payment for services
- Names of table personnel (timer, scorer) with whom they will work
- Amount of time allotted for pregame warm-ups
- Special pregame recognition ceremonies
- What type of beverage (water, sports drink) they would like at halftime
- Halftime entertainment schedule and halftime extensions (with agreement of the opponent)
- Process for egress at halftime and after the game, including any security required

Many conferences have established pregame procedures for specific activities, such as football, baseball, or softball. If that is the case, that schedule should be posted in the opponent's locker room as well as in the officials' changing area and reviewed with all parties before the game. If an athletic administrator has established a schedule of activities before a contest, the athletic directors of opponent schools must be provided a copy of those procedures in advance of the event.

In addition to providing adequate locker room facilities for each participating school, the host athletic administrator should ensure that both the home and visiting team bench areas are arranged to accommodate the needs of the coaches and student-athletes. Among the items that must be considered are

- an adequate number of seats to accommodate all team members;
- floor or field markings to designate coaches' boxes prescribed by NFHS or state-association rules;
- an adequate supply of water, cups, and towels on hand at all times;
- receptacles for used cups and trash; and
- a designated row behind the visitor's bench for varsity or nonvarsity teams to sit when not playing.

Many high school athletic administrators have followed the lead of collegiate programs and provide a multitiered cart to each team for water coolers, towels, cups, and medical supplies. The audiovisual carts housed in many school libraries are suitable for meeting this need.

Members of the print and electronic media who regularly cover a school's athletic teams can play a critical role in promoting the overall school athletic program and contributing to public relations. Although the accomplishments of a school's athletes and coaches provide the material for print and electronic media coverage, the role of the athletic administrator cannot be understated. The athletic director plays the central role in establishing and maintaining positive associations with the media. He is, in effect, "the key ambassador for not only [the] department, but also the entire school system" (Stevens 2008, 23). Often, the difference between receiving positive and negative coverage is a result of the athletic director's efforts to cultivate professional relationships with reporters who cover high school programs. By using specific procedures and proven strategies, an athletic director can enhance the public image of the athletic department along with that of student-athletes and coaches.

Being proactive in assisting the media before a contest pays great dividends for the athletic department. The athletic director should provide all print and electronic media outlets within the coverage area with accurate game schedules and give notice of special-recognition events such as honoring a coach's achievement or a milestone victory. The media must also be informed of postponements, cancellations, and rescheduled dates.

One of the most important game amenities an athletic administrator can provide to both spectators and media members is a printed game program or roster for each home contest. Many athletic administrators provide local commentators with electronic copies of all rosters before the first game or post them on the school website. As a general rule, team rosters should include the following information:

- The names of all participants, with jersey numbers listed in numerical order
- Current school grade of each student-athlete
- Position(s) played
- Height and weight, when appropriate

Like any publication produced by a school, team rosters must be reviewed before printing to prevent incorrect spellings or other errata. An athletic director or sports information specialist may also provide a helpful service to television and radio commentators by including phonetic spellings for difficult-to-pronounce names and, if practical, game scores and individual player statistics.

Athletic administrators can enhance the image of their schools and programs by forming positive relationships with the reporters who come to their facilities to cover events. Making the extra effort to greet and welcome media representatives to one's school creates a personal touch that is generally welcomed by the reporter. A regular practice should be implemented wherein the athletic director checks the individual needs of a reporter, ensuring she has

- a current roster or game program,
- a reserved desk or access to a specific space to cover the game,
- a quiet area to complete the writing of a story after the contest,
- access to the Internet to file stories electronically, and
- water or a sports drink.

An underutilized aspect of contest management is the development and deployment of a media relations plan that incorporates the responsibilities of the athletic administrator, coaches, and student-athletes. Given that most schools do not have the luxury of a paid sports information director, most of the daily contact with the media is part of an athletic director's job description. Media relations can be enhanced by ensuring that game results and statistics are reported in a timely manner to all print and electronic outlets. This duty is particularly important on those occasions when there is no on-site coverage of the event. Whether the person responsible for communicating game results is the athletic director or a coach, that process should be clearly stipulated as a duty. Similarly, the person with this responsibility should have access to the e-mail and telephone contact information of all local newspapers and television stations.

The athletic administrator should design a media relations plan that addresses postgame interview responsibilities and protocols for coaches and athletes. Practical strategies for interviews should address ways to respond to challenging questions or after a disappointing loss. Proven strategies include complimenting one's opponent, having coaches discuss needed team improvements, and having players discuss a personal need to improve. These are media discussion points that reflect the goals of interscholastic sport and also demonstrate credibility and sincerity.

Spectator Amenities

An athletic administrator must always remember that he is playing host not only to visiting teams and coaches but also to local and visiting spectators. Given the price of admission to professional and college athletic events, professional theater, and even the local cinema, high school athletics offers an excellent value for one's entertainment dollars. Even though people today have various options for spending free time, it is not uncommon for high school athletic directors to host one thousand or more spectators at a given athletic event. Many athletic departments rely heavily on gate receipts to fund their programs. Therefore, it is essential that athletic directors maximize the potential for income from this important source.

One of the most famous phrases in the history of Hollywood is "If you build it, they will come." An athletic administrator seeking larger gate revenues must remember that creating a positive atmosphere of competition and fair play for parents, students, and other spectators will create a more enjoyable experience and ensure that all will feel safe during a contest. The following is a list of items every athletic administrator should include on a checklist of spectator amenities:

- Ample parking and ease of access to the game venue
- Designated spectator seating areas for home adults and students and visiting adults and students
- Concessions
- Restrooms
- In-game entertainment

Parking and Access to the Game Venue

The quality of the spectator experience begins on entering the school campus or game facility. A common complaint heard by athletic administrators is that the amount of parking is inadequate or is located a great distance from the contest venue.

In accordance with federal and state law, patrons who have disability license plates are entitled to unrestricted marked parking spots in proximity to the gates of the facility. These factors combine to mandate development of public access strategies within the overall contest management plan.

A number of practices have proven successful in this regard. When anticipating a particularly large attendance at a contest, it may be prudent to hire additional police or a security firm to assist in parking. Visibility of a uniformed figure who proactively manages game-day traffic creates a positive first impression and contributes to a sense of order and security for people attending the game. Parking attendants should ensure that only vehicles with disability plates occupy marked parking slots and should direct traffic in a manner that creates an orderly flow both before and after the contest.

It is also prudent to consider alternative parking arrangements if the expected audience could exceed the capacity of a contest facility's parking lot. Some athletic administrators utilize vacant fields or other nonmarked areas on the school property to handle overflow parking. Others contact neighboring businesses that own large parking lots to request access to these areas on the date of a heavily attended game. Athletic directors who anticipate that game patrons may elect to park on the street should contact the local police authority to obtain its input and approval.

Another courtesy service that has proven popular when accommodating the needs of older or disabled spectators is the use of golf carts or other methods to transport people to the contest site from the parking lot and back to their vehicles after the game. Being shuttled great distances to and from their vehicles enables these people to enjoy the excitement of high school athletics and is a public relations strategy that increases the chances they will return. This highly visible service may encourage others to attend who would otherwise feel unable to.

Spectator Seating

A simple amenity expected by most spectators attending an athletic contest is a seat that affords a clear view of the game and that can be accessed safely. Most indoor arenas and gymnasiums and outdoor stadiums have permanent or retractable bleachers. Athletic administrators should work with their district maintenance directors to ensure that all bleachers meet safety guidelines and have clearly marked aisles. Railings should be firmly mounted and meet all safety codes. As part of their preseason routine, many athletic directors inspect all bleacher planks to check for loose, wobbly, or broken floorboards or areas that may be slippery. Seating areas that pose a safety risk to spectators should be closed until corrective measures are taken.

As part of their contest management preparations, athletic directors should project the anticipated attendance for an event and determine if the capacity of the arena or stadium can meet that demand. Seating capacities for all facilities should be posted, and limits should be strictly observed. If it appears that the size of the expected audience may exceed capacity (both in terms of seating and standing room capacity), the athletic administrator should consider one or more of the following strategies:

- Acquiring auxiliary seating to handle overflow spectators
- Conducting a precontest sale of tickets and limiting attendance to the event to ticketed patrons
- Moving the contest to another facility that will be able to hold the expected number of people
- Implementing a closed-circuit television viewing opportunity in the school auditorium.

The last three options should be explored only as a last resort. Limiting the number of tickets may pose public relations problems, particularly for longtime spectators who may attempt to purchase tickets after the game is sold out. At the same time, coaches usually have strong feelings about the home field advantage, and booster groups rely on spectator business at the concession stand as a major source of revenue. Regardless, any changes in event ticketing or game location should be announced early and often through the media, in e-mails to parents, and on the school's website.

The seating needs of disabled citizens must be incorporated in the larger plan for accommodating spectators. Many large outdoor grandstands include ramps for easy access to designated disabled seating areas in accordance with the Americans with Disabilities Act (ADA). Similarly, modern indoor seating units incorporate cutouts into the bottom row for wheelchair patrons. If a facility's bleachers do not include infrastructure designed specifically for these purposes, the athletic administrator should contact the school district business officer, legal counsel, and buildings and grounds supervisor to expedite compliance with these ADA requirements.

Spectator Management

One of the most important responsibilities assigned to an athletic administrator is spectator management at home contests. A number of factors contribute to the challenges associated with this occasionally daunting and difficult task. The rising popularity of televised sports, particularly college basketball, has exposed both adult and student fans to a variety of crowd behaviors, some of which are unethical and inconsistent with the values that underlie educational athletics. Student sections demonstrating nonsporting behaviors and chanting inappropriate cheers and comments form the background noise associated with televised college sports. These groups, in turn, become the role models for impressionable high school students who seek to emulate them.

Some adult behaviors also pose challenges for high school athletic personnel. Parents who are invested both monetarily and psychologically in their children or who live vicariously through their athletic experiences have become increasingly vocal at high school events. Similarly, "helicopter" parents who do not trust the coaches who work with their youngster have become a challenge for many athletic departments. As a result, coaches, officials, administrators, and even student-athletes have borne the brunt of parent tirades. Some adults have taken their negative behavior to an extreme by accosting or assaulting game officials or members of a coaching staff after a contest.

Given these challenges, athletic administrators need to design a spectator management plan as part of their overall contest management protocol. A starting point for any athletic director is to communicate the expectations for spectator behavior to all potential audiences through a variety of media. Many schools publish spectator guidelines in both parent and student handbooks, on the contest programs, and on their athletic websites. Athletic administrators often meet with key student leaders or captains' councils to reiterate these goals and to enlist their support in promoting positive behaviors at athletic events. Similarly, parent orientation and information meetings and booster club meetings are excellent forums to communicate the school's expectations to adults. Crowd expectations should also be posted on signs throughout the athletic venue and announced by the public address announcer before each half or at any time spectator conduct becomes unacceptable.

Many conferences and state athletic associations have adopted guidelines for spectator behavior to standardize both expectations and consequences for any transgressions. Among the prohibited behaviors identified by these groups include the following:

- Using noisemakers during the athletic contest
- Holding signs or placards that could be used as projectiles
- Wearing inappropriate attire or being bare-chested
- Using profanity or vulgar references or gestures
- Posting inappropriate signs in the facility

Athletic directors should also recruit adequate numbers of staff for each event to ensure appropriate numbers of school administrators, faculty leaders, and security personnel are available. All supervisors should wear a badge, a tag, or clothing that identifies them as authorized representatives of the school. Distinctive clothing or identification can be important when addressing unacceptable spectator behavior. As discussed earlier in this chapter, the roles of security officers should be well defined and coordinated with school personnel, and there should be regular communication between security staff and the school administration throughout the contest. Game security officers should be strategically placed throughout the venue to maximize visibility and permit easier coverage of potential trouble areas.

Many athletic administrators designate specific sections for both home and visiting student spectators. Often these areas are located at diagonal corners of the facility to minimize the amount of contact between student groups and to maximize the opportunity for positive competitive cheering. For rivalry games, it is also advisable to station school administrators from the home and visiting schools adjacent to their respective student spectators. This assignment is extremely important for contests that attract larger groups of student spectators and that elicit more passionate (and creative) cheering. In many cases, the visiting athletic administrator and other administrators may be in attendance and can assist in supervision. If the design of a facility permits, having separate entrance and egress points for groups of student fans may be a sound strategy to reduce the possibility of conflict.

Some conferences have adopted creative measures for monitoring spectator conduct during an athletic contest. In both New York State and southern Maine, for example, athletic administrators have utilized a card system for addressing inappropriate as well as positive behaviors. Adults or students who demonstrate inappropriate behavior that does not warrant ejection are given a yellow card on which is printed a warning that subsequent poor behavior may result in ejection. Spectators who are ejected from a contest are issued a red card stating that all privileges to attend athletic contests at the school are revoked until a meeting with school administration occurs. Finally, athletic administrators reward students or adults demonstrating positive sporting behavior with a green card that can be redeemed for complimentary food or beverages at the concession stand.

Emergency and Security Issues

During every athletic contest the athletic administrator must anticipate, prevent if possible, and be ready to intervene in a host of situations. Some potential problems can be anticipated, but others will come as a surprise. Although there is no substitute for experience, training, and plans for managing specific issues, a leader's greatest assets are sound judgment and excellent instincts.

Among the challenges experienced by contemporary high school athletic administrators are transporting a student who has sustained a major injury, managing evacuations of large crowds of people, storming of the court or field by student spectators, and dealing with violence in and around the competition site.

Major Injuries

Athletic administrators should develop site-specific emergency plans in the event a student or spectator is injured and requires transportation by emergency vehicles. The roles of the athletic administrator, law enforcement personnel, coaches, certified athletic trainer, and students should be clearly outlined. The access points for rescue personnel should be kept clear of parked vehicles and communicated to the dispatcher when a 911 call is made. Time-saving maneuvers can pay instant dividends; the athletic administrator may consider providing the local rescue company with campus maps and keys to all locked gates. All stadium gates and entry doors must be numbered with highly visible signage.

Crowd Evacuation

Whether it is related to weather, a natural disaster, or a problem within a facility's infrastructure, sometimes it is necessary for an athletic administrator to suspend a contest and evacuate a facility. As always, being proactive is the key to ensuring that an evacuation occurs smoothly and safely. Athletic administrators should work cooperatively with the student resource officer and other colleagues to design plans to manage crowd evacuations for a number of scenarios, including fires, lighting failure, dangerous weather, bomb threats, and natural disasters. Those plans should be duplicated and stored in a number of areas on campus. Once the spectators arrive and an event begins, the athletic administrator or his designee is the point person for decisions to suspend the event and to initiate the appropriate plan.

Many state associations have policies related to the postponement or cancellation of outdoor athletic events because of lightning or other natural phenomenon. The athletic director should carefully follow all guidelines to ensure spectator safety and to reduce risk of liability, particularly if these policies are established as a legal standard of care. In the absence of a thunder and lightning protocol, the NFHS mandates resuming play no earlier than 35 minutes after the last thunder or lightning event. If lightning is imminent, athletic administrators should communicate the plan to the head coaches of all teams and game officials, identifying one or more holding areas for evacuations of all facilities, including those in secondary or satellite areas. Upon arrival at the holding centers, attendance records should be taken of all coaches, players, and officials. The athletic director assumes responsibility for communicating with all parties involved and works closely with game officials to determine if the contest will be resumed.

The public address announcer plays a key role in evacuation situations. When it becomes necessary to vacate a building or outdoor facility, the announcer should maintain a calm voice and provide clear, specific directions identifying available areas of egress and the process being employed for evacuation. The athletic administrator should provide the game announcer with scripts for various evacuation scenarios.

Crowd Control

The number of disruptive and violent incidents during and following high school sports contests has increased dramatically in recent years. Police visibility and intervention has become common place in some areas. The athletic director and school administration have a responsibility to ensure that spectators support their team in a manner that is educationally sound and safe for all. A number of contest management considerations and strategies follow.

A thrilling goal-line stand to preserve a lead in the waning moments of a football contest and a buzzer-beating shot in a basketball game that translates into instant victory are among the most electric moments in high school

Contest Management Best Practices in Action: Accommodating the Large Crowd

People who are responsible for athletic programs may, on occasion, be challenged with unusual contest management situations. When two of the state's best teams appear to be destined for a late-season meeting in a facility that may not accommodate the expected crowd, the host athletic director is confronted with a major decision: to play the contest as scheduled at the home site or seek out a neutral venue with a larger capacity. A scenario such as this may have major competitive, financial, and public relations implications for the school and program. A hasty decision made without a thorough review of important factors could result in dozens of spectators being unable to attend the contest. An example follows.

Two of Maine's top large-school ice hockey programs sharing the same home arena faced this situation in 2010. In the first meeting of the season in January, the official capacity of the building was exceeded by more than 200 patrons. City and arena officials notified both athletic administrators that attendance for all future contests would be capped at 1,000. Given the quality of both high school hockey programs and the expected audience for a rematch one month later, both schools deliberated playing at their small home arena or taking advantage of an opportunity to play at a 6,000-seat venue located 20 miles (32 km) away. The administration and the coaching staffs of the two schools worked cooperatively to identify and assess all factors involved in the final decision.

Despite the fact that the home rink had been booked and that no refund for that rental would be offered, both athletic administrators opted to play at a neutral facility, with positive results.

More than 1,300 attended the rematch, which offset the costs associated with the loss of the home ice rental and the rental costs for the neutral venue. What could have been an image and customer satisfaction issue was, instead, a major public relations and financial success for both schools.

sports. For the athletic administrator, however, they also create high anxiety and, without appropriate planning, a potential loss of control of the event.

The game-ending play that brings a crowd to its feet can also provoke spectators to leave the stands and erupt onto the floor or field to share in the moment with the players and coaches. When students storm the court or field, however, they place the participants, coaches, game officials, and themselves in a highly dangerous and precarious position. The resulting melee has proven to be a serious cause of injuries to anyone who happens to be in the way.

Athletic administrators should utilize a variety of strategies to prevent an onrush of spectators from taking place. The school's philosophy related to postgame exit procedures should be part of the athletic handbook and reviewed with parents and students. On the day of the game, security personnel or faculty assistants should be placed in proximity to student sections and should clearly communicate postgame expectations with those in the front rows. In addition, the public address announcer should issue reminders over the intercom that all spectators should remain off the playing surface at the conclusion of the contest. (A script with specific language to that effect should be included within the public address announcer's packet.)

Violent Incidents

Based on the situations in their individual communities, some athletic administrators have utilized creative options to sell tickets and simultaneously enhance the safety of all participants and spectators.

In Racine, Wisconsin, violence levels rose to such a peak that Horlick High School athletic director Jay Hammes adopted a system of mandatory spectator identification and online ticketing. After being shot at by members of a local gang just a few yards from the front door of his gymnasium, Hammes decided to act and established a program to counteract the violent culture of his community. "The most important priority for sport contest and activity managers," he asserts, "is public safety." Hammes adds, "As school administrators and event managers who work in a contemporary society characterized by increasing violence and litigation, we have no choice" (Hammes 2010, 19).

All spectators attending football and basketball games at Racine Horlick High School are required to purchase tickets in advance through the Internet and are admitted only after showing a printed copy of the online ticket and a form of personal identification. Gate personnel do not collect money. Their major responsibilities involve welcoming spectators to the game and verifying the identity of each person entering the facility with a photo identification. Hammes has found that this approach creates a more efficient and orderly method for managing the spectators, which has greatly reduced the amount of gang activity at football and basketball games.

In turn, both the NFHS and the NIAAA have endorsed Hammes' Safe Sport Zone online ticketing program.

Summary

Successful contest management is not unlike coaching. Multiple activities occur simultaneously and require immediate response and management. In many cases, athletic administrators who are former coaches can call on learned skills to perform game-day duties more effectively. Whatever mechanism an athletic director selects to coordinate the details of an athletic event, the strategy must be extremely task oriented, intensely proactive, and highly organized. At the same time, the director must be flexible enough to customize his plan for specific venues or contests and for changing circumstances.

Veteran colleagues can be helpful mentors who can provide ideas about best practices and assessing one's own practices. Experience is also one of the best teachers; strategies that have proven unsuccessful should not be viewed as failures but instead as learning opportunities. As Evers (2012, 15) observed, "Many of our concepts have been born through the fire of successful situations" and developed "through the school of hard knocks."

In the final analysis, the majority of amateur sport in the United States is funded and directed by educational institutions. Competition and spectatorship must be held to educationally sound and compatible standards.

CHAPTER 12

Legal and Safety Concerns

Lee Green, JD

One of the greatest challenges facing athletic administrators in the modern environment of education-based athletics is the demanding task of complying with the myriad of legal mandates imposed on athletic programs and those who lead them. Today's athletic administrator is the equivalent of the CEO of a sizable enterprise. To exercise effective leadership over all aspects of the organization, an athletic director must have a thorough knowledge of sport law and its impact on every component of the athletic program.

Sport law is a broad term that encompasses numerous categories of the American legal system. In recent years, five key topics within sport law have emerged from case law, legislation, and agency rulings that affect education-based athletic programs:

1. Liability for sports injuries and legal mandates for the safety of student-athletes
2. Compliance with the sport-related gender equity requirements of Title IX
3. Constitutional and civil rights of interscholastic student-athletes
4. Prevention of hazing and bullying in interscholastic athletic programs
5. Prevention of sexual harassment in interscholastic athletic programs

Athletic administrators must develop a thorough understanding of each of these five areas of sport law because each applies to education-based athletic programs. High school sports administrators must also apply the derived legal principles to the management and leadership of their programs. Further, the contemporary high school athletic director must continually monitor changes in each area of sport law as new court cases are decided, new legislation is enacted, and new administrative rulings are issued. Table 12.1 is an examination of the framework of legal compliance within each of the five areas.

To exercise effective leadership over all aspects of the organization, an athletic director must have a thorough knowledge of sport law and its impact on every component of the athletic program.

TABLE 12.1 Five Key Legal Concerns of Education-Based Athletic Programs

Legal issues	Objectives for athletic administrators
Liability for sports injuries and legal mandates for the safety of student-athletes	Understand the 14 broad categories of duties imposed on athletic programs related to the safety of student-athletes.
Compliance with the sport-related gender equity requirements of Title IX	Understand the broad Title IX compliance framework and procedures for performing a Title IX self-audit for a school.
Constitutional and civil rights of interscholastic student-athletes	Understand issues of freedom of speech, freedom of expression, freedom of religion, due process, and equal protection.
Prevention of hazing and bullying in interscholastic athletic programs	Understand the behaviors defined as hazing or bullying by court cases and statutes and comply with prevention mandates.
Prevention of sexual harassment in interscholastic athletic programs	Understand the legal definition of sexual harassment and comply with legal reporting requirements and prevention requirements.

Sports Injury Liability

One of the most frequently litigated claims in education-based athletic programs arises when an injured student-athlete brings a tort-based lawsuit against a school district and its insurers, along with district employees, in a chain of vicarious liability for the injury. School district defendants may include the superintendent, district athletic director, principal, building athletic director, head coach, assistant coaches, athletic trainers, and any other employee or person within the orbit of possible responsibility.

A tort is a wrongful act that causes injury to a party and for which the injured person is entitled to compensation. In contrast to criminal suits, tort lawsuits are civil causes of action through which the injured party asserts that the cause of harm resulted from

- intentional misconduct by the allegedly responsible party,
- reckless misbehavior by the tortfeasor (wrongdoer), or
- a lack of reasonable care by the wrongdoer.

Intentional torts, because of the high level of culpability by the responsible party, result in the highest damage awards from courts. Reckless torts, because of the relatively lower level of culpability of the tortfeasor, result in proportionally lower damage awards to injured parties. Negligent torts, those arising from a lack of reasonable care by the wrongdoer, result in lower damage awards reflecting the responsible party's lower level of culpability. However, even the lower damage awards arising from negligence suits may be in the millions of dollars for people whose damages include large medical bills, ongoing medical care for catastrophic injuries, extreme pain and suffering, and punitive damages against the wrongdoers.

Negligence is the most commonly asserted claim in sports injury lawsuits. To recover damages in a negligence lawsuit, the plaintiff must prove four elements:

1. The defendant(s) had an affirmative duty of care under all of the circumstances to protect the plaintiff from harm.
2. The defendant(s) failed to exercise reasonable care to fulfill that duty of care.
3. A breach of duty by the defendant(s) caused the plaintiff's injuries.
4. The breach of duty by the defendant(s) resulted in measurable financial damages to the plaintiff.

Even if the plaintiff is able to establish all four elements of negligence, defendants have two defenses available through which liability may be avoided:

- The plaintiff assumed the risk of injury under all the circumstances of the situation. Only inherent risks may be assumed by a plaintiff—risks so obvious that the plaintiff was aware of the likelihood of injury or risks about which the plaintiff had been specifically informed in a thorough and effective manner so that the plaintiff fully appreciated the likelihood of injury.

- The plaintiff was liable for contributory negligence—the argument that the plaintiff's own lack of reasonable care was the cause of the injuries. Most American courts now use a comparative negligence approach through which either a judge or a jury apportion fault between the defendant and the plaintiff, and the defendant is responsible only for the assigned percentage of fault multiplied by the total financial damages resulting from the plaintiff's injuries.

In July of 2010, a settlement was reached in *Felix v. Barre Supervisory Union*, a catastrophic injury case that illustrates how the typical negligence case is litigated. The case involved a 16-year-old high school football player who sustained neck and spinal cord injuries resulting in permanent quadriplegia. The injury occurred in the first game of the 2005 season when the student-athlete, an out-of-state transfer new to his high school team, lowered his head and made helmet-to-helmet contact with an opponent. The lawsuit, filed in a Vermont state court, named as defendants the school district, its insurers, and a number of school personnel including the athletic director and all the football coaches. Duties allegedly breached included planning, proper technique instruction, supervision, warnings, proper monitoring of players for injuries and incapacities, medical assistance, and implementation of an emergency medical response plan.

As is common in sports injury negligence cases, the Felix case initially focused on the plaintiff's claims that the school and its personnel had a number of specific, affirmative duties of care to protect him from injury and that reasonable care was not exercised to fulfill those duties. In particular, the plaintiff asserted that coaches had failed to teach players the dangers of head-down contact and that he had been allowed to play without having completed a state association–mandated preparticipation requirement of 10 practices.

The school district countered that the case should be dismissed because the injured plaintiff had assumed the risk of injury by voluntarily participating in the sport of football. The district also argued that it and its personnel were shielded from liability by the state's statutory immunity law that insulates public institutions and public employees from liability for negligent actions that result in harm to a third party.

Before settlement, the Felix case was appealed to the Vermont Supreme Court to resolve the issues of assumption of risk and statutory immunity. The high court ruled that the injured player had not assumed the risk of such an injury because the doctrine applies only to obvious risks or to risks of which the injured party was specifically informed. Given his age and relative lack of football experience, the risks were not considered to be sufficiently obvious and inherent so as to be assumable. And because the player had not received specific technique instructions focusing on the avoidance of head-down contact, nor had he received warnings about the dangers of head-down, helmet-to-helmet contact, the latent risk of that specific type of catastrophic injury to a young and inexperienced student-athlete had not been converted into a known risk for the young man.

In addition, the Vermont Supreme Court made a ruling consistent with a national trend in sports injury negligence cases when it concluded that the school district and its personnel would not be shielded by statutory immunity. In recent years, there has been an erosion of the statutory immunity doctrine as a defense in sports injury cases involving student-athletes. Although the doctrine is still often invoked to shield other categories of public employees such as police and firefighters from liability for negligence, courts have increasingly ruled that schools and school personnel have a heightened duty to protect the young people in their charge from harm and that statutory immunity will not serve as an automatic bar to liability. Although occasionally a court will invoke statutory immunity to protect school personnel, the doctrine can no longer be considered a blanket-shield for schools and personnel.

After the rulings in the Felix case by the Vermont Supreme Court, the district and its insurers made the decision to settle the case. Although financial terms of the settlement were not disclosed, the structured payout was reported to be an amount sufficient to cover the cost of the injured student-athlete's lifetime medical care, an amount reported by various media outlets to be approximately $9 million given the boy's permanent quadriplegia.

The Felix case illustrates an important standard of practice for athletic administrators with regard to liability for sports injuries. The starting points for developing and implementing an effective risk management program are improving safety standards for student-athletes and reducing the legal exposure of the school and its personnel.

Attainment of both goals can be enhanced by a thorough understanding of the legal duties imposed by courts, legislatures, and administrative agencies on athletic personnel. In the modern environment of athletic administration, these legal duties can be divided into 14 broad categories, each of which includes multiple subcategories of duties.

1. Planning
2. Supervision
3. Selection and training of coaches and other athletic personnel
4. Proper technique instruction
5. Warnings
6. Safe playing environment
7. Protective athletic equipment
8. Evaluation of conditioning and initial preparedness to participate
9. Evaluation of injuries and incapacities affecting continuing participation
10. Matching and equating student-athletes for safe participation
11. Immediate medical assistance
12. Emergency medical response plan
13. Safe transportation
14. Full and accurate disclosure

Legal Duty 1: Planning

Planning is the threshold legal duty that encompasses all other duties. When an injured student-athlete sues, courts will rarely find that a school and its athletic personnel have exercised reasonable care unless a written, strategic plan is in place for fulfilling all aspects of all the duties owed to student-athletes to protect them from harm. Courts tend to impose liability on schools and athletic personnel in the following circumstances:

- No planning was done whatsoever.
- Planning was done, but it was poor or inadequate and failed to address all the categories of duties.
- Thorough planning was done, but the safety measures included in the plan were never implemented or were not adhered to in later years.

As with all the legal duties, it is imperative that athletic personnel "paper the trail" to demonstrate that reasonable care was exercised to fulfill the duty of planning. Papering the trail requires that the plan and all supporting documentation be in writing.

Duty to Plan—Case Law Application

In *Gill v. Tamalpais*, a 2008 California Court of Appeals decision, a female basketball player was injured in a collision with a metal post supporting a backboard and was sent, unsupervised, to an athletic training room. While awaiting the arrival of medical personnel, she fainted and fell, resulting in serious additional injuries requiring stitches and extensive reconstructive dental work. A $336,932 jury award at trial was upheld by the appellate court, which emphasized that the primary factor in its decision was the failure by the school district and its athletic personnel to develop a comprehensive plan for its athletic programs to ensure they fulfilled duties of supervision, safe playing environment, safe equipment, immediate medical assistance, and emergency medical response plan.

Legal Duty 2: Supervision

Courts impose two types of supervisory duties on schools and athletic personnel. The first is the duty of specific supervision—the responsibility to exercise reasonable care when supervising student-athletes engaged in the athletic activity itself, including practices, organized weightlifting and conditioning sessions, and contests. The second is the duty of general supervision—the responsibility to exercise care when supervising student-athletes for a reasonable period before and after the athletic activity and to exercise reasonable care in supervising sports environments such as gymnasiums, playing fields, weight rooms, locker rooms, and other athletic facilities, even when they are not in active use.

Duty to Supervise—Case Law Applications

In *Barretto v. City of New York*, a 1997 New York Court of Appeals decision dealing with specific supervision, a volleyball player was injured after his coach left the gymnasium for a few minutes, thereby leaving the team completely unsupervised. While the coach was absent, the plaintiff attempted to jump a volleyball net as it was being raised into place. The boy fell to the floor headfirst and sustained neck and spinal cord injuries, rendering him a paraplegic. A jury found the school and coach liable for failing to exercise reasonable care in supervising the team and awarded the injured athlete $18.8 million, reduced to $14.9 million because of the boy's contributory negligence. Although the verdict was eventually overturned, the jury's decision regarding the duty of specific supervision illustrates the importance for athletic programs to ensure that student-athletes are never left unsupervised and that supervision alternatives and contingencies should always be planned in advance for those circumstances where a coach needs to temporarily leave the athletic environment.

In *Yarber v. Oakland Unified School District*, a 1992 California Court of Appeals decision dealing with general supervision, a 13-year-old boy was killed while he and several friends were trespassing on a high school soccer field on the weekend. At the playing field, the group tipped over a soccer goal; while trying to lift it back into place, they lost control of the goal. As the goal fell, it struck Yarber on the head. The appellate court took into account the trespassing and vandalism aspects of the decedent's behavior but also concluded that reasonable care to fulfill the duty of general supervision required that the school take the simple measure of anchoring or otherwise securing the goals so they could not be tipped over and putting up warning signs on the field. It is important to note that the Yarber court, as do most courts, did not require the district and its athletic personnel to be the absolute guarantors of the safety of those in the athletic environment. The court did not conclude that the district should have built a 10-foot impenetrable fence around the fields. The court required only the exercise of reasonable care—commonsense safety measures such as anchoring the goals and posting signage—that could have easily been implemented and that might have prevented the boy's death.

Legal Duty 3: Selection and Training of Coaches and Other Athletic Personnel

The exercise of reasonable care in the hiring and training of coaches is a threshold duty necessary for the fulfillment of other duties such as proper technique instruction, warnings, medical assistance, supervision, and safe playing environments. Courts evaluate whether the coach's educational background was thoroughly vetted before the hiring; whether the sport-specific backgrounds of the personnel were carefully evaluated; and whether the coach had completed all essential certifications such as first aid, CPR, and required NFHS coaching courses or the alternative American Sport Education Program (ASEP) training courses.

Duty to Select and Train Coaches—Case Law Application

In *Britt v. Maury County Board of Education*, a 2008 Tennessee Court of Appeals decision, a cheerleader was injured in a fall from the top of a human pyramid. The primary issue in the ensuing litigation was whether the cheer coach's educational and sport-specific background had been adequately evaluated by the school and its athletic director before the coach had been hired. After a lower-court ruling in favor of the school, the appellate court reversed and found that the school did not have a personnel file paper trail sufficient to establish that the coach had the cheer-specific training necessary to provide proper technique instruction and to safely supervise participants during practices and competitions.

Legal Duty 4: Proper Technique Instruction

Courts tend to evaluate four issues related to whether an injured student-athlete received proper technique instruction:

1. Whether reasonable care had been exercised to hire qualified coaches (duty 3)
2. Whether the techniques that were taught to the athlete were safe and correct (expert witnesses will be retained to testify on behalf of plaintiff)
3. Whether adequate safety instructions were provided regarding the safest method for performing a particular activity (expert witnesses will be retained to testify on behalf of plaintiff)
4. Whether adequate risk instructions were provided regarding the dangers of and potential injuries that might occur from the use of improper techniques

Courts will also evaluate whether a reasonable progression of skills was taught to the injured athlete, taking into account her age, skill level, experience level, and other indicators of preparedness to participate in the activity in question.

Duty to Instruct—Case Law Applications

In *Acosta v. Los Angeles Unified School District*, a 1995 California Court of Appeals decision, a gymnast learning to perform a giant on the high bar missed the bar on a release-and-catch sequence. The missed catch component of the giant caused Acosta to fall and injure his spinal cord, resulting in permanent quadriplegia. The appellate court ruled that the failure of the coaches to use a safety harness for spotting, which was available on site, violated the duty of proper technique instruction because it was the injured boy's first attempt at performing the maneuver, and reasonable care related to progression of skill dictated the use of the harness.

Another often-litigated issue related to technique instruction is the question of whether a coach is liable for injuries sustained by a student-athlete while performing additional running, lifting, or other punishments involving excessive physical exertion. In *Gorthy v. Clovis Unified School District*, a 2006 U.S. District Court decision in California, a high school football player was disciplined for arriving late to practice by being forced to do bear crawls on an asphalt-covered area, with his bare upper body, hands, and legs pressed against the pavement. The temperature that day was 95 degrees Fahrenheit (35 degrees Celsius), and the athlete sustained second- and third-degree burns that required skin graft operations to repair. Although the school and its coaches argued they had the right to dispense reasonable corporal punishment, the court ruled that the technique instruction used to discipline the boy was grossly excessive and awarded damages to the injured plaintiff. The case illustrates the standard of practice mandating that athletic administrators carefully train and monitor all coaches and athletic personnel to ensure that proper technique instruction and methods of discipline are being used.

Legal Duty 5: Warnings

Courts have held athletic personnel accountable for warning student-athletes of the risks related to participation in sports activities. Warnings can improve safety standards for student-athletes, and proof that sport-specific warnings were communicated may limit the legal exposure of athletic personnel for injuries sustained by student-athletes. One of the primary defenses available in sports injury cases is assumption of risk, but courts have consistently ruled that student-athletes assume only the risk of inherent dangers that are fully comprehended. Inherent dangers are those of which any reasonable person would be aware or those about which a person has been specifically warned.

The key is to ensure that sport-specific warnings regarding general dangers of participation and specific dangers arising from using improper techniques are provided to student-athletes and parents or guardians in a thorough and understandable manner. Moreover, this information should be presented with high frequency and in multiple media forms. This might include oral statements, demonstrations, written warnings, instructional videos, printed material provided by sports equipment manufacturers, and assessment methodologies such as written tests or evaluative drills during practices. It is also suggested that written sport-specific warning statements conclude with a section wherein the athlete and at least one parent or guardian certify understanding of the content.

A related issue is the legal enforceability of written waivers of liability that student-athletes and parents have signed. Although many courts find such waivers to be in violation of public policy and refuse to enforce them as automatic disclaimers of liability, those same courts often use the information included in the written waiver as proof that clear, detailed, sport-specific warnings were provided to an injured student-athlete, and therefore the athlete was aware of and assumed the risk of the injury.

Duty to Provide Warnings—Case Law Application

In *Sharon v. City of Newton*, a 2002 decision by the Massachusetts Supreme Court, the information included in a waiver of liability was successfully used by a school and coach to establish the defense of assumption of risk. The injured party, a cheerleader who fell from a pyramid, had signed a detailed cheer-specific waiver of liability before participation. The waiver and the warnings therein had been thoroughly explained by the school's athletic director to all the cheerleaders and their parents at a preseason meeting. The court upheld the enforceability of the waiver and ruled that it did not violate public policy because participation in a scholastic sports program was a voluntary activity; the court also concluded that what might have been latent dangers related to cheer participation had been so thoroughly explained in the waiver and preseason meeting that the risks had been transformed into inherent dangers that were fully assumed by participants.

Legal Duty 6: Safe Playing Environment

Courts generally consider six issues in determining whether a safe playing environment was provided for student-athletes:

1. Whether reasonable care was exercised in the selection and setup of the environment
2. Whether reasonable care was exercised to ensure that regular inspections of the environment were performed for safety hazards
3. Whether repairs were promptly made when safety hazards were discovered in the environment
4. Whether the environment complied with local safe building codes
5. Whether reasonable care was exercised to protect third parties in the environment such as spectators, officials, and coaches
6. Whether reasonable care was exercised with regard to event management and event security

Duty to Provide a Safe Environment— Case Law Application

In *Leung v. City of New York*, a 2006 New York Superior Court decision, a high school track team member was injured during a team practice on a multi-use field when she was hit in the face by a lacrosse ball. Multiple track and field activities were in progress on the field at the same time as a lacrosse practice. The lacrosse players were throwing at least half a dozen lacrosse balls back and forth in the midst of the track athletes. The court ruled that the school and its athletic personnel had violated the duty to provide a safe playing environment by failing to exercise reasonable care in the setup, design, layout, and execution of the multiple activities that were taking place simultaneously on the field.

Legal Duty 7: Protective Athletic Equipment

Courts generally consider six issues in determining whether adequately safe protective athletic equipment was provided for student-athletes:

1. Whether the appropriate type of equipment was provided to student-athletes
2. Whether the equipment was of sufficient quality
3. Whether the criteria for distribution of the equipment was based on safety
4. Whether appropriate instructions were given for safe use of the equipment
5. Whether consistent use of the equipment was required
6. Whether regular inspections were made of the equipment for repair and reconditioning.

Duty to Provide Safe and Appropriate Equipment— Case Law Application

In *DiGiose v. Bellmore-Merrick Central High School District*, a 2008 New York Court of Appeals case that illustrates how a school and its athletic personnel effectively fulfilled the duty to provide protective equipment and satisfied all the duties imposed on athletic programs, a cheerleader injured during a tumbling stunt sued, claiming a violation of the duty to supply protective athletic equipment because of the lack of protective mats on the gym floor at the time she was injured. The court ruled that in the school's written comprehensive safety plan for its athletic program, careful consideration had been given to the use of protective equipment in all sports; with regard to cheer tumbling stunts, national governing body standards had been incorporated into the plan, and mats were deemed impractical given the nature of the tumbling routine being practiced. Extensive evidence, including a paper trail of sports participation agreements, cheer-specific waivers of liability, adequate supervision, proper technique instruction, and a safe environment, made it clear that the school, its athletic director, and the cheer coach had fulfilled all their legal duties to the injured athlete.

Legal Duty 8: Evaluation of Conditioning and Initial Preparedness to Participate

Evaluation of the initial preparedness of student-athletes to participate requires the assessment of six issues:

1. Whether athletic personnel were adequately trained to evaluate initial preparedness to participate

2. Whether physical exams were required of all student-athletes and whether the exams were sufficiently thorough and substantive so as to identify any incapacitating condition

3. Whether medical history questionnaires were completed by all student-athletes and whether those questionnaires were reviewed by a doctor for indications of any incapacitating conditions

4. Whether student-athletes were evaluated to ensure they possessed adequate cardiorespiratory and strength conditioning for safe participation or return to play after injury

5. Whether student-athletes were assessed to ensure they possessed adequate skill and experience to be able to safely compete at their intended level of competition

6. Whether reasonable measures were taken to evaluate whether student-athletes had ingested performance-enhancing drugs or sports supplements that might present a danger to safe participation

Legal Duty 9: Evaluation of Injuries and Incapacities Affecting Continuing Participation

This duty deals with the responsibility of athletic personnel to continuously monitor student-athletes after participation has begun for any indications that continued participation might be unsafe, including injuries or incapacities that might arise during practices and contests, as well as to decide when to return student-athletes to action after an injury.

In recent years, the most significant injury issue has been concussions and the question of when a student-athlete can safely return to action. Almost every state has enacted concussion protocol legislation imposing detailed concussion management requirements for school districts in its jurisdiction. These statutes function as a codification of reasonable care, and athletic administrators should be familiar with the governing state law on concussions. The National Football League's health and safety website includes a continually updated list of all states with concussion protocol laws and the detailed requirements of each state statute. For information, visit www.nflevolution.com/article/The-Zackery-Lystedt-Law?ref=270.

Legal Duty 10: Matching and Equating Student-Athletes for Safe Participation

Athletic personnel have the duty to exercise reasonable care to match and equate student-athletes for safe participation based on six criteria:

1. Size
2. Strength
3. Skill level
4. Experience
5. Age
6. Incapacitating conditions

This duty includes the responsibility both to prevent team mismatches that present an excessive risk of injury to student-athletes and to prevent individual mismatches that create a significantly heightened level of danger to players.

Matching and Equating Athletes— Case Law Applications

In *Benitez v. City of New York*, a 1989 New York Court of Appeals decision, a small and inexperienced high school football player sustained a broken neck when his small-class team played a big-class team populated by larger,

(continued)

(continued)

stronger, and more experience players. The case illustrates the need for athletic administrators to avoid team mismatches. In *Patrick v. Great Valley School District*, a 2008 U.S. Third Circuit Court of Appeals decision, a high school wrestler was forced during practice to compete against a teammate several weight classes above his. The teammate outweighed the plaintiff by 40 pounds (18 kg), had significantly more skill and experience than the plaintiff, and was two years older than the plaintiff. The case illustrates the need for athletic personnel to exercise reasonable care to avoid individual mismatches.

Legal Duty 11: Immediate Medical Assistance

Athletic personnel must provide immediate medical assistance in the event that a student-athlete sustains an injury, feels ill, or suffers any other participation-related medical crisis. The exercise of reasonable care to fulfill this duty requires athletic directors to ensure that all athletic personnel have received adequate training to recognize the signs of injuries or incapacities, that all personnel have required certifications such as first aid and CPR, and that appropriate medical equipment such as first aid kits and automated external defibrillators are readily available.

Legal Duty 12: Emergency Medical Response Plan

Schools and athletic personnel have the duty of developing an emergency medical response plan and ensuring it is ready to be activated in the event a student-athlete is injured, feels ill, or suffers any other participation-related medical crisis. The plan should address communication issues—given the nature of a particular injury, who should be contacted and how that contact is to be made. The plan should include contingencies for all levels of injuries that might occur, ranging from catastrophic to minor, and should also address medical information issues—are medical consent forms and medical history questionnaires readily available if an injury occurs during practice, at a home contest, or at an away game?

Legal Duty 13: Safe Transportation

This duty deals with the responsibility of schools and athletic personnel to exercise reasonable care to provide safe modes of transportation for student-athletes traveling to and from practices and contests. Courts often apply the doctrine of in loco parentis (in the place of a parent) in requiring schools to provide safe transportation from the school to all practice facilities and contests and then back to the school after practices and contests. Courts tend to impose liability on athletic directors and coaches when a student is injured in a car accident in transit to or from practices or contests unless the student was being transported in a safe school-owned or contracted vehicle driven by a properly licensed school driver or outside contractor.

Safe Transportation—Case Law Application

In *Clement v. Griffin*, a 1984 Louisiana Court of Appeals decision that is one of the landmark sports transportation cases, several baseball players were injured in an automobile accident while being transported in a dilapidated school van with worn tires that were low on pressure and which was being driven by one of the student-athletes, who did not have the chauffeur's license required by state law. The court found the school's athletic director and baseball coach personally liable for violating their duty to provide safe transportation.

Legal Duty 14: Full and Accurate Disclosure

In recent years, courts have increasingly found schools and athletic personnel liable for failing to provide full and accurate disclosure of certain categories of information to student-athletes, including information about insurance coverage (or lack thereof) by the athletic program and information about initial eligibility requirements for college sports. Typically, liability is imposed when athletic personnel erroneously communicate misinformation.

Full and Accurate Disclosure—Case Law Applications

In *Tri-Central High School v. Mason*, a 2001 Indiana Court of Appeals decision, liability was imposed on a school and athletic director for failure to adequately explain to student-athletes and parents that the insurance provided by the school carried a $25,000 deductible that had to be covered by the family of an injured athlete. An injured football player's broken leg resulted in $22,000 of medical expenses, and the court assessed that amount against the school and athletic director because of the negligent failure to explain the deductible.

In *Sain v. Cedar Rapids Community School District*, a 2001 Iowa Supreme Court decision, liability was imposed on a high school and school personnel for communicating erroneous information to a student-athlete about NCAA-mandated core course requirements for initial college sports eligibility. The misinformation resulted in the athlete's losing a college scholarship, and the court emphasized the superior knowledge of school personnel and the reliance of the student on that superior knowledge in awarding damages to the player.

Safeguarding Student-Athletes and Their Legal Rights

Sport law as it relates to athletic administration is much more than a mere collection of legal principles designed to limit the liability exposure of schools and athletic personnel. Sport law, in its most relevant and useful manifestation, represents a society-wide consensus as to what is required of athletic personnel with regard to safeguarding student-athletes against physical injuries and violations of their legal rights.

On a far too frequent basis, tragedies occur that serve as a reminder of the role athletic personnel play in protecting young people from harm. In October of 2010, in my hometown of Kansas City, such a tragedy occurred. A high school football player who had suffered a concussion during a previous game was allowed to return to action prematurely for his senior-night game, a big-rivalry contest for which he was cleared to play by his family doctor, a general practitioner who did not want to keep him from participating in the final game of his high school career. During the contest, he sustained a helmet-to-helmet hit that resulted in his death that night from second-impact syndrome.

Although it is impossible to say whether this young man's life would have been saved by closer adherence to the emerging nationwide legal standards of practice regarding traumatic brain injuries—state concussion protocol statutes mandating baseline testing and follow-up testing as a return-to-action prerequisite, annual concussion education for all athletic personnel, return-to-action requirements of medical clearance by a physician specializing in traumatic brain injuries, and an overarching err-on-the-side-of-caution strategy—greater knowledge of emerging legal standards may have resulted in a different outcome.

Every year, in multiple cases around the United States involving catastrophic injuries, heat exhaustion deaths, concussion fatalities, and similar instances of serious injuries, the families of student-athletes are left wondering whether more professional education for athletic personnel and a greater understanding of prevailing standards of practice might have saved the life or lessened the injuries of a young person. Athletic personnel should approach the study of sport law as an opportunity to enhance their knowledge of the cutting-edge standards in place to protect the health and safety of the young people in their charge.

Title IX Compliance

In 1969, Bernice Sandler, a college professor and activist who had encountered gender discrimination in her employment relationship with the University of Maryland, lobbied Congress to extend the existing laws against gender discrimination in employment to cover educational institutions. Sandler's endeavor resulted in the enactment of Public Law 92-318 of the Education Amendments of 1972, better known as Title IX, a 37-word statement that would have a profound impact in the decades to come on athletic participation opportunities for women:

"No person in the United States shall, on the basis of sex, be excluded from participation in, be denied the benefit of, or be subjected to discrimination under any education program or activity receiving Federal financial assistance."

In 1972, approximately 294,000 girls participated in high school sports programs, only one out of every 27 girls enrolled nationwide. By 2012, the 40th anniversary of Title IX's enactment, that number had grown to more than 3,000,000 girls participating in high school sports, roughly one out of every three girls enrolled nationwide.

The U.S. Department of Education's Office for Civil Rights (OCR) is the federal agency charged with enforcing Title IX. The sources of law governing Title IX compliance by college and high school athletic programs include a series of policy guidances and policy clarifications issued over the years by the OCR. These legal principles have been incorporated into the many settlement agreements negotiated by the OCR with educational institutions. They also contain the extensive body of federal-court case law interpreting Title IX.

Out of these sources of law has emerged a Title IX compliance framework (see figure 12.1) that serves as a blueprint for schools wishing to conduct Title IX self-audits to ensure they conform to all of the law's mandates.

If a Title IX complaint is filed with the OCR by a female student-athlete, a coach, a parent, or a member of an advocacy group, the ensuing investigation by the OCR will include all three broad components of the framework.

Component I: Sports Offerings

Initially, the OCR will evaluate whether the institution can demonstrate it is providing adequate participation opportunities to girls through compliance with any one of the three alternative options within the three-prong test. A school can show it satisfies the first prong—substantial proportionality—by demonstrating that its ratio of female athletic participation (female athletic participation opportunities divided by total athletic participation opportunities) is close to its ratio of female enrollment.

Component I: Sports Offerings

    a. Participation Opportunities: The Three-Prong Test

       Prong 1: Substantial proportionality *or*

       Prong 2: History and continuing practice of program expansion *or*

       Prong 3: Full and effective accommodation of athletic interests and abilities

    b. Levels of Competition: The Two-Prong Test

       Prong 1: Equivalently advanced competitive opportunities

       Prong 2: History and continuing practice of improvement

Component II: Financial Aid

Component III: Other Athletic Benefits and Opportunities [PLAYING FAIR]

  P Protective athletic equipment, uniforms, gear, and other supplies

  L Locker rooms, practice facilities, and competition facilities

  A Allocation of travel, transportation, lodging, and meal benefits

  Y Years of experience, quality, and compensation of coaches

  I Institutional housing and dining facilities and services

  N Nature of publicity, marketing, and media services

  G Game and practice scheduling, including times and days of the week

  F Facilities for and access to athletic training and medical services

  A Academic tutoring services provided to student-athletes

  I Institutional support services provided to teams and coaches

  R Recruiting resources provided to teams and coaches

FIGURE 12.1   Title IX compliance framework.

In general, the OCR defines substantial proportionality as a gap of less than 5 percent. In the alternative, if the school cannot demonstrate substantial proportionality, it may satisfy the OCR if it can show compliance with prong two's "history and continuing practice" option by proving a recent history and an ongoing pattern of the school's expanding sports participation opportunities for girls.

Finally, if the school cannot demonstrate compliance with prongs one or two, it may nevertheless satisfy the OCR by showing that the institution is in compliance with prong three's "full and effective accommodation" option by conducting surveys and using other assessment tools. Through the regular use of interest surveys, an athletic director can establish that there are no additional girls' sports the school could add in which a sufficient number of girls are interested in fielding a team. Details about how institutions should self-evaluate compliance with the three-prong test, along with all other aspects of conducting Title IX self-audits, can be found on the OCR's website at www2.ed.gov/about/offices/list/ocr/index.html.

In addition to assessing compliance with the three-prong test for participation opportunities, the OCR will use the two-prong test for levels of competition to evaluate whether the school is providing participation opportunities to girls at the same levels of competition as those provided to boys. A school may demonstrate compliance by showing it already offers equivalently advanced competitive opportunities for girls or that it has a history and continuing practice of improving the levels of competition for girls.

Fair Treatment—Case Law Application

In *Ollier v. Sweetwater Union High School District*, a 2012 U.S. District Court decision in California, the federal court ruled that the district was not in compliance with Title IX because of numerous inequities experienced by the Castle Park High School girls' softball team throughout the 11 areas of other athletic benefits and opportunities. The dispute began in 2006 after complaints by female players, their parents, and their coach about the poor condition of the school's softball facilities as compared to its baseball facilities.

In 2009, after an OCR investigation and the filing of a federal lawsuit, the court ruled that the school was not in compliance with any of the options within the three-prong test and was failing to provide adequate sports participation opportunities to the girls enrolled at the school. The remaining claims regarding inequities in the 11 areas of other benefits went to trial. After 10 days of testimony, the court ruled that inequities existed between girls and boys throughout all of the sports offered at the school, including facilities problems, locker room disparities, differences in uniforms and equipment, scheduling disparities, problems in the provision of athletic training and medical services, inequities in publicity and promotional support, and disparities in access to quality coaching. Furthermore, the court found the school district liable for retaliation for having fired the softball coach who had originally complained about the inequities experienced by his team and players. The case is a contemporary example of the precise manner in which the OCR and the federal courts interpret Title IX, and it provides numerous lessons for athletic administrators. The full text of the case may be read on the federal judiciary's website at www.las-elc.org/docs/cases/Sweetwater_Order.2012.02.09.pdf.

Component II: Financial Aid

With regard to the financial aid component of Title IX, the OCR will evaluate whether the amount of athletic-related scholarships or any other source of funding flowing to female student-athletes is proportional to that being provided to male student-athletes. Although financial aid is rarely an issue for public high schools, even the structure and administration of exceptions to pay-to-play systems—which indirectly create the equivalent of athletic-related funding flowing to certain student-athletes—must comply with Title IX.

Component III: Other Athletic Benefits and Opportunities

Most Title IX complaints filed with the OCR are rooted in a perception of inequity by female student-athletes, parents, or coaches in one or more of the 11 areas of other athletic benefits and opportunities. The OCR refers to these 11 areas as its "laundry list" of sports program features that must be allocated to female student-athletes in a manner equivalent to which they are allocated to males. The 11, represented in figure 12.1 by the acronym PLAYING FAIR, encompass all aspects of participating in an athletic program.

Constitutional and Civil Rights of Student-Athletes

Issues regarding the constitutional and civil rights of student-athletes tend to arise when discipline is imposed for violation of an athletic program's code of conduct, and a lawsuit is subsequently filed by the student challenging the sanction.

Social Networking Issues and First Amendment Abridgement

Since the launch of MySpace in 2003, Facebook in 2004, Twitter in 2006, Google+ in 2011, and their numerous social networking progeny, schools and athletic programs have been struggling with a new issue related to the constitutional rights of student-athletes. Legal challenges have focused on the extent of school legal authority over off-campus postings by students on social media websites and the question of whether the imposition of sanctions against athletes for inappropriate postings is a violation of the students' First Amendment freedom of speech and freedom of expression rights.

During 2011, five U.S. Court of Appeals rulings and a significant U.S. District Court decision were issued in cases addressing the extent of school legal authority over off-campus postings by students on social media websites. Three of the cases were decided in favor of students and three in favor of schools.

Equal Protection of Rights—Case Law Application

In *L.A. v. Board of Education of the Township of Wayne*, a 2011 decision by the New Jersey Office of Administrative Law (OAL), nine high school football players were suspended and thus barred from playing in the state championship game after they were arrested and charged with aggravated assault after a fight at an off-campus party. The players sought reinstatement by arguing that their constitutional rights had been violated. Specifically, the players cited abridgement of their Fifth and Fourteenth Amendment due process rights, their First Amendment freedom of speech and freedom of expression rights, and their Fourteenth Amendment equal protection rights.

With regard to due process, the players argued that their participation in sports was a property right of which they were being deprived without adequate procedural protections. The OAL relied on a long line of court-case precedents in ruling that participation in athletics is a privilege, not a constitutionally protected property right. With regard to the First Amendment, the players argued that the school's punishment for off-campus behavior was an impermissible violation of their rights to freedom of speech and expression. The OAL disagreed, noting the school's student-athlete code of conduct clearly stated that discipline would be imposed for on-campus or off-campus misconduct and that the players' actions did not fall within the orbit of the protections provided by the First Amendment. Finally, with regard to equal protection, the players argued that their punishment was arbitrary and disproportionate to sanctions imposed on other student-athletes for similar misbehavior. The OAL disagreed and ruled that the punishment was neither arbitrary nor disproportionate.

The standard of practice to be gleaned from these social media cases is that courts do not consider sanctions against students for off-campus postings on social media to be constitutional violations in situations where the information

- communicates a threat,
- constitutes bullying behavior, or
- results in a material disruption of the educational environment at school.

However, courts may conclude that the First Amendment protects off-campus postings that fall outside of the threats, bullying, and disruption standard and that student-athletes may not be sanctioned for those off-campus postings.

In *Doninger v. Niehoff*, the Second Circuit Court of Appeals ruled in favor of school administrators at Lewis S. Mills High School (Connecticut) who disciplined a student for profane postings on a blog; the court concluded that the blog satisfied the substantial disruption standard established by the U.S. Supreme Court in its 1969 decision *Tinker v. Des Moines School District*.

In *J.S. v. Blue Mountain School District*, the Third Circuit Court of Appeals held that the district violated the free speech rights of a Blue Mountain Middle School (Pennsylvania) student who created a fake MySpace profile of her school principal that incorporated profanity and falsely characterized him as a sex addict and pedophile, concluding that the student's actions did not cause a substantial disruption at school. In *Layshock v. Hermitage School District*, the Third Circuit ruled that the district violated the free speech rights of a Hickory High School (Pennsylvania) student who created a parody MySpace profile of his principal containing numerous vulgarities and sexual innuendos. The court concluded that the student's off-campus behavior did not create a substantial disruption on campus.

In *Kowalski v. Berkeley County Schools*, the U.S. Fourth Circuit Court of Appeals ruled that the district did not violate the free speech rights of a Musselman High School (West Virginia) cheerleader disciplined for creating a MySpace discussion group page designed as a vehicle to cyberbully another student at her school, concluding that bullying, cyberbullying, and other forms of harassment satisfy the Tinker substantial disruption standard.

In *D.J.M. v. Hannibal Public School District*, the U.S. Eighth Circuit Court of Appeals held that the district did not violate the free speech rights of a Hannibal High School (Missouri) student disciplined for using social media to communicate threats to use a gun against his classmates. The court concluded that a true threat—a statement that a reasonable recipient would have interpreted as a serious expression of intent to cause harm or injury to another—does not constitute protected free speech.

In *T.V. & M.K. v. Smith-Green Community Schools*, a U.S. District Court ruled that the school district violated the free speech rights of two Churubusco High School (Indiana) volleyball players disciplined for off-campus postings of profanely captioned photos on social media sites. These postings depicted the students at a summer slumber party in various states of undress while engaged in sexually suggestive poses with phallus-shaped lollipops. The court concluded that the behavior did not create a substantial disruption at school.

Hazing and Bullying in Athletic Programs

Hazing and bullying are widespread problems in high school athletic programs and one of the most highly litigated claims against districts and athletic personnel. Courts typically impose liability for failure to create an antihazing policy or for developing a policy that is substantively inadequate or ineffectively implemented.

The lesson to be learned from the rulings in court cases such as *Mathis v. Wayne County Board of Education* is that schools and athletic administrators should develop and implement an antihazing policy for their athletic programs using the following five-step process:

1. Definition: Create a working definition of hazing that includes a list of all the specific prohibited activities considered to constitute hazing.

2. Procedures: Create both a reporting procedure and an investigation procedure. The reporting procedure should avoid designating anyone with a potential conflict of interest as the person to whom reports should be made (e.g., the coach or athletic director); in most cases, a district's federally mandated Title IX officer would be an appropriate choice. The reporting

Hazing and Bullying—Case Law Application

In *Mathis v. Wayne County Board of Education*, a 2011 U.S. District Court decision in Tennessee, two basketball players were the victims of ongoing hazing of a sexual nature by older team members. The harassment generally occurred in the team's unsupervised locker room after practice and consisted of several specific hazing rituals, including "lights out"—an activity where the older players would shout "lights out," at which time the locker room would go dark and naked upperclassmen would surround unclothed underclassmen and begin "humping and gyrating on them." Another of the hazing rituals was "blindfolded sit-ups"—a hazing activity recommended to the upperclassmen by their coach in which underclassmen were blindfolded and forced to perform sit-ups into the naked rear ends of other players squatting over them. Other team hazing behaviors involved sodomy with foreign objects, including pencils and markers.

Despite complaints by the underclassmen and their parents to school officials, a limited investigation was conducted, and minimal punishment was imposed on the perpetrators. In response, the plaintiffs filed a lawsuit. The federal court refused to grant summary judgment to the district and its personnel, ruling that schools, administrators, and coaches may be held liable for hazing and peer sexual harassment when a school official in a position to take remedial action has knowledge that harassment is occurring and exhibits deliberate indifference to remedying the situation.

procedure should absolutely mandate that school personnel, student-athletes, or parents who suspect hazing must immediately file a report. The investigation procedure should set forth all the stages of the investigation process, a timetable for completion of the investigation process, and sanctions for parties determined to have violated the hazing policy.

3. Communication: Create a system for communicating the policy to athletic personnel, student-athletes, and parents. Incorporate the policy into coaching handbooks, student-athlete codes of conduct, and sports participation agreements signed by student-athletes and parents. Develop strategies for presenting and discussing the policy, including in-service programs for personnel and multimedia presentations to use at gatherings of student-athletes and parents.

4. Alternatives: Create positive alternative team-unity and character-building activities to replace prohibited hazing activities. Examples include leadership training courses, team-building activities, mentoring programs, community service initiatives, social activities, and fund-raising efforts. Involve team captains in the process of developing and implementing such activities.

5. Monitor: Create policies and procedures that can be continually implemented and monitored by athletic personnel. In addition, orientation to these procedures should be repeated annually as new coaches, student-athletes, and parents become involved in the athletic program.

Almost every state legislature has enacted laws mandating the creation of antihazing policies and antibullying policies by school leaders. To examine the detailed requirements of your state's antihazing statute, visit www.stophazing.org/laws.html. To examine the detailed mandates of your state's antibullying statute, visit www2.ed.gov/rschstat/eval/bullying/state-bullying-laws/state-bullying-laws.pdf.

For more information on strategies athletic administrators can employ to combat hazing and bullying in athletic programs, consult the U.S. Department of Education's Office for Civil Rights online publication titled Protecting Students From Harassment and Hate Crimes in the OCR Reading Room at www2.ed.gov/about/offices/list/ocr/publications.html.

Sexual Harassment in Athletic Programs

Beginning in the year 2000, a dramatic increase in sexual harassment litigation occurred. This increase followed issuance of five U.S. Supreme Court rulings in which strict liability was placed on employers and schools. Included in these decisions were suits seeking to impose liability for harassment of student-athletes by athletic personnel or harassment of student-athletes by other student-athletes.

Most of the lawsuits involving sexual harassment in athletic programs are litigated as hostile environment cases. Hostile environment sexual harassment occurs when unwelcome words or actions of a sexual nature that are sufficiently severe or pervasive so as to create a hostile or abusive environment are perpetrated on the victim. Implicit in hostile environment sexual harassment lawsuits are four elements:

1. Unwelcomeness
2. Words or actions of a sexual nature
3. Severe or pervasive actions
4. Creation of a hostile environment

In sexual harassment cases involving K-12 students, courts generally do not accept the consent of the student to be a defense for the perpetrator or for schools. Therefore, in cases involving a student-athlete who is the alleged victim of sexual harassment by athletic personnel or peers, only three issues are involved. Were there words or actions of a sexual nature directed at the victim? Was that behavior severe or pervasive? Was a hostile environment created?

Courts have consistently ruled that words or actions of a sexual nature include the following:

- Sexually explicit language directed at students
- Off-color jokes told to students
- Sexually oriented materials or photos being shown to students
- Excessively personal conversations including sexually explicit components with students
- Excessively personal letters, cards, and electronic communications transmitted to students
- Sexually oriented comments about physical appearance directed at students
- Inappropriate physical contact with students
- Romantic or dating relationships with students

In cases where the evidence establishes all three elements, the U.S. Supreme Court has imposed a strict liability standard on schools and athletic personnel. Districts and personnel in the chain of potential vicarious liability will automatically be held responsible when a school employee in a position to take remedial action has knowledge that sexual harassment is occurring and exhibits deliberate indifference to correcting the situation.

It is imperative that athletic administrators create a sexual harassment policy—one consistent with the district policy on the issue for all students—and that the athletic program policy be communicated to all athletic personnel, student-athletes, and parents. The policy should be incorporated into coaching contracts and coaching handbooks to make it clear to athletic personnel that violation of the policy is grounds for termination. The policy should also be included in student-athlete codes of conduct. In addition, sports participation agreements must make it clear that peer sexual harassment is grounds for discipline against the offending student-athlete. As with sports warnings, hazing and bullying prohibitions and sexual harassment prohibition should require written acknowledgment of these policies by athletes and a parent or guardian.

A related legal issue is the failure by school officials to report such harassment to law enforcement or social services agencies as required by applicable state laws governing child abuse. Athletic administrators should research reporting requirements established by state law and board of education policy, incorporate those requirements into the athletic program's sexual harassment policy, and ensure that the designated authorities are immediately contacted when any instance of improper conduct is discovered.

For more information on strategies athletic administrators can employ to prevent sexual harassment in athletic programs, consult the U.S. Department of Education's Office for Civil Rights online publication, Sexual Harassment: It's Not Academic, in the OCR Reading Room at www2.ed.gov/about/offices/list/ocr/publications.html.

Summary

Five key topics within sport law have emerged from case law, legislation, and agency rulings that affect education-based athletic programs:

1. Liability for sports injuries and legal mandates for the safety of student-athletes
2. Compliance with the sport-related gender equity requirements of Title IX
3. Constitutional and civil rights of interscholastic student-athletes
4. Prevention of hazing and bullying in interscholastic athletic programs
5. Prevention of sexual harassment in interscholastic athletic programs

Athletic administrators must develop a thorough understanding of each of these five areas of sport law because each applies to education-based athletic programs. High school sports administrators must also apply the derived legal principles to the management and leadership of their programs. Further, the contemporary high school athletic director must continually monitor changes in each area of sport law as new court cases are decided, new legislation is enacted, and new administrative rulings are issued.

PART III

Financial Matters

The two chapters in part III address the financial aspects of running an athletic program. Chapter 13 discusses how to market your program and develop important relationships within the community, such as parents, fans, alumni, and local businesses, and how to turn those relationships into money to support your program. Chapter 14 provides athletic administrators with the tools to formulate, execute, and follow a budgeting plan.

CHAPTER 13

Marketing and Fund-Raising

Bob Buckanavage

The essence of marketing isn't about goods and services. It isn't about sales. It isn't about profits. It really is all about developing relationships with customers so they will be loyal to a particular brand of product or service.

If you were to ask five people to define marketing, more than likely you would get five different definitions. Because marketing encompasses such a broad scope of activities and ideas, trying to settle on one definition is difficult.

When this understanding is applied to sport marketing, the process gets more complicated. Defined, sport marketing is the process of planning and executing the conception, pricing, promotion, and distribution of sport ideas, goods, services, organizations, and events to create and maintain relationships that will satisfy individual and organizational objectives.

What makes sport marketing more complex is that the sport arena has certain characteristics that are truly unique. Sport itself is very subjective to the consumer because impressions, experiences, and interpretations may vary from person to person for the same event. Such factors as player injuries, weather, and team momentum significantly create inconsistent and unpredictable outcomes for spectators. Sport is about emotions. Spectators become emotionally attached to their teams. They become the consumers of sport products and services as their way of identifying with their sports teams.

Nontraditional Marketing

The traditional boundaries of marketing extend beyond the for-profit enterprises that exist in our society to nonprofit marketing. The most obvious distinction between a for-profit business and a nonprofit organization is the overall profitability of the organization. A for-profit business measures success in sales and revenues generated, while a nonprofit organization hopes it generates enough revenue to meet its goals or cause.

The athletic director needs to develop relationships with a variety of prospective customers. Within every high school sport community, the potential market includes parents, friends, fans, alumni, and local businesses. They make up the market for your goods, services, advertising, sponsorships, and more.

In our society, nonprofit organizations are big business and employ millions of people who generate billions of dollars with a broader appeal to people, places, causes, events, and organizations. The five major categories of nontraditional marketing are (1) person marketing, (2) place marketing, (3) cause marketing, (4) event marketing, and (5) organization marketing.

Person marketing refers to the efforts of a celebrity to attract attention to, interest in, and preference for a target market. The best example of person marketing from my own experience involves former NFL star player Troy Vincent. When Troy played for the Philadelphia Eagles he returned to the community in Bucks County, Pennsylvania, where he graduated from Pennsbury High School and was a standout student-athlete in football, basketball, and track. Since I was his athletic administrator in high school, we already had a positive relationship. Troy had established a foundation and was oriented to giving back to the community, so I took the initiative and scheduled a meeting with him to solicit funding for a fitness center to be named in his honor at Pennsbury High School. Our meeting went exceptionally well, and Troy came on board to donate the cost of the fitness equipment. We also took advantage of dedicating the Troy Vincent Fitness Center by inviting the local media and Philadelphia sports media to the high school for this special occasion. The day was electrifying because the student body was well aware of what was going on, and the media coverage positively promoted the center to the public. Troy was extremely pleased and humbled to have the fitness center dedicated in his name.

To this day, after all these years, the center continues to host physical education classes, interscholastic athletics, and employee fitness and community services programs. It serves as a wonderful lesson for all athletic administrators that there are key persons in our communities who are willing to give back to high school sports because they believe in the value of sports participation and the lifelong lessons learned from the competitive experience.

Another category is place marketing, whereby an agency attempts to attract customers to a particular geographic area. Cities and states promote their tourist attractions to entice travelers. For example, the 9/11 Memorial in New York City is now beginning to attract huge crowds to view the tribute that is emerging for the victims of that tragic day.

The third category, which has gained considerable traction in recent years, is cause marketing. In this scenario, an organization aligns itself with a social issue or cause to raise awareness in selected markets. One that I have personal experience and success with is the Coaches vs. Cancer program, which generates revenue from fund-raising focused on high school basketball. The promotion of a social issue also shows that the athletic program cares about the community.

Event marketing refers to the marketing of sporting, cultural, and charitable activities to specific markets. If you use the NFL Super Bowl as a prime example of a sporting event, the effectiveness of sponsorships on increasing brand recognition is apparent.

The final category is organization marketing, which involves attempts by an organization to influence members to accept their goals or services or to contribute in some capacity. For example, as an organization, the NIAAA does an excellent job of promoting its member benefits to athletic administrators across the country.

Relationship Marketing

The athletic director needs to develop relationships with a variety of prospective customers. Within every high school sport community, the potential market includes parents, friends, fans, alumni, and local businesses. They make up the market for your goods, services, advertising, sponsorships, and more. An athletic director should compile a list of these potential supporters or update existing lists as necessary.

Another aspect of relationship marketing is developing partnerships and alliances with business contacts, suppliers of sporting goods and services, and other corporate partners. This takes place early in the marketing process. It starts with the top-quality products and services provided to the athletic department that meet the needs of the coaches and student-athletes. It continues with excellent customer service after purchases are made, helping to develop brand loyalty for future purchases.

This aspect of the job gives the athletic director an opportunity to develop relationships with the sales and marketing people in the sporting goods industry. At the local community level, most athletic administrators have contacts with sporting goods suppliers. It's how the administrator fosters these relationships that makes the difference in the long run when it comes to pricing and service. For example, a strong relationship with a vendor can come in handy when the athletic department has a special-needs request such as an odd-size uniform or a piece of equipment to be delivered the day of a game.

In the marketing industry, there are four universally known elements, referred to as the four Ps: product, price, place, and promotion. A product is a tangible or intangible asset (good or service) that meets a customer's needs. Price represents the cost of that asset, whether it's a good or service, that the customer is willing to pay. The higher the value of the product as perceived by the customer, the higher the price. Place refers to where the customer may obtain the product, also known as distribution channels. Promotion is the marketer's communication link between sellers and buyers. Many companies are now moving toward integrated marketing strategies to coordinate the promotional mix of advertising, publicity, Internet, and sales.

Interscholastic Sport Marketing Process

The importance of planning is best stated as follows: "If you don't know where you are going, then any road will get you there." Every school and athletic department should have a mission statement that defines its purpose and differentiates it from others. This mission statement serves as a reference point for all decision making and is especially vital in strategic planning.

Strategic planning is defined as the process of determining an organization's goals and then developing an action plan to achieve these goals. A useful tool in that process is the SWOT analysis. SWOT is the acronym for strengths, weaknesses, opportunities, and threats. This analysis will reveal the program's strengths—what it does well—and weaknesses or limitations. From this an athletic administrator can make key decisions, such as how to market its products.

In general, an education-based interscholastic marketing plan should follow these steps:

- Step 1: The process starts with an analysis of the sport product to determine its tangible and intangible worth. Tangible goods includes uniforms, coaching apparel, footwear, helmets, bats, balls, and other equipment. Services are the activities that support the game or event itself, including game officials, trainers, the band, cheerleaders, concession stands, cable TV, and the media. The game or event represents the core of the sport product and is usually viewed as a form of entertainment. It includes the sport-specific participants, the coaches, and the competition.

So, for most athletic administrators, this task is all about the tradition of the local high school. What do the coaches, athletes, and community take the most pride in when representing the school? Traditionally, it's about the school colors and making certain they are worn and displayed consistently from sport to sport and season to season. This builds school pride in wearing the colors and positively influences how the public views all the participants.

- Step 2: Positioning the sport product is about differentiating it from competing products by creating a positive image for the consumer. Working cooperatively with the public and responding to their interests is an effective communication tool. Athletic directors should keep in mind that they have an extensive market, including participants, spectators, game personnel, advertisers, sponsors, and the media.

Athletic administrators are responsible for understanding the philosophy of the school district as it relates to athletics and ensuring it is adhered to.

How an athletic director behaves and carries himself in full view of the public will separate him from the pack. The athletic administrator wants the product—the student-athletes—to be first-class competitors, to exhibit good sporting behavior, and to respect the game. This becomes a mantra, the way to conduct business, how first impressions are made. All of this and more will help differentiate a school's product from others.

- Step 3: The astute marketer will analyze the target audience—the consumer—and develop a strategy to reach them. On the high school level, the target market is clearly defined by the respective community. This is where a careful balance of the marketing mix factors into the strategy (i.e., the product, price, place [distribution], and promotion).

The 21st-century athletic administrator faces great challenges in this regard because of current economic conditions in the high school sports market. Understanding the market and building relationships with the consumers will help position the athletic program for success. Building a knowledgeable and dedicated coaching staff committed to excellence is imperative to attract an audience that will financially support the program. If it's necessary to charge a participation fee to help defray the cost of the athletic program, parents will support a successful program that is education based, that provides value to their child's experience, and that is a positive force in the community.

- Step 4: Pricing a sport product involves determining the value and setting profitable and justifiable prices. In setting a pricing strategy, it is imperative to consider the consumers' needs, preferences, and purchasing patterns or behaviors. Competition is another factor to consider along with laws, ordinances, government regulations, and the political environment.

Pricing a sport product is not an easy task because only a few sports are characterized as revenue producing (e.g., football, basketball, wrestling). This may vary from state to state and even within regions of the same state, but not all sports produce revenue. So, the athletic administrator needs to consider the so-called going price for admission within his league or conference and decide on ticket prices for students and adults. This is where the athletic administrator can become creative with different pricing strategies and incentives (e.g., general admission, student rates, family package reserve seating, special event days for elementary schools, senior days). Again, a successful athletic program will make the task of pricing the product easier as compared to a program that is not successful.

- Step 5: Promoting a sport product is all about communication between the sellers and the buyers (i.e., the athletic program and the community). It involves implementing a mix of activities that will best present the desired image of the product to the selected target audience, such as advertising and publicity; promotions (coupons); community, public, and media relations; and personal selling. This integrated marketing approach at the high school level will be beneficial in reaching the athletic department's desired goals.

For example, the enterprising athletic administrator may consider some of the following promotional activities to increase game attendance and add value to her program: door prize drawings, food coupons, clothing raffles, items with the school logo and colors, intermission contests, themes and special events, concession stand coupons, and alumni days. Many of the items and gifts that are raffled are donated by local businesses, which can give local merchants game exposure and build relations.

- Step 6: Placing the sport product refers to its various locations. It should be readily accessible, attractive in appearance, convenient, pleasant, safe, and secure. Sport is unique in that the selling and buying of a product occurs at the same time and place as the staging of games or events. The use of electronic media has emerged in recent years as another avenue to market a sport product, along with the distribution of contest tickets.

One of the more popular media activities that has emerged at the high school level is cable TV. This media program can attract some of the most creative students into the sport arena. The students get involved in video-recording and streaming games onto the local cable TV channel; they script the content, track data through game stats, interview coaches and players, edit the program, and so on. One of my former coaches, Al Wilson, an English teacher, caught the attention of the superintendent and was appointed as the Media Coordinator for the school district. In this role, he developed a video production class that became part of the curriculum in the high school. In this class, he was able to identify students who had an avid interest in media and went on to develop an outstanding media program for the district. Many of his former students pursued college careers in media production and today are successfully working in the industry for all of the major networks including ESPN.

- Step 7: The final step in this process focuses on the importance of evaluating the marketing plan. The feedback from inside and outside the athletic department must be analyzed to determine the extent to which the plan achieved the organization's mission. Linking the mission to what the organization does well (core competencies) will determine to what extent the marketing plan was successful.

The process of evaluation is extremely important in determining whether the marketing plan was successful or not. The athletic administrator will need to evaluate the pricing structure of tickets and the impact on gate receipts; the effectiveness of the promotional activities on game attendance; the impact of in-kind donations from merchants on game promotions; and the viewership of cable TV.

The evaluation of the product, the coaches, and ultimately the student-athletes is most critical to this process. A coaching evaluation instrument that documents and assesses performance based on behavioral competencies is important for retaining competent coaches and also for improving their performance.

A successful sport marketing plan is driven by positive communication. If the mission of the strategic plan reflects the core values and competencies of the athletic department, then implementing the marketing plan based on this process will achieve the desired results. By employing an integrated marketing strategy, athletic directors will successfully sell products using effective pricing, distributions, and promotions to their target audience.

Booster Clubs

Booster clubs are an example of relationship marketing. The athletic director creates a relationship with the booster club, and the booster club in turn creates a relationship with other organizations and the community. Since the advent of Title IX in 1972 and the positive impact it has had on interscholastic sport participation, booster clubs have also experienced a comparable and parallel growth in our schools. The past 40 years in high school sports have been incredibly exciting on one hand and equally challenging on the other.

When schools offered just a handful of sports, primarily for the boys, booster clubs focused on only the so-called revenue-producing sports such as football and basketball. Fast forward to the present day, and the 21st-century athletic administrator is now dealing with multiple booster clubs for both boys' and girls' sports programs alike.

There are several key components to building a successful booster club organization. First and foremost, the athletic director needs to determine whether the booster club is a de jure type of club, one that is approved by the school board, or a de facto type that exists without explicit, formal approval of the school board.

The obvious choice is to make certain that all booster clubs are approved by the school board to ensure that safeguards are incorporated into the constitution, bylaws, or school district guidelines. There are too many horror stories of fraudulent acts or absconded funds associated with poorly organized and managed booster clubs.

The school district should have guidelines for all its booster clubs. Among those guidelines should be the provision of clear and complete information about the club as to its name, purpose and function, membership qualifications, board of directors, officers, member and board duties, meetings, finances, fiscal year, and basic policies of operation.

A well-developed section on finances will spell out the following: disbursement of funds, establishment of nonprofit status under 501(c)3 of the IRS tax code, deposits, payment of expenses, bonding of treasurer, budgets, expenditure limits, and annual audit. Once these guidelines and procedures are in place and school board approved, they will then provide the framework for creating a positive and successful relationship with the booster club.

Although stories abound about the headaches some parents create for athletic directors and coaches, booster clubs that are properly constructed and managed can have a positive and profound effect on the athletic program. Parents, who typically support booster clubs, can become powerful allies.

Taking an active role in the booster clubs helps parents understand the athletic budget, fund-raising guidelines, and how the money raised should be spent. Many parents are either involved in businesses in the community or have connections to the business community that help raise funds for athletics. Equally important, sport parents provide assistance in building support, generating school spirit, maintaining school pride and tradition, and promoting a sense of fair play. All these things create a positive image in the community of the school's athletic program.

There are countless examples of how today's athletic administrators have led booster clubs in funding major capital improvement projects that directly benefit the athletic program. For instance, one of my most gratifying experiences involves the football parents club. Traditionally, we always played our home football games on Saturday afternoon because we had no stadium lights. The parents approached me about conducting a major fund-raising project for stadium lights, and they wanted my support. They needed school board approval and administrative support as well. There was no hesitation on my part because I was very familiar with the key members of the parents club, and their funding plan was comprehensive and well thought out.

After several planning meetings, we prepared a proposal and presented it to the school board, which unanimously approved the fund-raising project at no cost to the district. The $80,000 project received widespread support from the parents club, the business community, and the football enthusiasts. There were in-kind general contractor donations as well as electrical donations, and the school district cooperated fully. This is a great example of how the athletic director can effectively build relationships with key members of a booster club and collaborate on a worthwhile project that will benefit the athletic program.

Title IX Considerations for Booster Clubs

Whether the athletic director is responsible for an all-sports booster club or booster clubs for individual sports, he needs to be mindful of the Title IX implications.

According to national expert, Peg Pennepacker, on Title IX issues at the high school level, Title IX does not require boys' and girls' budgets to match dollar for dollar, but the benefits provided must be equal. The Office for Civil Rights (OCR) interprets Title IX further by stating that "educational institutions cannot use an economic justification for discrimination" (Pennepacker 2011).

When a high school athletic department accepts funding from a booster club, the athletic department can use the money as specified by the booster club. However, it cannot use the funding as a reason or excuse to discriminate. For instance, if the booster club funds were used to purchase boys' basketball warm-ups, then the athletic department is obligated by law to find the funding to ensure that the girls' basketball team has the same benefit (warm-ups).

OCR's position is crystal clear on this issue. The source of the funds is really not the issue, but the equal benefit is the measure of the law. Although this might be difficult to understand and accept, it is vitally important that school administrators—superintendents, principals, and athletic directors—comply with the law. Booster clubs need to be on the same page with Title IX compliance and educated about it. "Most Title IX complaints come from students, parents, or coaches based on disparities between boys and girls related to other benefits that accompany participation" (Pennepacker 2011).

Advice From School Boards

Most local school boards will provide sound advice to athletic directors when dealing with booster clubs in order to develop sound policies.

1. Require insurance at limits established by the board, naming the district as an additional insured.
2. Acknowledge familiarity with the obligation to comply with district policies on sexual harassment, Title IX, hazing, discrimination, smoking, weapons, and so on.
3. Require an annual audit, with copies to the superintendent and all board members.
4. Require a surety bond for the treasurer or fund custodian.
5. Limit fund-raising activities involving student labor to a maximum number of hours or activities per week.
6. Maintain proper registration and reporting under state charitable solicitation laws.

Along with following this advice, it is equally important to determine the local school board's policy and procedure for (1) use of the school district's name; (2) use of a logo, mascot, and school colors; (3) fund-raising; and (4) accepting donations (cash or in-kind).

Further, who has oversight regarding the selling of ads in sport-specific programs? Are ads from beer or liquor distributors acceptable? Is advertising permitted on ballpark or stadium fences? If so, it is subject to open-forum law and First Amendment issues (e.g., if you take one ad, you cannot selectively refuse others). What is the school district's policy on games of chance (e.g., 50/50 draws)? The athletic director needs to adequately address these questions so that all approved booster clubs have a clear understanding of the school district's position on each issue.

Typically, most school boards will have well-developed and approved policies and procedures for booster club organizations. Most school boards recognize and appreciate the efforts and countless hours these community-based clubs contribute in supporting district-approved programs and activities. Collaboratively, booster club fund-raising activities should be consistent with the philosophy and goals of the school district. It is within the leadership role of the athletic director to ensure that the lines of communication and understanding between all parties remain open and transparent.

Corporate Sponsorships

For the past 10 years, corporate sponsorships have emerged as one of the hottest trends in interscholastic sports. National and state associations and local school districts across the United States have discovered that sponsorships are mutually beneficial to both parties and have begun embracing the sponsorship opportunities the corporate and business world has to offer. Corporate sponsorships are another example of relationship marketing. By creating relationships with various corporations, an athletic director has the opportunity to promote the program through those relationships, in more ways than just financing. If an athletic director works with a local sporting goods store, for example, both the store and the athletic program can benefit from the exposure each receives.

Sponsors have learned that integrating sponsorships into the promotional mix of personal selling, advertising, sales promotion, and public relations creates important links in the marketplace. Marketers have astutely used sponsorships as a means to leverage the value inherent in sport properties. They have found that sponsorship is an efficient way to reach specific markets and quickly create brand awareness. In our society, sport is part of the American fabric, and sponsorships have become an integral part of the tapestry.

By definition, a sponsorship happens when a company or business provides cash or in-kind resources to an event or activity in exchange for direct association with that event or activity. The company or business buys access to the customer's audience and other assets of the property.

In 2002, Dr. Eric Forsyth, Bemidji State University, partnered with the Pennsylvania State Athletic Directors Association (PSADA) to publish a practical guide for high school athletic directors and coaches titled *The Sponsorship Connection*. The research conducted answered the important questions of who, why, what, and how in regard to making the sponsorship connection in the interscholastic sports market, translating into a useful how-to guide for athletic directors. According to the research experts on this issue, Dr. Forsyth has been the leading contributor in understanding why businesses sponsor high school sports. Let's examine the research more closely (Pierce and Bussell 2011).

The purpose of the study was to determine whether small and large companies differ in their motives to sponsor, in their level of management involved in evaluating proposals, and in their decision-making criteria.

Sponsorship Sources

The primary reason small and large companies engage in sponsorships at the high school level is their willingness to give back to and support the educational market. Beyond that rationale, they differ as follows:

Small companies	Large companies
Support education	Support education
Sponsorship goodwill	Public image
Personal enjoyment	Sponsorship goodwill
Public image	Company's exposure
Provide scholarships	Increase business objectives
Company exposure	Provide scholarships
Increase business objectives	Enhance prestige
Enhance prestige	Personal enjoyment

The correlation between incorporating more benefits into sponsorship proposals and success is quite evident. The more the company will realize a positive return on investment (ROI), the more likely it will sponsor an event or athletic program. This is a valuable point of emphasis for the athletic director in developing an attractive sponsorship proposal.

Within each company is a key group or person who will make the final decision. An athletic director needs to know who those decision-makers are. This will require familiarity with the company in terms of its size, its products and services, the target market or audience, and the cost of the sponsorship. The key decision-makers for small and large companies are as follows:

Company	Upper management	Middle management
Small	Owner	Office manager
Large	CEO	Marketing director
	Owner	Advertising director
	President	Finance director
	Vice president	Office manager

Corporate Sponsorships: It's All About Connections

From my years of experience in the high school sport arena as a teacher, coach, and administrator, I truly believe that when it comes to sport marketing and fund-raising, it's all about relationships.

One of the best examples of how this comes together and essentially connects all the dots is the true story of how a successful business in the fitness industry was started in Pennsylvania.

(continued)

(*continued*)

During the 1996 March conference of our state association, I was approached by two experts in the fitness and wellness industry about whether our state athletic directors association would be interested in endorsing and promoting a series of seminars across the state. After several meetings and discovery sessions, we began to relate to each other and found we had common interests and enthusiasm for developing fitness opportunities for the student-athletes and coaches in the Pennsylvania market.

We launched a series of seminars during the 1996-1997 school year for the specific purpose of creating fitness centers and programs in our schools' physical education and athletic departments. The seminars were titled How to Develop a Fitness Center When You Have No Budget, No Space and No Support.

The seminars attracted an audience that included superintendents, principals, athletic directors, business managers, coaches, and school board members. The content focused on how to improve physical education, sport-specific fitness training, facilities and equipment, curriculum renewal and assessment, community services, and creative funding options. The response from the participants was overwhelmingly favorable, and so we began the process of connecting the key players to make this a reality in our schools.

One of the primary presenters of the seminar series was Mr. Thomas Webster. From this experience and because of the relationship he and I established, Tom started his own fitness business—Webster's Fitness Products, Inc. To this day, our respect for each other has grown tremendously, and the relationship is as sound as the day is long.

Webster's Fitness Products, Inc., has evolved to become the premier provider of fitness equipment and service in the Pennsylvania market. Since 2000, it has been one of the most loyal and respected corporate sponsors and partners of the Pennsylvania State Athletic Directors Association. The credibility that Tom Webster has earned with our member schools and athletic directors speaks for itself. His company has installed approximately 200 state-of-the-art fitness and wellness centers in Pennsylvania schools that provide opportunities for physical education classes, interscholastic athletic teams, and community-based programs.

At the end of the day, it's all about developing relationships, finding common ground, and working together to achieve attainable goals.

Sponsorship Criteria

Once the reasons companies sponsor high school athletic events and programs have been established, the next logical step is to examine what criteria are used in the decision-making process. This step is extremely helpful for the athletic director in developing a successful sponsorship proposal. The rank order below illustrates the point. However, there will be sponsors who are seeking a specific return on their investment (ROI), and it will require the experienced athletic administrator to customize the sponsorship proposal to the defined needs of the prospective sponsor.

1. Cost of the sponsorship
2. Quality of the sponsorship
3. Company's exposure
4. Reaching the target market
5. Return on investment
6. Competition between competitors

Additional criteria that may be incorporated into a sponsorship proposal include the following: benefits to student-athletes, the sport-specific relationship, the partnership with the athletic department, the relationship of the company within the community (employees), and the personal relationship between the company and the athletic director and coaches.

Sponsorship Value

There are approximately 20,000 high schools in the United States and according to the National Federation of High Schools (NFHS), there are 7.6 million student-athlete participants. Although there are similarities in terms of what each high school has to offer in sport marketing, there are many differences. Each athletic administrator needs to take inventory of the athletic department's own marketable assets to determine its sponsorship worth. For example, the typical assets of any high school might include some or more of the following:

- Size of the market or audience
- Available signage
- Sport-specific publications (game programs)
- Mascot, logo, school colors
- Sport-specific events and programs
- Access to website
- Local media access (newspaper, radio, cable TV)

- Student database
- Facilities (stadiums, gymnasiums, fitness centers, ballparks)
- History and tradition of sport
- Booster club(s)
- Hospitality events

Once the assets are identified, the athletic director should consider combining the benefits or entitlements into multiple levels to maximize the sponsorship revenue. For instance, one popular approach is to designate levels such as bronze, silver, and gold, each with specific benefits and costs ranging from $2,500 to $10,000.

The assets of the athletic program could be divided into two distinct categories: tangible and intangible. Both will have an impact on how the athletic director goes about pricing each asset. Tangible assets may include the following values: sport-specific advertising in game programs, signage on the property (stadiums, gymnasiums), advertising on radio or cable TV, game or event tickets, log-on apparel, mailing lists, scoreboards, website banners, booth space, and concession stands. Intangible assets that may also have value are the reputation of the school and sports program, the success of a sport-specific program, community support and loyalty to the school, media coverage the school provides, category exclusivity, networking with other sponsors, and a proven track record with the sponsor.

Seeking a Sponsorship

For the high school athletic director, the process of seeking a sponsorship may seem rather daunting, especially if it's a new experience. There is no silver bullet that will close the deal for a sponsorship, but there is one constant: the "ask." Somewhere in the process, you must position the ask for what you are proposing.

The following steps outline the process in seeking a corporate sponsorship:

1. Interact with the businesses in the community.
2. Become familiar with their products and services.
   a. Find out who the decision-makers are.
   b. Determine what promotional mix they use.
3. Contact the decision-maker.
   a. For a small business, contact the owner; for a large business, the marketing department.
   b. Make the connection; build a relationship.
   c. Schedule a face-to-face meeting.

4. Have a conversation with the decision-maker.
   a. Engage in flow of information about the sport program.
   b. Share the value and benefits of the proposal.
   c. Position the proposal for favorable review.
5. Present the sponsorship proposal.
   a. Seek careful consideration of the offer by the company.
   b. Explore through discovery what the company wants.
   c. Exercise flexibility, but do not compromise standards.
   d. Explain fully the entitlements included in the proposal.
   e. Express confidence and passion in delivering what is promised.
   f. Share any testimonials from current sponsors.
   g. Tailor the proposal to the prospective business category.
   h. Discuss the accountability for return on investment.
   i. Build the relationship; develop teamwork.
6. Close the deal with the ask.
   a. Summarize the value and benefit of the sponsorship.
   b. Focus on the prospect's interests and priorities.
   c. Determine during the meeting the right time for the ask.
   d. Emphasize the impact the sponsorship will make on the athletic program.
   e. Make the ask based on what the school is seeking in dollars or in-kind.
   f. Maintain eye contact and stay silent.
   g. Allow the prospect to respond to the request.
   h. Follow up within 24 hours with a thank you and hopefully a confirmation letter or signed proposal.

Most of my experience with corporate sponsors is at the state athletic director association level, starting in 1990 to the present time. I learned on the job as the executive director of the Pennsylvania State Athletic Directors Association. The information detailed in this section has been very helpful because I have applied it in the corporate world with success. I've been fortunate to raise more than $100,000 per year for the past 12 years and more than $1.3 million since I began in 1989-1990. Today, many athletic administrators are being asked to engage in fund-raising and attracting corporate sponsors. The process outlined in this section is a successful one and with experience is applicable at the local community level. But keep in mind the value of building and establishing those relationships in order to seal the deal.

Educational Foundations and Fund-Raising

The new fiscal reality in public education will greatly influence the way interscholastic athletic programs are funded now and in the future. Research supports the emergence of alternative revenue sources to fund high school athletics. The data clearly reveal that athletic directors are increasingly seeking alternative revenue from three sources: (1) fund-raising, (2) sponsorships, and (3) participation fees.

So far this chapter has addressed the impact that booster clubs and sponsorships have on athletic budgets. This final section explores the role of local educational foundations (LEFs) and fund-raising.

Educational foundations and endowments have been in existence for a long time, especially at the collegiate level. In the past decades, LEFs have become more prominent at the local school district level in most states. With public education under attack and underfunded, LEFs are now emerging as another viable and consistent source of funding for the K-12 educational environment. Successful LEFs are making a difference in our schools by providing educational resources that have been cut from the budget. There have been instances in Pennsylvania where an LEF has made a significant contribution to the local high school athletic budget.

As the axiom states, "If anything is worth doing, then it is worth doing right." Any organization needs to take the first-things-first approach to success. You need to plan. You need to be organized. You need to maximize your people resources. You need to understand that less is more. And you need to know where you want to go. It all sounds familiar.

Successful foundations are recognized and remembered. As such, they should clearly and concisely answer the following questions: Who are we? Why are we here? How do we do what we do? When do we do what we do? Where does this happen? All these questions and answers pertain to the challenges that educational foundations face.

To gain an awareness and understanding of its who, why, how, when, and where, the foundation needs to develop a focused, repetitive, meaningful, and believable message. The audience that the educational foundation can target with this message consists of school boards, superintendents, administration, staff, teachers, parents, students, families, residents, businesses, vendors, and alumni.

Once a plan is in place for the foundation, the executive director needs to identify its priorities, focus on a clear message, and target the primary audience. In doing so, it is important to match the method of communication to the priorities, message, and audience. There are several choices for communicating this message to the target audience (e.g., advertising, using direct mailings, engaging in social media, posting on the website, using public relations).

The bottom line in all philanthropy is the individual. Most sources cite that anywhere from 75 to 85 percent of giving comes from individual donors.

So what does the director need to understand about individual giving to create a successful educational foundation that will benefit the local high school athletic program?

What Motivates a Person to Support?

Basically, everyone enjoys some form of recognition, and most people feel good about giving. There is an emotional component associated with giving. We know, from experience and research, that the vast majority of philanthropy comes from individuals.

The least compelling reasons that motivate a donor are guilt or obligation, fancy proposals and promotional materials, and tax considerations. The most compelling reasons are as follows:

- The donor's belief in the mission of the organization
- Community responsibility and civic pride
- The fiscal stability and health of the organization
- High regard for the staff and volunteer leadership
- Serving on a board or committee and being involved

Individual donors also have their own personal goals for giving. These goals include the prestige of the association, recognition, self-worth and immortality, memorializing a loved one, feeling good about themselves, religious obligation, and just pure philanthropy. Research further tells us the following about individual giving:

- The organizations most likely to receive attention are connected to the donor's experience.
- The stronger and more emotional the connection, the greater the gifts.
- A willingness to commit is nurtured and expanded by direct involvement with the organization.
- Personal contact with constituents is critical.
- Donors want and need continual feedback about the use of gifts.

Where Does the LEF Start?

The logical starting point for any foundation is to identify the need. The LEF board of directors and executive director must develop a compelling case for support, including a well-defined, understandable need for a gift. The ask needs to be specific and straightforward. The foundation should create a timely and urgent (especially online) sense of giving from its targeted audience. There also should be transparency in how the gift will be used and what it will accomplish. For example, when the director translates the needs into an ask, she should properly communicate them as follows:

- Help fund a coaching education program for all varsity high school coaches: 30 coaches = $2,000.
- Help send the boys' and girls' soccer teams to summer camp: $1,000 per team of 30 players each.
- Help purchase pitching machines for both the baseball and softball varsity teams: $5,000.
- Help fund the installation of lights at the high school stadium: $80,000.

Who Should the LEF Ask?

Most established foundations with a history of success have priorities in terms of whom to ask. For instance, the number one priority might be the board of directors and major donors; number two may be current donors and last year's donors; number three could be any donors that have lapsed; number four may be parents, alumni, e-mail and social media contacts, event donors, volunteers, and the general community.

There is a degree of art and science to fund-raising. How do directors determine the appropriate amount to ask? The following is a guide:

- Major gift donors: Tailor the ask to their interest level, capacity, and previous philanthropic donations.
- Regular donors: Match the ask amounts to their past giving history.
- Non-donors: Don't ask too much. A lower ask amount will lead to more new donors.

An integrated approach to fund-raising gives donors the opportunity to donate through different methods. For example, personal solicitations, direct mails, e-mails (urgent and timely), envelopes with other marketing materials, and website buttons provide opportunities for online promotions and donations.

How to Ask in Person

The advantage of the face-to-face ask is that it is more likely than any other method to generate an increased gift. The donor is also more likely to renew because of the relationship the director can develop with the donor by showing passion and enthusiasm for the foundation. The following step-by-step process shows how to make the personal solicitation work:

1. Identify all prospects.
   a. Include the board, volunteers, and past donors.
   b. Make a list of new prospects (start with yourself, friends of the board, and volunteers).

2. Qualify the prospects.

   a. Is there a direct link to the LEF?

   b. Have they previously given to the organization?

   c. Can they make this gift level?

3. Assess their readiness.

   a. People who have given a recent gift are ready!

   b. People who haven't given but are close to someone in the organization might be ready.

   c. People who are interested in the cause but don't know anyone in the organization need cultivation.

4. Cultivate those who need to be cultivated (tours of the school, informal meetings, events, and so on), and ask those who are ready to be asked.

5. Set up a meeting.

   a. Send an introductory letter.

   b. Follow up with a phone call.

   c. Make an appointment.

6. Make the ask.

   a. Prepare. What are the prospect's interests, priorities, and giving amount?

   b. Ask in pairs—have two people present when the ask is made.

   c. If possible, have a volunteer who has made a gift of her own make the ask.

   d. Never make an ask if you haven't already given yourself.

   e. Pick the right place to ask.

   f. Talk about the impact the organization has through personal stories. Focus on the benefit, the impact, and the vision.

   g. Ask! "Can you help us with a $250 contribution?" Or "We are hoping you can give us a donation of $500 to $1,000 this year."

   h. Keep looking at the prospect.

   i. Stay alert.

   j. Allow the prospect to respond to the request.

7. Follow up with a thank you within 24 hours and, if appropriate, a confirmation letter.

Remember: The asker's passion for and commitment to the cause is one of the most important influences on the prospect.

Summary

The challenges that the 21st century athletic administrator faces are not insurmountable, but they are complex. Fortunately, the NIAAA and the NFHS have been collaborating on important initiatives about the benefits and value of high school sports that will greatly assist members as we go forward.

Sport marketing and fund raising are not new to the arena, but they have gained considerable traction because of the economic crisis facing our country. The fiscal landscape has changed dramatically for athletic administrators, and they are now tasked with a daunting challenge of finding new revenue sources to deliver quality athletic programs. The new fiscal reality in public education has impacted school boards in every state and they are further challenged with increased health care costs and underfunded pensions.

More and more high schools have experienced an increase in the use of corporate sponsors, pay-to-participate fees, and fund raising as additional revenues sources to fund athletic programs.

CHAPTER 14

Budgeting and Purchasing

John Evers, CMAA

Because sports are extracurricular activities, there is no requirement or mandate for athletic teams or competition in schools. An athletic department that is bleeding money, consistently spending beyond its means, is in danger of losing sports and perhaps being shut down. Therefore, it is the duty of the athletic administrator to be a good steward of all funds that come under the control of the athletic department. Sound practice and policies, backed by accurate record keeping, are the hallmark of a strong athletic department.

Athletic administrators and members of the athletic department must be held accountable for all dollars spent. There must be accurate assessment of all financial data to show wise use of funds.

Seldom do interscholastic athletic programs fail to demonstrate their worth. High school athletics are, in general, a very good investment of dollars. Most school sports programs engage up to one-third of the student body, yet they use less than 2 percent of the school's operating budget. The per capita expenses for athletics are far less than those for instructional purposes. Regardless, there must be a constant state of awareness and review of funds allocated and spent to allow for the growth of all athletic programs.

Every state has different rules, statutes, and regulations governing the manner in which athletic funds are obtained, earmarked, distributed, and documented. Individual districts may also impose specific rules and regulations on the manner in which funds are procured, items are purchased, and funding is approved. The athletic administrator must follow all funding and spending guidelines at all times in order to comply with mandates imposed on the athletic department.

The process of building an athletic budget may be lengthy. The actual budget may go through several rewrites and may need to be approved at different levels of administration. Sometimes the budget may even have to go to a public vote, such as approval of a tax levy. Such a system of checks and balances is necessary to ensure all parties have an equal chance to view and review the budget. A budget that does not provide such oversight often

There must be a constant state of awareness and review of funds allocated and spent to allow for the growth of all athletic programs.

fails to address all areas necessary to fund a well-rounded and complete athletic department. Reviewing and assessing the budget over a period of time is a method of instilling public confidence in the work of the athletic administrator.

Most school districts employ a treasurer or bookkeeper to write all checks, make all deposits, and keep an accurate balance and debit account for the school and athletic department. The athletic administrator must be able to take the data received from the school's financial officer and use this information to formulate, execute, and follow the budgeting plan.

When formulating and executing an athletic budget, athletic administrators must strictly follow state and local guidelines and develop a clear and transparent plan of action. But regardless of the state or district, certain constants will always remain. The athletic director should seek to accomplish five basic goals when constructing and following a budget (Evers 2001):

1. Understand the budget structure. Although not a financial expert, the athletic administrator must have a firm understanding of what funds are going in and out of the department. A general understanding of where and how funds are distributed is paramount in the budgeting process. Any major financial or legal questions can be referred to those with more financial knowledge.

2. Explain the budget to all stakeholders. The development and execution of an athletic budget is part of a shared trust between an athletic administrator and the public being served. There should be no secrets, and all information should be freely shared with administrators, coaches, patrons, and student-athletes on a regular basis.

3. Modify the budget, when necessary, to meet new challenges. New challenges present themselves to an athletic administrator on a daily basis. What was a low priority in spending on one day could become a major need a day later. It is imperative that the budget be flexible enough to meet new needs and demands as they arise without compromising the integrity of the process.

4. Sell the budget to all parties. Many budget decisions involve hard choices. An effective athletic administrator must be able to develop a relationship with coaches, athletes, and patrons. Once a relationship is built, hard choices can be explained to all involved. Explanation that is accompanied by empathy is the key to selling a comprehensive budget plan to all stakeholders. This allows an athletic department to survive during financial good times as well as bad times.

5. Document all phases of the budget process. An athletic administrator will handle, funnel, earmark, and spend enormous amounts of money when

conducting the business of an athletic department. It is crucial that there be a method and mode of documentation for every transaction. Accurate documentation is not only a legal matter but also a matter of absolute trust that must be garnered through exhaustive measures to ensure a complete paper trail at all times.

Budgeting Process

The process of building a budget is one that requires great care and thoughtful management. Several steps must be taken before completing the budget for each sport and the department. These steps should be measured and are vital to the overall success of all programs.

Review the Athletic Budget History

The first step in formulating an athletic budget is to review what has taken place in the athletic department in the past. This history should go back at least 5 years and possibly as long as 10 years and include all sports at all levels.

A review of past spending is next to be completed. This review should highlight all spending by sport and as a department, as well as spending from sources outside the department. Such sources might include booster clubs, vending machines, concessions, and corporate sponsorship.

Next, the athletic administrator should review any past capital improvements, facility work, or other major renovations. Any past issues or concerns related to gender equity must also be analyzed and documented.

Finally, all requests and needs that have been generated by coaches, administrators, patrons, and athletes over the past years should be organized. Once all phases of the review have been completed, an accurate picture of past spending and purchasing patterns will become clear.

Envision a Realistic Future

Once the past has been assessed, the next step in the process of building a budget is to envision a realistic future. This future must be based on facts and jointly developed by the athletic administrator, school administration, and coaching staff. This shared vision can be generated in group or individual meetings of all parties.

Part of developing a realistic vision is attempting to estimate participation numbers for each of the sports or activities over the next five years. This is a difficult task, but information garnered from youth and middle school sports teams can help build a framework from which solid estimates can emerge.

The next step in the process is to develop and project spending needs in the short term. Much of the information gathered in developing an accurate history can be a great assistance in developing short-term spending needs assessments. Spending from one year to the next usually does not show great variance unless some outside forces intervene. The more difficult task is to develop spending projections over the long term. The more time involved, the more opportunity for unforeseen circumstances to surface. Much more input is required in this step. The athletic director may need to obtain information on student enrollment and feeder-league participation well down into elementary school levels. Assessments of facility needs and possible capital funding issues might need to be addressed at the district level or beyond. These discussions might delve into topics that could be covered in a district master plan or a district building improvement policy.

Another part of envisioning a realistic future is addressing potential additions or deletions of sports, sports team, coaching staff, or support personnel. Many school districts have prescribed plans and procedures for adding or abolishing existing teams or levels. Some districts react to changes on an individual basis.

Often changes in sports support and sponsorship are brought on by compliance with mandated guidelines. Such forces for change include the Americans with Disabilities Act (ADA) and Title IX.

Although some changes are the product of a district movement toward compliance, others are the product of concerns or complaints lodged with the Office for Civil Rights (OCR). Complaints filed with OCR can result in investigations of schools and school districts. Schools found not to be in compliance are usually given several avenues to address concerns. Many schools complete needed remedies with few problems. Others are directed by OCR to institute major changes in funding, support, recruitment, facilities, schedules, and policies for boys' and girls' teams and for coaches. Often the changes schools must institute to reach compliance levels will add increased stress to athletic budgets.

Determine a Budget Type

As mentioned earlier in this chapter, a variety of laws and statutes govern athletic funding and budgeting across the United States. Often the funding rules that apply to a state or district will dictate the type of budget or funding that is adopted. Regardless of the state or district rules, budgets across the United States usually fall into one of four major categories. Budgets are typically classified as zero based, incremental, shared responsibility, or combination. This section explores the similarities and differences between the four types of budgets.

Zero-Based Budgets

A zero-based budget is one in which the athletic administrator and coaching staff annually negotiate all funding based on documented need. The negotiation starts at zero and is expanded depending on current need in each program. Past history is usually not taken into consideration. Some of the areas that become part of such a negotiation might include the following (NIAAA 2010):

- The number and experience level of members of the coaching staff
- The participation numbers (i.e., whether increasing or decreasing)
- All inventory levels and projected needs for the sport
- Travel to all competitions at all levels
- Cost of officials for all home events at all levels
- The repair, maintenance, cleaning, and replacement of all items in inventory
- Possible repair or maintenance of game and practice facilities

Incremental Budgets

For an incremental budget, the athletic administrator is authorized to approve specific increases or decreases in the tax- or tuition-funded portion of the athletic budget. Such changes are usually driven by the need to accommodate long-term growth and development or a possible long-term decrease in numbers in each program. Regardless of the decision made by the athletic administrator, coaches are advised to keep and document on-hand inventories as well as long-range developmental plans and future participation estimates. The athletic administrator has the autonomy in this model to shift funds from one sports budget to another. There can also be shifting within a sports budget to augment funding from booster clubs and fund-raising.

Several factors can affect incremental budget allocations. Such factors include the current economic climate in the district, changes in state or federal assistance, new legislative mandates, state and local tax levy changes, collective bargaining agreements, and local elections.

Documentation in the form of written assessment data is needed to minimize the possibility of incremental reductions. Data that should be gathered include the following (NIAAA 2010):

- Data pertaining to participation statistics for present and future classes
- Long-range planning and status reports for participants and facilities
- Mandated changes such as those for ADA, Title IX, or risk management issues
- Player and parent assessments in the form of surveys, exit interviews, and interest studies

Partial or Complete Responsibility Budgets

In this type of budget, the athletic administrator has some degree of responsibility for raising funds to operate the athletic department. This usually involves corporate support, major fund-raising initiatives, game contests and promotions, season ticket sales, and advertising campaigns. This method of procuring funds usually becomes part of the fabric and culture of the school and community. In some states, physical plant operation, transportation, and the salaries of coaches can be funded by the school's overall general-fund budget.

Combination Budgets

Combination budgets usually build base salaries for coaches with tax or tuition funds within an incremental or zero-based model. Once the base budget is built, the total budget may be adjusted in several ways. Some of the methods of augmenting the base budget include booster club activities, vending machine revenues, concession sales at home events, candy bar sales, fun runs, outreach efforts to local businesses, and corporate sponsorship. In some school districts the contest revenues and season ticket sales may be placed in the school general fund as an offset against the local tax levy. Given an increase in the number of Title IX challenges by OCR or actual Title IX lawsuits, all components of the basic Title IX compliance framework must be considered.

Develop an Organizational Budgeting Policy

When planning an athletic budget, the athletic administrator must develop a sound and well-planned set of policy guidelines that can serve as guidelines for all decisions. The policies and guidelines must be aligned with the mission and philosophy of the school and district. Some areas that should be addressed in budgeting are discussed in this section.

Pay to Participate

Pay to play has been around for a long time in our schools. During the budget crisis of the 1980s and 1990s, the implementation of paying to play sports in high school was shocking. When school boards across the country began to address the budget gaps, they found themselves in a no-win situation between laying off teachers and continuing to support nonacademic activities.

During that era, voters almost everywhere were reluctant to raise their property taxes—the main source of revenue for K-12 education—at a pace that matched inflation. Also, the changing demographics are partly at fault. As our population ages, the number of American households that have school-age children may continue to shrink. The challenge to school budgets will only intensify.

Since that crisis, school administrators have learned that "pay to participate" is a more user-friendly way to raise funds for the athletic budget. The connotation makes a distinction that student-athletes are not guaranteed to play but will have the privilege of participating in the interscholastic athletic program for a fee.

Today, pay to participate has emerged as an accepted way for school boards to raise funds to offset the cost of sports programs and activities. In these turbulent economic times, the cuts to school district budgets have taken their toll on all facets of the academic and nonacademic offerings. Almost every state budget has been affected by the economic downturn since 2008, and implications are widespread. The new fiscal reality finds that all school revenues are in decline. The federal funds have pretty much disappeared, most state budget funding has been cut dramatically, and the local revenue sources are flat or reduced because of unemployment and property assessment appeals.

As school districts begin to face this new fiscal reality, they are finding that the growth in mandated costs (e.g., pensions and health care) will consume a sizable share of any revenue growth. This will not be offset by any increase in federal or state funding. So the watchword going forward is *fiscal discipline*.

Almost half of the total number of districts and schools that charge students to participate in interscholastic sports earmark the funds for specific expenditures, including revenue for the athletic budget, facilities improvement, busing, the fitness center, the athletic trainer's salary, insurance, and the cost of physical exams.

So with this new fiscal reality, is the landscape beginning to change in terms of how interscholastic sports are funded? Are education-based activities endangered? Are they in jeopardy of being replaced by the community-based model that has been gradually gaining traction over the years in towns across the United States? Are the old ways of funding education-based sports in transition to another or new way of funding?

If schools are required to fund-raise to pay for their sports programs, then athletic directors will need the necessary training to learn a little more about sport marketing. Although there are detractors in every community about the affordability of sports programs, high school sport participation continues to grow. According to National Federation of State High School Associations (NFHS) data, 7.6 million students participated in sports during the 2009-2010 school year (Howard 2011). Interest in high school sports has never been higher, and the benefits of high school sport participation are well documented: better attendance records, lower dropout rates, higher grade point averages, improved self-esteem, and preparation for a successful career. However, a survey of NFHS member state associations in 2009 revealed that participation fees were being charged by schools in 33 states, and it is likely that more states and schools will consider this option going forward beyond 2012 (Gardner 2011).

Athletic directors will have to consider many issues when pay to participate becomes part of the internal strategy to raise funds for the athletic program. Activity fees vary widely across the country. Charges have been reported from as low as $20 per year to as high as $500 per sport. The amount often hinges on whether coaching salaries and transportation fees are covered by the assessments. Here are several issues to consider:

• Check the legality in your state: Laws and courts have decided on both sides of this issue in a number of states based on the constitutionality of the practice. Most states, however, allow for school boards to impose the fee. Current practices have become creative in terms of identifying a specific fee for a specific expenditure (e.g., transportation, insurance).

• Examine fee structures in other districts in your state: Athletic directors like to share information about their programs. So brainstorm at your next meeting or conference to find out what works best with your neighboring schools, and put together a list of dos and don'ts to consider or recommend to your administration and school board.

• Set a maximum yearly fee structure per student and family: Students and families should not be penalized for participating in multiple sports with multiple children each year. They should not be forced to choose a sport because of the fee structure.

• Establish a schedule of when the fees are to be collected and by whom: If possible, keep the coaches out of collecting the fees. Typically, fees are collected in the athletic director's or principal's office. One practice that works well for most schools is to make the fee payable after the first practice but before the first contest. Payment is mandatory for participation in the first contest.

• Establish criteria for refunds: In this case, use common sense, but refund sparingly. All aspects of athletic participation need to be considered in terms of injuries, quitting the team, or dismissal because of student conduct violation.

• Establish criteria for those unable to pay the fee: Most school districts use qualifications for free or reduced-cost lunches as means of identifying students and families needing assistance. In this case, maintaining confidentiality is paramount for these students.

• Establish a specific purpose for the funds: Parents want to know where the money collected is going and how it will be used. It is an individual school's choice to identify how the funds will be used to offset expenditures, whether it be uniforms, travel, insurance, or something else. One practice that is frowned upon is to use the fees for coaching salaries. This has the potential to create too many problems for coaches and athletic directors.

• Establish the participation aspect of the fee: The fee does not guarantee playing time, only the privilege to participate in a sport. This should be made clear to the parents and students from the onset. Coaches determine who will play.

• Include the participation fee in the policies and procedures manual: It is vitally important to communicate this school board-approved policy to all parties before each sport season, including the students, parents, coaches, and community. Some schools have students and parents sign a form acknowledging their awareness of the policy and its rules.

- Develop consensus with all stakeholders: When developing the guidelines for how a participation fee schedule will be implemented, it is imperative to include all the stakeholders—students, parents, coaches, and administrators—so they have a sense of ownership in the program. If the process is conducted properly from the beginning, all parties will share the importance of maintaining education-based athletic programs and the benefits that young people acquire from participation.

Booster Clubs

Booster clubs can be a great assistance if properly organized and informed. Such organizations can also cause problems for the athletic administration if their practices deviate from state, local, and school policies. It is essential that booster clubs be organized in a manner that is compliant with the mission and philosophy of the school as well as being conducted within the laws that govern the athletic department.

The athletic administrator must guide the booster clubs in developing a constitution, complying with school oversight procedures, conforming to all rules of legal liability, and operating in a manner that does not bring the school out of compliance with Title IX rules and regulations. Most athletic departments that develop problems with booster clubs are those that allow extra benefits (e.g., uniforms, travel, meals, overnight stays) for some teams, while other teams do not receive similar treatment from their boosters or the athletic department.

Corporate Sponsorship

The level and amount of corporate sponsorship that can be used to supplement a budget is usually under the control of the school district. Prudent athletic administrators ensure all agreements made between corporate sponsors and athletic departments meet district guidelines and receive district approval at the highest level.

Some areas of corporate sponsorship that are popular in interscholastic athletics today include vending contracts, venue sponsorship, naming rights, scoreboard sponsorship, uniform sponsorship, and game sponsorship. In most cases, a contract should exist between the sponsoring group and the school district. The school legal counsel should also approve any contractual agreements.

Gender Equity Policies

All decisions relative to budgeting and purchasing must be completed within the Title IX compliance framework. Although funding of boys' and girls' sports need not be equal, it must reflect fairness and contribute to a sense of balance throughout the athletic department. The athletic administrator must build and maintain sound policies that prevent a major imbalance in spending between male and female sports teams. Areas that should be addressed by gender equity policy include oversight procedures, documentation methods, tracking of capital improvements, and yearly reporting of all spending by each sport as well as the overall athletic department.

The three-prong test employed by the OCR to determine gender equity compliance includes a study of participation numbers, financial aid, and other benefits and services. The area of compliance that most directly affects interscholastic athletics in a financial manner is other benefits and services. Some of the other benefits and services that could be traced directly to budgeting and purchasing include equipment, supplies, travel expenses, lodging, meals, and support services.

Supplemental Fund-Raising

As with corporate sponsorship, many school districts have strict policies on methods of supplemental fund-raising. Some districts ban fund-raising completely. Others strictly control and regulate who can raise funds, when they can operate, where they can execute the fund-raiser, and how funds are documented and dispersed. It is imperative that athletic directors develop similar guidelines that are in agreement with all school and district mandates. If a group representing the athletic department or team violates state laws or breaches the rules of legal liability, the ultimate responsibility will fall back on the athletic administrator. Oversight of all levels of supplemental fund-raising should be a high priority for the athletic administrator (Evers 2007).

Travel Policies

With the cost of fuel, driver payments, and maintenance constantly on the rise, the athletic administrator can control costs by developing an athletic travel policy for all teams. Local travel is usually dictated by the size of the team and the availability of school buses or smaller conforming vehicles (small buses or vans).

Long road trips can cause two types of problems. The first problem is cost. Often long trips require large amounts of gas and may produce higher driver costs in the form of hourly wages as well as overnight accommodations. The second problem that can arise is an equity issue. Many teams prefer a charter bus for longer trips. Charter buses allow teams to travel in comfort, but they usually cost much more than school bus rates. If some teams are allowed to travel in charters, while others are forced to ride school buses, equity issues will quickly arise. Policy that is fair and equitable to all sports can prevent many problems.

Uniform Rotation

The athletic administrator must develop and distribute an accurate and complete system for replacing uniforms. This plan must consider costs of uniforms, purchases in the same calendar year, and fairness between boys' and girls' sports. The athletic director must be certain that all uniforms purchased comply with rules and regulations set forth by the NFHS. A sound uniform rotation will be successful if athletic personnel follow a long-term plan, maintain an accurate inventory, and properly care for all uniforms.

Complimentary Tickets

Complimentary tickets are given to people who are deemed to be significant contributors to the district, the school, or the athletic department. Many districts have rules about who is eligible to receive such tickets. The athletic director must keep accurate records of all recipients to satisfy school as well as accounting guidelines. Some areas to consider include the number of complimentary tickets issued, who receives these tickets, and how many people are admitted on each complimentary ticket. District and local bargaining agreements might also affect the policy.

Develop a Basic Organizational Policy for Purchasing

All purchases made by or for the athletic department must be approved and accepted by the athletic administrator, whether the department purchases an item directly or accepts a donation from an outside source. The athletic administrator must maintain balance in all purchasing by developing a basic organizational policy. Such a policy is best implemented when approved by the local school district and published where all coaches, patrons, and boosters can have access.

It is vital that any purchase made on behalf of the athletic department meet strict guidelines. Such strict control of purchasing can reduce or eliminate possible concerns with fraud, abuse of school or booster funds, and possible equity violations. This section discusses some areas that might be included in a basic organizational purchasing policy.

Approval Policy for Purchasing

The athletic administrator is ultimately responsible for every purchase made by the athletic department or on behalf of the athletic department. Whether the purchase is made by the athletic administrator, one of his assistants, a coach, or an athletic booster group, the ultimate responsibility for the purchase, receipt, and use of such items rests on the shoulders of one individual. Therefore, the athletic administrator must develop, maintain, and share a clear and concise method of approval for every expenditure. It is imperative that the established chain of command and procedural process be followed to the letter every time a purchase is made. It is also extremely important that all documentation (in the form of itemized receipts) be retained and that all purchasing follow the guidelines set forth by the state as well as the school district.

Role of the Athletic Administrator and Coach in Purchasing

The head coach and athletic director should meet on a regular basis. At the conclusion of each competition season, the two normally meet to complete a formal written evaluation. A portion of this meeting should be dedicated to drafting a budget for the following year. It is at this time that hard decisions can be made on what was purchased in the past year and what is needed for the upcoming season. At this meeting, the framework for what will be purchased for the next year can be formally constructed. The athletic administrator can give direction to the coach on what will be purchased by the athletic department and what will require supplemental fund-raising by the coach or a booster group. Regardless of who purchases the items, all basic departmental procedures must be followed.

Role of Supplemental Fund-Raising

The role of supplemental fund-raising in interscholastic athletics can depend on several variables. All state and local statutes must be obeyed. Some schools are not allowed to fund-raise because of limits imposed by their district or administration. Many schools and school districts have specific rules and guidelines for the type of fund-raising, the methods of fund-raising that will be allowed, who will be allowed to complete the fund-raising duties, and where the money will be spent once it is gathered. Regardless of school or district rules, it is also extremely important that accurate records of inventory, sales, and expenditures be kept and shared.

Role of Athletic Booster Clubs

Booster clubs can be organized as an overall school group or as a dedicated fund-raising and support group for an individual sport or team. Such clubs must comply with all school and district missions and philosophies. Booster groups should have written bylaws; well-established goals; an organizational hierarchy; and a method of communication between the booster group, the head coach, and the athletic administrator. It should be clear to all that the booster groups serve the school at the request, and under the guidance of, the athletic administrator. All activities and fund-raising endeavors should be approved by the school and athletic administrator. Any activities that could bring discredit to the school or could violate school or district guidelines should be eliminated.

Once funds are raised, the athletic administrator must serve as the ultimate arbiter of how the funds will be spent, allowing her to control spending and ensure it is equitable. In some cases, booster groups with large numbers and many members could raise funds that might lead to a major imbalance in spending between similar sports. If a boys' basketball booster group is allowed to raise huge amounts of funds to benefit the boys' teams and the girls' teams is not given the same treatment, a situation could arise that indicates an inequity. When such imbalances occur, it is the duty of the athletic administrator to create balance. A firm handle on spending will help prevent problems between sports within the athletic department.

Use of Purchase Orders

One of the basic operational procedures of every athletic department should be the use of a purchase order for all transactions. A purchase order is a buyer-generated document that authorizes a purchase transaction. When accepted by the seller, it becomes a contract binding on both parties. A purchase order sets forth the descriptions, quantities, prices, discounts, payment terms, date of performance or shipment, and other associated terms and conditions, and it identifies a specific seller.

The purchase order protects both the buyer and seller from changes in pricing and costs. It also serves as an additional safeguard and documentation method to prevent spending that has not been approved or authorized. If a purchase order is required for purchases on behalf of the athletic department, it reduces the chances that spending will occur that might produce unfair benefits between sports. The purchase order is also a tool to assist the athletic administrator in keeping track of spending within the department.

Bidding Policy

Most states have rules for educational institutions related to the amount of money that must be involved before a bid process is required for purchasing. Many schools and districts have polices that match the state statute or are even more restrictive. It is the duty of the athletic director to be aware of all state statutes as well as school and district policy on the bidding process.

Every purchase that approaches or exceeds the required limits must be let out for bid. A sound and consistent policy on bidding on purchases will ensure fairness for all vendors. Such a policy will also protect the school and athletic director by producing a final cost that is the most advantageous for all parties. A quality bid process will also instill a sense of trust between the athletic administrator and the vendors. Such a process can also demonstrate a level of accountability for the athletic administrator.

Accounting Procedures

As with all other financial matters, the state and local governing bodies usually have a prescribed method of accounting that must be followed at all times. Most schools and districts undergo an audit procedure on a regular basis to ensure that all accounting procedures are followed in purchasing. Some complete an audit every year and some every two years. Proper records, methods of receiving funds, and methods of distributing funds are reviewed for accuracy and compliance with all rules and regulations. A paper trail that includes proper documentation for funds received and adequate proof of spending in the form of itemized receipts can be evaluated by an independent accounting organization. This process allows for growth and improvement and can correct minor deficiencies before they become major problems.

Budgets and the Athletic Administrator

A new athletic director was hired in a large suburban high school. He came to the job after many years as an assistant and head coach in several schools and in several sports. His background was highlighted by an ample amount of experience in leadership and coaching and by knowledge of most sports. He was highly organized and able to multitask with ease. The one area lacking in his efforts to master his new assignment was budgeting, financing, and purchasing.

The new administrator had been familiar with how to budget for the sport he was coaching, but he had no experience in the concept of financial management for a department with 19 sports, 45 teams, and more than 600 athletes. His view of the big picture was quite limited when it came to money.

He struggled for the first few years, trying to get a handle on how to plan, how to get coaches to plan, and how to organize a system to track all requests and purchases. Soon the requests came for data on how he was in compliance with Title IX regulations, how boys' and girls' teams were treated financially, and how he was going to fund changes in sports and facilities. He had few answers.

With the help of many local athletic directors, he developed a system for tracking and documenting not only his projected budget but also all spending during the course of the year. He used Excel spreadsheets to take the information he received from the school treasurer and convert it to a simple and easy electronic tool. Soon he was able to track his spending, document spending for all sports and all athletes, and plan for future budgets with his coaching staff. He was also able to share documented information with local governing bodies and his superiors.

The development of a system that was both functional and easy to share with many parties was the first step to success. He followed that by developing electronic tools for the per capita tracking of spending on all athletes. Soon all his coaches were able to work with the athletic director each year to develop, follow, and continue a sound system for financial planning. As a result, the anxiety level for all was reduced and efficiency was increased. The athletic director, his coaching staff, his student-athletes, and their parents were all better served through this sound system of financial planning and documentation.

Although most schools have one person who is ultimately responsible for all accounting procedures, the athletic administrator must assist in all manners possible to make sure the athletic department's spending and purchasing methods comply with all mandated guidelines.

State, Local, and School Policy Guidelines

As with the bidding policy just discussed, many local schools or districts can employ guidelines that rise to a level above what is required by the state. It is the duty of the athletic director to be fully aware of any such variations from state statute.

Documentation

Documentation of athletic budgeting and spending can come in many forms. Most treasurers or bookkeepers produce reports on a monthly basis to chart expenditures and receipts. These reports are detailed accountings of every check and every deposit made on behalf of an athletic department. Massive amounts of data can be produced each year in the basic operation of an interscholastic athletic department. The key to documentation is to place these raw data in a format that is both usable and easy to understand. With the increased use of the computer and readily available software, this type of documentation has become well within the ability of today's athletic administrator. Whether the vehicle of documentation is Quicken, Excel, or any other type of spreadsheet, the result is a well-organized and simple record of documented spending.

For the purpose of this chapter, we show spreadsheets produced using the Excel portion of the Microsoft Office package. All the examples shown in this text have been produced and used by actual high school athletic departments. These spreadsheets are simple to construct, are easy to modify, and can be stored and shared.

Budget Categories

When developing budget-tracking software, the first step is to produce a list of the most common budget categories. This master list will be used to place expenditures in the spreadsheet to help track purchases. Some of the more common categories seen in interscholastic athletic department spending include the following (NIAAA 2010):

- Awards
- Capital improvements
- Equipment
- Facility rentals
- First aid and training supplies
- League, conference, or state dues
- Officials and game expenditures
- Professional development

- Repairs and cleaning
- Salaries and benefits
- Tournament fees and costs
- Travel, meals, and overnight housing
- Uniforms and warm-ups

There might be other areas of expenditure that are common to a local school or district. Regardless of the expenditure, it is advantageous to classify all spending into 20 categories or fewer.

Budget Documentation Sample Reports

In this chapter, we show examples of six different types of reports for documenting an athletic department's spending. All these reports document specific information that can be used to track both income and expenditures. Such documentation can provide a simple paper trail as well as an instrument for analyzing past spending and purchasing. The documents contained in this section can also be a great aid when the athletic administrator and coach begin planning for future expenditures.

Yearly Financial Report (By Sport)

A school treasurer or financial officer normally produces a report once a month or at least once a quarter to document receipts and expenditures. This report normally comes in the form of a prescribed document produced by some type of accounting software. Such reports include raw data and are often in a format that is difficult to follow. All spending and receipts are usually included in a long printout, with some type of coding to place all transactions in the various sports categories.

To produce accurate and clear documents, the athletic administrator can place the monthly or quarterly raw data in a format that can be simply adjusted as each new report comes in; this can serve as an accurate tracking device for current levels of income as well as expenditure. An Excel spreadsheet allows for all sports to be tracked in one simple and easy-to-understand document. All sports can be placed on one spreadsheet, or a spreadsheet can be produced that has a tab for each sport and a summary tab that can display overall spending for all sports. Individual sheets and columns can be color-coded to indicate sports that are bringing in more money than they are spending (in black) as well as sports that are spending more money than they are bringing in (in red).

Other tabs can be constructed to track receipts and expenditures occurring during the daily business of an athletic department that might not be directly assigned to one or more sports. Examples include donations and all-sport passes that can be used for multiple sports. Some expenditures that might be found on these sheets include training supplies, capital improvements, and overall facility maintenance.

A typical sheet used in this mode of documentation should include categories and amounts for all forms of receipts and a similar structure for all forms of expenditures. The overall net gain or loss for each sport should also be included. Such a spreadsheet can be updated after each raw data report is received. At the end of the year, the final update produces a year-end report of all spending and the net gain or loss for each sport. The athletic director can use this report as an informational tool when meeting with coaches, patrons, parents, administrators, and student-athletes. To see an example of a yearly financial report for a single sport in an Excel spreadsheet format, see figure 14.1.

Yearly Financial Report (By Department)

A spreadsheet that can document the spending for an entire athletic department can be produced quickly and easily using the same Excel format as for an individual sport. All the individual sheets representing each sport can be linked to a separate sheet that indicates total levels of receipts and expenditures for each sport, other receipts, and other expenditures. This summary sheet can give a quick snapshot of the total financial status of all sports and the department that is easy to understand and follow. This is an excellent tool to express the financial health of an athletic department when discussing spending and purchasing with all stakeholders. To see an example of a yearly financial report for an entire high school athletic program in an Excel spreadsheet format, see figure 14.2. The sports are listed in order of their completion during the school year. The sports go from fall, to winter, and then spring.

Yearly Per Capita Report (By Gender)

Title IX guidelines do not require exact levels of spending by comparable boys' and girls' sports. Variables can exist between programs that produce a wide swing in spending when examining year-end totals. One program might have numbers that allow for three levels of competition (varsity, junior varsity, and frosh), while other sports might have only two levels because of lower participation.

A more accurate depiction of the financial support given to a sport can be produced by documenting per capita spending in one sport and then comparing those numbers with a comparable sport. Per capita spending levels reflect the actual spending per athlete in each sport. If an athletic department spends $100 for each girls' basketball player and $500 for each boys' basketball player, questions could arise related to the equity of support offered by the school. There might be legitimate reasons for such inequity for a single season. Analysis of similar data over several seasons that shows similar trends could raise the athletic administrator's concerns (Evers 2010).

A documentation tool for per capita levels of support can be easily constructed using an Excel spreadsheet. A similar spreadsheet can be produced in the same file that will follow the same numbers and the same categories each year. The final document would serve as a historical record that reflects

2011-2012 Athletic Financial Report

FOOTBALL

Receipts	
Varsity gate	$54,600
Reserve gate	$2,079
Freshman gate	$2,301
Season tickets	$5,930
Sectional share	$3,279
Jerseys and helmets	$1,260
Meals	$200
Sectional 1 expenses	$36
Regional football expenses	$2,208
Total receipts	**$71,893**
Expenditures	
Meals	$358
Equipment reconditioning	$4,595
Transportation	$1,757
Officials	$2,458
Uniforms	$1,272
Equipment	$6,685
Helmets	$2,329
Workers	$5,586
Clinics	$700
Security	$2,331
State tickets	$225
Coaches' shirts	$256
FB seat markers	$74
Decals	$514
Scouting	$68
Shoes	$60
Regional football expenses	$2,138
Porta-johns	$300
Field maintenance	$1,090
Total expenditures	**$32,796**
2000 net gain	**$39,097**

FIGURE 14.1 An example of a yearly financial report by sport.

2011-2012 Athletic Financial Summary

Sport	Receipts	Expenditures	Gain/loss
Football	$71,893	$32,796	$39,097
Boys' soccer	$8,324	$10,883	($2,559)
Boys' tennis	—	$444	($444)
Boys' cross country	$549	$1,167	($618)
Girls' cross country	$275	$774	($499)
Girls' golf	$1,325	$1,515	($190)
Girls' soccer	$3,021	$3,861	($840)
Volleyball	$3,961	$6,981	($3,020)
Girls' swimming	$2,116	$3,190	($1,074)
Boys' basketball	$25,824	$11,232	$14,592
Girls' basketball	$16,178	$17,445	($1,267)
Wrestling	$3,935	$5,623	($1,688)
Boys' swimming	$1,683	$2,328	($645)
Girls' tennis	$290	$1,662	($1,372)
Boys' golf	$189	$612	($423)
Girls' track	$695	$2,193	($1,498)
Boys' track	$1,533	$3,789	($2,256)
Softball	$3,185	$4,301	($1,116)
Baseball	$6,385	$6,294	$91
Cheerleading		$1,039	($1,039)
Other receipts	$14,370	$14,380	$14,380
Other expenditures		$45,448	($45,448)
2000-2001 totals	$166,191	$163,577	$2,614

FIGURE 14.2   An example of a yearly financial report by department.

per capita spending for all girls' and boys' sports over any period. Analysis of the yearly progression of per capita spending can produce a better picture of the support levels offered to boys' and girls' sports by an athletic department. Large variations in spending between like sports can be identified and addressed in an orderly manner and with accurate documentation to assess changes and improvements (Evers 2010). To see an example of per capita spending and support for boys' sports in a typical year in Excel spreadsheet format, see figure 14.3.

OCR Report (Composite Report for Title IX Purposes)

In the event of a formal complaint to the Office for Civil Rights, the OCR may request a review of all programs and data. The OCR will provide its own documents for completion before any meetings or visits. This process can be both lengthy and tedious. Vast amounts of numerical and anecdotal data will be requested for compilation and study. Legislative measures related to accountability for high schools are currently being studied by the U.S. Congress. Many of these measures would require similar levels of compliance and accountability in written form to be completed yearly at the interscholastic level (as is done at the collegiate level today).

One way to stay ahead of possible OCR issues is to construct and complete a yearly composite report. This report addresses many of the issues of equity and compliance that a typical OCR visit and study would evaluate. The athletic administrator can also use such a document to complete a self-study of all spending and support services for boys' and girls' sports each year. By completing such a study, and using the results to guide spending, purchasing, and overall support, the school and athletic administrator could stay ahead of the curve in dealing with potential equity problems. Such a document could also serve as a record of past support. Improvements in spending and support practices shown in this report could indicate willingness on the part of the school or district to address inequities in spending and support in a proactive manner (Evers 2010).

5- or 10-Year Financial Summary (By Sport)

Long-range planning is essential for the continued growth and development of any athletic department. Such planning can occur only as part of a cooperative effort between the athletic administrator and the head coach of each sport. Part of that planning can be to study participation numbers and overall changes to the physical plant. Any study of the past must center on the receipts and expenditures for the entire department. Usually a composite summary of spending of up to 5 years will give an accurate picture and help develop a view of trends that have been established. If possible, a 10-year summary might give even more clarity (Evers 2001).

When a coach and athletic administrator are able to view and study summary reports for multiple years, they are able to approach planning from a solid base of documented information. This gives them the ability to envision and plan a much more effective and realistic financial framework. Small variations that occur from year to year are taken out of the equation, and a solid background for planning and executing the department's budgeting and purchasing can emerge.

As with the single-year financial summary, the 5- or 10-year report can be broken down by individual sport. Separate worksheets can be constructed within such a document to track other spending and receipts that do not fall under the control of a single sport.

Such a document is a great aid to the athletic administrator, not only when planning for the future but also when communicating past trends. A 5- or 10-year summary can be shared with school administrators, student-athletes, parents, patrons, and all other relevant parties to reinforce the costs of operating an interscholastic athletic program. When times are good, such a document is a great testament to the effective use of resources. In leaner times, the document can reinforce the need for caution and assist in any campaign to reduce costs and increase accountability.

A 5- or 10-year summary document can be especially useful for booster groups or those that wish to engage in large-scale fund-raising. Such summary documentation can accurately portray the level of spending for each sport. This type of information can support the need for funding to continue programs at current levels and can serve as motivation to raise additional funds in the future to accommodate potential growth.

5- or 10-Year Financial Summary (By Department)

The most effective tool in budgeting and purchasing that an athletic administrator can possess is a 5- or 10-year financial summary report for the entire department, which can display in one page the average amount of income for each sport as well as the average amount of expenditures over a prolonged period. The net gain or loss for each sport can be displayed on the same document. By using color highlights in an Excel spreadsheet, it's easy for the most casual observer to determine what sports are losing money (coded in red) and what sports are making money (coded in black) over an extended period.

A 5- or 10-year financial summary is only a snapshot, but it is focused on the overall financial health of an athletic department. Such a tool can be effective when developing long-range plans for spending. Whether an athletic department is growing or on the decline, such documentation can serve as rationale for spending and purchasing policies. Whether drastic changes are in order or subtle adjustments are needed, the summary of spending and income over such a period can serve as the needed impetus for change. When the question is raised about the need for change, the numbers reflected in a long-term summary can be powerful tools to back the judgment of the athletic administrator. To see an example of a 10-year summary report of receipts, spending, net gains, and net losses in a typical high school in an Excel spreadsheet format, see figure 14.4.

Boys' Sports 2009

	Football	Cross country	Tennis	Soccer	
Number of athletes	110	15	15	35	
Number of contests	27	10	28	33	
Total expenditures	$29,073	$190	$2,134	$7,740	
Total receipts	$59,376	—	—	$6,067	
Levels of competition	3	2	2	2	
Cost per athlete	$264.30	$12.67	$142.27	$221.14	
Gain/loss per athlete	$275.48	($12.67)	($142.27)	($47.80)	
Practice time	3:00 p.m.	3:00 p.m.	3:00 p.m.	Vary	
Practice length	2 hr	2 hr	2 hr	2 hr	
Practice location	So. fields	Vary	Courts	So. fields	
Number of paid coaches	6	1	2	2	
Number on staff	7	1	2	2	
Number of unpaid coaches	3	0	0	0	
Head coach salary	$8,851	$2,901	$1,934	$5,784	
Assistant coach salary	$4,860	$0	$1,298	$2,927	
Varsity official pay	$59	n/a	n/a	$47	
Reserve official pay	$35	n/a	n/a	$35	
Gate admission price	$5	n/a	n/a	$4 and $3	
Season ticket price	$14	n/a	n/a	n/a	
Visiting locker rooms	Yes	No	No	No	
Home locker rooms	Yes	Yes	Yes	No	
Access to trainer	Yes	Yes	Yes	Yes	
Trainer at home events	Yes	No	No	No	
Director at home events	Yes	No	No	Yes	
Weight room access	Yes	Yes	Yes	Yes	
Host IHSAA tourney	Yes	No	No	No	
Host conference tourney	n/a	No	No	No	
Host invitational tourney	No	Yes	No	Yes	
Preseason meeting	Yes	Yes	Yes	Yes	
Coach:player ratio	16:1	15:1	8:1	18:1	
Years experience on staff	85	31	34	22	
Avg. years experience	14	32	17	11	
Reporters at contests	Yes	No	No	Yes	
Call in results to media	Yes	Yes	Yes	Yes	

FIGURE 14.3   An example of a per capita report by men's sports.

Basketball	Wrestling	Swimming	Track	Golf	Baseball
35	28	37	40	10	35
58	38	11	15	18	75
$12,712	$8,516	$2,431	$4,045	$1,418	$7,933
$28,601	$9,676	$1,985	$2,160	$195	$6,191
3	3	2	3	2	3
$363.20	$304.14	$65.70	$101.13	$141.80	$266.66
$453.97	$41.43	($12.05)	($47.13)	($122.30)	($49.77)
Vary	3:00 p.m.	Vary	3:00 p.m.	3:00 p.m.	Vary
2 hr	2 hr	2 hr	2 hr	2 hr	2 hr
Gyms	Wr. Room	Pool	Track	R. Hills	Field
4	2	2	2	1	3
5	4	3	2	1	3
1	2	1	1	0	2
$8,851	$5,784	$5,784	$5,784	$1,934	$5,784
$4,860	$2,927	$2,927	$2,927	$0	$2,927
$59	$50	$56	$48	n/a	$47
$39	$44	n/a	n/a	n/a	$36
$5	$4 and $3	$4 and $3	$4 and $3	n/a	$4 and $3
n/a	n/a	n/a	n/a	n/a	n/a
Yes	Yes	Yes	No	No	No
Yes	Yes	Yes	Yes	No	Yes
Yes	Yes	Yes	Yes	Yes	Yes
Yes	Yes	No	No	No	No
Yes	Yes	Yes	Yes	No	Yes
Yes	Yes	Yes	Yes	Yes	Yes
No	Yes	No	No	No	No
Yes	Yes	Yes	Yes	No	No
No	Yes	No	Yes	No	No
Yes	Yes	Yes	Yes	Yes	Yes
9:1	14:1	19:1	20:1	10:1	13:1
40	28	24	50	6	39
10	14	12	25	6	13
Yes	Yes	No	No	No	Yes
Yes	Yes	Yes	Yes	Yes	Yes

Athletic Financial Report Summary 1995-2005

Sport	Receipts	Expenditures	Gain/loss	Average
Football	$629,648	$291,755	$337,893	$33,789
Boys' soccer	$46,907	$58,316	($11,409)	($1,141)
Boys' tennis	$863	$8,156	($7,293)	($729)
Coed cross country	$3,399	$13,404	($10,005)	($1,001)
Girls' golf	$4,117	$7,415	($3,298)	($330)
Girls' swimming	$15,440	$24,034	($8,594)	($859)
Girls' soccer	$34,867	$47,672	($12,805)	($1,281)
Volleyball	$38,814	$55,406	($16,592)	($1,659)
Boys' basketball	$254,180	$132,360	$121,820	$12,182
Girls' basketball	$112,682	$129,193	($16,511)	($1,651)
Wrestling	$38,482	$48,439	($9,957)	($996)
Boys' swimming	$12,834	$18,392	($5,558)	($556)
Girls' tennis	$932	$8,883	($7,951)	($795)
Boys' golf	$933	$9,180	($8,247)	($825)
Girls' track	$7,960	$19,892	($11,932)	($1,193)
Boys' track	$19,867	$35,496	($15,629)	($1,563)
Softball	$53,758	$59,158	($5,400)	($540)
Baseball	$73,195	$69,266	$3,929	$393
Cheerleading		$8,082	($8,082)	($808)
Other receipts	$243,074		$243,074	$24,307
Other expenditures		$537,582	($537,582)	($53,758)
10-year totals	$1,591,952	$1,582,081	$9,871	$987
10-year average	$159,195	$158,208	$987	

FIGURE 14.4 An example of a 10-year summary by department.

Communication

The type of documentation highlighted in this chapter is of no use if it remains in a file or on a computer. The key to using documentation to drive progress is the ability to communicate the results to all members of the school community. Effective athletic directors use every avenue available to disseminate information to those most affected.

The athletic administrator should meet with the coaching staff on an annual basis and share the information contained within the financial documentation. Such communication should also extend to parents, patrons, and student-athletes. School and district administrators must be made aware on a regular basis of the financial progress of the athletic department. Potential donors and corporate sponsors can also benefit from such knowledge.

The financial side of operating an interscholastic athletic department is about transparency. When secrets are kept, public trust can become damaged. It is imperative that the athletic administrator be forthright with all aspects of the financial side of the department. By showing all stakeholders a willingness to be open and transparent, the athletic administrator can build a department that functions openly and facilitates a culture of shared responsibility, allowing for maximum growth and development.

Summary

Budgeting and purchasing are two of the most crucial skills that today's athletic administrator must master. Unfortunately, many athletic leaders come into the job with very little experience in these areas. Hard work, study, and collaboration with colleagues can help the athletic administrator to develop a plan for success. This plan should include several layers of involvement from multiple stakeholders. A system must be developed to help in planning, tracking, and documenting all financial matters. Such an approach will help the athletic administrator be more effective in service to his coaches, parents, and student-athletes.

PART IV

Physical Assets

The two chapters in part IV discuss equipment and facilities. Purchasing, inventorying, and maintaining equipment is covered in chapter 15. The consideration of renovation versus building, as well as general physical plant maintenance, is discussed in chapter 16.

CHAPTER 15

Equipment

Joni Pabst, MA, CAA

The operation of a high school athletic department is much like a puzzle. Many pieces must fit into place to ensure that athletes have a positive and safe experience. The puzzle takes form and shape when budgets, guidelines, and procedures are established and implemented when purchasing equipment and uniforms. When a single piece of this puzzle is missing, dissatisfaction builds, athletes may be harmed, and lawsuits could follow.

This chapter is intended to help athletic directors make effective decisions when determining the necessary equipment and appropriate uniforms for their programs and teams. It also provides recommendations for monitoring the status of equipment usage to ensure that no athlete is being placed at risk.

Equipment Management

When considering equipment for the athletic department, it is important to divide the inventory initially into indoor and outdoor sports equipment and subsequently into permanent and portable equipment categories. The needs of each sport vary, and certain specifications must be satisfied for equipment that remains outdoors as opposed to stored in a gymnasium. NIAAA Leadership Training Course 618 provides in-depth information on a variety of player equipment procedures and issues.

The athletic administrator and coaches should inventory all department equipment for quantity and condition. A spreadsheet is probably the best way to record the needed information. If a faculty athletic equipment manager has been designated, this person should assist in the inventory process to understand the need for documentation and the implications for immediate and long-range budgeting. It is also important to communicate to coaches that an equipment inventory is being compiled. Coaches will have the latest information on equipment that may have been damaged or stolen during the season and may be able to identify equipment that has been purchased through a booster club or separate fund-raising. Duval (2003) has provided detailed guidance on this process.

When a comprehensive and accurate inventory of all inside and outside equipment has been compiled, decisions can be made as to which equipment can be repaired and which should be discarded and replaced for safety issues. Later in the chapter is a checklist of indoor and outdoor equipment for use during the inventory process.

When requests from all coaches have been received, budget assets determined, and the rotation plan reviewed, the athletic administrator can initiate the purchasing process. Some schools are permitted to purchase directly from a vendor of their choice. In other cases, a strict purchasing process must be implemented that requires bid solicitations and price comparisons among various vendors for items of an identified quality standard.

Regardless of the process, it is very important to provide all potential vendors with the specific product information and to document all communications (written, spoken, or e-mail) to ensure teams receive exactly what they ordered. Once orders have been received, check all uniforms against the equipment specifications ordered, and document immediately if anything is damaged or not received as originally ordered. Once orders have been received, coaches or a faculty equipment manager must check all uniforms.

When a comprehensive and accurate inventory of all inside and outside equipment has been compiled, decisions can be made as to which equipment can be repaired and which should be discarded and replaced for safety issues. Later in the chapter a checklist of indoor and outdoor equipment is provided for use during the inventory process.

Purchase Considerations

When purchasing permanent and portable equipment, the athletic director must consider several factors. One is the assessment of available fields for outdoor sports such as soccer, nonvarsity football, and field hockey.

For example, for girls' and boys' soccer teams each offering two or three levels of competition, field space and field conditions can become significant issues. Injuries, unsafe playing conditions, and equity issues may all arise without responsive planning. One solution that provides a suitable practice environment for both boys and girls is to use portable soccer goals. A team may not have a regulation field for practice, but with portable goals, the coach can set up a partial field that allows all tactical and strategic components of the game to be covered in practice. Portable goals can easily be moved in the event of muddy or worn areas on the field that increase the potential for injury. They may also be moved to allow for special drills that involve all players during a practice session.

Portable goals are less expensive than permanent goals. Because most high school athletic directors are not able to provide dedicated sport-specific space, portable goals allow for flexibility when a new playing field is not possible. Similar creativity must be considered for all capital equipment items.

Equipment Safety Checks

All indoor and outdoor equipment items must be checked for damage and hazards. Unsafe equipment must be removed from practice and competition until repaired or replaced. Following is a basic guide for the coaches, athletic director, or equipment manager. More detailed checklists are provided in NIAAA Leadership Training Course 504 or 799.

Baseball and Softball

- Check all pitching machines to make sure they have a grounded plug, are accurate, and in good working order. Make sure the coach has posted rules for use.
- Make sure the mesh in the backstop and batting cages is in good shape, void of holes or tears where balls may fly out and strike someone. Again, make sure that rules for use are posted.
- Check to see if chain-link fencing around the field is free of holes or protruding metal that could injure someone. Also make sure the tops of the outfield fences are capped and the protective caps are in good condition.
- If there are light poles within the field area, make sure the padding is in good shape and adequately covers all areas with which a player may collide.

Basketball

- Check backboards to make sure the padding covers the bottom and sides. Check padding for damage; if it is hanging down in places, either fix or replace it.
- When looking at the backboards, make sure the ceiling suspensions do not show signs of cable stress and that the motors to raise and lower them are in good working order.
- Check all electrical equipment in the gym—lights, sound system, and scoreboards. Make sure all have grounded plugs and are in good working order. Make sure the gymnasium PA system and emergency lights are powered by a generator in the event power is lost.
- Check the scorer's table and team benches or chairs for any broken parts, and have them repaired before the season starts.
- Although it is considered part of the facility, make a cursory check of the floor for warped or damaged boards or loose anchor plates that make the playing surface uneven and unsafe.

Football

- Inspect goalpost pads for any tears or lost padding and ensure the fasteners that hold the pads securely in place.
- Make sure that sideline markers and pylons are soft and pliable and are made of brightly colored material.

- Prior to competition, check that all sprinkle heads are fully retracted and that sideline drains are covered.
- All tackling dummies and sleds need to be checked for torn pads, broken springs and sleeves, and any metal stress.

Golf

- Check all indoor nets and driving-range nets for holes and tears to keep balls from going through.
- Check all clubs for any signs of metal stress.

Gymnastics

- Check all mats, landing pits, and padding for tears and damage that could cause injury. Repair or replace as needed.
- Make sure the surfaces of all bars, beams, vaults, rings, and pommel horses are free of splintering, peeling, warping, cracking, or tearing.
- Assess springboards and Reuther boards for worn nonslip surfaces; worn screws, bolts, or threads; and springs that are worn, loose, or protruding on the vaulting surface.
- Carefully check all support cables to make sure they are not frayed and that the hardware is in good shape, turn buckles are fully engaged, and floor plates are stable under pressure. Check the padding as well.

Soccer

- Check all goal nets for holes and tears, making sure that hooks and fastening devices are not protruding toward the field of play.
- Check the scorer's table and players' benches for damage.

Track and Field

- For jumping and vaulting areas, make sure the landing pad covers are in place and secured and that landing pad foam is in good repair. Fill holes in any runways.
- Throwing areas must have proper cages, with no holes or tears. Make sure toeboards are securely fastened and not damaged.
- Check hurdles for broken parts. Make sure they can be locked into the proper height and are counterweighted.
- Check throwing implements, pole-vault poles, and batons for any surface damage or cracks. Crossbars and standards need to be checked for damage as well.

Volleyball

- All standards and poles need to be checked for damage. Make sure all anchor plates are secured to the floor and that all padding for the standards is free of tears.
- Check all nets for frayed cables and worn pulleys. Also check nets for tears and damage.

- Assess the official's stand for any damage, and make sure the padding on the stand is in good shape.

- Check the scorer's table and bench area for damage. Check the scoreboard and PA system to make sure they have grounded plugs and are in good working order.

Weight Room

- Check that weight machines are well lubricated and free of metal stress or fraying. Check all anchor points, safety stops, and pulleys or

Managing Protective Equipment and Athletes' Safety

The safety of all student-athletes must be a high priority regardless of sport or gender. As a related matter, protective equipment is an important consideration. In particular, football helmets and shoulder pads are safety items that require continual review and management. Following are examples illustrating the ongoing implementation of safety measures for helmets and shoulder pads at a large Arizona high school.

The equipment manager and head coach keep an accurate record of all helmets in the school inventory. A computer spreadsheet is used to list each helmet's serial number, size, date of inspection, and date cleared for return to inventory as a safe, usable helmet. Records are kept for the life of each helmet by serial number, detailing which seasons the helmet was used and which athletes wore it. (Note: Some helmet manufacturers will not guarantee the safety of a helmet shell after a specified number of years.)

The equipment manager, along with the certified athletic trainer, has been trained to fit helmets in accordance with the manufacturer's guidelines. Athletes are taught to make sure the chin straps are always securely snapped when entering the field of play. Care is also taken to ensure that shoulder pads are properly fitted and that all straps are properly secured to afford maximum protection.

At the end of the season, all helmets and shoulder pads are inspected and sanitized by a certified reconditioning vendor in preparation for the next season.

The sanitation of both helmets and shoulder pads has become increasingly important because outbreaks of methicillin-resistant *Staphylococcus aureus* (MRSA) have occurred in some schools. When the helmets and shoulder pads are returned to the site, they are accompanied by safety documentation along with a list of helmets that have been rejected. Rejected helmets are taken out of inventory and noted on the master inventory (e.g., "Rejected 2012").

This critical protocol has been put in place to ensure safe and effective protective equipment for our teams throughout the years.

cogwheels for metal stress or corrosion. Make sure all machine foot pedals have nonskid material to prevent injury.

- Check free weights and collars to make sure threads are not stripped and collars aren't bent. Weld collars on any fixed weight bars.
- Check all weight benches for torn or ripped surfaces as well as making sure they are braced firmly and that nuts and bolts are welded.
- High-density flooring mats should be checked for any damage.

Wrestling

- Check all mats to make sure there are no tears and that they are securely anchored and taped. Make sure they are being properly cleaned to avoid the spread of any infection.
- Check all wall mats for tears, and make sure they are properly secured to the wall. Make sure all thermostats, fire extinguishers, light switches, and fountains are recessed into the wall.
- Have the scales calibrated properly by the appropriate personnel.
- Check the scorer's table, scoreboard, PA system, and lights for problems or damage.

Rotation Plans for Uniforms and Consumable Playing Equipment

With contemporary pressures on school and district budgets, a long-range rotation plan for acquisition of new uniforms has become commonplace. In most schools across the United States, when new varsity uniforms are purchased, the existing inventory is passed to nonvarsity teams within the program. Because of physical size differences, there may be times when new purchases are required for nonvarsity teams as well, particularly for frosh athletes. Regardless of the process used by a school or district, the athletic director must develop a rotation process that is transparent and logical for all parties involved. The average number of years in a uniform rotation cycle is four or five. However, local budget pressures and school or district policy will guide these decisions.

An important component of a uniform rotation process is examining the overall needs of each sport program. In this regard, the athletic director begins with the available budget funds for uniforms and then considers factors such as the following:

- Which sports need complete replacement uniforms?
- Which sports need additional inventory (e.g., fill-in numbers and sizes)?
- Which uniform sets require large numbers or have high costs (e.g., football)?

- What role can a booster club play to ensure full inventories, service to as many teams as possible, and equitable uniform purchases?
- Which lower-cost uniform purchases (e.g., golf, tennis) can be paired with the higher-cost items to provide uniforms for as many teams as possible in any school year?

Some districts and schools allow individual teams to raise funds in order to get their uniforms earlier than the approved rotation plan stipulates. In cases such as these, it is crucial that all members of the school coaching staff, booster club, and parent groups be aware of the rotation, have a copy of the rotation form, and receive an explanation of the reason for variance. Publishing a public uniform acquisition document is a helpful tool that can prevent misperceptions of fairness.

The athletic administrator must ensure that all purchasing procedures are followed and must be ready to provide documentation and reasons for all purchases made on behalf of the athletic department.

A sample uniform acquisition and rotation plan for a high school is shown in figure 15.1.

After developing an equitable rotation plan, the athletic director must implement a process for gathering information from each of the head coaches in the sports program. In some school districts, rigid budgetary timelines are defined, in which case it is imperative that coaches be given adequate time and information for submitting their uniform and equipment requests.

An example of a school policy from Sahuaro High School in the Tucson Unified School District is included in figure 15.2 (Sahuaro High School 2008).

Equipment Repair and Reconditioning

Reconditioning and repair of existing inventory are indicators of prudent management of assets that were originally financed with tax or tuition funds. The manual for NIAAA Leadership Training Course 618, Management of Interscholastic Athletic Player Equipment, comments on this issue:

"There can be many uses for old uniforms and equipment. After a few years, schools can donate old uniforms to such organizations as churches, YMCAs, and boys clubs. Many high schools are looking for old uniforms for school raffles. Saving old uniforms for alumni games is also a good idea. However, make sure to account for all equipment, whether it is now someone's desk lamp or has been donated to the local YMCA" (NIAAA 2006).

At the end of a sport season, uniforms, helmets, and other equipment are often returned to the inventory battered, broken, and in need of repair. Most high school athletic budgets do not allow for replacement of expensive equipment each year, so many schools and districts engage in reconditioning. There are companies that will recondition equipment for a fraction of the cost of total replacement. The value of reconditioning is far more than dollars saved. Of greater importance is the value of the risk reduction and

Athletic Department Memorandum

TO: ___High School coaching staff___

FROM: ___Athletic administrator___

SUBJ: ___Uniform rotation___

To meet student needs, while establishing equity within the athletic department and meeting financial restraints of the district, the following uniform rotation has been developed. This rotation is based on a four-year schedule and identifies only uniform needs and not other capital items for each particular sport. Other athletic items still need to be identified each fiscal year by the head coach and then submitted to the activities director.

The four-year rotation will be implemented on the following schedule:

Year A	Year B	Year C	Year D
Football	Baseball	Boys' golf	Boys' and girls' cross country
Girls' soccer	Boys' soccer	Boys' volleyball	Boys' basketball
Boys' and girls' tennis	Girls' volleyball	Girls' basketball	Boys' and girls' swimming
Boys' and girls' track	Softball	Spirit line	Wrestling
	*Football		

School year	Uniform
2004-2005	Year A
2005-2006	Year B
2006-2007	Year C
2007-2008	Year D
2008-2009	Year A
2009-2010	Year B
2010-2011	Year C
2011-2012	Year D

*If needed

FIGURE 15.1 Sample uniform acquisition and rotation plan for a high school.

Sample Policy: Ordering of New Equipment and Uniforms

Coaches or sponsors must meet all school and district guidelines and timelines for these requests. The activities office will work with all pricing submitted by each coach or sponsor; therefore, it is essential that all pricing be included when submitting the requests. Some items that are often overlooked and not included in prices submitted are lettering, numerals, and striping. Please be sure the prices submitted include these items. Lettering, numerals, logos, and other design features should be listed on requests as a separate line for clarification.

The activities office does not automatically order items needed for each program and will not assume that coaches or sponsors need items if items are not requested. Please keep in mind that monies may not be available to order balls and other items if omitted from the original order.

When reviewing the orders for each program and trying to meet the financial restraints placed on each school by the district, the assistant principal for activities, in consultation with the athletic director, has the final decision-making authority as to which items will be ordered and which items will not be ordered for that year. The assistant principal for activities and the athletic director will make every attempt to consult with coaches or sponsors when changes, deletions, or additions in items requested are necessary before the school order is submitted to the district.

Please note that coaches and sponsors do not have the authority to approve or change orders with vendors when it is school or district money that is paying for items ordered.

FIGURE 15.2   School policy from Sahuaro High School in the Tucson Unified School District.
Reprinted, by permission, from Sahuaro High School Coaching Handbook, 2011.

safety of the reconditioned equipment. Abeshaus (1996) has written extensively on this topic.

Reconditioning is more than just cleaning worn-out helmets and equipment. It is a process of repairing and sanitizing athletic equipment, ranging from helmets used in various sports, shoulder pads, and softball and baseball catcher's equipment to lacrosse sticks, tackling dummies, padding for volleyball uprights, and pits for high jump and pole vault. An important task is to educate coaches about reconditioned equipment and the related processes.

When selecting a company to recondition the athletic department's equipment, it is critical that the company meet national safety standards. It's not just about washing and fixing equipment—it is about doing what is right and providing athletes with safe equipment in accordance with the standards of the National Operating Committee on Standards in Athletic Equipment (NOCSAE) and the Athletic Equipment Managers' Association

(AEMA). NOCSAE was formed in 1969 to reduce the incidence of injuries to athletes by setting standards for all protective equipment.

Another important selection factor is finding a company that carries product liability insurance that will adequately cover any injury claim from an athlete. Reconditioning companies should be asked to produce a certificate of product liability insurance before entering into negotiations. Many schools and districts request that their insurance representative evaluate the reconditioning company's policy to ensure adequacy of coverage.

Athletic directors should take the time to call other athletic administrators to research their satisfaction levels with their current reconditioning service providers. Ask about the company's reputation for quality work, the degree to which it meets all NOCSAE standards, and its longevity in the area of reconditioning athletic equipment.

After selecting a certified reconditioning company, the athletic director should document all equipment sent out for servicing, with serial numbers if applicable. When the equipment is returned, the reconditioner should also supply appropriate records of the work accomplished and records of all equipment that was rejected as unrepairable along with the reason for rejection.

Inventory Control

To provide teams with the highest-quality uniforms and equipment within the defined budget restraints, the athletic director must begin with an inventory of the uniforms and equipment assigned to each team (including all competitive levels). NIAAA Leadership Training Course 511 provides details on budgeting and budget management for high school athletic directors.

The inventory process can be daunting, but it is necessary in order to be more financially responsible with the athletic budget. All equipment and uniforms the athletic department owns should be tabulated on a yearly basis. When making the inventory list, note the quality of the uniforms and equipment and whether certain uniforms or equipment are no longer serviceable or safe for use. Unacceptable equipment and uniforms should be disposed of according to school or district guidelines. Of particular importance is secure disposal of protective equipment so that young athletes do not acquire and wear items that do not afford adequate protection for smaller players.

If a school staff athletic equipment manager has been designated, this person must be involved in the inventory process. Providing the staff equipment manager with a computer and an appropriate spreadsheet software program in the equipment room will enhance retrieval and inspection of inventory data as needed. A computer and appropriate software will save time, result in more accurate data, and allow the equipment manager to discard paper records in order to keep up with the inventory. If there is no computer, inventories can be recorded on card stock, copies of which are retained in the equipment storage area and the athletic director's office.

Anything added to or taken from the equipment room is recorded on the card. It is thus imperative that all athletic department personnel be trained to record withdrawals and additions so an updated inventory is available when needed.

In the event an equipment manager is not available to the athletic department, coaches must be active participants in the inventory process. Each coach must be responsible for issuing uniforms and equipment along with collecting all issued items at the end of their respective seasons. When coaches are involved in this process, it is the responsibility of each coach to inform the athletic administrator of damaged uniforms or unsafe equipment when submitting their end-of-season inventory. Examples of both athletic department inventory checklists and individual sports team checklists are included in figure 15.3, which is a sample from the course manual for NIAAA LTC 504, Legal Issues I (Risk Management). A large number of equipment accounting procedures are also described in NIAAA LTC 502.

Accountability

Accountability for uniforms and equipment is a responsibility of all stakeholders in the athletic department. This includes the athletic administrator, the equipment manager, coaches, athletes, and parents. Equipment record forms can be used to establish a record of accountability; these forms can be modified to fit individual school needs. Examples are included at the end of this section.

When the uniform and equipment inventory has been established for all sports teams, it is important that each head coach retain a copy of the total inventory of uniforms and equipment for their respective sports.

The next step is to develop a procedure for issuing equipment and uniforms to the athletes. One type of accountability is to make up a player or athlete card that lists information on uniforms, practice gear, safety equipment, and shoes. Each athlete signs the card, which indicates he received the items. The coach or equipment manager signs and dates the card as well. Many schools or districts make sure an athlete has met all eligibility requirements and paid any required fees before issuing uniforms and equipment.

At the end of the season, the athlete returns the uniform and equipment to the coach or equipment manager, and both the adult and the athlete sign and enter the date of return on the equipment issuance card.

On occasion, it can be difficult to collect fines for lost or damaged equipment from athletes who terminated membership on a team or who may be graduating. It is wise to have a policy in place for these types of situations. Here are some examples (Stevens 2010):

- Athletes may not receive end-of-year awards or letters, or they may not be able to attend the end-of-season banquet or be eligible for the next sport season until all uniforms and equipment have been returned.

1. Athletic administrator

___Awards   ___Secretarial help   ___Publications

___Trophies   ___Postage   ___Office supplies and equipment

___Plaques   ___Rentals   ___State and conference dues

___Letters   ___Custodial duties   ___Banquets and parent nights

___Numerals   ___Athletetes' physicals   ___Video equipment

___Certificates   ___Meeting expenses   ___Tickets

___Engraving   ___Portable restrooms   ___Jackets

___Frames   ___Flowers   ___Sweaters

___Sports pins   ___Director's mileage

2. Baseball and Softball

___Balls   ___Helmets   ___Batting gloves

___Bases   ___Masks   ___Rule books

___Bats   ___Scorebooks   ___Ball bags

___Bat bag   ___Shoes   ___Belts

___Body protectors   ___Sliding pads   ___Catcher's equipment

___Backstop   ___Uniforms   ___Lineup cards

___Caps   ___Game   ___Water bottles

___Gloves   ___Practice   ___Whistles

___Jackets   ___Resin   ___Leg guards

___Undershirts

3. Basketball

___Backboards   ___Pants   ___Air pump

___Balls   ___Scorebooks   ___Ball rack

___Shirts   ___Rule books   ___Possession indicator

___Shoes   ___Timers   ___Scrimmage vests

___Glass guards   ___Warm-ups   ___Water bottles

___Nets   ___Whistles   ___Rebounding rim

___Uniforms   ___Game   ___Practice

4. Football

___Balls	___Rule books	___Laces
___Blocking dummy and charger sleds	___Down and distance markers	___Rib, shoulder, knee, thigh, forearm, hand, elbow, and hip pads
___Chin straps	___Sideline coats	
___Cleats	___Tackling dummies	___Belts
___Face masks and bars	___Helmet tape	___Equipment bags
	___Helmets	___Decals
___Neck collars	___Kicking shoe	___Kicking cage
___Sun glare	___Tees	___Scrimmage vests
___Whistles	___Sideline markers	___Corner markers
___Warm-ups	___Uniforms	___Mouthpieces
___Game	___Carbon stat sheets	___Practice

5. Golf

___Balls	___Driving mats	___Tees
___Match	___Driving net	___Gloves
___Practice	___Shirts	___Clubs
___Bags	___Jackets	___Rain gear
___Ball shagger	___Sweaters	___Shoes
___Rule books		

6. Gymnastics

___Balance beam	___Chalk	___Uneven bars
___Digital scorer	___Hand and wrist guards	___Vaulting horse
___Springboard	___Ankle supports	___Floor exercise mat
___Chalk tray	___Mat tape	___Horizontal bars
___Warm-ups	___Landing mats	___Equipment covers
___Parallel bars	___Pommel horse	
___Water bottles	___Watches	___Rule books
___CD/tape player	___CDs/tapes	___Tumbling/twisting belts
___Uniforms	___Rings	___Reuther board
___Meet	___Scorebooks	___Practice

(continued)

(continued)

7. Training Room or Medical Room

___Tape   ___Ice machine   ___Assorted pads and bandages

___Foam rubber   ___Bandages, asst. sizes   ___Elastic bandages

___Stretcher   ___Crutches   ___Skin lube

___Air splints   ___Gauze roll   ___Gauze pads, asst. sizes

___Cotton   ___First aid cream   ___Whirlpool(s)

___Foot powder   ___Braces   ___Hydrocollator

___Ankle wrap   ___Ankle roller   ___Strawberry ointment

___Tape scissors   ___Ice packs/bags   ___Helmet removal tools

___Freezer   ___Medicine kits

8. Soccer

___Balls   ___Flags   ___Net hooks

___Nets   ___Goals   ___Scrimmage vests

___Shin guards   ___Scorebooks   ___Rule books

___Warm-ups   ___Corner flags   ___Goalie gloves

___Water bottles   ___Air horn   ___Goalie jersey(s)

___Whistles   ___Shoes   ___Uniforms

___Game   ___Practice

9. Swimming and Diving

___Caps   ___Scoresheets   ___Scorebooks

___Rule books   ___Starter's pistol   ___Blanks

___Goggles   ___Ear plugs   ___Nose plugs

___Pacer clock   ___Suits   ___Swim paddles and aids

___Warm-ups   ___Stop watches

10. Tennis

___Balls   ___Rackets   ___Restringing supplies

___Nets   ___Straps   ___Racket covers

___Rule books   ___Scorebooks   ___Shoes

___Uniforms   ___Match   ___Practice

11. Track and Field/Cross Country

___Hammer	___Hurdles	___Standards
___Markers	___Scorebooks	___Batons
___Equipment bag	___Shoes	___Tape measures
___Finish line tape	___Watches	___Toeboards
___Hammer circle	___Takeoff board	___Vaulting poles and boxes
___Javelin	___Javelin stop board	___Landing pit covers
___Flags	___Landing pits	___Spikes, long and short
___Crossbars	___Crossbar lifters	___Lap counters
___Discus	___Shot (for shot put)	___Starting blocks
___Water bottles	___Starter's pistol	___Blanks
___Whistles	___Exchange zone flags	___Warm-ups
___Uniforms	___Meet record cards	
___Meet	___Practice	

12. Volleyball

___Balls	___Standards	___Net straps
___Nets	___Standard pads	___Tension net fasteners
___Antennae	___Scorebook(s)	___Libero sheets
___Rule books	___Knee pads	___Official's stand/pads
___Water bottles	___Whistles	___Shoes
___Uniforms	___Game	___Practice

13. Wrestling

___Tights	___Singlets	___Conditioning suits
___Mat tape	___Mats	___Mat covers
___Head gear	___Chin straps	___Timer
___Whistles	___Water bottles	___Rule books
___Scorebooks	___Knee pads	___Shoes
___Warm-ups	___Uniforms	

FIGURE 15.3 Sample inventory checklist.

- Graduating seniors may be restricted from prom attendance, end-of-year senior activities, or even participating in graduation ceremonies until uniforms and equipment are turned in.

Any proposed policies for assisting in the retrieval of uniforms and equipment must be approved by the school or district leadership to ensure support if it becomes necessary to enforce these policies. To prevent these situations, some coaches collect uniforms after the final game of the season before the athletes leave the locker room.

Whatever policy is developed and approved by senior administration, the athletic director must make sure it is consistently enforced by all coaches within the athletic department. "Choose your penalty to obtain the best results. Whatever penalty is chosen, make sure that the staff strictly enforces the penalty for *everyone*, not just a chosen few. If coaches and the athletics director are strict and explain the rules in the beginning, problems will be minimal" (NIAAA 2006).

Developing and implementing an accountability system for issuing and returning uniforms and equipment ensures that the athletic department will save financial resources by not having to replace lost or stolen uniforms or equipment. Figures 15.4 and 15.5 show examples of forms in current use.

Name_____ Sport_____

Date issued_____ Type of uniform_____

Uniform number (top)_____ Uniform number (bottom)_____

I agree to be solely responsible for the above-described uniform issued to me by the

_____ Athletic Department. In the event that the uniform is lost, stolen, destroyed, or damaged, I will pay the replacement cost of

$_____. I also understand that if I wear the uniform without permission at any time other than at the athletic contest in which I'm scheduled to participate, I will forfeit the right to retain the use of the uniform.

_____
Signature of athlete

_____
Signature of parent/guardian

FIGURE 15.4   High school athletic department uniform issuance record.

Uniform item	Total quantity	Good condition	Fair condition	Replace

Sport:_____ Year:_____

Level: Varsity JV Frosh   Coach:_____

FIGURE 15.5   Athletic department uniform inventory form.

Care of Equipment and Uniforms

The care of uniforms and equipment is critical. Proper care ensures that the inventory doesn't require unforeseen replacement due to improper use or laundering. If a school is fortunate and has an equipment manager who not only issues and receives uniforms but also launders them, the athletic administrator must ensure the equipment manager is educated about properly laundering and sanitizing all uniforms and equipment.

Some schools have industrial-size washers and dryers because of the large loads of towels and uniforms they must deal with on a regular basis. Conversely, other schools are able to afford only regular-size washers and dryers that are found in a home. Regardless of which laundry equipment the school laundry agent has, be sure she is thoroughly educated on the operation of all equipment and the types of detergent that are best for large quantities of soiled laundry. Many vendors and manufacturers can provide suggestions for products to use for cleaning, removing stains, and sanitizing.

Soiled laundry needs to be collected in some type of hamper or bin that has wheels for easy portability and, if possible, tilting capabilities for loading and unloading. Industrial-type bins or hampers are made of fabric or vinyl and should be sanitized daily while the dirty laundry is out and before clean laundry is put back in.

Uniform Fabric Considerations

When laundering uniforms, equipment managers must take care to examine the type of fabric and fabric content of each set of uniforms so they use proper washing products and techniques to ensure the most effective cleaning process.

Sorting the laundry gives the equipment manager an opportunity to check for tears or damage and to check pockets for items that could damage the machine or impair its ability to properly clean. If torn or damaged uniforms are found during the sorting process, the equipment manager should complete all needed repairs before the uniform is reissued. Some schools use volunteer parents for easy repairs or a seamstress at a local dry cleaning establishment.

During the laundry sorting process, the equipment manager may find heavy stains that require pretreating so as to not waste water and detergent by rewashing a load of uniforms. Another reason for sorting is to separate the various uniform colors to avoid transfer of colors to white uniform parts. If the school's designated laundry agent does not follow the manufacturer's guidelines, white pants may be contaminated with other colors, and some jerseys and pants may be subject to shrinkage.

After the laundry has been washed, care must also be taken in the drying process. Again, labels and drying instructions must be followed to ensure that uniforms are dried at a proper temperature that won't cause shrinkage or damage to the lettering and numbers. Using a timer when drying uniforms will help prevent overdrying, shrinkage, and wasted electricity. If the school dryer doesn't have a timer, have one installed or supply a simple kitchen timer.

Folding Versus Hanging Uniforms

The issue of whether to fold or hang uniforms depends on the type of storage available in the school equipment room. Regardless of the method used, it is important to fold or hang the uniforms immediately to ensure they do not wrinkle. Part of the responsibility of the equipment manager is to make sure the uniforms look good for competition and aren't full of wrinkles and tears. When folding or hanging the uniforms, the equipment manager should make sure the numbers on the uniforms are easily visible and that they do not have to be refolded in an effort to locate numbers. The manual for NIAAA's LTC 618 shares this thought:

"Usually, the person who does the folding or hanging also acts as a final inspector. Checks are made for stains, tears, or any other problems that can be remedied. A final inspection when folding or hanging can definitely add to the life of the garment, as well as prevent embarrassment" (NIAAA 2006).

Storage

Some schools have the luxury of a large and accessible equipment room where every sport has cabinets or closets to store its respective uniforms and equipment. Other schools have a number of rooms in which uniforms and equipment are stored, and the coaches are responsible for the care of their inventories. Regardless of the situation, some basics must be followed to ensure equipment and uniforms are secure and kept clean:

- Open shelving is advantageous for items that require daily access during the season.
- Closed closets or shelving provides a dust-free environment for uniforms.
- Proper ventilation is essential to prevent mold and other microorganisms that can contaminate uniforms and equipment.
- It is recommended that dirty uniforms be kept separate from clean uniforms to avoid recontamination of laundered items.
- The equipment room must be secure and preferably not keyed to a lock to which others have access.
- If a school has one large equipment room that houses all uniforms and equipment, it is advisable to have locks on the cabinets and closets to provide extra security for each sport.

There are many companies that manufacture and sell components for equipment room storage. Sales personnel from these companies will come to a school to analyze the space and help design a system that meets the specific needs of the athletic department. If that option is not affordable, the athletic director should consider contacting the school booster organizations or parent volunteers who may be willing to build the storage items needed.

When designing a school athletic equipment storage room, the athletic director would be prudent to work with a committee of parents, construction specialists, and a vendor who specializes in equipment room storage. This committee will need to know the approximate amount of space needed for each sport. Table 15.1 provides some average estimates. Each school will have different needs according to the sports that are sponsored.

It is the responsibility of the athletic administrator to provide secure storage so that coaches are not required to store uniforms and equipment in classrooms, cars, or homes. A school's athletic inventory investment is better protected if uniforms and equipment are properly stored. Wenger Corporation (2006) provides detailed information on a wide range of equipment storage systems.

Summary

This chapter has been designed to help athletic directors make informed decisions regarding the uniforms and equipment needs of their athletic programs. Equipment and uniform inventory, purchase, rotation, cleaning, maintenance, and storage needs were covered. As each school's sport offerings may vary, there are check lists and guidelines throughout this chapter

TABLE 15.1　Average Estimates of Space Needed By Each Sport

Girls' programs	Approximate storage size
Basketball	75 to 150 sq ft
Cheerleading	75 sq ft
Cross country	50 to 75 sq ft
Golf	65 to 75 sq ft
Soccer	50 to 100 sq ft
Softball	75 to 150 sq ft
Swimming and diving	50 to 100 sq ft
Tennis	50 to 75 sq ft
Track and field (no field equipment)	65 to 75 sq ft
Volleyball	100 to 150 sq ft
Total	**655 to 1,025 sq ft**
Boys' programs	**Approximate storage size**
Baseball	100 to 200 sq ft
Basketball	75 to 100 sq ft
Cross country	50 to 75 sq ft
Football	300 to 500 sq ft
Golf	65 to 75 sq ft
Soccer	50 to 100 sq ft
Swimming and diving	50 to 100 sq ft
Tennis	50 to 75 sq ft
Track and field (no field equipment)	65 to 75 sq ft
Volleyball	100 to 150 sq ft
Total	**905 to 1,450 sq ft**

to assist the athletic director in handling all the areas concerned and to assist in providing safety for their athletes. The chapter also touched on the area of indoor and outdoor and permanent versus portable equipment, and considerations to be made when making those decisions. Also included is an assessment of all equipment for safety issues. Safety is paramount in all areas of educational athletics and the athletic director must stay on top of those issues. Also included are the cleaning and storage considerations for uniforms and equipment and the reconditioning when applicable of player equipment. Some guidelines for storage by square footage and by sport have been included.

CHAPTER 16

Facilities

Carter Wilson, CMAA

A high school campus is more than the sum of its buildings. It is the physical expression of the institution, its activities, and its purpose. A campus provides a sense of place and feeling that is created by the physical quality of its buildings, athletic fields, and landscaping. A high school is a singular place in our culture that brings together offices, libraries, classrooms, athletic fields, gymnasiums, and maintenance shops.

The facilities that make up a high school campus are inextricably connected with the institution's mission. Campus facilities support the activities of students, coaches, and administrators. The campus creates an environment that nurtures the development of ideas and intellectual and physical growth.

Physical Plant

The physical plant of a high school athletic department consists of all indoor and outdoor facilities and equipment that are intended to conduct sports, instruction, practices, and competitions for a range of boys' and girls' sports programs. Management of the physical plant department must be coordinated with other school and district resources to ensure that institutional goals can be met now and in the future.

The mission of a school's physical plant department is to enhance the learning environment of the physical education and athletic department through high-quality services and wise stewardship of its physical assets. To accomplish this goal, the physical plant division supports the school's instructional services and athletic activities through maintenance of all operational equipment and other physical plant assets.

To ensure efficient achievement of the goals of both the athletic and the physical plant departments, the management and maintenance of a school's academic and athletic facilities must be supported by an annual operating budget. The purpose of this resource is to keep all facilities in usable condition. Any modifications to a school's physical facilities must be supervised

It is essential to evaluate campus physical plant facilities to ensure these resources meet the needs of students, faculty, and local constituents. To provide an ongoing assessment of both indoor and outdoor athletic facilities, physical plant personnel should be trained and required to conduct regular facility and equipment inspections on a regular basis.

and monitored or performed by the physical plant department. This ensures that physical plant personnel have knowledge of the exact condition of the physical facilities at all times and also whether construction or remodeling complies with current legal codes and standards. To maintain that knowledge, physical plant personnel should assist in planning remodeling, new construction, or any alteration to structures and ground areas at the school.

The physical plant department consists of three divisions: (1) maintenance, (2) custodial, and (3) grounds. The maintenance division is responsible for general building and equipment maintenance. Workers perform routine repairs as well as preventive maintenance. Such activities include building upkeep, light carpentry work, installation of furniture, glass replacement, vehicle maintenance, and minor hardware inspections for bleacher supports, electrical outlets, and lighting devices.. The maintenance department is also critical in the support of special events, lighting, repairs to HVAC systems, and electrical and plumbing repairs.

The custodial division is responsible for general cleaning and minor repairs of the athletic facilities. Each day, members of this department generally perform the following duties:

- Empty trash in offices, classrooms, weight room, locker rooms, and gymnasium.
- Sweep and mop floors.
- Clean whiteboards and chalkboards.
- Clean restrooms and restock paper supplies.
- Vacuum carpets.

The grounds division is responsible for all maintenance and upkeep on the campus grounds and athletic fields. The purpose of the grounds division is to create a positive outdoor environment that is safe, pleasant, and supportive of academic and athletic pursuits.

It is essential to evaluate campus physical plant facilities to ensure these resources meet the needs of students, faculty, and local constituents. To provide an ongoing assessment of both indoor and outdoor athletic facilities, physical plant personnel should be trained and required to conduct facility and equipment inspections on a regular basis. Sport-specific checklists (see figures 16.1 and 16.2) should be available for the inspection of all equipment and facilities.

School _____ Date_____

Location _____ Room_____

Instructions: Note each item below as "S" (satisfactory) or "U" (unsatisfactory). Add any pertinent comments and the location of hazards for each item checked "U" (unsatisfactory).

BASEBALL FIELDS/SOFTBALL FIELDS

	Field level and free of holes and foreign objects
	Area free of debris and broken glass
	Fencing in good condition
	Storage buildings in good condition
	Dugouts and seating in good condition
	Backstop in good condition
	Base anchors secure
	Shrubs and trees maintained—no branches hanging over or through fence
	Bleachers in good condition (no loose nuts, bolts, broken braces, or sharp edges)

FOOTBALL FIELDS/SOCCER FIELDS

	Field level and free of holes and foreign objects
	Area free of debris and broken glass
	Fencing in good condition
	Concrete anchors for fence posts not exposed
	Storage buildings in good condition
	Shrubs and trees maintained—no branches hanging over or through fence
	Bleachers in good condition (no loose nuts, bolts, broken braces, or sharp edges)
	Sprinkler heads retract after watering
	Area properly drained

JOGGING TRAIL/TRACK

	Trail/track level and free of holes and foreign objects
	Area free of debris and broken glass
	Grassy areas maintained

(continued)

341

(continued)

TENNIS COURTS

	Court surface in safe condition
	Area free of debris and broken glass
	Cracks filled or repaired
	Leaves removed

CORRECTIVE ACTION TAKEN (indicate if work order has been initiated)

Name_____ Date _____

FIGURE 16.1 Outdoor facility safety inspection checklist.

Instructions: Note each item below as "S" (satisfactory) or "U" (unsatisfactory). Add any pertinent comments and the location of hazards for each item checked "U" (unsatisfactory).

GENERAL FACILITY AREA FLOOR

	No wet areas or slip, fall hazard
	No trip hazard
	No cords across walkway
	Emergency procedures clearly posted

GYMNASIUM

	Gym rules clearly posted
	All equipment properly stored
	Area clean and free of debris
	Area free of tripping hazards
	Court surface in safe condition
	Bleachers free of splinters
	Bleachers in good condition (no loose nuts, bolts, broken braces, or sharp edges)
	Hoops, nets, and backboards in good condition
	Lighting adequate

WEIGHT ROOM

	Area supervised
	Area free of debris and broken glass
	Weights and equipment properly racked and stored
	Machine cables secured and in good condition
	Aisles free of tripping hazards
	Floor matting available where applicable

LOCKER ROOM AREAS

	Clean and free from tripping and slipping hazards
	Metal lockers maintained, free of sharp edges
	Benches and chairs in safe condition
	Electrical systems in safe condition
	Lighting adequate

CORRECTIVE ACTION TAKEN (indicate if work order has been initiated)

Name_____ Date _____

FIGURE 16.2 Indoor facility safety inspection checklist.

Upon discovery of damaged or inoperable equipment, physical plant personnel must file a report with the athletic administrator or facility manager. These reports should be in writing and should specify the nature of the damage along with the date and time of discovery. Any dangerous or inoperable equipment should be replaced or removed from the premises. Students must be denied access to the damaged facilities and equipment until repair is completed.

Turf Management

Natural and synthetic turf fields must meet two basic requirements: (1) They must be large enough to allow a sport to be played according to the competition rules, and (2) they must have a surface that allows the players to compete safely and efficiently. Because many sports surfaces are also used for nonsports activities such as band practice or drum corps competition,

Bleacher Safety

An important priority for athletic directors throughout the United States is to provide a safe indoor and outdoor environment for all event spectators. Frequent checks of a school district's bleacher systems are critical in protecting spectators who attend athletic contests. Checking a bleacher system once a year for deterioration may not be adequate to keep the system in optimal working order. In a large Georgia school district, a description of their safety assessments illustrates how the bleacher systems are kept safe.

After each season, the director of maintenance and the district facilities manager conduct a visual inspection of the school's bleacher system. This inspection takes place both on seating and walkway surfaces leading to the bleachers as well as on the support system beneath the seating area. A seating chart of the facility is used to ensure that each section of the bleacher system is inspected during the process. Any problem areas are identified and noted on the seating chart, and a detailed report is created. Upon completion of the inspection report, bleacher maintenance work orders are developed and are divided into two categories: (1) routine and (2) serious.

The detailed report is kept on file in the office of the district maintenance department and is reviewed at the conclusion of each school year. A pattern of routine or serious problems can be quickly spotted through regular use of this report.

Routine repairs, such as replacing and tightening bolts, are performed by the maintenance department. For items considered serious, such as broken seats and bent frames, the bleacher installer or other repair company is called in to make the necessary repairs and replacements. As a risk management procedure, records are kept of all school district maintenance, and the repair company gives the school district a certificate indicating the bleacher system is safe and ready for use during the next athletic season.

This protocol has been implemented to provide a safe environment for all outdoor and indoor athletic events throughout the school year. For example, if bleachers are heavily used or are showing cracks and deterioration, more frequent inspections may be necessary.

the surface must be adequately durable to withstand the cumulative stresses associated with sports and nonsports activities. Patton (2009), Sprecher (2011), and Steinbach (2011) have developed comparisons of the strengths and issues related to artificial and natural sport turf surfaces.

Natural Turf Considerations

There are many factors to consider in selecting turf grass for a sports field. Everyone has a favorite type of surface. There is no "right" choice across the board; there is only the choice that is right for a particular installation and the kinds of activities conducted in that facility.

Turf grass advantages include the following:

- Environmentally friendly. Twenty-five hundred square feet of living, growing, grass plants release enough oxygen for a family of four for a year. Grass absorbs carbon dioxide, helping to reduce global warming.

- Cooler surface. Grass provides a cooler place to play than bare dirt, cement, or artificial turf. This occurs because the photosynthetic process in the grass intercepts sunlight, using the sun's energy to make plant sugars instead of warming the dirt. Plants evaporate water as part of the process, which also cools the air.

- Clean surface. Grass roots, thatch, and leaves provide a clean surface for activity.

- Better appearance. The visual appearance and aroma of grass are pleasing to people.

- Recycling medium. Because turf grass nurtures the growth of micro-organisms, it is an excellent recycling medium. Unlike artificial turf, natural grass fields do not require removal of leaves, chewing gum, peanut shells, sunflower seed hulls, and bits of paper. In addition, infectious diseases such as MRSA that could be transferred from a player to the grass are naturally counteracted. Grass fields do not need disinfecting.

- Self-repair. Given reasonable rainfall and temperate climates, natural grass fields repair themselves.

Grass gives good footing but not great traction. *Good traction* means that when players collide, natural turf tends to stretch, which is better for human joints. *Great traction* can be bad because human skeletal joints can be damaged when a player's foot is anchored against high-traction artificial turf.

All sports fields sustain wear and damage when used. Although natural grass fields have the ability to repair and regenerate themselves, artificial surfaces feature durability despite multiple hard usage patterns and climatic extremes.

Artificial Turf Considerations

Astroturf was originally designed to encourage people to be more active outdoors. It started to appear on athletic fields in the early 1960s. In 1966, it was installed in the world-famous Houston Astrodome, where professional athletes played for many years on the bright-green carpet. In 1967, artificial grass was installed in its first outdoor sports arena—Memorial Stadium at

Indiana State University in Terre Haute, Indiana. Despite early enthusiasm, Astroturf demonstrated a number of issues.

According to Dr. Michael Meyers, head of the department of sports and exercise sciences at West Texas A&M and lead author of a study on turf injury rates, "Basically, Astroturf was a glorified carpet over concrete" (Meyers 2004, 1626 - 1638). Astroturf was blamed for a variety of sports injuries, including "turf toe" and concussions, because its surface was harder than that of natural grass.

Yesterday's artificial turf is very different from today's synthetic in-fill systems in that the new in-fill technology creates a field that looks much more like natural grass and has improved shock-attenuation properties.

New-generation synthetic turf can have a high initial installation cost, but manufacturers say the savings in maintenance will make up for it. Unlike natural grass fields, synthetic turf playing fields do not need watering, mowing, reseeding, or painting (field markings are woven directly into the fabric). For those reasons, modern synthetic turf products are less expensive to maintain.

By comparison, keeping a natural turf field in top condition is also more complicated than keeping up a synthetic turf field. Turf grass must be aerated and treated with herbicides and pesticides. These maintenance tasks usually fall to the school grounds staff. Unfortunately, classroom-related issues relegate turf needs to a lower-priority rank. By choosing to install a synthetic field, school administrators may save money on maintenance and relieve some of the burden on their maintenance workers.

Synthetic turf can be considered eco-friendly or "green" compared with pesticide-dependent, water-demanding natural grass. It has been estimated that synthetic turf prevents billions of gallons of water and millions of pounds of fertilizers and pesticides from being applied every year. Synthetic turf also prevents hundreds of thousands of pounds of carbon from being spewed from turf-care equipment into the atmosphere. Finally, the recycled particulate rubber in a typical fill-in synthetic football field will prevent between 18,000 and 20,000 car tires from being rolled into landfills.

Because synthetic turf won't freeze or get muddy like natural grass, it can be used year round, in conditions that would normally cause a game to be called on account of rain. Synthetic turf fields have built-in drainage channels to keep the fields from flooding even in a downpour.

Both synthetic turf and natural turf have the potential to cause injuries. Dr. Meyers conducted a study of high school football injuries on natural turf and on synthetic turf. The study, which was published in the *American Journal of Sports Medicine*, indicated that various types of injuries were linked to turf differences.

Myers indicated, "This new generation of synthetic turf typically results in far fewer injuries than we see on the old-generation Astroturf, the old synthetic artificial carpeted turf" (Myers 2004, 1626 - 1638). The study found fewer joint problems, less major joint damage, and fewer ACL injuries on synthetic turf than on natural grass.

Because artificial turf (in-fill type) is a relatively new product, its complete life span and maintenance requirements are not fully known. The athletic director should answer the following questions before making a major investment:

- Will the artificial turf manufacturing and installation company provide a warranty specifying the expected life of the product?
- Will the selling firm provide a warranty bond for the life of the product? This will ensure there is some legitimate recourse in the event of a product failure even if the seller is no longer in business.
- What is the longest period of time this specific artificial field has been in use at another school, college, or university?
- What conditions or maintenance practices will void the field's warranty?
- Does a single warranty cover all aspects of the artificial field's soil base preparation, base materials, artificial turf materials, and so on? Will there be separate warranties and voiding conditions for each element?
- What level of technical training is supplied, recommended, or required for the maintenance crew in order to properly maintain the area and the warranty conditions?

For schools, colleges, and recreation departments that must endure long, cold winters, an artificial turf product might be best. In more temperate climates, the lower initial costs of natural grass might make it more attractive. Only after a careful consideration of the pros and cons of each type of surface can administrators decide which type of playing field is right for their programs.

Gymnasium Floors

From a competition perspective, the sports floor is probably the most important equipment component of any sports facility. It is a fundamental item that must be considered from the outset of any construction or remodeling project when the overall objectives are being set.

Sports flooring requires careful considerations before construction or floor covering installations are initiated. Special flooring can meet the needs of athletes in diverse sports such as basketball, tennis, track, weightlifting, and indoor soccer. School gymnasiums and other multipurpose sports facilities present unique sports flooring needs. These floors must be extremely durable and economical to maintain while providing a surface on which several different activities can be scheduled in a short time frame.

The most important feature of a sports floor is that it prevents injuries. This must be true for competitive athletes as well as elementary school children getting their first chance to play on a sports floor.

Sports flooring can be made from a variety of natural and synthetic materials. When the athletic director is choosing sports flooring, the options can seem overwhelming. Starting with the basics, there are six types from which to choose:

1. Wood
2. Resilient pure vinyl
3. Poured urethane
4. Polypropylene interlocking tile
5. Solid rubber
6. Vinyl composition tile

Sports flooring differs immensely from floors designed for any other purpose. Because the needs of athletes come first, safety, performance, and comfort are basic considerations. Three characteristics are important for a safe indoor athletic surface: (1) shock absorbency, (2) impact attenuation, and (3) surface friction. Kollie (2012) has provided informative facts and guidance on flooring solutions.

Proper shock absorption is highly important. As an athlete strikes a sports surface, the force of impact is translated into two resultant forces: one absorbed by the floor and the other returned to the athlete.

Some hard surfaces such as concrete and asphalt provide little or no force reduction during running or jumping activities. Ideally, a sports floor system should absorb a certain amount of these forces. The degree to which this goal is accomplished can be measured and compared to the less effective impact reduction afforded by hard surfaces. For example, a sports floor with a force reduction value of 40 percent will absorb 40 percent of the impact force and return 60 percent of that force to the athlete. It is widely accepted in the indoor sports flooring industry that a minimal desired percentage is 50 percent. A majority of wood gymnasium floors installed at the high school, collegiate, and professional levels will meet this rating.

Impact attenuation refers to the impact of an athlete's body part with the surface. Athletic surfaces can be rated on the two general characteristics of area elasticity and point elasticity. Cushioned wood athletic floors, like those found in most school gyms, are area-elastic and are more forgiving to a falling athlete. Most synthetic floors, namely those installed directly on concrete, are less area-elastic. Point elasticity refers to the degree to which a floor absorbs and returns energy over a small area. Wood gym floors are less point-elastic than synthetic floors. Thus, they return less energy to a smaller point such as the foot, ankle, or upper extremity of a falling athlete.

Surface friction is used to measure a floor's inherent prevention of sliding by athletes on the playing surface. For an indoor sports floor, the surface friction must be high enough to prevent premature and uncontrollable slippage but also low enough to permit sliding when an athlete falls with significant momentum or as a result of an extreme force. For wood floors, surface friction is a direct function of the finish on the surface. For most synthetic floors, surface friction measurements are higher.

Wood Floors

Athletes and other performers, coaches, trainers, owners, and architects overwhelmingly cite maple as the preferred sports floor surface. In fact, maple is the flooring of choice for 70 percent of the sports floors installed in the United States. Maple has been called nature's perfect flooring surface. It exhibits flexibility, resilience, and durability and has low maintenance demands. The surface provides dependably uniform grip and traction to athletic footwear. Safety is greatly enhanced with the maple surface compared to a synthetic floor. In a study by the Ducker Research Company in 1991, athletes were 70 percent more likely to sustain a floor-related injury on a synthetic floor than on a maple floor (Maple Flooring Manufacturers Association 2009).

For professional and college programs, wood floors enjoy a stronghold on the sports flooring market. However, there are other gymnasiums in which wood flooring is not an affordable option. For cost-efficiency purposes, some operators of multipurpose gymnasiums install synthetic surfaces on their activity courts.

Synthetic Floors

Alternatives to hardwood flooring are available in three basic synthetic forms: (1) poured-in-place urethane, (2) rolled sheet goods made of vinyl or rubber, and (3) injection-molded polypropylene tiles.

Poured urethanes can be further broken down into two categories:

1. Those that utilize prefabricated rubber sheet goods as a base, which then receive coats of urethane that results in a seamless surface
2. Those installed with multiple levels of poured urethane, starting at the concrete substrate

When properly installed, poured-in-place urethane floors bond permanently to the raw concrete substrate and exhibit tremendous elasticity, tensile strength, and tear strength. Elasticity represents how far a floor can be stretched horizontally before it tears.

Tensile strength refers to the amount of vertical pressure a floor can withstand without tearing. A floor's tear strength relates to the amount of force required to lengthen or expand an existing tear. These characteristics determine the degree to which a urethane floor will handle stresses ranging from shifts in the substrate to loads exerted by bleachers.

Sheet goods commonly used in gymnasium flooring applications include vinyl, recycled vinyl, and recycled rubber. These products offer facility operators a range of aesthetic and playability characteristics along with ease of installation. Individual sheets of flooring that range in width from 4 to 6.5 feet (1.2 to 2.0 m) are adhered directly to the concrete substrate. At that time, seams are chemically welded or heat welded. Sheet goods cost between $4.50 and $7.00 per square foot installed. In comparison, a recreational maple floor can cost $9.50 per square foot. Sheet goods offer another distinct health and safety advantage. They can be chemically treated to help prevent the spread of bacteria and germs.

In terms of aesthetics, both rubber and vinyl flooring products are sold in a variety of colors, allowing the installation of floors with contrasting colors to delineate court boundaries, free throw lanes, and center jump circles. This minimizes the amount of paint required and thus reduces the need for repainting.

Snap-together modular tiles are the least expensive option of all synthetic gym floor systems. These tiles cost between $3.50 and $6.00 per square foot installed. In addition to being low cost, this system is highly versatile. From elementary sports to the highest levels of competition, injection-molded polypropylene tiles have advanced as rapidly as any synthetic surface in terms of multiuse applications.

Another distinct advantage of snap-together modular tile floors is their relative immunity to moisture damage. Water damage to a wood floor often requires replacement of the entire floor. Conversely, damage to a synthetic floor requires that only a section of the floor be replaced.

The primary reason institutions install synthetic floors relates to cost. Synthetic floors typically cost one-third the price of a wood floor. Wood floors will always have their place among gymnasium purists, who extol its time-tested beauty and performance. But for many schools, synthetic floors are a good choice. They provide a lot of comfort and versatility.

Permanent Equipment

Permanent equipment includes capital items such as bleachers, railings, weight machines, sound systems, scoreboards, basket lifts, gymnastics equipment and gymnastics floor anchorage systems, wrestling and gymnastics floor exercise mats and crash pads, volleyball systems, backstops, dugout fencing and fence caps, electronic timing devices for pools, diving boards and starting blocks, indoor and outdoor track judge stands, and pole-vault and high-jump standards and landing mats.

The first step in purchasing permanent equipment for a high school or other institution is for the athletic director to determine the intended use of each piece under consideration. Will the equipment be used for sports practices and competition? It is important to choose the correct equipment in order to achieve the desired results. The next step is to conduct research on the demographics of the clients who will use the facility. A gymnasium that will be used by physical education classes, athletic teams, and community youth-league sports should be equipped differently from a facility used as the competition site for varsity basketball and adult recreation teams only.

After considering all usage possibilities, the next important but occasionally limiting factor is determining the budget. Project managers and athletic directors should have a tentative budget in mind before conducting cost research on permanent equipment. It is easy to be attracted to innovations and the latest features on the market. But as stewards of public trust, it's important to work within a budget to control spending. As a guideline, administrators should consider buying the best equipment a budget allows even if it means buying less. There are two major pitfalls when buying lower-cost, poor-quality products. First is compromised safety for clients. Second is that it will be more prone to breakdowns.

Another important consideration when selecting permanent equipment is the amount of space available for setup. An overcrowded facility can give the impression of being cluttered and thus reduce the facility's overall appeal. Proper spacing should allow for easy access, safe usage, and transportability. Transportability should facilitate cleaning both the equipment and the activity space in which it is used. The project manager should also take into consideration the weight of the equipment and conduct research to ascertain whether the floor underneath is strong enough to support the equipment's mass. Structural engineers should be consulted to determine whether heavy weight machines can be installed on the upper floors of an activity site and utilized safely by teams and classes.

Simplicity of usage is another issue in the purchase of permanent equipment for an athletic facility. Any adjustments that must be made by coaches or students should be simple to implement and few in number. Numerous, difficult adjustments will discourage use by coaches and can be particularly troubling to users with injuries.

A final factor for consideration when selecting permanent equipment is quality. To emphasize an earlier point, an athletic director should buy the best equipment that is affordable. Purchasing high-quality equipment can lead to more frequent usage. The facility manager must have the equipment serviced at regular intervals in order to maintain its performance and increase longevity.

Building Renovation Versus New Construction

One of the most important decisions a school district must make is whether to renovate an existing athletic facility or replace it completely. At a time when school districts are experiencing budget cuts and teacher furloughs, the decision to renovate facilities is being examined more closely.

Because of the increasing costs of new construction and a need for improved utilization of existing space, the emphasis in facility planning has changed from new construction to other more realistic and relevant choices. In today's economy, new construction has become an option of last resort and then only after careful study of other alternatives. Hill (2005) and Klingensmith (2011) provide extensive guidance for planning athletic and physical education facilities.

As a result of economic pressures, communities have fewer options and less flexibility when deciding whether to construct a new facility or retain the current building. Whether the decision is to renovate or build, the ultimate objective is the same—provide the best possible place for students to grow and learn.

Weighing the advantages and disadvantages of renovating an older facility requires expertise, experience, and creativity. The potential for renovation is occasionally dismissed without full consideration of the facts and long-term implications.

A feasibility study must be conducted to examine all benefits and deficits of renovation. This is a time-tested way to evaluate the compatibility of an old building with contemporary educational uses. A feasibility study helps determine whether renovation of a historic school is possible and practical. This research would also determine whether a renovated building can meet the identified educational needs. In addition to providing a cost–benefit analysis, a feasibility study evaluates technology needs and barriers, outlines a schedule for completing the school construction project from start to finish, determines options and alternatives, and identifies the potential implications of decisions to the surrounding neighborhood and community.

Cost is one of the most important factors that drive the decision-making process. Whenever a recommendation to construct is made, faculty and coaches must understand that it could be very costly to renovate. On the other hand, school athletic department personnel must recognize that a school facility could have historical value or may serve a special function in a community.

Questions that a school athletic department should consider include the following:

- Does the building have historical significance?
- Do the costs of rehabilitating the current facility outweigh the costs of new construction?
- Can the facility be renovated to accommodate 21st-century instructional delivery practices and modern technologies?
- Have new construction codes been enacted that can complicate renovation and add to the costs?
- Will it be necessary to retain some sections of the existing facility? Are there sections that should be replaced?

- Is the facility of adequate size for the school population of today and of the future?
- Is the building well lighted, spacious, and comfortable?
- Does the environment impart a feeling of safety and well-being?

Schools renovate athletic facilities for a variety of reasons. One is a statutory mandate called the Americans with Disabilities Act (ADA) of 1990, which defines accessibility standards. Many older stadiums were not in compliance, and the required facility renovations offered an opportunity to bring facilities into compliance while also enhancing the education and sports experiences of the students. The National Trust for Historic Preservation (2010) provides insight concerning feasibility studies related to renovation projects.

The ADA pertains to the design, construction, and alteration of buildings and facilities. When an older facility is renovated, the project must include alterations and updates to make it accessible and ADA compliant. ADA requirements state that if "existing elements, spaces, or common areas are altered, then each such altered element, space, feature, or area shall comply" with the same provisions as new construction projects. And "if alterations of single elements, when considered together, amount to an alteration of a room or space in a building or facility, the entire space shall be made accessible" (ADAAG 2002).

Before initiating a renovation project, a school must consider a number of issues. The first step is to evaluate the school's goals, formulate a plan, and hire an architectural planner who can help with problematic planning issues.

The next step is to determine if the integrity of the system will remain after the expansion. A majority of the outdoor facilities that were built 20 or 30 years ago were constructed with welded steel that may have been adversely affected by the weather. In addition, electrical codes have changed over time. If an older section of a building is connected to a renovation, it may be necessary to change all older electrical components to meet current code requirements.

In summary, building renovation should be considered if the following requirements in the identified buildings can be met:

- Have a particular architectural or cultural value
- Can be adapted to meet the latest requirements more cheaply than the construction of a new building
- Are structurally sound
- Do not contain any toxic materials (asbestos, lead piping, paint containing heavy metals)
- Can be adapted in accordance with the highest safety standards (evacuation, fire protection, earthquake resistance)

- Can be equipped with modern installations (electrical circuits, air conditioning, communications)
- Offer local socioeconomic benefits outweighing those linked to the construction of a new building

Maintenance

Maintenance personnel are essential for periodic inspections, preventive maintenance measures, and repairs that directly contribute to the safe operation of athletic facilities. The early detection of facility problems and the expedited response by these staff may directly influence the success of all academic and athletic personnel. To ensure the school's facilities are adequately maintained, the school district should develop and implement scheduled preventive and reactive strategic maintenance plans for all its facilities. Records of completed preventive maintenance work and the dates completed should be maintained and securely filed.

The structure and organization of the preventive maintenance program must be communicated to administration and staff before effective maintenance work can be initiated. Operations and maintenance departments should establish a cross-discipline preventive maintenance work center. The purpose of this center is to inspect various systems and components and write maintenance work orders. After the inspection, a specific section of the maintenance department (e.g., plumbing, electrical) is assigned to do the actual work tasks.

In rural and smaller school districts, challenges may exist when establishing an organizational structure for preventive maintenance. The availability of trained workers, limited accessibility, and logistical concerns are among factors that influence the maintenance department in these settings. A common structure for many rural or smaller districts is to supplement the work of one or two on-site custodial and general maintenance personnel with a traveling crew of maintenance workers with journeyman skills in the various building trades. Rau (2010) discusses some of the legislative and political issues related to maintenance of sport facilities.

Another option is to augment a small in-house workforce with open contracts to provide private-sector preventive maintenance service or maintenance repair services. Open-ended mechanical, electrical, and plumbing contracts are common ways to augment the in-house workforce.

Liability can be a major issue for sports facilities. Often, maintenance of the facility plays a role in litigation. There are three main areas of potential litigation involving sports facilities:

1. Problems exist with the initial design and facility construction or installation and any subsequent renovations.
2. The actual facility usage differs from the purpose for which the facility was designed.

3. Hazardous maintenance issues and facility conditions resulted from failure to inspect for and identify potential problems and rectify them.

"Adequate and appropriate," "reasonable and proper," and "foreseeable and fixable" are phrases that crop up repeatedly when discussing facility issues and liability for injury or loss in legal proceedings. Although there may not be published industry-wide standards for all aspects of sports fields, generally accepted reasonable expectations apply. Athletes anticipate an appropriately graded playing field that is free of debris, holes, divots, depressions, ridges, lips, and other potential safety hazards. This expectation also pertains to loose seams, worn patches, or uneven in-fill on synthetic fields.

Field maintenance should focus first on safety. Thus, maintenance personnel or the groundskeeper should inspect the playing field surface before each contest. When potential risks of injury are identified, they should be rectified before play begins. The challenge is consistently providing fields and other facilities that meet or exceed safety expectations and documenting that preventive maintenance has been implemented.

Dr. Gil Fried, a sport management professional, is a longtime advocate of risk management programs. The steps he has developed for this process are outlined here (Fried 2013).

1. Reflect: Determine your primary interest in safety and develop a comprehensive plan to address it.

2. Deflect: Utilize appropriate strategies of deflection (e.g., contracts, insurance) as a tool to help manage ultimate financial and legal liability.

3. Detect: Critically examine the facility to determine what type of disasters could occur and what issues, occurrences, or events will trigger each disaster.

4. Inspect: Inspect the information gathered during the detect phase, seeking potential problem areas and developing potential solutions.

5. Correct: Whenever problems or concerns are identified, correct them. Proceeding with a problem is an invitation for disaster and potential liability.

6. Reinspect: After problems have been corrected, reexamine the concern to ensure the correction is appropriate and adequate. Once a facility manager knows about a problem, he cannot hide behind the excuse that he ordered something to be corrected and assumed the work had been done.

7. Reflect: After an event, analyze what occurred, gathering input from all parties involved, jointly exploring methods of improvement.

When establishing a maintenance plan for indoor and outdoor athletic facilities, the key is to develop and follow a written plan. Although the format for the inspection of individual facilities can vary, certain basic criteria apply for daily, weekly, and seasonal inspections. During an inspection, each inspection item should be dated and documented. Identified problem areas must be rectified and the work dated; detailed records of the repair or maintenance process should be retained. The duties owed to invitees to an athletic facility are as follows:

- Keep the premises in safe repair.
- Inspect to discover hidden hazards.
- Remove hazards or warn users.
- Anticipate foreseeable usage needs (e.g. football, soccer, field hockey, rugby).
- Conduct operations safely.

Siedler and Miller (2008) have provided important insights concerning risk management measures for sport facilities. Trusty (2010) provides specific guidance on risk management related to sport field management.

High-quality operating and maintenance procedures can strengthen a well-planned eco-friendly construction or renovation project. Effective maintenance is necessary to ensure equipment operates more efficiently while consuming less energy. Although maintenance personnel were once focused solely on basic upkeep, today's professional workers must be well-versed in a number of environmentally friendly techniques and materials. Their skills and knowledge must include awareness of the latest energy issues; toxic materials management; storm water drainage methods; and best practices for the operations of heating, ventilation, and air conditioning systems.

Over time, reliable building performance can be ensured through measurement, adjustment, and upgrading processes. Aside from the financial and environmental benefits, eco-friendly building systems do not require an excessive amount of upkeep. A preventive maintenance schedule can be put in place with little effort and minimal expense.

Current Athletic Facility Trends

The trend in new athletic facility construction is driven by the idea that sports facilities should be multipurpose venues containing some architectural flair. The green movement, compliance issues, safety concerns, potential liability, and economic realities also shape facility designs.

One of the new trends in the construction of athletic facilities deals with lighting. Gymnasiums in the 1960s relied on inefficient fluorescent lamps that produced poor lighting along with a buzzing sound. Then came other types of lighting (metal halide, high-pressure sodium, halogen) that were brighter but had other drawbacks. Some had cool-down and warm-up times, so if the power went out in the middle of a sporting event, all action would come to a halt for as long as 15 minutes.

New products on the market offer superior lighting as well as energy and cost savings. High-intensity fluorescent lights are extremely bright yet have compact fixtures. They are the norm for new facilities and offer a relatively quick return on investment. Recreation departments, high schools, colleges, and professional teams are all interested in saving money through improved efficiencies.

Gymnasiums of the past tended to be without windows, whereas newly constructed facilities make use of natural light for purposes of energy efficiency and occupant comfort. Standard windows produce unwanted glare and have the potential for breakage. A safer option is translucent fiberglass wall panels, which allow natural lighting into the gym.

Bleacher manufacturers have also reacted to changes in the construction of new athletic facilities. A newer retractable bleacher offers optimal traction on the different types of athletic flooring and finishes as opposed to traditional wood products. Patron comfort and aesthetic appeal are also important. These considerations have led manufacturers to develop plastic modular bleachers that look better, resist vandalism, and are easier to clean and maintain. Potential liability, consumer safety, and code compliance issues have driven the biggest changes in the design of bleachers.

Although the economy continues to force budget cuts, public expectations for sports facilities have grown. Instead of being cement cubes, gymnasiums and other sports facilities are now more architecturally interesting. Instead of corridors connecting spaces designed for programmed activities, it is not uncommon to find a lounge area with Wi-Fi capabilities where students can do homework or chat with friends. No longer is it about the gym or the pool; rather, the emphasis has shifted to spaces that connect and enhance the overall educational, athletic, and social experience.

Concern about the environmental impact of new construction is another force that is driving sports facility design. Eco-friendly sports facility design considers the architecture, site, region and climate, building envelope, construction materials, building systems, and other variables. Support for green construction remains strong across the country.

Athletic Master Plan

High schools spend millions of dollars each year on new athletic facilities. Because these projects are significant investments, construction proposals must be formalized, evaluated, and approved. Further, the process and actual proposal must be publicized, discussed, and explored in exacting details. It all begins with an athletic master plan.

The physical plant master plan, a long-term vision for campus improvements, has been around for decades. It encompasses everything from the science labs to the career technology department and is based on user input, surveys, planning initiatives, and economic conditions. Every dollar is precious to school district officials and to taxpayers. Having a master plan ensures that every dollar is spent wisely and that each project is carefully planned and orchestrated for the most efficient use of funds. The master plan provides a framework for growth.

As important as the master plan is to the school district as a whole, the athletic physical plant master plan is equally critical to the growth and success of the athletic department. The athletic master plan provides an analysis of a school district's athletic facilities and needs. It encompasses hundreds of schematic drawings, financial analyses, and architectural renderings. It analyzes infrastructure, parking, and landscaping needs; evaluates the campus' ability to sustain growth; and prioritizes construction projects.

Developing a comprehensive, long-range athletic master plan requires a team of trained professionals. The members of this planning committee, which is typically led by a design firm, could include buildings and grounds personnel, athletic department officials, and campus administrators. Duties of this committee include the following:

- Assessing the needs and wishes of the athletic department
- Determining which projects are realistic, affordable, and doable
- Prioritizing and scheduling renovations and construction
- Devising short- and long-term strategies to carry out the plan
- Developing fund-raising strategies and finance plans

The athletic master plan is developed in several stages, but the first three stages set a tone for the process. These are (1) programming, (2) benchmarking, and (3) brainstorming.

During the programming phase, members of the athletic master plan committee gather input from all levels of the school district, including student-athletes. They talk with the athletic director, coaches, teachers, and members of the maintenance staff to discern their specific needs and ideals for a new construction project. Surveys are often used to compile wish lists for areas that are lacking or need improvement. During this stage, the committee develops and prioritizes a comprehensive plan that encompasses all potential improvements. This plan may acknowledge that financial realities could limit the project.

The benchmarking stage is a chance for school officials to visit other institutions to see how effective various facility improvements have been on other campuses. These visitations also allow analysis of methods used to develop these facilities as part of a comprehensive athletic master plan.

The process is simple. A school district sends representatives to three or more schools to identify various factors they find attractive about these schools. This process helps establish levels of quality by looking at comparable data to determine what may be appropriate for their institution.

The interactive brainstorming session, often called a charette, integrates all desirable construction factors. Decisions about building locations and how renovations should be implemented are considered. The thinking should be "outside the box," challenging the status quo to devise creative, innovative solutions. Looking months and years ahead, the team determines when additions should come online, eventually pinpointing the dollar amount needed for each component of the plan.

Developing and implementing an athletic master plan is a daunting task for an individual athletic department. But failure to do so could have harmful effects on the athletic department and the school district at large. Better facilities, more efficient land use, and better value for dollars spent can result in greater overall success.

Summary

The mission of a school's physical plant department is to enhance the learning environment of the physical education and athletic department through high-quality services and wise stewardship of its physical assets. Maintenance or replacement of worn out or outdated operational equipment and other physical plant assets is essential, but must be balanced with the economic realities of the school or district. The athletic director also needs to make important decisions in choosing new equipment, which can include gym floors and outdoor fields. Cost, performance, and safety must be considered and balanced with the needs of the school.

Priority Issues Ahead in Interscholastic Sports

Eric Forsyth, PhD, CAA

John Olson, PhD, CMAA

This closing section provides an overview of five emerging issues of significance for high school athletic directors throughout the United States:

1. Budget and resources: Increased costs, reduced budgets, pressure to expand programs without increased resources, pressure to eliminate programs.

2. Budget effects on student participation and administrative factors: Participants are expected to pay participation fees for the first time in their school or district, or participation fees are increased; supplemental funding has become a necessity; booster club members want a voice in department policies and personnel decisions (hiring and firing).

3. Social networking (Facebook, Twitter, texting): Threats, harassment, denigration *by* athletes, denigration *of* athletes, violent retaliation, disruption of school programs.

4. Increased specialization among high school athletes: An athlete or parents select one sport for which the athlete's training and competition are continuous, to the exclusion of other high school sports participation. Athletes develop a sense of entitlement to playing time because of their specialization. Families develop unrealistic expectations for a college athletic scholarship because of specialization.

5. Quality of coaches and continuing education: Problem areas cited include coaches being unaware of the educational purposes of sport; coaches not using appropriate motivational methods; coaches being unaware of or not using scientific conditioning principles; coaches not knowing or not using risk management practices for specific sports; budgets for the continuing education of coaches being reduced or eliminated.

These concerns were initially identified through opinion surveys of NIAAA sectional representatives and the executive staff of the Minnesota

State High School League (Forsyth 2007). To determine the impact of these issues throughout the United States, several NIAAA leadership groups expanded Forsyth's research methodology. These NIAAA leaders have an average of 25 years' experience in high school athletic administration. Collectively, these veteran directors confirmed Forsyth's earlier identification of five significant issues in high school sport. Further, they suggested that each has the potential to negatively affect high school sports and athletic administration in future years unless reversed or resolved.

NIAAA members were surveyed electronically to get their opinions about the severity of these emerging and potential future issues. This survey was administered separately to NIAAA members in each of the eight NIAAA sections shown in figure 17.1.

The survey data were separately tabulated for each NIAAA section. Survey participants assessed the current severity of each of the five issues and also ranked them in terms of current impact. Separate assessments were conducted within each of the eight NIAAA sections in order to provide information to individual state athletic director associations and NIAAA's executive board. It is hoped that the findings will enhance decision making with regard to future research, publications, and leadership training topics as well as identify workshop presenters who can suggest successful strategies for responding to each issue.

The data listed in table 17.1 are the percentages of NIAAA athletic directors in each of the eight sections who believe the five contemporary issues have negatively affected current programs at major to severe levels. Further, they believe these issues will worsen unless innovative measures are implemented. Survey participants selected the number and description that best

FIGURE 17.1   Eight NIAAA geographic sections.

represents the impact of these issues on their current programs. The choices on the severity scale are as follows: 1-2 = little effect, 3-4 = some effect, 5-6 = significant effect, 7-8 = major effect, 9-10 = severe effect.

Table 17.2 ranks the five issues in terms of severity, where 1 is most severe and 5 is least severe.

TABLE 17.1   Percentage of NIAAA Survey Participants Who Rated the Current Effect of Five Interscholastic Sports Issues as Major or Severe

NIAAA section	Budget/ finance	Budget reduction	Social networking	Specializa- tion by athletes	Coaches quality
Section 1 (n = 128)	78.2	72.5	74.1	84.4	66.3
Section 2 (n=148)	79.6	83.8	70.9	82.4	72.9
Section 3 (n=71)	55.0	68.0	73.4	78.9	59.0
Section 4 (n=206)	91.2	76.3	64.8	84.6	73.2
Section 5 (n=107)	85.7	67.0	68.1	80.9	76.7
Section 6 (n=42)	83.3	85.6	88.0	85.7	59.5
Section 7 (n=58)	94.9	83.3	64.6	89.8	75.7
Section 8 (n=46)	86.7	68.9	68.9	79.9	73.3

TABLE 17. 2   Cumulative Rank Order of Issues by NIAAA Members

Issue	Rank	% rating	Severity level
Specialization by athletes	1	83.3	Major effect
Budget and finance	2	81.8	Major effect
Budget reduction effect on participation	3	75.6	Major effect
Social networking	4	71.6	Major effect
Quality coaches and professional growth	5	69.5	Significant effect

Specialization by Athletes

In some cases, parents and athletes become overly optimistic about collegiate and professional aspirations by making early commitments to a single sport. Often, these commitments entail competing with a local high school team during the state association–approved season and then bypassing other school sport programs to play with an amateur team in that same sport for a major portion of the remaining school year.

As a variation on this theme, some athletes entirely bypass a particular high school sport to pursue extended-season play and travel with a private-sector amateur sports team. These extended schedules may also keep the athlete from participating in other school sports seasons. In addition, private-sector coaches may strongly encourage specialized conditioning routines. These activities are offered at significant cost along with specialized instruction by coaches who have played at a collegiate, international, or professional level of competition.

An unfortunate aspect of specialization occurs when entry-level athletes, frosh, and JV players must specialize as early as the grade-school years in order to develop adequate skills to qualify for nonvarsity team membership.

During orientation programs for new students and entry-level athletes, athletic directors would be prudent to cite the following facts:

- Although a small number of specialized athletes do receive college grant-in-aid athletic scholarships, that number is extremely small. NCAA data indicate that about $1 billion in athletic-related financial aid is awarded each year at Division I and II institutions. However, of 7.6 million high school athletes (NFHS 2011), 126,000 (1.6 percent) received grant-in-aid athletic scholarships (NCAA 2012a). Grants-in-aid are awarded and administered directly by each institution, not by the NCAA. Division III members do not offer athletic-related financial aid (NCAA 2012a).

- For the two most popular boys' and girls' high school sports, the percentage of athletes who receive grant-in-aid scholarships is also very small. More than 1 million teenage boys play high school football, but just 28,300 (or 2.83 percent) received a scholarship from a Division I or II school (NCAA 2012a). Track and field is the most popular high school sport for teenage girls. In 2010, more than 600,000 participated, but fewer than 10,000 athletes were awarded track scholarships (Registered Rep 2010).

- Eight in 10,000 (.8 percent) of high school senior boys playing interscholastic football will eventually be drafted by an NFL team (NCAA 2012b).

Table 17.3 provides an overview of the percentage of student-athletes transitioning from high school to college athletics and from college to professional sports (NCAA 2012b).

When an athlete focuses on one sport and the related conditioning regimens, the student and family may develop a sense of entitlement to

TABLE 17.3   Transition From High School to College and Professional Sport Competition

Student-athletes	Men's basket-ball	Women's basket-ball	Football	Baseball	Men's ice hockey	Men's soccer
High school seniors	155,955	125,409	316,697	134,579	10,546	113,815
College athletes	17,500	15,708	67,887	31,264	3,944	22,573
College frosh	5,000	4,488	19,396	8,933	1,127	6,449
College seniors	3,889	3,491	15,086	6,948	876	5,016
High school to college	3.2%	3.6%	6.1%	6.6%	10.7%	5.7%
College to profes-sional	1.2%	0.9%	1.7%	11.6%	1.3%	1.0%
High school to profes-sional	0.03%	0.03%	0.08%	0.60%	0.10%	0.04%

significant playing time on a high school team because of the specialized commitment. As a balance to these beliefs, orientation programs must focus on the responsibilities of a coaching staff to assess candidates fairly along with the obligation of coaches to select the most-skilled and best-conditioned players for competition.

Finally, parents need to be made aware of the number and length of trips expected and the costs associated with private-sector competition, travel, and lodging. In addition, parents need to ask private-sector coaches if the athlete's school attendance will be frequently interrupted and if the private-sector coaching staff will monitor academics, personal conduct, and school attendance of the specialist athlete as prerequisites to playing time.

Budget, Finance, and Resource Shortfall

NIAAA survey data make it clear that inadequate resources have had a negative effect on high school athletic programs (table 17.2). This issue is expected to worsen unless creative and innovative funding strategies can be identified (see chapter 13).

For the immediate future, it is imperative to keep the public and educational decision-makers well informed. Proactive information and community relations presentations should include the following:

• Documentation of the effect of participation, with emphasis on the improved academics, attendance, and personal conduct of athletes. A special focus should be the positive effects of participation by at-risk student populations.

• Testimonies by current athletes and alumni to the media and to educational governance boards concerning the life-changing effects of sport participation that reversed criminal behaviors and other forms of negative conduct.

• Documentation of efficient and maximal use of existing resources. These include extended maintenance and repairs of existing uniforms and equipment inventories. Emphasis should also be given to successful efforts to prevent loss, theft, and misuse of equipment.

• Evidence of cooperative efforts by supplemental funding organizations. The existing school and district athletic budget must be used as a foundation for targeted fund-raising. Title IX equity considerations must remain at the forefront of all supplemental funding efforts.

• Innovative marketing and fund-raising efforts to increase supplemental revenues. Refer to chapter 13 for examples of fund-raising initiatives and corporate sponsorships. It is imperative to recognize and thank athletic program donors and sponsors.

Effect of Fees on Participation Stability

The NIAAA survey participants identified declines in student participation as a result of fee requirements or increases as the third major issue in interscholastic sports. If fund-raising is instituted to help offset the impact of fees on students, it is important to gain approval from the state association for any efforts to assist poverty-level students with payment of athletic fees. To avoid violation of an amateur status eligibility rule, these efforts typically entail contributions to a school fund administered by a committee that makes athletic fee decisions based on poverty documentation.

Often, students who are approved for assistance are those who currently receive free and reduced school meals and subsidized bus passes or other fee waivers. School counselors and community outreach and support staff can be especially helpful in validating requests for subsidized payments. Fee waivers are another option. As with fee subsidies, waivers require similar procedures to document a legitimate need for assistance.

Electronic Social Networking

Local school district athletic policy and athletic administrator decisions must be based on recent court findings related to this emerging issue. Recent judgments suggest that disciplining athletes for off-campus electronic networking is an overly broad sanctioning procedure that abridges the First Amendment (Green 2012).

Athletic policies should focus on the potential for violent acts and school disruptions as retaliations for comments on electronic networks. In addition, dangerous situations may evolve as an outgrowth of social networking (e.g., gang threats and retaliatory violence). Because of broader safety issues for the school and community, athletes may be instructed to cease networking activities with known gang members under threat of athletic suspension until local police or gang task force personnel are advised and involved.

Actual involvement of athletes in school disruptions or violent responses to electronic networking can be appropriately disciplined in accordance with local school prohibitions against fighting, school disruption, or conduct unbecoming.

Quality of Coaches and Continuing Education

One of 14 legal duties expected of athletic directors is the "selection and training of coaches" (Green 2009). This legal guidance strongly suggests continuing education of coaches to maintain the highest levels of instruction, supervision, and safety, with an ultimate goal of preventing injuries to and losses of athletes.

In numerous school districts throughout the United States, up to 50 percent of coaches are not licensed teachers and are not employed at the sponsoring schools. For this reason, the NFHS has developed a fundamental training course for coaches who lack formal training. This course is titled Coaching Principles and is described in greater detail at NFHS.org. The course may be taken online, in a traditional classroom setting, or in a blended online and classroom format. Coaching Principles provides a foundation for all continuing education to enhance skills and knowledge while meeting the mandate of the legal duty of training coaches.

Other courses of relevance for a coach's continuing education curriculum include the following:

- Concussion management
- Taping and bracing clinics
- Nutrition and hydration concepts taught by a certified professional nutritionist
- Roles and responsibilities of the certified athletic trainer, the strength and conditioning coordinator, and the team physician

- Sport-specific risk management methods and strategies
- Emergency care procedures, including site-specific emergency management plans and responses

In some geographic areas, college and university faculty or medical clinic staff have the responsibility to provide free services to and instruction to state or local residents. Using this source of expertise, athletic directors may be able to access contemporary research and emerging innovation or best practices at minimal cost. In addition, colleges and universities increasingly offer professional growth opportunities and graduate degree programs through online learning technology. In this model, students interact with college faculty by way of home computers to pursue course work or graduate degrees. For further information, consult the website of the NIAAA (www.NIAAA.org).

Summary

In closing this book, the chapter authors present basic strategies and responses for five significant issues facing interscholastic sports. Investigative findings and best practices of collegiate and private-sector researchers were suggested as topics for workshops and presentations at national and state athletic director conferences along with subject matter for NIAAA publications and Leadership Training Institute courses.

References

Introduction

Bureau of Labor Statistics. 2012. Occupational outlook handbook. 2010 edition. Available: www.bls.gov/oco/ocos251.htm.

Forsyth, E. 2007. *Current Issues Surrounding Interscholastic Sports: Survey Report*. Indianapolis, IN: NIAAA.

Forsyth, E. 2010. Contemporary issues surrounding interscholastic sports: What they mean to athletic administrators. Unpublished research paper. Bemidji, MN: Bemidji State University.

Forsyth, E. 2013. *Contemporary Issues Surrounding Interscholastic Sports: Parents Issues*. Indianapolis IN: NIAAA. Vol. 39, No. 3, pp. 16-17.

NFHS. n.d. Case for high school activities. Available: www.nfhs.org/search.aspx?searchtext=case for high school activities.

NFHS. n.d. High school athletics participation survey. Available: www.nfhs.org/content.aspx?id=3282.

NFHS. 2011. 2010-11 athletics participation summary. *NFHS Handbook 2011-12*. Indianapolis, IN: Author.

Robinson, M., M. Hums, R. Crow, and D. Phillips. 2001. *Profiles of sport industry professionals: The people who make the games happen*. Gaithersburg, MD: Aspen Publishers.

Chapter 1

Becker, B. 1993. Activities participation: best predictor of success. *National Federation News* 10(1): 29.

Blackburn, M. 2000. Best bargain in education? High school activity programs. *Interscholastic Athletic Administration* 26(4): 23.

Blackburn, M. 2004. Effects of interscholastic athletic participation on grade point averages of high school students. Unpublished research paper. Indianapolis: Indiana Wesleyan University.

Born, T. 2007. High standard for GPA means a competitive disadvantage. *Minneapolis Star Tribune*, May 14. Available: www.highbeam.com/doc/1G1-163493439.html.

Broh, B. 2002. Linking extracurricular programming to academic achievement: Who benefits and why? *Sociology of Education* 75(1): 69.

Bukowski, B. 2001. A comparison of academic athletic eligibility in interscholastic sports in american high schools. *The Sport Journal*, 4(2).

Bureau of Labor Statistics. 2009. Occupational outlook handbook. 2010-11 edition. Available: www.bls.gov/opub/mlr/2009/11/art5full.pdf.

California Interscholastic Federation. 2009. A case for athletics. Available: http://205.214.168.16/sports/state/volleyball_girls/pdf/index.html.

Forsyth, E. 2010. Contemporary issues surrounding interscholastic sports: What they mean to athletic administrators. Unpublished research paper. Bemidji, MN: Bemidji State University.

Fredricks, J. Eccles, J. (2006). Is extracurricular participation associated with beneficial outcomes? Concurrent and longitudinal relations. *Developmental Psychology*, 42(4), 698.

Heath, D.H. 1992. *Fulfilling Lives: Paths to Maturity and Success*. San Francisco: Jossey-Bass.

Indiana Women's History Association. 2003. *For the Sport of It!* Indianapolis: IWHA.

Interscholastic Equity Committee. 1994. *Gender Equity in Interscholastic Athletics*. Columbus: Ohio High School Athletic Association.

IAHSAA. 1992. Benefits of high school activities. Iowa Athletic High School Activities Association. Available: http://www.iahsaa.org/resource_center/Character_Sportsmanship_Safety/Benefit_of_Activities_Handout.pdf.

Jeziorski, R.M. 1994. *The Importance of School Sports in American Education and Socialization*. New York: University Press of America.

Koebler, J. 2011. High schools sports participation increases for 22nd straight year. US News Education. Available: www.usnews.com/education/blogs/high-school-notes/2011/09/02/high-school-sports-participation-increases-for-22nd-straight-year.

Kosteas, V. (2010). *High School Clubs Participation and Earnings*. Cleveland State University. Available: http://papers.ssrn.com/sol3/papers.cfm?abstract_id=1542360

Michigan High School Athletic Association. (n.d.). *Funding educational athletics* [Videotape]. East Lansing. MI: Author.

NASBE Special Commission. 2004. *The Report of the National Commission on High School Athletics in an Era of Reform: Athletics & Achievement*. Alexandria, Virginia: National Association of School Boards of Education.

National Center for Educational Statistics. (1995). Extracurricular Participation and Student Engagement. Institute of Educational Sciences. Available: http://nces.ed.gov/pubs95/web/95741.asp.

National Collegiate Athletic Association. 2012. Undergraduate scholarships. Available: http://www.ncaa.org/wps/wcm/connect/public/NCAA/Academics/Resources/NCAA+Scholarships.

NCHSAA. 2012. Case for high school athletics. North Carolina High School Athletic Association. Available: http://www.nchsaa.org/page.php?mode=privateview&pageID=49.

NFHS. 1977. Three studies document values of activity programs. *National Press* 11(38): 115.

NFHS. 1980. *Survival Kit for Activity Directors*. Kansas City, MO: NFHS.

NFHS. 2006. National spotlight: Value of high school athletics confirmed by survey. *NFHS News* 23(4): 10. Indianapolis, IN: NFHS.

NFHS. 2011a. 2010-11 athletics participation summary. *NFHS Handbook 2011-12*. Indianapolis, IN: NFHS.

NFHS. 2011b. History. *Annual Report 2010-11* (p. 2). Indianapolis, IN: NFHS.

NFHS. 2012. The case for high school activities. Available: www.nfhs.org/content.aspx?id=3262.

NIAAA. 1992. *Future Funding for School Athletics*. Indianapolis, IN: NIAAA.

NIAAA. 2010. *Professional Development Program*. Indianapolis, IN: NIAAA.

NIAAA. 2011a. *A Profile of Athletic Administration*. Indianapolis, IN: NIAAA.

NIAAA. 2011b. *Athletic Administration: A Comprehensive Guide*. [Video/DVD]. Indianapolis, IN: NIAAA.

OSAA. 2012. The case for high school activities. Oregon School Athletic Association. Available: www.osaa.org/osaainfo/08CaseForHSActivities.pdf.

Overton, G. 2003. By wide margins in massive statewide academic study. NCHSAA. Available:

https://www.nchsaa.org/intranet/downloadManagerControl.php?mode=getFile&elementID=7680&type=5&atomID=9981.

Pedersen, P., J. Parks, J. Quarterman, and L. Thibault. 2011. *Contemporary Sport Management*. 4th ed. Champaign, IL: Human Kinetics.

Riess, S.A. 1995. *Sports in Industrial America: 1850-1920*. Wheeling, IL: Harlan Davidson.

Roberts, J. 1993. Activities, motivation and education. *MHSAA Bulletin* (February): S2-3.

Sawyer, T, K. Boone, T. Gimbert, J. Kuhlman. December 17, 2012. *The Value of Interscholastic Sport: Impact of Athletic Participation on GPA and Graduation Rates*. Workshop presentation at National Athletic Directors Conference, San Antonio, TX.

Sheehy, H. 2002. *Raising a Team Player*. North Adams, MA: Storey Books.

Stevenson, B. 2007. Title IX and the evolution of high school sports. *Contemporary Economic Policy* 25(4): 486-505.

University of Maine. 2006. *Sports Done Right*. Orono: University of Maine.

Vaccaro, C. 2011. Attendance at HS sporting events tops 500 million. SachemPatch. Available: http://sachem.patch.com/articles/attendance-at-hs-sporting-events-tops-500-million.

Whitley, R. 2003. High school athletes outperform non-athletes by wide margins in massive three-year academic study. Available: http://www.nchsaa.org/page.php?mode=privateview&pageID=85.

Chapter 2

Blackburn, M. 2007. Creating foundations for sound decisions and simplifying your role. *Interscholastic Athletic Administration* (Summer): 16-19.

Hoch, D. 2010. Where does winning fit? *Coach and Athletic Director* (December): 16-17.

Hoch, D. 2011. Benchmarks to measure success of your athletic program. *High School Today* (May): 18-19.

Hoch, D. 2012. Athletic directors: Dealing with unrealistic expectations. *High School Today* (February): 28-29.

Kidder, R. 2010. Valuing ethics in athletics. *Interscholastic Athletic Administration* (Summer): 12-13.

NIAAA. 2005. NIAAA Code of Ethics.

NIAAA. 2010. Top 10 survival tips. *Interscholastic Athletic Administration* (Winter): 22-23.

Chapter 3

Metcalf, T. 1997. Listening to your clients. *Life Association News* 92(7): 16-18.

Walker, K. 2002. Communication basics. *LEADS Curriculum Notebook Unit II*, Module 2-1. Manhattan: Kansas State University.

Chapter 4

Gardner, R., and N. Van Erk. 2011. Standards for measuring success not based on number of victories. *High School Today* (January): 1.

Hoch, D. 2005. Writing a better coaching evaluation narrative. *Interscholastic Athletic Administration* (Summer): 18-19.

Hoch, D. 2007. Accountability and documentation. *Interscholastic Athletic Administration* (Fall): 10-11.

Hoch, D. 2007. Coaching evaluations: It's not all about the forms. *Managing School Athletics* (November): 6.

Hoch, D. 2007. Is winning all that matters? *High School Today* (November): 16-17.

Hoch, D. 2008. The key to a better evaluation process is helping your coaches understand it. *Interscholastic Athletic Administration* (Winter): 18-19.

Hoch, D. 2009. Coaching evaluations in education-based athletics. *High School Today* (November): 8-9.

Hoch, D. 2009. Conducting the coaching interview. *Coach and Athletic Director* (November): 8-9.

Hoch, D. 2009. Education-based athletics: Only in the United States. *High School Today* (February): 8-9.

Hoch, D. 2010. An integrated mentoring program for your coaches. *Interscholastic Athletic Administration* (Fall): 18-19.

Hoch, D. 2010. Consistent questions give insight on prospective coaches. *Managing School Athletics* (December), p. 6.

Hoch, D. 2010. Strategies for hiring the best coach for your school. *High School Today* (March): 8-9.

Hoch, D. 2010. The athletic director as a personnel manager. *Interscholastic Athletic Administration* (Summer): 24-25.

Hoch, D. 2010. The athletic director as the coach of coaches. *High School Today* (April): 20-21.

Hoch, D. 2010. Where does winning fit? *Coach and Athletic Director* (December): 16-17.

Hoch, D. 2012. *Hiring, Mentoring and Evaluating Coaches: An Integrated Process*. Brookfield, WI: Lessiter Publications.

NASPE. 2006. *National Standards for Sport Coaches*. 2nd ed. Reston, VA: National Association for Sport and Physical Education.

Chapter 5

Anderson, J.C. 2005. Stretching before and after exercise: Effect on muscle soreness and injury risk. *Journal of Athletic Training* (40): 218-220.

Braddock III, Jomills, Henry. 1981. The issue is still equality of educational opportunity. *Harvard Education Review* (51.4): 490-96.

Dale, G., and J. Robbins. 2010. *It's a Mental Thing!* Durham, NC: BW&A Books.

Eisenman, P.A., S.C. Johnson, and J.E. Benson. 1990. *Coaches Guide to Nutrition and Weight Control*. Champaign, IL: Human Kinetics.

Feingold, David. 1992. Pediatric Endocrinology. *An Atlas of Physical Diagnosis, Second Edition*. 2nd ed. N.p.: W.B. Saunders, 1992. 16-19.

Fejgin, N. 1993. Participation in high school competitive sports: A subversion of school mission or contribution to academic goals? *Sociology of Sport Journal* (10.1) 18-43.

Janssen, J., and G. Dale. 2001. *The Seven Secrets of Successful Coaches: How to Unlock and Unleash Your Team's Full Potential.* Cary, NC: Janssen Peak Performance.

Marsh, Herbert W. 1993. The effects of participation in sport during the last two years of high school. *Sociology of Sport Journal* (10.1): 18-43.

Martens, R. 1987. *Coaches Guide to Sport Psychology.* Champaign, IL: Human Kinetics.

Martens, R. 2012. *Successful Coaching.* 4th ed. Champaign, IL: Human Kinetics.

Melnick, M.J., Sabo, D.F., Vanfossen, B. 1994. Effects of interscholastic participation on the social, educational, and career mobility of hispanic girls and boys. *International Review for the Sociology of Sport* (27.1) 57-75.

NCAA Eligibility Center. n.d. 2011-12 guide for the college bound student athlete. Available: http://www.ncsasports.org.

Sharkey, B.J. 1986. *Coaches Guide to Sport Physiology.* Champaign, IL: Human Kinetics.

Thompson, J. 2007. *Positive Coaching in a Nutshell.* Palo Alto, CA: Balance Sports Publishing.

Yeager, J., J. Buxton, A. Baltzell, and W. Bzdell. 2001. *Character and Coaching: Building Virtue in Athletic Programs.* Port Chester, NY: National Professional Resources.

Chapter 6

Eugene Ashley High School. n.d. Athletic department mission statement. Available: http://www.nhcs.k12.nc.us/ashley.

Glenbard Township High School. n.d. Glenbard Township High School district 87. Athletic department strategic plan. Available: www.athletics2000.com/GlenbardWest/Documents/09-Athletic%20Department%20Strategic%20Plan.pdf.

Kestner, J. 1996. *Program Evaluation for Sports Directors.* Champaign, IL: Human Kinetics.

Loveland High School. n.d. Loveland High School Athletic Department Mission Statement. Available: www.loveland.k12.oh.us/lhs/athletics/pages/Mission_Statement.pdf.

NIAAA. 2008. National Interscholastic Athletic Administrators Association LTC 707: Assessment of Interscholastic Athletic Programs and Personnel, Indianapolis, IN.

Olson, J., and M. Blackburn. 2010. Athletic assessment. *Interscholastic Athletic Administrator* (Fall), 20 -21.

Chapter 7

Bakker, D. 2005. NCAA initial eligibility requirements: The case law behind the changes. Available: http://laworgs.depaul.edu/journals/sports_law/Documents/NCAA%20eligibility%20by%20Bakker.pdf.

Bureau of Labor and Statistics. 2012. Occupational outlook handbook. 2010-11 edition. Available: www.bls.gov/oco/ocos077.htm.

CDC. 2012. Adolescent and school health. Health and academics. Available: www.cdc.gov/HealthyYouth/health_and_academics.

Child Growth Foundation. 2012. Puberty and Tanner stages. Available: http://www.childgrowthfoundation.org/CMS/FILES/Puberty_and_the_Tanner_Stages.pdf.

National Athletic Trainers' Association. 2012. Guidelines for the development of an affiliated site agreement. Available: www.nata.org/education/educational-programs/affiliated-site-agreement.

National Strength and Conditioning Association. NSCA code of ethics and principles. NSCA 2008.

NIAAA. 2007. Leadership Training Course 617. Administration of Interscholastic Sports Medicine Programs. Indianapolis, IN: NIAAA.

NIAAA. 2009. Leadership Training Course 504. LTC 504 Athletic Administration: Legal Issues I (Risk Management). Indianapolis, IN: NIAAA.

NIAAA. 2009. Leadership Training Course 625. Athletic Administration: Management of Game and Event Announcing. Indianapolis, IN: NIAAA.

NIAAA. 2010. Leadership Training Course 630. Athletic Administration: Interscholastic Contest Management—Planning, Preparation and Methods. Indianapolis, IN: NIAAA.

NIAAA. 2011. Leadership Training Course 627. Athletic Administration: Administration of Interscholastic Sports Strength & Conditioning Programs. Indianapolis, IN: NIAAA.

San Jacinto Unified School District. 2012. Volunteer contract 2011-2012. Available: www.sanjacinto.k12.ca.us/documents/studentsupport/volunteer_contract.pdf.

Chapter 8

Bates, R. 2003. Middle school athletics: Not a mirror of the high school program. *Interscholastic Athletic Administration* (Spring): 10-11.

Dyer, M. 2009. Nation's high schools cope with recession. *High School Today* (September): 8-9.

Eastern South Dakota Athletic Conference. 2009. Constitution and bylaws. Brandon, SD: ESDAC.

Fellmeth, L. 2010. Participation in high school sports tops 7.6 million. *High School Today* (October): 10-11.

Floyd, D.G. 2011. Use of facilities rental plan should be clearly defined. *High School Today* (January): 30-31.

Giebel, N. 2003. Scheduling checklist: Survival guide for new athletic administrators. *Interscholastic Athletic Administration* (Winter): 18-19.

Hoch, D. 2002. Basic rules for good gym management. *Scholastic Coach & Athletic Director* (September): 16-17.

Krotee, M.L., and C.A. Bucher. 2007. *Management of Physical Education and Sports*. 13th ed. New York: McGraw-Hill.

Lamb, J. 2011. Addressing budget issues without cutting services. *High School Today* (April): 10-12).

NIAAA. 2007. *Leadership Training Course 799, Standards of Excellence in Interscholastic Athletic Programs*. Indianapolis, IN: NIAAA.

NIAAA. 2009a. *Athletic Administration: A Comprehensive Guide*. Indianapolis, IN: NIAAA.

NIAAA. 2009b. *Interscholastic Athletic Administration*. Special Supplement Edition.

NIAAA. 2010a. *A Profile of Athletic Administration*. Indianapolis, IN: NIAAA.

NIAAA. 2010b. Leadership Training Course 504, Legal Issues I: Risk Management. Indianapolis, IN: NIAAA.

NIAAA. 2010c. Leadership Training Course 506. Legal Issues II: Title IX and Sexual Harassment. Indianapolis, IN: NIAAA.

Olson, J.R. 1997. *Facility and Equipment Management for Sports Directors*. Champaign. IL: Human Kinetics.

Pennepacker, P. 2010. Making budget cuts while staying in Title IX compliance. *High School Today* (May): 8-9.

Purdy, R.L. 1973. *The Successful High School Athletic Program*. West Nyack, NY: Parker.

Vachlon, M. 2009. The four-day school week and how it impacts activity programs. *High School Today* (January):14-15.

Chapter 9

Aldana, K. 2012. Consumer advisory: NHTSA reissues 15-passenger van safety caution. *Press Releases and Research*. National Highway Traffic Safety Administration. Available: http://www.nhtsa.gov/CA/10-14-2010.

National Association of State Directors of Pupil Transportation Services. 2004. Survey of state laws on 12 and 15 passenger vans used for school transportation. Available: http://www.nasdpts.org/documents/VansSurveyFeb04.pdf.

National Association of State Directors of Pupil Transportation Services. 2011. Our mission and purpose. Available: http://www.nasdpts.org/.

National Transportation Safety Board. 1999. Bus crashworthiness issues. *Highway Special Investigation Report*. Available: http://www.ntsb.gov/doclib/reports/1999/SIR9904.pdf.

Chapter 10

DeMaria, M. 2012. More students taking online courses. *USA Today College*. Available: www.usatodayeducate.com/staging/index.php/ccp/more-students-taking-online-courses.

Frombach, E. 2010. Promoting your athletic program through technology. NFHS Coaching Today. Available: www.nfhs.org/CoachingTodayFeature.aspx?id=6542.

Maxwell, J. 1995. *Developing the Leaders Around You*. Nashville, Injoy.

Nagel, D. 2009. Most college students to take classes online by 2014. Available: http://campustechnology.com/articles/2009/10/28/most-college-students-to-take-classes-online-by-2014.aspx.

O'Quinn, L. & Corry M. (2002, December 16). Factors that deter faculty from participating in distance education. *Online Journal of Distance Learning Administration, 5* (4). Retrieved October 4, 2003, from http://www.westga.edu/~distance/ojdla/winter54/Quinn54.html

Ottalini, D. 2010. Students addicted to social media. Available: www.newsdesk.umd.edu/sociss/release.cfm?ArticleID=2144.

Power, D. 2010. What is social media? Available: http://dssresources.com/faq/index.php?action=artikel&id=226.

Stengel, R. 2009. Technology and culture. *Time*. Available: www.time.com/time/magazine/article/0,9171,1902836,00.html.

Chapter 11

Evers, J. 2012. Development and use of an event management handbook. *Interscholastic Athletic Administration* 38: 14-15.

Hammes, J. 2010. Identify all spectators to enhance contest safety. *Interscholastic Athletic Administration* (37): 18-19.

NIAAA. 2010. Leadership Training Course 630. Athletic Administration: Interscholastic Contest Management. Indianapolis, IN: NIAAA.

Rumble, B. 2003. *The Voice Above the Crowd: A Professional Manual for Announcing Amateur Athletic Contests and Events*. Washington: Brad Rumble and Associates.

Stevens, G. 2008. Managing the fifth estate: An athletics director's guide to working with the media. *Interscholastic Athletic Administration* 35: 22-23.

Stevens, G. 2009. The road to "game day": Fundamental strategies for planning and hosting successful athletic events. *Interscholastic Athletic Administration* 35: 10-12.

Stevens, G. 2011. Timeless traditions: Rivalries in American high schools and the role of the athletics administrator. *Interscholastic Athletic Administration* 38: 18-22.

Chapter 13

Boone, L., and D. Kurtz. 2004. "Customer-driven marketing" (chapter 1) and "Strategic planning and the marketing process" (chapter 2). In *Contemporary Marketing*. Mason, OH: Thomas Learning.

Downey, L., and R. Lilly. 2011. How to market a successful athletics program. *High School Today*. (November): 34-35.

Dyer, M. 2010. Schools develop strategies to retain sponsors in tough economy. *High School Today*. (November): 9-10.

Evans, D. 2005. *Building a successful booster organization*. Indianapolis, IN: NIAAA.

Forsyth, E. 2001. *The Sponsorship Connection: A Practical Guide for High School Athletic Directors and Coaches*. Fayetteville, AR: Athletic World Advertising

Harrington, J. 2011. Who Are You and What Do You Do. Presentation by the Pennsylvania Consortium of Educational Foundations Leadership Academy. Harrisburg, PA.

Irwin, R., W. Sutton, and L. McCarthy. 2002. "The Promotional Role of Sport Sponsorship." In *Sport Promotion and Sales Management*, 205-237. Champaign, IL: Human Kinetics.

Itczak, A., and K. Bodey. 2010. *Closing the Deal: Corporate Sponsorship at the Local Level*. Indianapolis, IN: NIAAA.

Joeckel, S. 2008. "Wildcat power" from the Millard West athletic booster club. *High School Today*. (Fall): 8-10.

Laird, C., and A. Bolognese. 2009. *Building an Effective Sport Sponsorship Program: Guidelines for Maximizing Corporate Partnerships*. Indianapolis, IN: NIAAA.

NIAAA. 2009. Leadership Training Course 611. Concepts and Strategies for Interscholastic Marketing, Promotions and Supplemental Fund-Raising. Indianapolis, IN: NIAAA.

Owen, D. 2002. Booster Clubs: Is the Tail Wagging the Dog? Joint presentation by the Pennsylvania School Boards Association and the Pennsylvania State Athletic Directors Association. Mechanicsburg, PA.

Parker, J., B. Zanger, and J. Quarterman. 1998. "Sport marketing." In *Contemporary Sport Management*, 171-183. Champaign, IL: Human Kinetics.

Pennepacker, P. 2011. Booster clubs and Title IX: Tough times and tough decisions. *High School Today*. (September): 12-13.

Pierce, D., and L. Bussell. 2011. National survey of interscholastic sport sponsorships in the United States. *Sport Management Journal* (7): 43-60.

Prevosto, J. 2009. Creating a positive and effective working relationship with your booster club. *High School Today*. (April): 8-9.

Ukman, L. 2008. *IEG's Guide to Sponsorship: Everything You Need to Know About Sports, Arts, Event, Entertainment and Cause Marketing*. Chicago: IEG.

Chapter 14

Evers, J. 2001. Building and implementing a sound athletic financial philosophy. *Interscholastic Athletic Administration* 28(1): 16-17.

Evers, J. 2002. Gender equity: A proactive approach to compliance. *Interscholastic Athletic Administration* 29(3): 12-15.

Evers, J. 2007. Legal issues in fund-raising. *Interscholastic Athletic Administration* 34(1): 28-29.

Evers, J. 2010. Gender equity compliance and justification through documentation. *Interscholastic Athletic Administration* 37(1): 14-16.

Gardner, B. 2011. Even with pay-to-play, high school sports are a bargain. *High School Today* (May): 1.

Howard, B. 2011. Education Funding Crisis Affects Activity Programs. *High School Today* (May):10-12.

NIAAA. 2010. Leadership Training Course 511. Concepts and Strategies for Interscholastic Budgeting and Finance Using Excel Spreadsheets. Indianapolis, IN: NIAAA.

Chapter 15

Abeshaus, A. 1996. Reconditioning of old equipment makes sense, saves dollars and cents. *NFHS Coaches' Quarterly* (Winter).

Duval, D. 2003. Athletics budgeting process. *Interscholastic Athletic Administration* (Winter): 14-16.

NIAAA. 2006. Leadership Training Course 618. Athletic Administration: Management of Interscholastic Athletic Player Equipment. Indianapolis, IN: NIAAA.

NIAAA. 2010a. Leadership Training Course 502. Athletic Administration: Principles, Strategies and Methods. Indianapolis, IN: NIAAA.

NIAAA. 2010b. Leadership Training Course 511. Concepts and Strategies for Interscholastic Budgeting and Finance Using Excel Spreadsheets. Indianapolis, IN: NIAAA.

Sahuaro High School. 2008. *Coaching Handbook*. Tucson, Arizona: Sahuaro High School.

Stevens, G. 2010. Prelude to summer: An athletics director's end-of-year itinerary. *Interscholastic Athletic Administration* (Spring) 28-29.

Wenger Corporation. 2006. GearBoss sports storage systems. *Athletics Facility Planning Guide*. Owatanna, MN: Wenger Corporation.

Chapter 16

ADAAG. 2002. ADA accessibility guidelines for buildings and facilities (ADAAG). Available: www.access-board.gov/adaag/html/adaag.htm.

Apallas, A.K. 2005. Artificial turf vs. natural turf. *School Construction News* (July/August). Available: www.schoolconstructionnews.com/2005/12/9/artificial-turf-vs-naturalturf.

Fouty, A. 2005. A sport field manager's perspective: Synthetic turf considerations, maintenance costs and concerns. Presentation at the Synthetic Turf Infill Seminar, May 11, 2005, Detroit.

Fried, G. 2013. *Sport Finance*. 3rd ed. Champaign, IL: Human Kinetics.

Hill, F. 2005. Planning playgrounds and athletics facilities: Part of the educational specifications planning process. Available: http://www.schoolfacilities.com/_coreModules/common/entitySearchList.aspx?keywords=SchoolFacilities.com.

HNTB. 2010. Athletics facilities on campus: Master planning and the athletics master plan. Available: http://news.hntb.com/white-papers/athletic-facilities-on-campus-master-planning-and-the-athletic-master-plan.htm.

Klingensmith, D. 2011. Trends in sports facility design: Design for all times. *Recreation Management* (July). Available: www.recmanagement.com/feature_print.

Kollie, E. 2012. Sports flooring solutions for your athletics facility. *School Planning & Management*. (June). Available: www.peterli.com/spm/resources/articles/archive.

Maple Flooring Manufacturers Association. 2009. Today's preferred sports surface. Available: www.maplefloor.org/literature/MFMAPreferredSportsSurface.pdf.

Meyers, M., and B.S. Barnhill. 2004. Incidence, causes, and severity of high school football injuries on field turf versus natural grass. *American Journal of Sports Medicine* 32: 1626-1638.

National Trust for Historic Preservation. 2010. Older and historic schools: Restoration vs. replacement and the role of a feasibility study. Available: www.preservationnation.org/information-center/saving-a-place/historic-schools/additional-resources/school_feasibility_study.pdf.

Parker, D. 1997. Turf wars. *Cornerstones*. Available: www.sandfordgroup.com/editoriallibrary/athletics_library/turfwars. Patton, A. 2009. Synthetic (artificial) turf vs. natural grass athletics fields. Available: http://turf.uark.edu/turfhelp/archives/021109.html.

Rau, A.B. 2010. ASU, legislators explore ways to pay for fixes to athletics facilities. *Arizona Republic*, February 16.Available: www.azcentral.com/news/articles/2010/02/16/2010026stadiumdistrict.

Seidler, T., and J. Miller. 2008. Providing safe facilities. *Athletics Business* (June 17). Available: www.athleticbusiness.com.

Sprecher, M.H. 2011. Natural grass or synthetic turf? *Landscape Architect Business Magazine* (September 26). Available: www.northstarpubs.com/articles/lab/natural-grass-or-synthic-turf.

Steinbach, P. 2001. Athletics field maintenance isn't rocket science. *Athletics Business* (April 1). Available: www.athleticbusiness.com.

Steinbach, P. Synthetic surface alternatives find niche in multipurpose gyms. *Athletics Business* (November 1). Available: www.athleticbusiness.com.

Trusty, S. 2010. Sports facility liability: Prevent injury and protect yourself. *SportsField Management* (October). Available: www.sportsfieldmanagementmagazine.com/print-5974.aspx.

Closing

Forsyth, E. 2007. *Current Issues Surrounding Interscholastic Sports: Survey Report*. Indianapolis, IN: NIAAA.

Forsyth, E. 2012. *Contemporary Issues Surrounding Interscholastic Sports: Finance Issues*. Indianapolis, IN: NIAAA. Vol. 39, No. 1, pp. 16-18.

Forsyth, E., and J. Olson. 2012. *Current and Emerging Issues in High School Sports Cited By NIAAA Members*. Indianapolis IN: NIAAA.

Green, L. 2009. 14 legal duties for coaches and sport administrators. Leadership Training Course 504. Negligence and Risk Management. Indianapolis, IN: NIAAA.

Green, L. 2012. Sport law: Year-in-review, 2011. *High School Today* (January) 24-28.

NCAAa. 2012. Available: http://www.ncaa.org/wps/wcm/connect/nli/nli/document+library/athletic+scholarshipwww. NCAAb. 2012. Available: www.ncaa.org/wps/wcm/connect/public/ncaa/issues/recruiting/probability+of+going+pro.

NFHS. 2011. 2010-11 high school athletics participation survey. *NFHS Handbook 2011-12.* Indianapolis, IN: NFHS.

Raosoft. 2004. Raosoft online calculation tool for confidence determination of survey sample data. www.raosoft.com/samplesize.html.

O'Shaughnessey, Lynn. 2010. Your client's kid eyeing a sports scholarship? *Registered Rep. Electronic financial newsletter.* Available. http://wealthmanagement.com/college-planning/your-clients-kid-eyeing-sports-scholarship.

Index

Note: Page references followed by an italicized *f* or *t* indicate information contained in figures and tables, respectively.

A

academic achievement
  athletic department goals 76, 96, 111, 114, 140
  athletics as complement 3-4, 15, 22, 80
  higher education attainment 5, 140
  scholarships and intercollegiate sports 92-93, 138-140, 257
  special education 137
  student-athlete successes xii, 4-6, 22, 75, 297
accounting procedures 303-304, 306-307
Acosta v. Los Angeles Unified School District (California, 1995) 251
administrative support
  scheduling duties 143, 144, 154, 157, 158, 171
  staff communications 45-46, 49, 72
administrators. *See* athletic administrators; school administrators
advertising 110, 205, 209, 279, 280, 281. *See also* marketing
allied educational services 119-124, 121, 141
  academic support and counseling 126, 137-139, 140
  strength and conditioning 132-136
  student health services 125-131, 136-137
amateur status 93, 366
Americans with Disabilities Act (1990) 137, 235, 294, 353
anti-discrimination statues. *See* Title IX
appreciation methods 34, 72, 73, 78, 366
artificial turf 345-347
assets, school athletic programs 274, 283-284
assumption of risk 245, 246, 251-252
athletes. *See* student athletes
athlete-to-coach ratios 107-108, 111, 312*t*, 313*t*
athletic administrators. *See also* contest management; legal issues; scheduling; transportation
  budgeting 291-293, 294, 295, 296, 297, 298, 300, 304, 315, 328, 351
  forecasts and priorities 361-368
  philosophy components and development 19-35, 107, 122, 221
  professional development 12-13, 31-32, 106, 368
  professional profiles ix-xi, xiv, xv-xvi, 9-11, 13, 15, 16-17, 18, 23-30, 31-34, 55-73, 98-100, 105, 106, 122, 169, 203-204, 232, 241, 304, 315, 361-368
  purchasing 301-302, 325, 327, 328
  recruiting and hiring x-xi, 11, 55, 367
  skill sets x-xi, 9, 10-11, 23-24, 33, 34, 50-53, 237, 241, 304, 315
  training and preparation xi, 11-14, 181
athletic officials
  communications and scheduling 46, 157, 167, 168, 230
  game management 226-227, 230
  guidelines 167-168, 223, 226-227
athletic practices 158
  athletic director support 44-45
  coach evaluations 63-64

football 246, 251
  scheduling 162-163
  supervision duties 248-249
athletic programs 14-17, 76, 93, 95-116, 274
  budgeting and purchasing 291-315, 308*t*, 309*t*
  communication 27-28, 37, 44-52, 97
  evaluations 90-91, 91*f*, 98, 104-107
  goals and objectives 99-103, 104, 113, 116
  growth and development 107-109, 111
  marketing and fund-raising 203-204, 205, 207, 209, 271-290, 361, 366
  new sport additions 104, 261, 294
  operating costs 291, 308*t*, 309*t*, 312*t*-313*t*, 314*t*
  sports offerings 259-260
  strategic planning 109-115, 247, 248, 254
athletic trainers
  allied services 120, 131, 132, 134
  certification and training 132, 134, 223, 227
  personnel management 55, 71, 72, 134
  strength and conditioning tasks 132, 135
  technology use 216-217
authority chains of command 98, 129, 131, 134-135
automated external defibrillators (AEDs) 130, 216, 227

B

Barreras, Ken x-xi, xii, xiii, xiv
Barretto v. City of New York (New York, 1997) 249
baseball
  equipment checklists and safety 321, 330*f*, 341*f*
  statistics tracking 216
  team transportation 160, 257
basketball
  equipment checklists and safety 321, 330*f*
  injuries and cases 248
  player goals 83*t*, 92
  schedules 144, 149, 150, 154, 158, 159
behavior expectations
  sexual harassment 267-268
  spectators 236, 237
  teams 63, 80, 97, 106, 180, 263, 266, 268, 367
Benitez v. City of New York (New York, 1989) 255-256
Berseth, Steve 143-169
bidding policies 303, 305, 320
Blackburn, Mike 3-18, 113
bleachers 234, 235, 344, 357
boards of education 16, 98, 146
  athletic program support 112-113
  booster clubs oversight and advice 277, 279-280
  communication 46-47
booster clubs
  communication 48, 49-50, 81
  contributions and roles 16, 50, 98, 204, 277-278, 278, 296, 302, 325, 361
  organization and guidelines 277, 279, 299, 302
  Title IX considerations 277, 278-279, 299, 302
Bowers, Bill 95-116
branding
  corporate sponsorships 280, 281
  Internet marketing 204, 205

branding *(continued)*
   school/athletic departments 110, 206, 207, 208, 274, 279, 327
   sport and team loyalty 95, 271, 274
Britt v. Maury County Board of Education (Tennessee, 2008) 250
Buckanavage, Bob 271-290
budgeting, athletic departments. *See also* education funding and budgets; purchasing
   budget creation 291, 292, 293-294, 302
   budget reviews and reports 291-292, 305, 306-315, 308t, 309t, 312t-313t, 314t
   expenditure categories 305-306, 306-307
   organizational policies 296-301, 328
   process 293-296, 304, 319-320
bus travel 156, 157, 171, 175, 182. *See also* transportation
   charters 176-178, 300
   emergencies 178-179, 181

C
cable television 276
caloric consumption 88, 88t, 136-137
carbohydrates 88, 88t, 89
case law applications
   duty examples 248, 249, 250, 251, 252, 253, 254
   equal protection of rights 263
   fair treatment 261
   hazing and bullying 265
   matching and equating athletes 253-256
   negligence and injury 246-247
   safe transportation 257
   social networking 264
   Title IX 259
cause marketing 272-273
certification and programs
   administrators and coaches, NFHS 60, 71, 105, 109, 130, 194, 250, 367
   administrators and coaches, NIAAA xi, 11-14, 14, 32, 120
   allied support services 120, 121
   contest and event management 167, 223, 226-227
   drivers 182-183, 187
   emergency- and health-related 71, 130, 182, 183, 227, 250, 256
   trainers 132, 134, 223, 227
change and change management 25-26, 27, 44
   professional development 31-32
   technology 25-26, 189, 204, 209
character education
   anti-hazing 266
   athletic department goals 76, 93-94, 96, 101, 111-112
   athletics participation xiv, 4, 7, 8-9, 15, 17, 75, 95, 297, 366
   sporting behavior xiv, 15
charter coach buses 176-178, 300
cheerleading injuries and cases 250, 252, 254
Chorosiewski, Kim x, xi, xii, xiii, xiv, 119-141
civil rights 243, 244t, 262-264, 268, 367
Clement v. Griffin (Louisiana, 1984) 257
coaches
   communication and relationship management (administrators) 34, 44-45, 47, 50, 108
   duties and player management 17, 63-64, 77-79, 83-86, 90, 92, 99, 135, 175, 251
   equipment knowledge and requests 319-320, 325, 327, 329
   evaluations 23, 60-68, 69-70, 105, 106, 108, 276
   experience and hiring xi, 11, 55, 56-57, 71, 108, 250

firing 61, 69, 261, 268
   goals and values 20, 23, 56-57, 75-76, 79, 93, 96, 100
   influence on team success 19, 86-87, 93-94, 275
   parents and xiii, 58, 235-236
   professional development 11, 60, 68, 76, 96, 105, 108-109, 111, 191, 195, 250, 361, 367-368
   quality concerns 361, 363t, 367-368
   salaries 66, 297, 298, 312t-313t
   schedule preferences and duties 150, 152, 154, 155, 156-157, 163
   teacher-coaches *vs.* non- 21, 108, 171, 367
   technology use 191, 192, 213-216
coach-to-athlete ratios 107-108, 111, 312t, 313t
codes of conduct 11, 15, 80, 97, 262, 263, 266
college planning 137-138, 139, 140
collegiate athletics 7
   high school compared ix, 365t
   NCAA eligibility and scholarships 17, 92, 138, 257, 364
   pre-college preparation 137-138, 139, 140
communication, nonverbal 38, 39-40, 41
   emotional awareness 43
   listening 39, 48, 78, 203
communication process 37, 38, 45. *See also* marketing
   and levels of operations 47
   message/content consideration 201, 202-203, 203
   modern technologies 193, 194, 195, 199-200, 201-202, 203
communications, verbal
   athletic administrators' attention and skill 30, 31, 33, 34, 37, 38, 44-46, 47-53, 72, 284-285
   athletic contests 227-228, 232-233
   emotional awareness 43-44, 48-49
   evaluating 105, 106
   humor 43, 77
   importance 34, 37, 38, 52-53, 203
   listening 38-39, 48, 78, 203
   player management 77, 78
   proposals and "asks" 284-285, 288-289
   school and larger community 44-48, 50-53
   stressful situations 42-43, 48-49
communications, written. *See also* documentation; e-mail; social media
   athletic administrators' attention and skill 27, 30, 64, 66-67, 201, 202-203, 206-208
   athletic administrators' purview 11, 27, 31, 41-42, 44, 51-52, 58, 59-60, 62, 91, 97, 99, 101, 208
   budgets and finance 311, 315
   etiquette 41, 57, 201
   event planning and management 221-222
   personal communication management 196, 201
   pre-event and game-day 229-230, 231-232
   program mission statements 23, 101-103
   scheduling-related 155, 157, 161-162, 169, 171-172, 206
   sports news 51-52, 155, 206
   students' online writings, and civil rights 264, 367
   transportation-related 171-172, 174
community-based sport programs
   alternatives to school athletics xii, xiii, xv, 112, 297
   event scheduling 145, 161-162, 163, 164, 165, 166-167

community service 22
community stakeholders
    athletic program budgets 292, 311, 315
    communication 32, 48-52, 112, 204, 205, 292
    contributions and power 16, 25, 50, 110, 278
    event scheduling 143, 165, 166-167
    marketing and PR 204, 205, 274-275, 277, 278
    strategic planning processes 109-110, 112
community values
    football focus 151, 277
    philanthropic giving 287
    winning focus xiii, 15, 20
competition contracts 153-154, 159
competition rules 7, 27, 226-227
competitiveness 126
    balance, athletic administrators/programs
        15, 19, 20, 23, 27-28, 56, 95
    benchmarks beyond winning xiii, 20-22
    coach evaluations considerations, winning
        over-focus 23, 61, 62, 69-70, 105
    focus on winning xiii, 15, 76, 96
    student athletes, and sporting attitudes 15,
        20, 76, 158
comprehension and acknowledgement state-
    ments 187, 298, 334f
concussion management and safety 127, 131,
    132, 217, 255, 258
conferences (athletic divisions)
    constitutions and by-laws 147-148, 156
    event scheduling 144, 145, 146-149, 150, 153-
        154, 159, 229
    football teams' influence 151
    officials and crew scheduling 168
conferencing, online 191-192, 194, 210, 212-213
confidence
    building methods 10, 82, 87-88
    leaders 40-41, 76, 87
construction
    athletic facilities 166, 278, 340, 356-359
    plans and costs 357-359
    renovation vs. 351-354
contest management. See also facilities and facili-
    ties management
    athletic administrators' duties 221-222, 224,
        225, 227, 228, 229-231, 235, 236, 241
    game management 215, 216, 226-233
    spectators and safety 233-241
contributory negligence 245
corporate sponsorship 280-282, 296, 299
CPR, certification and readiness 71, 130, 182, 183,
    227, 250, 256
custodial departments 340
D
decision making processes 24-25, 35
dieticians 136-137
DiGiose v. Bellmore-Merrick Central High School
    District (New York, 2008) 254
disabled populations, access 226, 234, 235, 353
discipline 63, 251, 263. See also behavior expecta-
    tions
disease risks, student athletes 5, 125, 323
divisional scheduling 148-149
D.J.M. v. Hannibal Public School District (Missouri,
    2006) 264
documentation
    comprehension and acknowledgement state-
        ments 187, 298, 334f
    contest management guides 221-222
    equipment inventory/purchasing 319, 320,
        328-329
    evaluations 62, 67, 70, 104-105, 106-107

financial 291, 292-293, 295, 302, 304, 305-314,
    315, 366
    goal setting 82, 100
    legal 153-154, 248, 250, 252, 254, 299-300, 310
    maintenance work 354, 355-356
    participation effects 366
    professional recordkeeping 70-71, 73, 121,
        128, 193, 310-311
    safety-related 97, 131, 248, 250, 252, 254
Doninger v. Niehoff (Connecticut, 2008) 264
driver certification 182-183, 187, 257
dual competitions 153, 154, 159, 160
due process rights 263
E
education. See also academic achievement; allied
        educational services
    by athletic administrators 27-28
    of athletic administrators 11-14, 32
    education-based athletic programs 4, 5-6, 15,
        17-18, 20-23, 27-28, 61, 65, 95, 98, 116, 243,
        244t
    sports and extracurriculars as xiii, xiv, 3, 4,
        5-6, 95, 98
    substance abuse programs 97, 131
    technology innovations 190, 191-192, 194
education funding and budgets. See also fund-
        raising
    athletic administrators and xi, xii, xv-xvi, 113,
        361, 363t, 365-366
    athletic scheduling and transportation 152,
        160-161, 175, 177-178, 184-187
    budget cuts 95, 204, 286, 290, 296, 297, 361,
        363t, 365-366, xii, xv-xvi
    construction effects 351-352
    educational foundations 286-289
electronic communication. See communications,
        written; e-mail; social media
elementary-level athletics
    intramurals 164-165
    participation 110, 111, 294
    scheduling 144, 158-159, 164-165
    sport specialization 364
eligibility, athletes
    academic 137-138, 140
    medical 131-132
    recruiting and scholarships 92-93, 138, 257
    reports 24, 106
    rules 80, 138, 366
e-mail
    event and transportation scheduling 153, 155,
        157, 161-162, 169, 171-172, 174
    marketing 206
    providers and management 196, 198
emergency situations
    communication tools 198-199, 218, 228, 238,
        240
    event management 228, 237-241
    medical response plans 248, 256-257
    readiness and communication 48-49, 97, 129-
        130, 228, 238
    standards of practice 24, 121, 128
    transportation-related 174, 177, 178-179, 181
emotional composure
    communication issues 38, 39, 42-43, 48-49,
        203
    event management 221
employee management. See personnel manage-
        ment
entitlement attitudes 75, 361, 364-365
environmental issues 345, 346, 356, 357
equal protection rights 263

equipment 319-338. *See also* uniforms
  athletic administrators' purview 10-11, 58, 72,
    97, 319, 325, 327, 328, 330*f*, 334, 337-338
  checklists and accounts 320, 329, 330*f*-333*f*,
    334, 340, 341*f*-342*f*, 343*f*
  contest management 222, 224, 230, 231
  gender equity 261, 278-279
  inventory and purchasing 319-320, 323, 324-
    325, 328-329, 330*f*-333*f*, 335*f*
  managers 158, 162, 319, 320, 321, 323, 328-329,
    335-336
  permanent 320, 350-351
  repair and reconditioning 325, 327-328, 343,
    344
  safety items 251, 253, 254, 323, 348
  safety planning and checks 130, 247, 248, 253-
    254, 321-324, 327-328, 338, 340, 341*f*-342*f*,
    342*f*-343*f*
  sharing 22, 320
  strength and conditioning 136, 215, 323-324
  transportation and storage 174, 180, 181, 328,
    336-337, 338*t*
ethics
  athletic departments 11, 135
  neutrality needs 167, 228, 239
  personal attributes 6, 28-29, 34, 223-224
  sporting behavior issues xiv, 235
evaluation, athletes
  goal review and assessment 101, 107
  methods 87-88, 91*f*, 107
  negative feedback 78, 87
  participation 80, 254
evaluation, programs 90-91, 91*f*, 98, 104-107
  marketing plans 276
  Title IX compliance 261, 310
evaluation, staff. *See also* personnel management
  coaches and officials 60-68, 105, 106, 108, 168,
    276
  self-evaluation 64-65, 108
  tools 65, 90-91, 91*f*, 105, 106-107, 108
event management. *See* contest management
Evers, John 291-315
exit points and procedures, venues 230, 237, 238,
    240
extracurricular activities 7, 109, 115
  as education xiii, xiv, 3, 4, 5-6, 95, 98
  scheduling 143, 145-146, 156, 158, 160, 161-
    162, 163-164
  students, balance xii, xiii, 5

F
Facebook 202, 206
  athletic departments use 27, 31, 112, 200, 201,
    207, 208, 216
  marketing 206-207
facilities and facilities management 112, 115, 339-
    359. *See also* contest management; equip-
    ment; safe environment, legal duty
  athletic administrators' purview 10-11, 16, 22,
    55, 97, 136, 221, 233, 343
  construction 166, 278, 340, 351-354, 356-357,
    358-359
  flooring/turf 342*f*, 343-350
  gender equity 261
  liability issues 165, 166-167, 354-356
  safety planning 129-130, 228, 233, 234-235,
    236, 237-241, 341*f*-342*f*, 342*f*-343*f*, 344,
    355-356
  sharing 22, 161-163, 165, 166-167
  site agreements 133-134
  trends 356-357
fair treatment, under Title IX 260*f*, 261, 262, 299

Family Educational Rights and Privacy Act
    (1974) 128
fat, in diets 88-89, 88*t*
Felix v. Barre Supervisory Union (Vermont, 2010)
    246-247
Fifth Amendment rights 263
financial aid, college 138, 262
financial aid, pay-to-play structures 298, 366
financial documentation and reporting 305-315
  per capita by gender 307, 310
  by sport 307, 308*t*, 309*t*, 311, 312*t*-313*t*, 314*t*
financial management
  booster clubs 277
  budgeting 291-301
  fund-raising 279, 280, 296, 300, 302
  purchasing 301-305
First Amendment rights 262-264, 279, 367
fitness levels 85, 86, 254
flooring 342*f*, 347-350
football
  equipment checklists and safety 321-322,
    331*f*, 341*f*
  financial reports 308*t*, 309*t*, 311*t*-312*t*
  game management staff 226
  injuries and cases 151, 152, 246, 251, 255-256,
    257, 258, 345
  parents' clubs 278
  practices 246, 251
  scheduling 144, 147, 148, 151-152
Forsyth, Eric 280-281, 361-368
Fourteenth Amendment rights 263
freedom of speech and expression, social media
    262-264, 367
friendship and professionalism 33-34
fund-raising. *See also* booster clubs; sponsorships
  athletic programs' methods 205, 207, 209, 278,
    284-285, 286-289, 296-299, 302, 366
  athletic programs' needs 204, 286, 287-288,
    290, 295-297, 325, 361
  educational foundations 286-289
  equipment targeted 278, 288, 325
  guidelines 279, 280, 296, 300, 302
  interscholastic marketing process 274-277
  supplemental 300, 361, 366
  tickets and concessions 224, 233, 235, 296

G
game film exchange 214
gang activity 240, 367
Gardner, Robert 61
Garvis, Scott 110
Gill v. Tamalpais (California, 2008) 248
goal setting
  athletes and teams 81-82, 83*t*, 87, 100-101, 158
  athletic programs 99, 100, 104-107, 116, 218, 274
  review and assessment 101, 104-107, 108, 116
golf, equipment checklists and safety 322, 331*f*
good sportsmanship. *See* sporting behavior
Google 207, 210, 212, 262
Gorthy v. Clovis Unified School District (California,
    2006) 251
Graham, Tim 171-188
Green, Lee 243-268
*A Guide for College-Bound Student-Athletes and
    Their Parents* (NFHS and NIAAA) 138
Guide for the College-Bound Student-Athlete
    (NCAA) 138
gymnasiums 342*f*, 347-350, 356-357
gymnastics 251, 322, 331*f*

H
Hagman, Warren L. 37-53
Hammes, Jay 240-241

hazing and bullying
    off-campus and online actions 263, 264, 361, 367
    professional relationships 26
    sports law and case law 243, 244*t*, 264, 265
    student athletes, and program policies 15-16, 97, 116, 264, 265-266, 268
head trauma
    blows and accidents 249, 253, 258
    concussion management 127, 131, 132, 217, 255, 258
health. *See* disease risks, student athletes; injuries; life balance; student health; substance use and abuse
Health Insurance Portability and Accountability Act (1996) 128
high school campuses 339, 340, 357-358
Hoch, David 19-35, 55-73
home *vs.* visiting teams. *See also* transportation
    crowd size considerations 239
    double round robin scheduling 159
    scheduling 148, 149, 152, 153, 154, 156
    spectator areas 236-237
humor 43, 77

I

immediate medical assistance, legal duty 256
Individuals with Disabilities Education Act (1990) 137
information management and security 123, 198
informed consent, and documentation 130-131, 252
initial preparedness to participate, legal duty 254
injuries
    allied educational services programs 119, 120, 126, 131
    athletic trainers' roles 72, 131, 216, 217, 227
    avoidance and prevention 83, 84*t*, 85-86, 131, 132, 255
    concussion management 127, 131, 132, 217, 255
    football 151-152, 246, 251, 255, 257, 258, 345
    guidelines 58, 81
    informed consent and sport-specific warnings 130-131, 251-252
    legal cases 246-247, 248, 249, 250, 251, 252, 253, 254, 255-256, 257
    liability issues 151, 152, 243, 244-245, 244*t*, 247-258, 328
    sports practices 63, 246, 251, 255
    transportation following 237-238
    transportation-related 179, 180, 256-257
    turf differences 345, 346-347
in loco parentis policy 127, 256
in season issues 83-90
in-service education 59-60
instruction, legal duty 246, 250-251
insurance 257
    booster clubs 279
    facility rental use 165, 166-167
    transportation-related 176, 185, 186
integrity attributes 28-29, 223-224
interscholastic athletics. *See also* athletic administrators
    forecasts and priorities 361-368
    marketing process 274-277
    origin and framework 6-7, 17-18
    program design 14-17, 95-99
    size and scope ix, xiv, 3, 21, 283
interviews 57
    exit surveys 218
    post-game 232-233

intramural sports, scheduling 162, 163, 164-165
investigations, hazing 265-266

J

job descriptions 56, 61, 81, 108, 222
joint-use agreements 165, 166-167
J.S. v. Blue Mountain School District (Pennsylvania, 2011) 264

K

Kestner, James L. 107
Kowalski v. Berkeley County Schools (West Virginia, 2011) 264

L

L.A. v. Board of Education of the Township of Wayne (New Jersey, 2011) 263
lacrosse 104, 253
law enforcement personnel 225, 226, 234
Layshock v. Hermitage School District (Pennsylvania, 2005) 264
leadership skills
    athletic administrators 9-10, 12-13, 26-27, 33, 77, 91, 100, 243
    methods and traits 32-33, 76-77, 100, 237, 241
    student athletes 6, 76-77
Leadership Training Institute, NIAAA 12-13, 14, 106, 113, 228
legal issues 243, 258, 268. *See also* case law applications; liability issues
    hazing and bullying 265-266, 268
    informed consent 130-131, 252
    program/administration legal duties 243, 244*t*, 245, 246, 247-258
    sexual harassment 266-268
    student-athlete constitutional and civil rights 243, 244*t*, 262-264, 367
    Title IX compliance vx, 11, 16, 159, 243, 244*t*, 259-262, 294, 296, 299-300, 310
Leung v. City of New York (New York, 2006) 253
liability issues 257. *See also* legal issues
    athletic administrators' purview 10, 11, 81, 243-244, 268
    comprehension and acknowledgement statements 187, 298, 334*f*
    equipment 319, 327-328, 344
    facilities 165, 166-167, 354-356
    football 151, 152, 246, 251, 257, 258
    harassment 265-268
    injuries 151, 152, 243, 244-245, 244*t*, 247-258, 328
    spectator safety 238, 344
    staff and volunteers 122, 123-124, 223, 227
    transportation 156, 176, 180, 185-186, 256-257
liability waivers 252, 254
life balance xii, xiii, 5, 18, 30-31
life success 5-6, 8, 17
lighting 356-357
lightning 216-217, 238
Likert scales 65, 91
listening skills 38-39, 48, 78, 203
locker rooms 229-230, 231
    gender equity 261
    hazing and bullying 265
    safety checks 343*f*
    sport availability 312*t*-313*t*
    supervision duties 248, 249
long-range planning 109, 114-115
    facilities/physical plant 115, 357-359
    financial 310-311, 314*t*
    participation rates 107-108, 310

M

maintenance departments 340, 343, 354-356
management styles 26-27

marketing 273-274
    corporate sponsorship 280-282, 296, 299
    interscholastic processes 224, 274-277, 297
    nontraditional 271-273
    relationship-based 273-274, 277-278, 366
    social media 204, 205, 206-208
    sport-specific 271, 283, 290
    technology methods and applications 203-
        209, 276
matching and equating athletes, legal duty 255-
    256
Mathis v. Wayne County Board of Education (Ten-
    nessee, 2011) 265
media
    administration communications/relations 48,
        51-52, 157, 202, 205, 231-233, 276
    athletic schedules sharing 154-155, 157, 229
    team coverage 21, 51, 231, 232
medical exams and histories, athletes 254, 256,
    258
meetings and workshops
    athletic departments 44, 60, 61, 62, 106, 108
    marketing-related 281-282, 284-285, 289
    school and parent meetings 50-51, 58, 80-81,
        100, 106, 186, 236, 298
    virtual, and technology 191-192, 194, 197, 210,
        212-213
memorandums of understanding 165
mental and emotional health services 126, 141
mentoring 58-60, 112, 241
methicillin-resistant *Staphylococcus aureus*
    (MRSA) 323
mission statements 109, 274
    athletic administrators' oversight 11, 99, 101
    examples 23, 101-103
    performance measures related 104, 105, 276
    school districts 99, 106-107, 109-110
mobile apps 194, 216, 218, 219
multisport athletes 4-5, 21-22, 114, 115
music, athletic events 228-229
N
National Federation of State High School As-
    sociations (NFHS) 7
    certification and coaching programs 32, 60,
        68, 71, 105, 109, 111, 130, 250, 367
    participation survey data 151, 297
National Highway Traffic Safety Administration
    183, 184
National Interscholastic Athletic Administrators
    Association (NIAAA) ix, 7, 362f
    certification programs xi, 11-14, 32, 120, 194
    Code of Ethics 28, 29, 122
    essay/scholarship program 8-9
    Leadership Training Institute 12-13, 14, 106,
        113, 228
    priority issues in interscholastic athletics 361-
        363, 363t, 366-368
National Operating Committee on Standards in
    Athletic Equipment (NOCSAE) 327-328
National Safety Council 178
National Strength and Conditioning Association
    135
National Transportation Safety Board 178
natural turf 345, 346
NCAA eligibility and scholarships 17, 92, 138,
    257, 364
negligence 245-246
neutrality 167, 228, 239
newsletters 198, 204, 208
nonconference event scheduling 145, 149-150,
    152, 153, 154

nonprofit organizations 271-272
nutrition 88-89, 88t, 136-137
O
Office for Civil Rights, U.S. Department of
    Education
    complaints and accountability 294, 296, 310
    hazing and harassment documentation 266,
        268
    Title IX 259-261, 262, 278-279, 294, 300
officials. *See* athletic officials
Ollier v. Sweetwater Union High School District
    (California, 2012) 261
Olson, John 361-368
online collaboration and instruction 190, 191-192,
    194, 197, 210-213
operating systems 192, 197, 200
organization marketing 272, 273
Other Athletic Benefits and Opportunities (PLAY-
    ING FAIR), Title IX 260f, 261, 262, 299
outdoor playing surfaces 343-347
outdoor sports equipment 320, 321, 341f-342f
P
Pabst, Jodi 319-338
paralysis, sports injuries 246, 247, 251
parental involvement xii-xiii
    academics support 96, 138, 140
    athletic program ties and communication 16,
        27, 39, 47, 48-50, 52-53, 58, 64, 69, 80-81, 90,
        97-98, 100, 208, 236, 298
    booster clubs 277-278
    challenges and conflicts xiii, 39, 48-49, 235-
        236, 361, 364-365
    child health 97, 126, 127
    in loco parentis policy 127, 256
    school administrator ties and communication
        46-47, 208
parking 225, 233-234
participation rates, athletic programs
    athletic department goals, benchmarks, and
        tracking 21, 23, 76, 107-108, 111, 261, 294,
        295, 310, 366
    football 151, 364, 365t
    by gender/Title IX 259-261, 277, 300, 307, 310
    interscholastic statistics xiv, 3, 21, 283, 297,
        365t
part-time personnel 55, 71, 73, 223-227
Patrick v. Great Valley School District (2008) 256
"pay to participate" model in athletics 185, 262,
    275, 296-298, 361, 366
per-capita spending 307, 310, 312t-313t
performance-enhancing substances 97, 254
Perkins, James, Jr. 110
personal attributes. *See also* character education
    coaches 56-57, 94
    leaders 29-30, 33, 76-77, 100, 237, 241
    student athletes 5-6, 7, 8-9, 15, 76-77
person marketing 272
personnel management 26-27, 55-73. *See also*
    evaluation, programs; evaluation, staff
    adjunct staff 71-73
    athletic trainers 55, 71, 72, 134
    coaches 34, 55, 56-71
    communications 44-45, 66-67, 72, 105, 218
    contest/event staff 222-226, 230
    documentation and recordkeeping 250
    strategic planning 110-111
philosophy development, athletic administrators
    19-35, 107, 221
physical development and maturation
    athlete matching consideration 255-256

football players, age differences 152, 255-256
student athletes 83, 84*t*, 85
physical plant
  departments 339-340, 343, 359
  long-range planning 357-359
place marketing 272
planning, legal duty 248
population density issues 150, 296, 297
Positive Coaching in a Nutshell (Thompson) 77, 93
positive reinforcement 87, 105
postseason 90-93
power
  vs. authority 32-33, 35
  coaches' 63, 77, 79
PowerPoint, use 31, 51, 192, 197
practices. *See* athletic practices
pre-college counseling and planning 137-138
pre-existing conditions, athletes 254
pre-game
  announcements and music 227-229
  team and staff protocols 230-231
preseason 80-82, 100, 106, 108, 186, 298
prioritization, tasks and duties 23-24, 30, 195-197
private-sector amateur teams 364, 365
private-sector transportation options 173, 175, 176-177, 183
productivity 193-195, 195-200
profanity
  music 228-229
  sexual harassment 267
  social networking and civil rights 264
  spectator behavior 236
professional athletics ix, xiv, 365*t*
professional development 59-60
  associations 120
  athletic administrators 12-13, 31-32, 106, 368
  coaches 60, 68, 76, 105, 108-109, 111, 191, 361, 367-368
  technology skills 190, 191, 209
professionalism 120-121
  friendship issues 33-34
  personnel evaluations 67
  recordkeeping 70-71
  social media use 41, 51-52
property taxes 296, 297
protective equipment 253-254, 323. *See also* equipment
protein, in diets 88, 88*t*, 89
public address staff and duties 223, 227-229, 238, 240
public relations
  athletic administrator role and influence 231, 232, 274-275
  methods 112, 275, 281
  revenue links 203-204, 205, 209, 235, 366
  ticket sellers 223-224
publishing software 198, 208
purchasing 301-305
  equipment 319-320, 327, 350-351
  tracking and patterns 293-294, 300, 302, 304, 305, 307

Q
quantitative analysis 106-107, 116

R
raffles 276, 325
recognition and appreciation 34, 72, 73, 78, 366
recordkeeping. *See* documentation
recruiting and hiring. *See also* personnel management
  by administrators 11, 55, 56-57, 71, 108, 134, 168, 275, 367

of administrators x-xi
  coaches, legal relevance 250
  volunteers 124
recruiting of athletes 92, 138-140, 140, 257
relationship marketing 273-274, 277-278, 280
relationships, professional
  friendship issues 33-34
  management and communication style challenges 26-27
rental agreements 166, 176, 186-187
repair and reconditioning, equipment 325, 327-328, 343, 344
rescheduling, contests and events 147, 154, 155-157, 175-176, 202
risk management. *See* assumption of risk; liability issues; safety
rosters 231-232
round-robin scheduling 144, 147, 148, 149, 154, 159, 164

S
safe environment, legal duty 252-253
safety
  athletic administrators' priorities 24, 97, 233, 240
  athletic administrators' purview, and programs 10, 16, 238, 240, 243, 247, 268
  coaches' priorities and communication 81, 250
  emergency readiness and communication 48-49, 97, 129-130, 178-179, 216-217, 227, 237-241
  equipment and facilities checks 321-324, 327-328, 341*f*-342*f*, 342*f*-343*f*, 355-356
  event and spectator issues 221, 224, 228, 233, 234-241
  transportation 156, 157, 176, 178-184, 188, 256-257
Sain v. Cedar Rapids Community School District (Iowa, 2001) 257
salaries 185
  budgeting types and salary sources 296, 297, 298
  coaches 66, 297, 298, 312*t*-313*t*
Sandler, Bernice 259
scheduling
  athletic administrators/administration 24, 29-30, 143-144, 143-145, 150, 152, 153-155, 156-158, 161-162, 164, 167, 169, 171, 173-174, 175-176, 199, 229, 238
  communication 44, 46, 47, 48, 49, 58, 81, 161-162, 169, 171-172, 202, 206, 229
  education funding and budget 152, 160-161
  facilities and equipment 136, 161-167
  football 144, 147, 148, 151-152
  gender equity issues 153, 154, 159, 162, 261, 300
  methods 144, 145, 146, 147, 148-149, 153
  officials 46, 157, 167-168
  rescheduling, events 147, 154, 155-157, 175-176, 202, 229
  software 168-169, 173, 176, 199, 229
  transportation 143, 144, 146-147, 150, 154, 157, 171-176, 185
  varsity and subvarsity 147, 152, 154-155, 158-159, 160
scholarships 17, 92, 262, 364
  academics and athletics 92-93, 138, 139, 257
  student/family focus and overfocus 21, 92, 361, 364
school administrators. *See also* athletic administrators; boards of education
  communication 26-27, 37, 46-47, 198-199
  duties 16-17, 24, 98

school administrators *(continued)*
  event scheduling 145-146
  power and authority 32-33, 98
  relationship management 17, 26-27, 112-113
  staffing management 56, 66, 67
school calendars 145-146, 153, 155, 160, 163-164
school community 44, 109
  communications 27, 44-52
  scheduling issues 143, 144, 145-146
school counselors 126, 137-139
school districts 20, 99, 106-107, 109-110
  finance 292, 296, 305
  meeting facilities 164
  weather policies 157
school rivalry contests 148, 224, 237
school safety, management 198-199
school sizes and divisions 19-20
scouting 154, 155
security personnel 223, 225-226, 234, 236, 240
self-evaluations
  coaches 64-65, 108
  Title IX compliance 261, 310
self-transport 186, 257
sexual harassment 243, 244*t*, 265, 266-268
Sharkey, B.J. 85, 86
Sharon v. City of Newton (Massachusetts, 2002)
  252
signage 209, 236, 238
skill and fitness development
  athlete matching consideration 255-256
  goals and planning 111, 158
  skill progression instruction 251
soccer
  equipment checklists and safety 322, 332*f*,
    341*f*
  goals 249, 320
social media 193, 195, 201, 203, 204
  athletic administration use and management
    27, 31-32, 41-42, 51-52, 112, 191, 201-202,
    202-203, 206-208, 210
  freedom of speech 262-264, 367
  marketing 204, 205, 206-208
  negative impact 202, 361, 363*t*, 367
  positive impact 201-202, 206, 208
softball
  equipment checklists and safety 321, 330*f*,
    341*f*
  statistics tracking 216
  team transportation 160
special education 137
specialization in sport 21-22, 76, 361, 363*t*, 364-
  365
spectator amenities 233-235, 344, 357
spectator conduct and management 235-237
  challenges, and athletic administrators' duties
    221, 228, 235-236, 240
  crowd control and security 225-226, 237,
    238-240
  declining standards and behavior xiv, 235-236
  supervisors 223, 236
spinal cord injuries 246, 247, 251
sponsorships 283-284
  corporate 280-282, 296, 299
  seeking and securing 110, 280, 281-282, 284-
    285
sporting behavior
  awareness and focus xiv, 15, 20, 27-28, 96, 275
  coaches 57
  declining standards 235-236, xiv

guidelines and rules 80, 236
  winning, over-focus xiii, 15, 20, 96
sports law 243, 258, 268
sports medicine 131-132, 134, 216-217, 227
sport-specific financial reports 307, 308*t*, 309*t*,
  311, 312*t*-313*t*, 314*t*
sports psychology 82, 86-87
spreadsheet software
  budgeting and accounting use 304, 305, 306,
    307, 309*t*, 310, 311
  equipment inventory 319, 323, 328
  features and general use 197-198
standardized tests (academic) 93, 138-139
standards of practice
  civil rights 263
  emergency situations 121, 128, 258
  professional 120-121
  safety and liability 247, 251
state-association-level contests
  scheduling 144, 145, 146, 155, 159
  staff certification 223, 226-227
state laws
  anti-abuse 266, 268
  finance, athletic departments 291, 292, 294,
    298, 300, 303, 305
  transportation 180, 182, 184
statutory immunity 246-247
Stead, Dave x, xi, xii, xiii, xiv
Stevens, Gary 221-241
Stice, Sheri 75-94
strategic planning
  athletic departments 109-115, 274
  safety and liability 247, 248, 254
strength and conditioning programs 132, 134-136
  adolescent development and 84*t*, 85
  evaluation 254
stress
  and communication 38, 39, 42-43
  contest and event management 221, 222,
    235-236
  student athletes 86, 126
stretching 85-86
student athletes. *See also* academic achievement;
  education; eligibility, athletes; parental
  involvement; participation rates, athletic
  programs; student health
  civil rights 243, 244*t*, 262-264, 367
  coach focus and management 56, 57, 61, 62,
    63, 69, 75-79, 93-94, 96
  communication 45, 47, 48, 49, 77
  development 75-94, 95, 158-159
  entitlement attitudes 75, 361, 364-365
  first-person accounts 8-9, 366
  preparedness to participate 254
  psychological aspects 86-87, 89-90
  relationship propriety 34, 77, 267, 268
  spending 307, 310, 312*t*-313*t*
student data 198
student health 119, 120, 125-126. *See also* injuries
  administration 127-131
  mental and emotional 126, 141
  nutrition 88-89, 136-137
  sports medicine 131-132
  strength and conditioning 132-136, 254
substance use and abuse 4, 15, 80, 97, 123, xiv
substantial proportionality, sports participation
  259-261
subvarsity athletics. *See* elementary-level athletics; varsity and subvarsity teams
supervision, legal duty 248-249

support services, education. *See* allied educational services
surveys
    athletic facility planning 358
    health information 131-132, 254, 256
    priority issues in interscholastic athletics 361-368, 363*t*, 365*t*
    program development 107-108, 109
    sports interest 104, 260-261
    sports participation data and equity 151, 254, 260-261, 297
    staff and player evaluations 105, 106, 108, 218
SWOT analysis 274-276

T

team goals 81-82, 115
team selection 80
technique instruction, legal duty 246, 250-251
technology
    athletic administrator duties and careers xi, 10, 25-26, 31-32, 189, 204, 209, 218-219
    athletic performance and competition 213-218
    changes and change management 25-26, 189, 193, 204, 209
    collaboration 191-192, 194, 197, 210-213
    educational 190, 191-192, 194
    electronic communication 31, 41-42, 193, 200-209
    event scheduling and communication 154-155, 168-169, 173, 176, 199, 201-202
    office 193-200
telephone communications 30, 31, 45, 52, 213
tennis, equipment checklists and safety 332*f*, 342*f*
termination of employment
    coaches 61, 69, 261, 268
    sexual harassment 268
ticket offices and sellers 223-225, 235, 240-241
    complimentary tickets 224, 301
    gate receipts 308*t*
    ticket prices 223, 224, 233, 275, 312*t*-313*t*
timing systems 216
Tinker v. Des Moines School District (1969) 264
Title IX
    booster clubs 277, 278-279, 299, 302
    compliance xv, 11, 16, 159, 243, 244*t*, 259-262, 294, 296, 299-300, 310
    participation and effects xiv-xv, 7, 97, 259-261, 307, 310
track and field 226
    equipment checklists and safety 322, 333*f*, 341*f*
    female participation 364
    injuries and cases 253
traction, playing surfaces 345, 348-349
training, physical
    measurement methods 215
    student athletes 83, 84*t*, 85-86
    technology aids 215, 216-217
training, professional 110-111, 222, 227-228, 250. *See also* certification and programs
training rooms, safety 332*f*
transparency, information and communication 33, 80, 257, 280, 287, 315
transportation
    budgetary concerns and expense cuts 160, 175, 177-178, 184-187, 297, 300
    communication 156, 157, 171-172, 174-175
    emergency vehicles 237-238
    guidelines 171, 175, 178, 180, 182-184, 300
    liability issues 156, 176, 180, 185-186, 256-257
    options 175-178

    remotely-located schools 150, 156, 157
    safety 156, 157, 176, 178-184, 188, 256-257
    scheduling 143, 144, 146-147, 150, 154, 156, 157, 171-175, 185
travel teams 364, 365
Tri-Central High School v. Mason (Indiana, 2001) 257
turf management 343-347
Turner, Roy 189-219
T.V. & M.K. v. Smith-Green Community Schools (Indiana, 2009) 264
Twitter 262
    athletic departments use 32, 112, 200, 201-202, 206, 208, 210
    game reports 216

U

uniforms
    inventory 320, 328-329, 330*f*-333*f*, 335*f*
    issuance and accountability 329, 334, 334*f*
    ordering and care 325, 327, 335-337
    rotation 300-301, 324-325, 326*f*
University of Maryland 259
URLs 205

V

Van Erk, Nina 61
van travel 176, 182, 183-184, 187, 257
varsity and subvarsity teams
    event scheduling 147, 152, 154-155, 158-159, 160
    football ticket sales 308*t*
    uniforms 324
video production and sharing 204, 205, 207-208, 214, 276
video review 139, 176, 214
Vincent, Troy 272
violent incidents 76, 236
    hazing 16, 97, 265
    management 237, 240-241
    off-campus and online threats 263, 264, 367
visiting team locker rooms and benches 230, 231
The Voice Above the Crowd (Rumble) 228
volleyball
    accidents 249
    equipment checklists and safety 322-323, 333*f*
    goal examples 83*t*, 92, 100-101
    schedules 149, 150, 158
volunteers 121-122, 123-124, 123*f*-124*f*

W

warnings, legal duties 130-131, 251-252
weather
    event postponement and rescheduling 155-156, 157, 175-176, 238
    warning systems 194, 216-217, 218
Web conferencing tools 191-192, 194, 210, 212-213
Website development 199, 205, 207, 208
weight room equipment checks and safety 323-324, 343*f*
whiteboards 192, 194, 215, 230
Whitehead, Bruce xi, xii, xiii, xiv, 3-18
Wilson, Carter 339-359
winning, focus. *See* competitiveness
wood flooring 348, 349, 350
wrestling 256, 324, 333*f*

Y

Yarber v. Oakland Unified School District (California, 1992) 249
yearly financial reports 306-308, 308*t*
YouTube 204, 206, 207, 208

Z

zero-based budgets 294-295

About the Editors

Michael L. Blackburn, PhD, CMAA, is the associate executive director for the National Interscholastic Athletic Administrators Association (NIAAA) in Indianapolis, Indiana. He began his service with the NIAAA in 2005.

He earned a doctorate in educational administration in 2007 from Indiana State University and an educational specialist degree in 2001 from the same institution. He holds a master's degree from the University of St. Francis and a bachelor's degree from Indiana State University. Blackburn is certified as a master athletic administrator, superintendent, and principal.

As the NIAAA associate executive director, he has been involved with initiatives that increased membership by nearly 70%, secured accreditation through North Central Association CASI, and implemented the association's Hall of Fame. Among other communications efforts, he is the publisher of *Interscholastic Athletic Administrator* magazine. He has worked with NIAAA leadership groups and affiliates on preparations for national conferences, budgeting, and professional outreach efforts including certification and the Leadership Training Institute (LTI).

Blackburn has served as director of athletics and assistant principal responsible for athletics for nearly three decades at Northwestern High School in Indiana. His secondary school experience includes serving in three school districts as a teacher, coach of three sports, and FCA sponsor. At Northwestern he led an equitable athletic program including 70 athletic teams and over 100 coaching and athletic personnel. An average of over 75% of students participated in athletics and benefited from a variety of programs that encourage academic achievement, participation, and positive conduct. Since 1977 he has been involved with the NIAAA, serving as chair of the Publications Committee, a member of the first strategic planning committee, an LTI instructor, and liaison. He was president and longtime secretary of the IIAAA. He was on the executive committee and board of directors of the state high school athletic association, for which he also served as vice chair.

Blackburn received the NIAAA Award of Merit, Swalls Scholarship Award in Educational Administration, NIAAA Distinguished Service Award, NFHS Citation, State Award of Merit, NCSSAD Midwest Athletic Director of the Year, IIAAA State Athletic Director of the Year, and IAEOP State Administrator of the Year. He has also been inducted into the NASPE Presidential Hall of Fame.

He and his wife, Brenda, have three children and six grandchildren.

Eric Forsyth, PhD, CAA, is a professor at Bemidji State University in Bemidji, Minnesota. Forsyth has published in both referee and trade journals, presented at various conferences on the national and international levels, and written several textbook chapters on issues related to high school athletics.

Forsyth is a founding author of the interscholastic athletic administration graduate curriculum standards endorsed by the National Association for Sport and Physical Education (NASPE) and the NIAAA. He also served as a consultant in the development of a new leadership training course pertaining to interscholastic sport corporate sponsorships. He is coauthor of a chapter on interscholastic sports in the textbook *Contemporary Sport Management, Fourth Edition.*

Forsyth earned his doctorate in sport administration in 1995 from the University of New Mexico in Albuquerque. In 2012 he completed the NIAAA certification program, achieving the certified athletic administration (CAA) distinction. Forsyth resides in Wilton, Minnesota, with his wife, Evelyn, and children, Sarah and Ryan.

John R. Olson, PhD, CMAA, is an adjunct faculty member in sport administration at Ohio University in Athens, Ohio, and Edgewood College in Madison, Wisconsin. He also spent seven years as an instructor in coaching, sport administration, and program administration at the University of Wisconsin at Madison. Olson has 40 years of public education experience in coaching, sport administration, school administration, and school district administration.

He is the author of two undergraduate textbooks on sport administration, numerous professional journal articles, and 17 NIAAA leadership training courses. He developed the NIAAA Certification Examination to establish competencies for high school athletic administrators as well as the NIAAA Program Quality Assessment Protocol, which outlines established standards of excellence for high school athletic programs. Olson has served as NIAAA curriculum director, NIAAA college and university liaison, and consultant for advanced standing degrees in sport administration.

He is a member of the Hall of Fame for the NIAAA (2011), National High School Coaches Association (2010), National Council of Secondary School Athletic Directors (2006), and the National Federation of State High School Associations (2000). He and his wife, Marlene, live in Madison, Wisconsin.

Bruce D. Whitehead, CMAA, has been executive director of the National Interscholastic Athletic Administrators Association (NIAAA) since 2007. A number of key initiatives have occurred during his years leading the NIAAA, including accreditation of the organization, increased staff, expansion of the Leadership Training Institute and Certification Programs, establishment of the Hall of Fame, association outreach and affiliations, and financial growth.

He has been involved in interscholastic athletics for over four decades as a coach in baseball, basketball, and tennis; and official, athletic administrator, and leader of athletic administrator organizations at state and national levels. He was an athletic administrator for 25 years at Crawfordsville High School in Indiana and coordinated the design of athletic facilities in the construction of a new high school. Whitehead was among the first class of those to earn the CAA in 1988 and became a certified master athletic administrator in 2001. He earned both bachelor's and master's degrees in mathematics from Purdue University and has served as an adjunct professor at two universities. Before serving as NIAAA executive director, he was assistant to the executive director for more than six years.

Whitehead was president and a board member of the Indiana Interscholastic Athletic Administrators Association and was secretary-treasurer of the NIAAA board. He was a member of the Indiana High School Athletic Association Board of Directors and Executive Committee, serving as vice chairman. While affiliated with the IHSAA board, he chaired the multiple-class committee as well as a committee that formulated implementation of coaches' education. In addition, he helped formulate an IIAAA mentoring program for directors of athletics. He has served the NIAAA as a conference presenter, author of articles, instructor in the Leadership Training Institute, and LTI course coauthor. He was chairman of the NIAAA Resolutions Committee.

In 2004 Whitehead was inducted into to the National Council of Secondary School Athletic Directors Hall Fame. He also received the Award of Merit from the NIAAA and the Citation award presented by the National Federation of State High School Associations, the NIAAA Distinguished Service Award, NIAAA/IIAAA State Award of Merit, and the Charles Maas Distinguished Service Award. In 2007 he was inducted into the Crawfordsville High School Athletic Hall of Fame.

Whitehead lives with his wife, Pamela, in Westfield, Indiana.